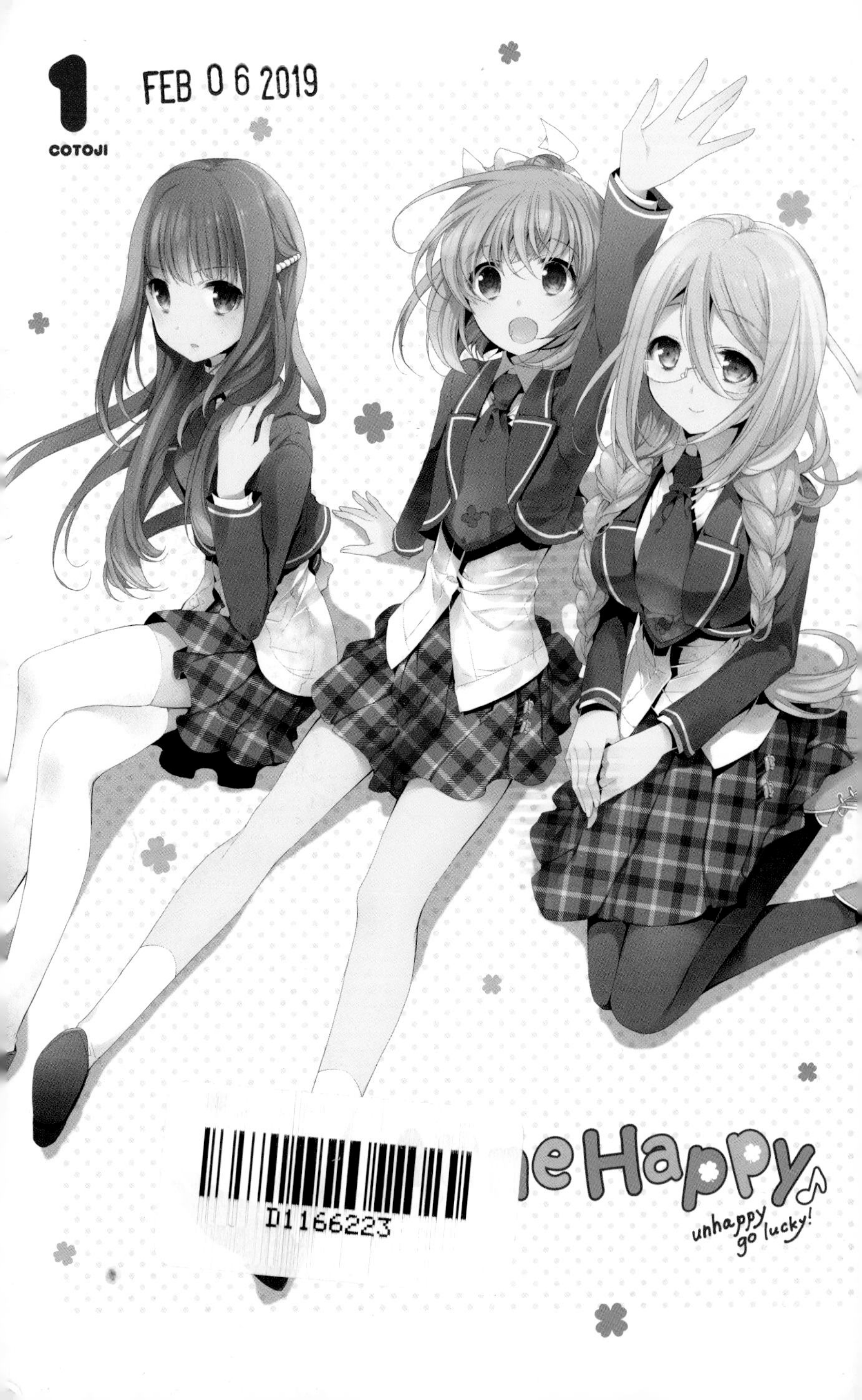
1
COTOJI
eHappy
unhappy go lucky!

CONTENTS
ANNE HAPPY
VOLUME ONE
COTOJI

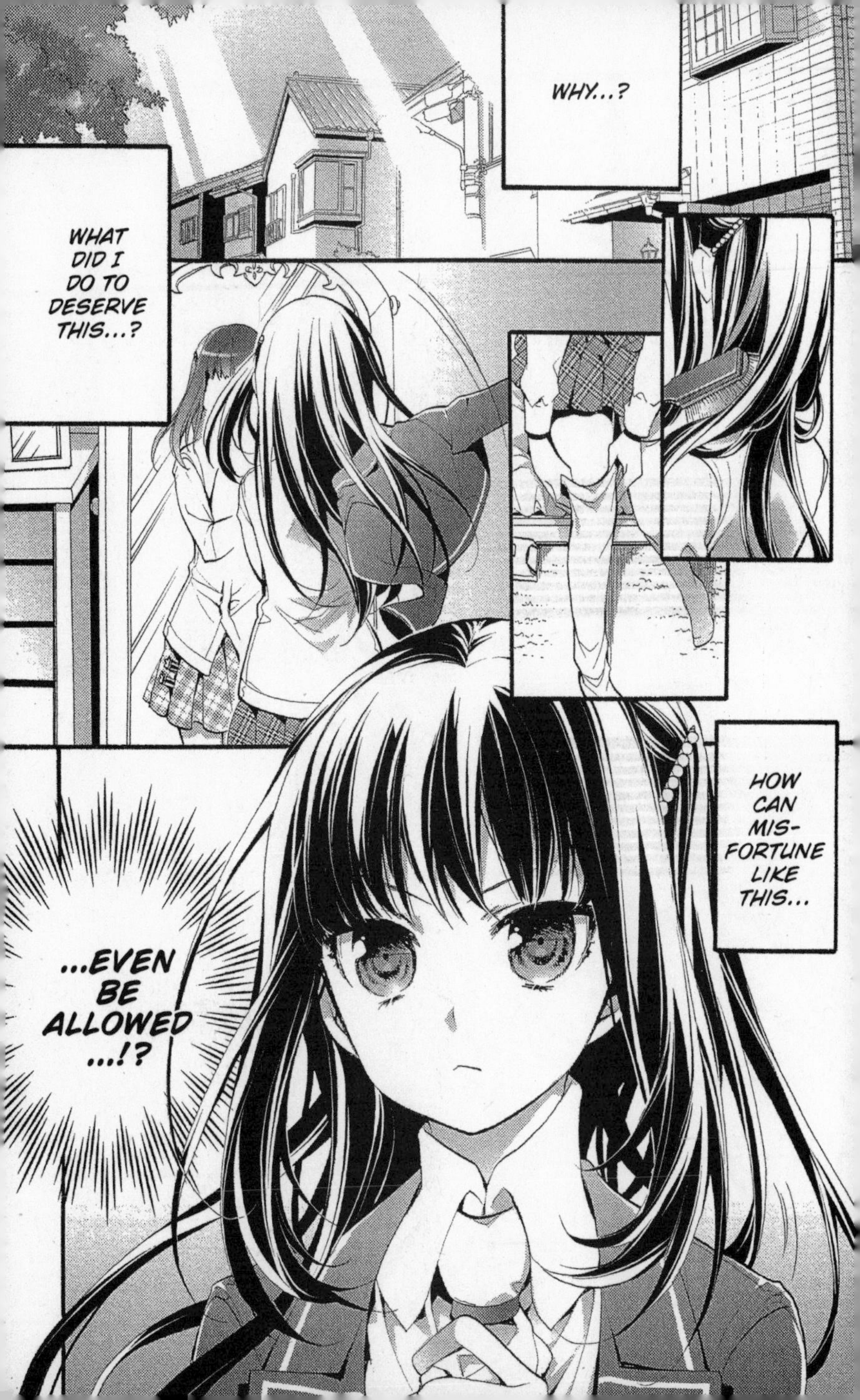
WHY...?
WHAT DID I DO TO DESERVE THIS...?
HOW CAN MIS-FORTUNE LIKE THIS...
...EVEN BE ALLOWED ...!?

✽ Lucky. 1

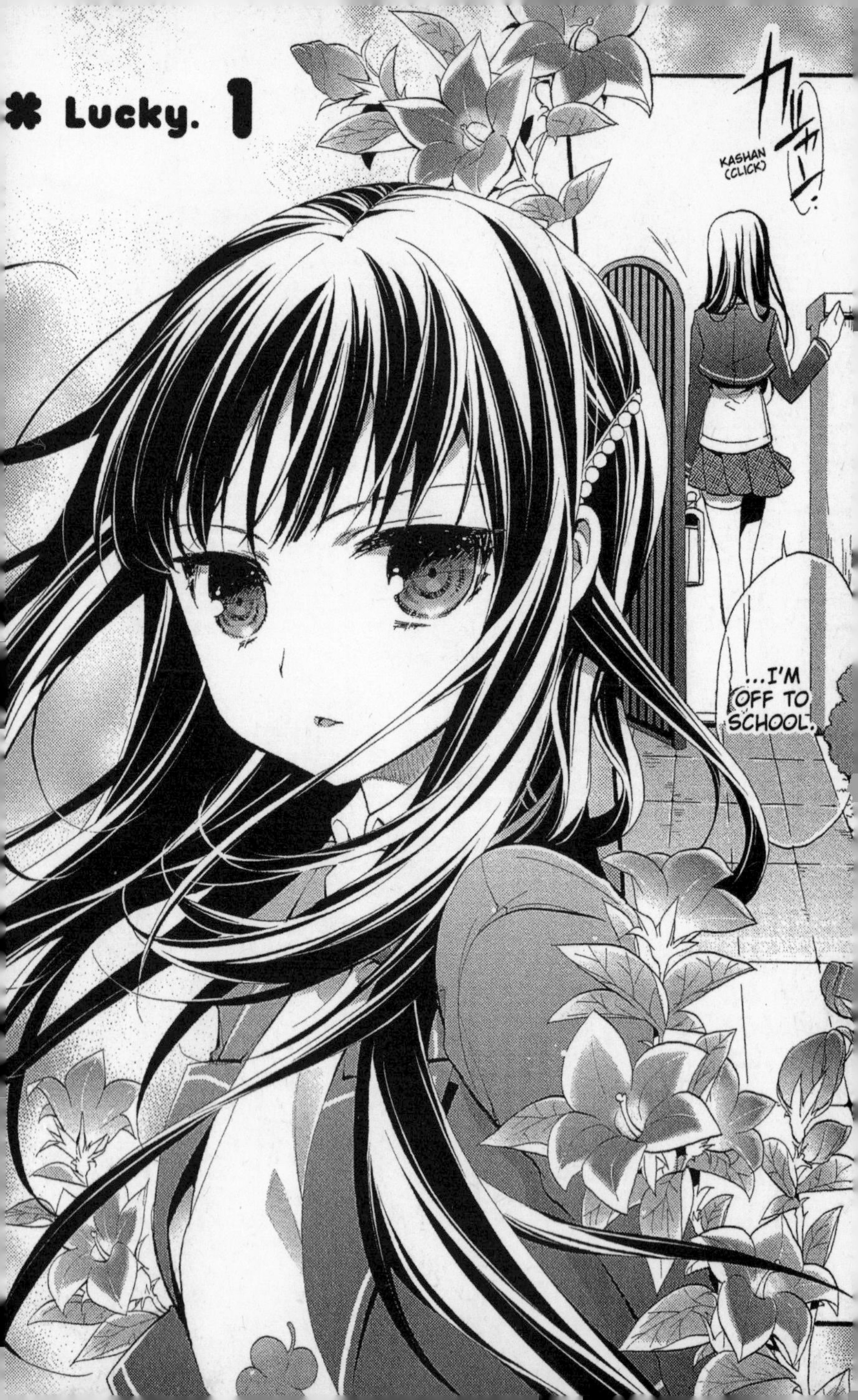
KASHAN (CLICK)
...I'M OFF TO SCHOOL.

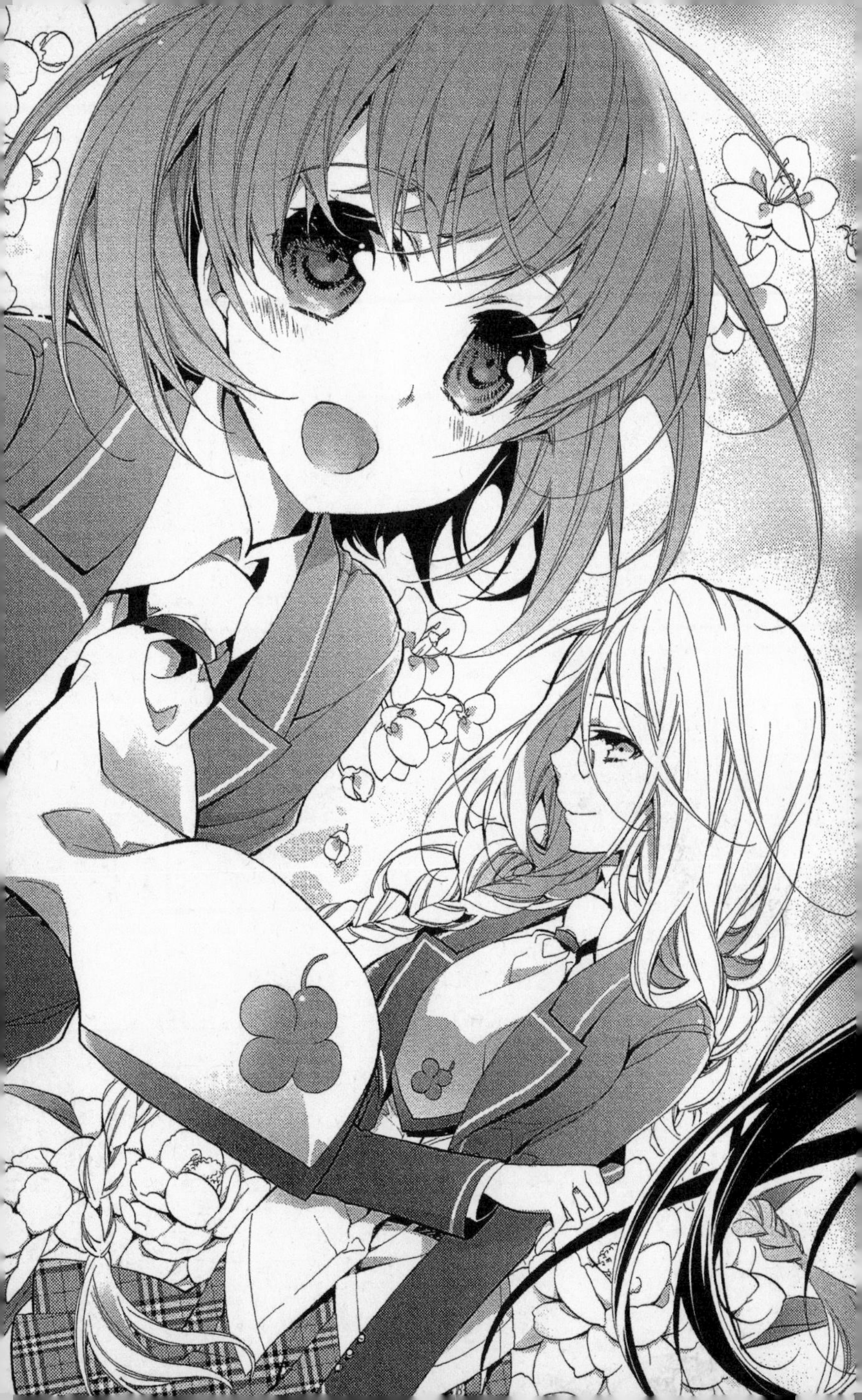

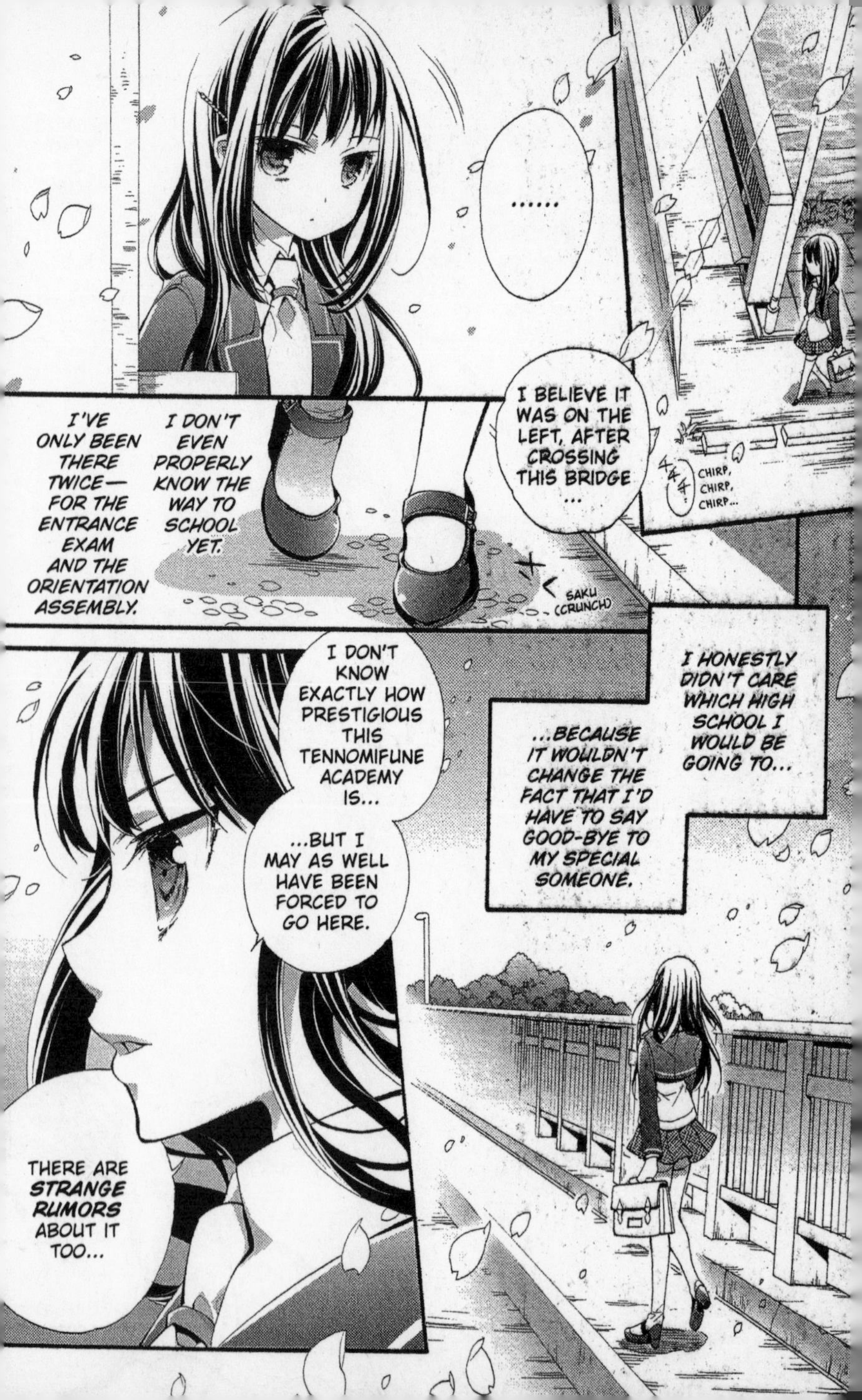
I BELIEVE IT WAS ON THE LEFT, AFTER CROSSING THIS BRIDGE ...
CHIRP, CHIRP, CHIRP...
......
I DON'T EVEN PROPERLY KNOW THE WAY TO SCHOOL YET.
I'VE ONLY BEEN THERE TWICE— FOR THE ENTRANCE EXAM AND THE ORIENTATION ASSEMBLY.
SAKU (CRUNCH)
I HONESTLY DIDN'T CARE WHICH HIGH SCHOOL I WOULD BE GOING TO...
...BECAUSE IT WOULDN'T CHANGE THE FACT THAT I'D HAVE TO SAY GOOD-BYE TO MY SPECIAL SOMEONE.
I DON'T KNOW EXACTLY HOW PRESTIGIOUS THIS TENNOMIFUNE ACADEMY IS...
...BUT I MAY AS WELL HAVE BEEN FORCED TO GO HERE.
THERE ARE STRANGE RUMORS ABOUT IT TOO...

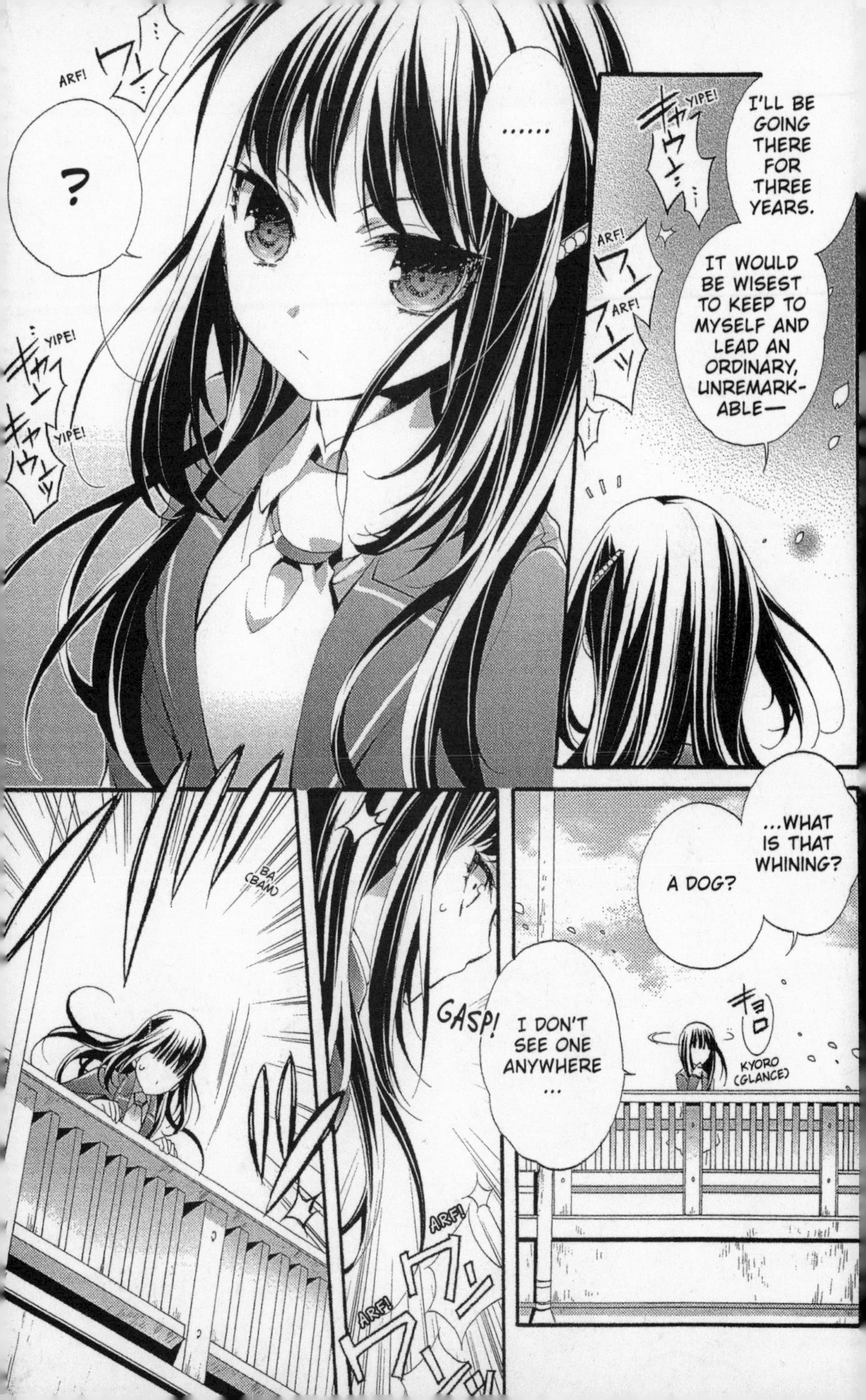
YIPE!
ARF!
ARF!
I'LL BE GOING THERE FOR THREE YEARS.
IT WOULD BE WISEST TO KEEP TO MYSELF AND LEAD AN ORDINARY, UNREMARK-ABLE—
......
ARF!
?
YIPE!
YIPE!
...WHAT IS THAT WHINING?
A DOG?
KYORO (GLANCE)
I DON'T SEE ONE ANYWHERE ...
GASP!
ARF!
ARF!
BA (BAM)

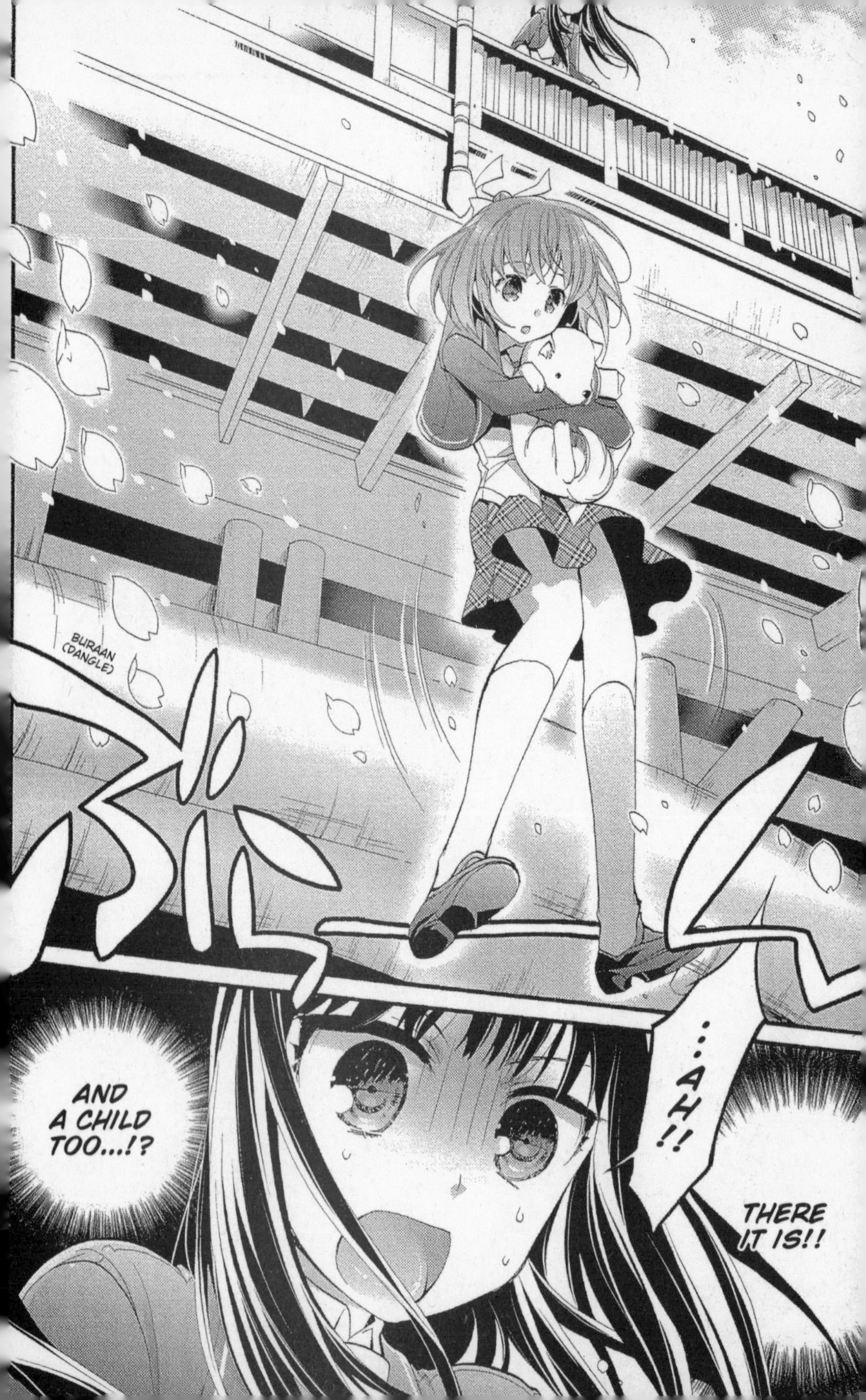
BURAAN (DANGLE)
...AH!!
THERE IT IS!!
AND A CHILD TOO...!?

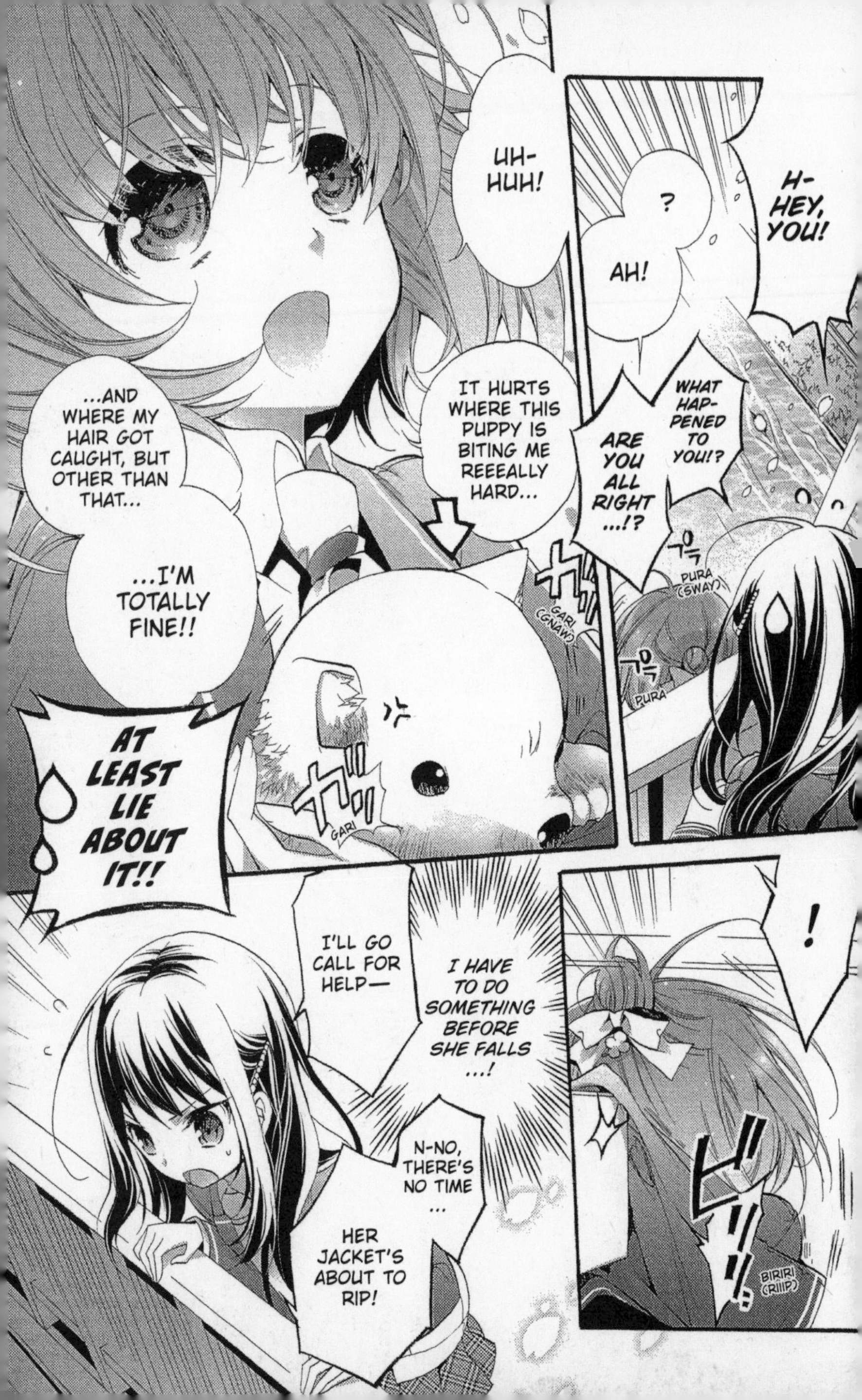
H-HEY, YOU!
?
AH!
WHAT HAPPENED TO YOU!?
ARE YOU ALL RIGHT ...!?
PURA (SWAY)
PURA
UH-HUH!
IT HURTS WHERE THIS PUPPY IS BITING ME REEEALLY HARD...
GARI (GNAW)
...AND WHERE MY HAIR GOT CAUGHT, BUT OTHER THAN THAT...
...I'M TOTALLY FINE!!
GARI
AT LEAST LIE ABOUT IT!!
!
BIRIRI (RIIIP)
I HAVE TO DO SOMETHING BEFORE SHE FALLS ...!
I'LL GO CALL FOR HELP—
N-NO, THERE'S NO TIME ...
HER JACKET'S ABOUT TO RIP!

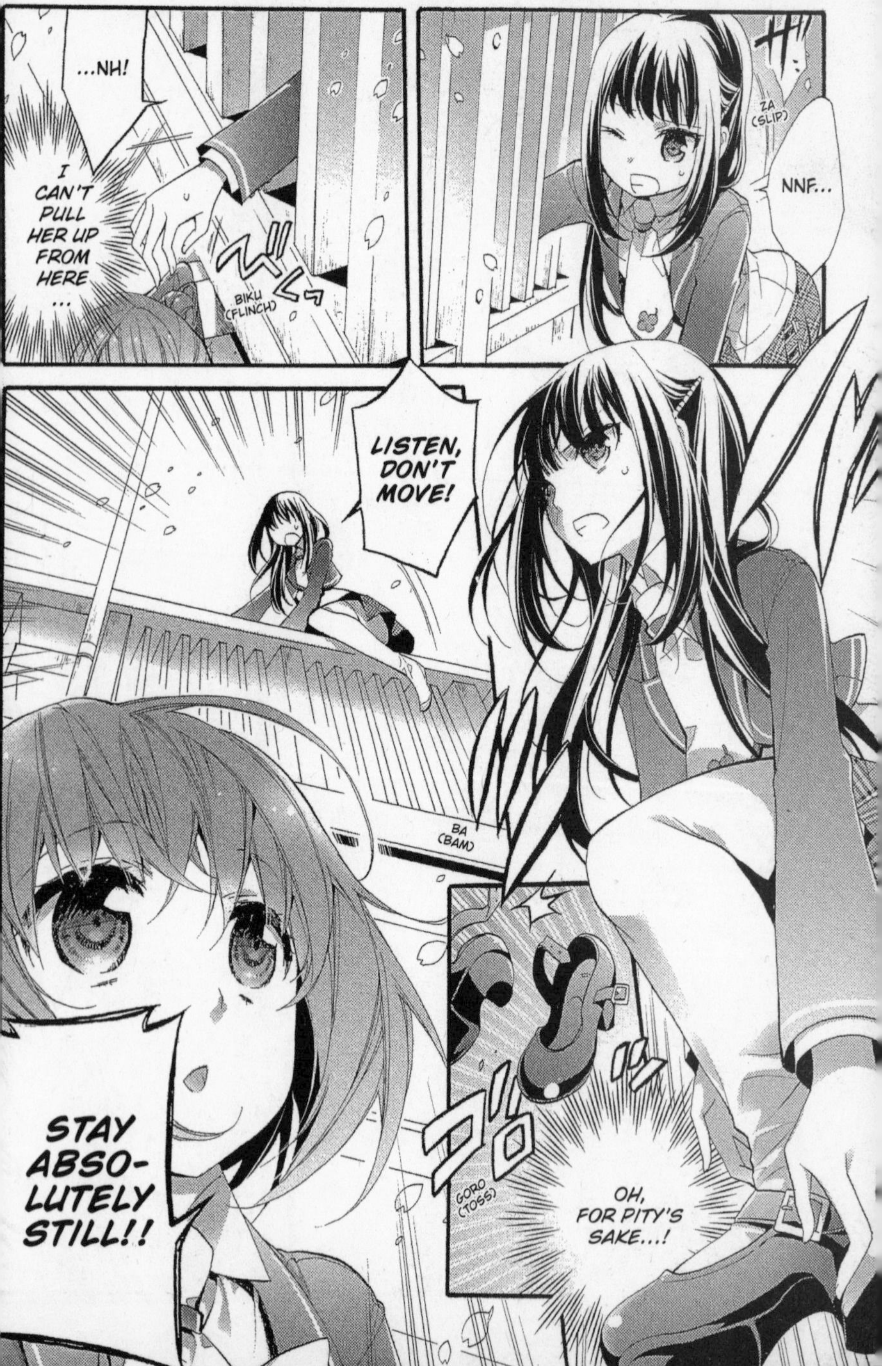
ZA (SLIP)
NNF...
...NH!
I CAN'T PULL HER UP FROM HERE...
BIKU (FLINCH)
LISTEN, DON'T MOVE!
BA (BAM)
GORO (TOSS)
OH, FOR PITY'S SAKE...!
STAY ABSO-LUTELY STILL!!

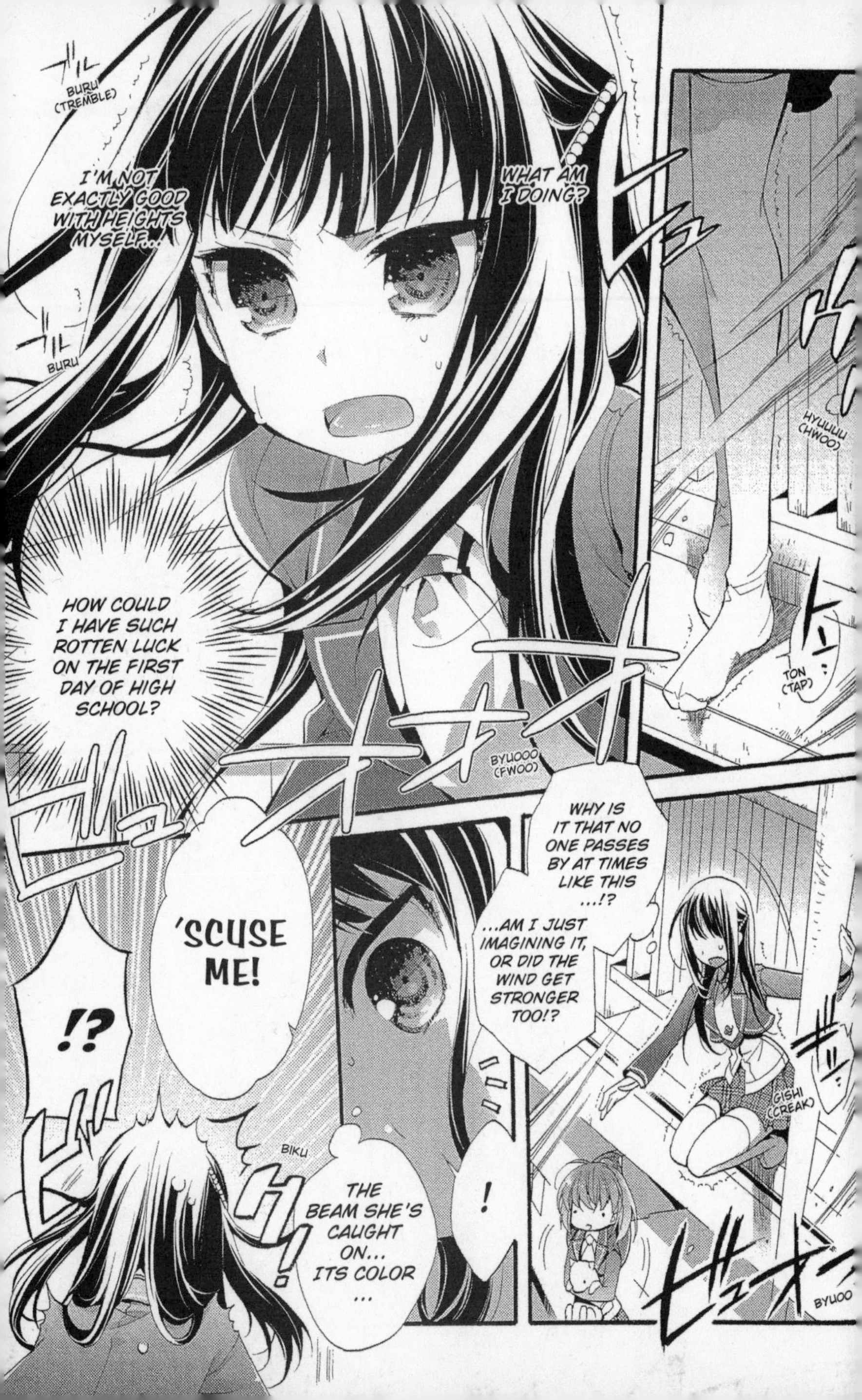
HYUUUU (HWOO)
TON (TAP)
WHAT AM I DOING?
BURU (TREMBLE)
I'M NOT EXACTLY GOOD WITH HEIGHTS MYSELF...
BURU
HOW COULD I HAVE SUCH ROTTEN LUCK ON THE FIRST DAY OF HIGH SCHOOL?
BYUOOO (FWOO)
WHY IS IT THAT NO ONE PASSES BY AT TIMES LIKE THIS ...!?
...AM I JUST IMAGINING IT, OR DID THE WIND GET STRONGER TOO!?
GISHI (CREAK)
BYUOO
!
THE BEAM SHE'S CAUGHT ON... ITS COLOR ...
'SCUSE ME!
!?
BIKU

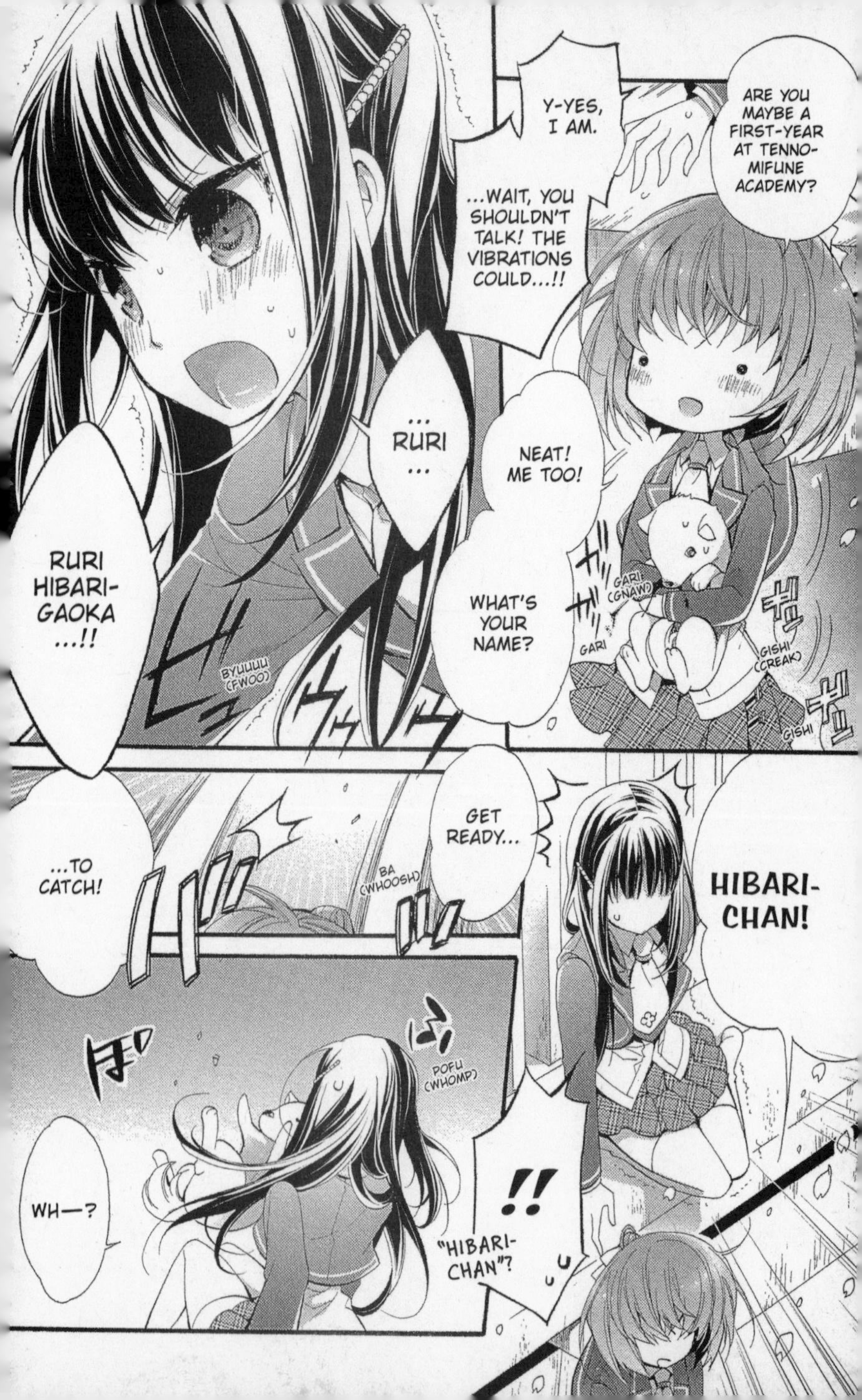
ARE YOU MAYBE A FIRST-YEAR AT TENNO-MIFUNE ACADEMY?
Y-YES, I AM.
...WAIT, YOU SHOULDN'T TALK! THE VIBRATIONS COULD...!!
NEAT! ME TOO!
WHAT'S YOUR NAME?
GARI (GNAW)
GARI
GISHI (CREAK)
GISHI
...RURI...
RURI HIBARI-GAOKA...!!
BYUUUU (FWOO)
HIBARI-CHAN!
GET READY...
!!
"HIBARI-CHAN"?
BA (WHOOSH)
...TO CATCH!
POFU (WHOMP)
WH—?

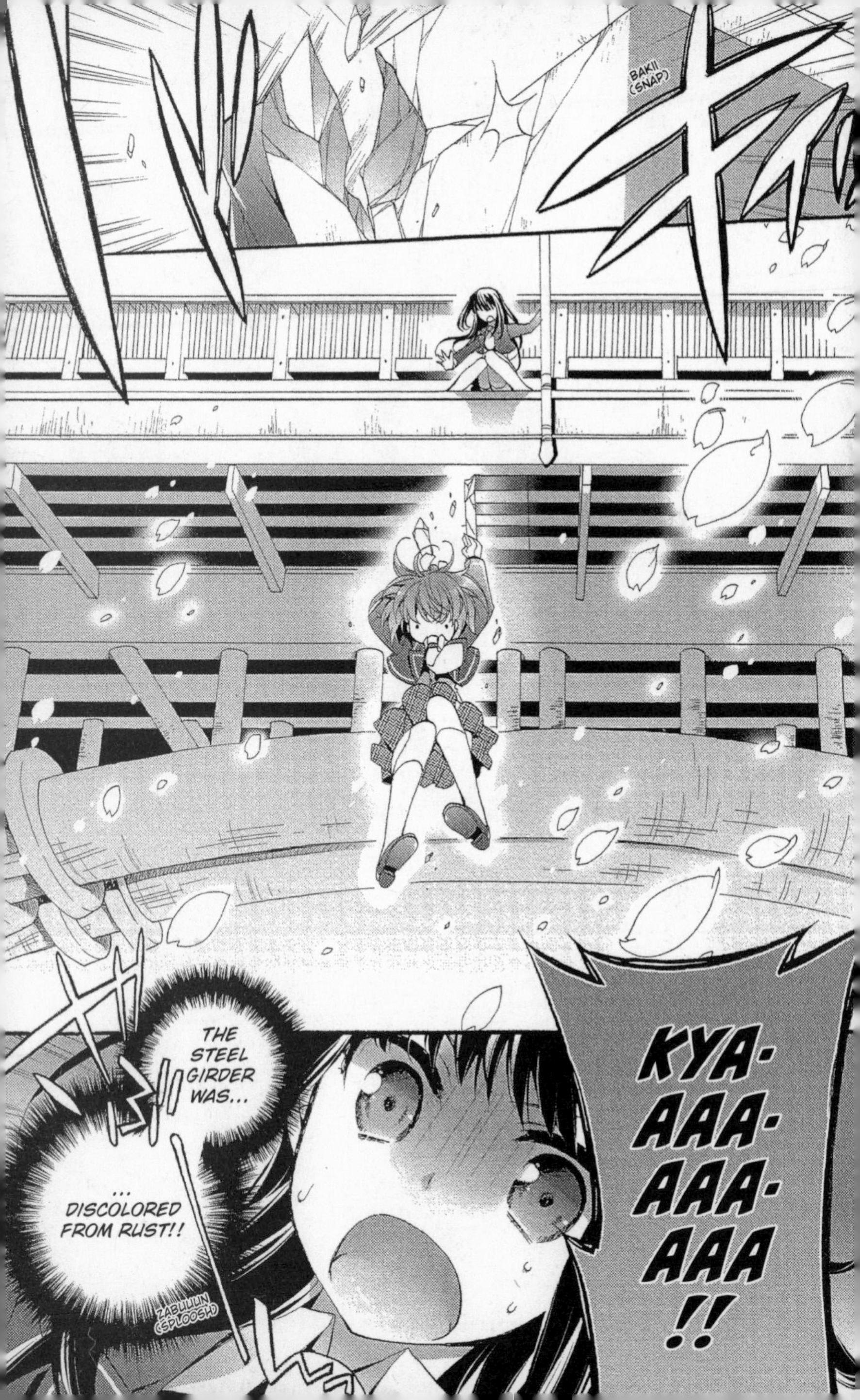
BAKII (SNAP)
KYA-AAA-AAA-AAA!!
THE STEEL GIRDER WAS...
...DISCOLORED FROM RUST!!
ZABULULIN (SPLOOSH)

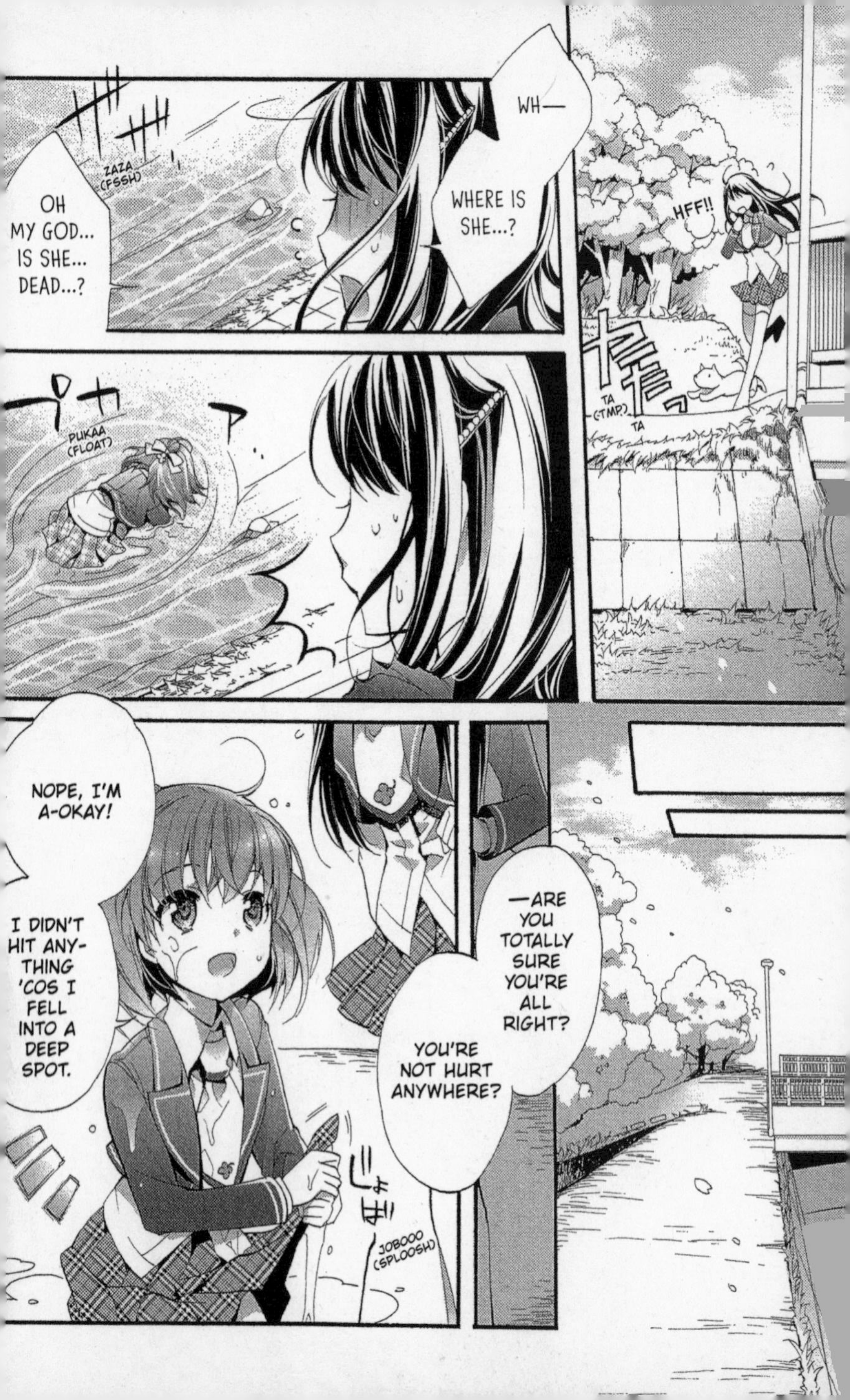
HFF!!
TA (TMP) TA
WH—
WHERE IS SHE...?
ZAZA (FSSH)
OH MY GOD... IS SHE... DEAD...?
PUKAA (FLOAT)
—ARE YOU TOTALLY SURE YOU'RE ALL RIGHT?
YOU'RE NOT HURT ANYWHERE?
NOPE, I'M A-OKAY!
I DIDN'T HIT ANY-THING 'COS I FELL INTO A DEEP SPOT.
JOBOOO (SPLOOSH)

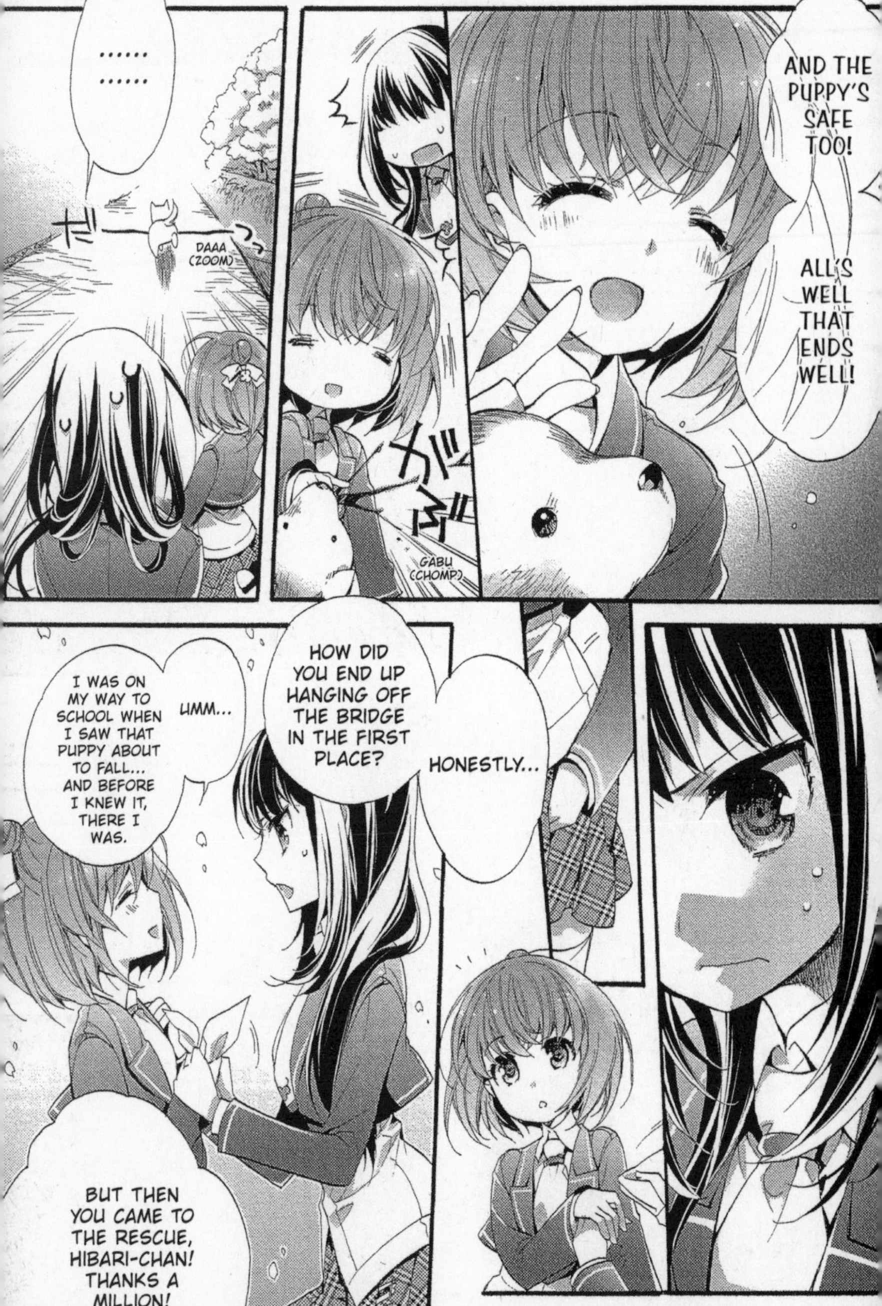
AND THE PUPPY'S SAFE TOO!
ALL'S WELL THAT ENDS WELL!
GABU (CHOMP)
......
......
DAAA (ZOOM)
HONESTLY...
HOW DID YOU END UP HANGING OFF THE BRIDGE IN THE FIRST PLACE?
UMM...
I WAS ON MY WAY TO SCHOOL WHEN I SAW THAT PUPPY ABOUT TO FALL... AND BEFORE I KNEW IT, THERE I WAS.
BUT THEN YOU CAME TO THE RESCUE, HIBARI-CHAN! THANKS A MILLION!

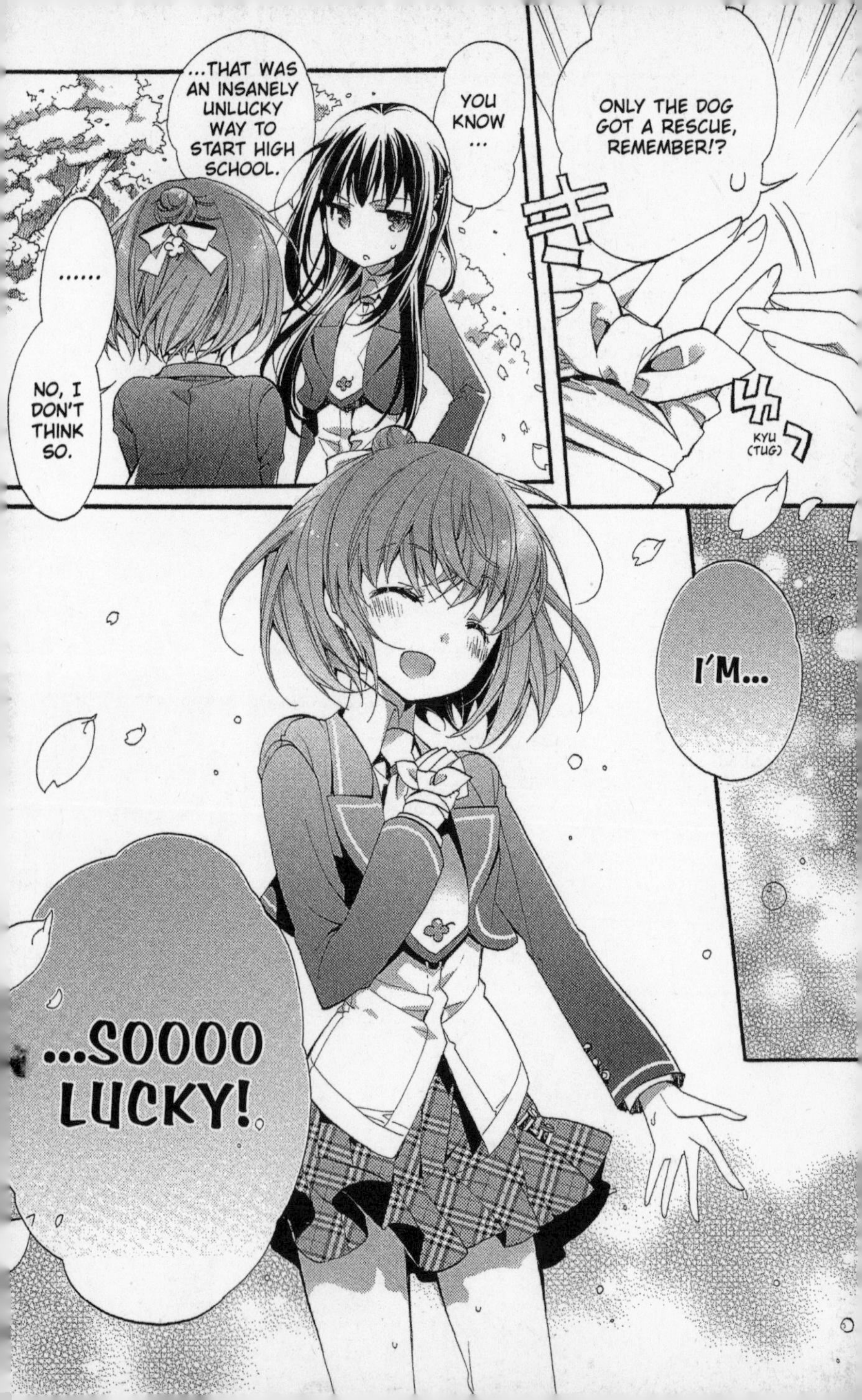
ONLY THE DOG GOT A RESCUE, REMEMBER!?
KYU (TUG)
YOU KNOW...
...THAT WAS AN INSANELY UNLUCKY WAY TO START HIGH SCHOOL.
......
NO, I DON'T THINK SO.
I'M...
...SOOOO LUCKY!

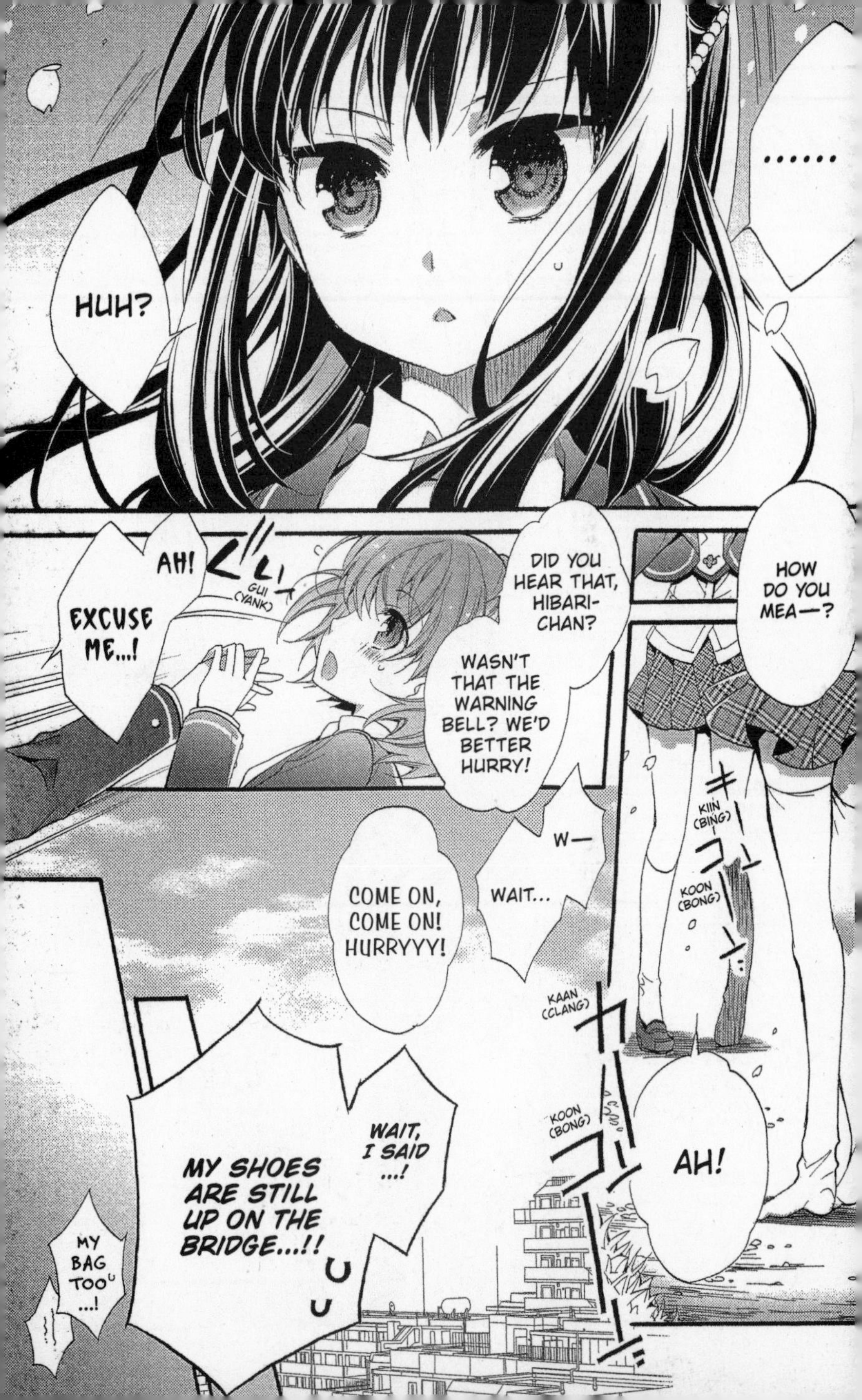
......
HUH?
HOW DO YOU MEA—?
KIIN (BING)
KOON (BONG)
DID YOU HEAR THAT, HIBARI-CHAN?
WASN'T THAT THE WARNING BELL? WE'D BETTER HURRY!
GUI (YANK)
AH!
EXCUSE ME...!
KAAN (CLANG)
KOON (BONG)
AH!
W—
WAIT...
COME ON, COME ON! HURRYYY!
WAIT, I SAID ...!
MY SHOES ARE STILL UP ON THE BRIDGE...!!
MY BAG TOO ...!

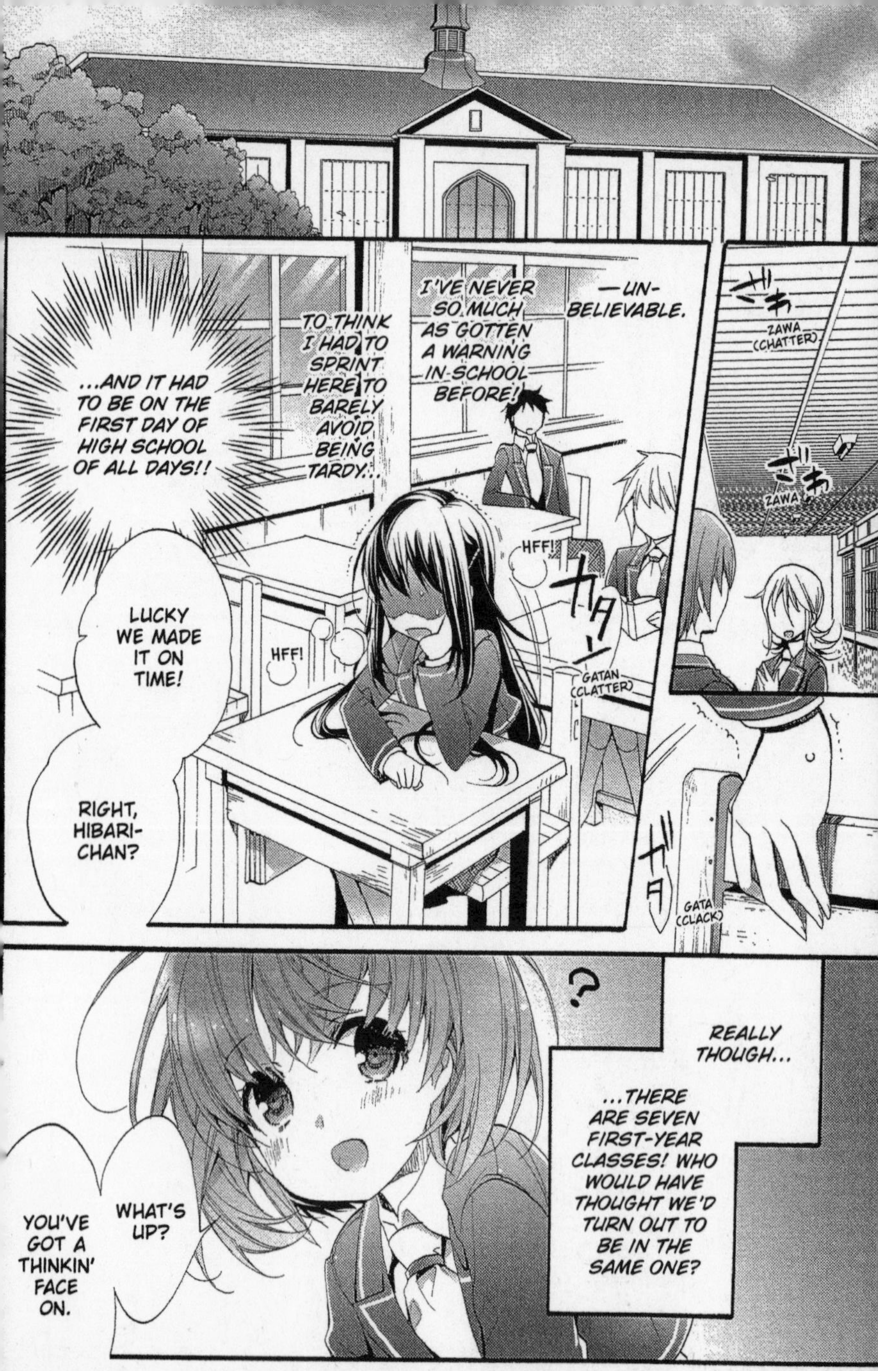
ZAWA (CHATTER)
ZAWA
—UN-BELIEVABLE.
I'VE NEVER SO MUCH AS GOTTEN A WARNING IN-SCHOOL BEFORE!
TO THINK I HAD TO SPRINT HERE TO BARELY AVOID BEING TARDY...
...AND IT HAD TO BE ON THE FIRST DAY OF HIGH SCHOOL OF ALL DAYS!!
HFF!
GATAN (CLATTER)
HFF!
GATA (CLACK)
LUCKY WE MADE IT ON TIME!
RIGHT, HIBARI-CHAN?
?
REALLY THOUGH...
...THERE ARE SEVEN FIRST-YEAR CLASSES! WHO WOULD HAVE THOUGHT WE'D TURN OUT TO BE IN THE SAME ONE?
WHAT'S UP?
YOU'VE GOT A THINKIN' FACE ON.

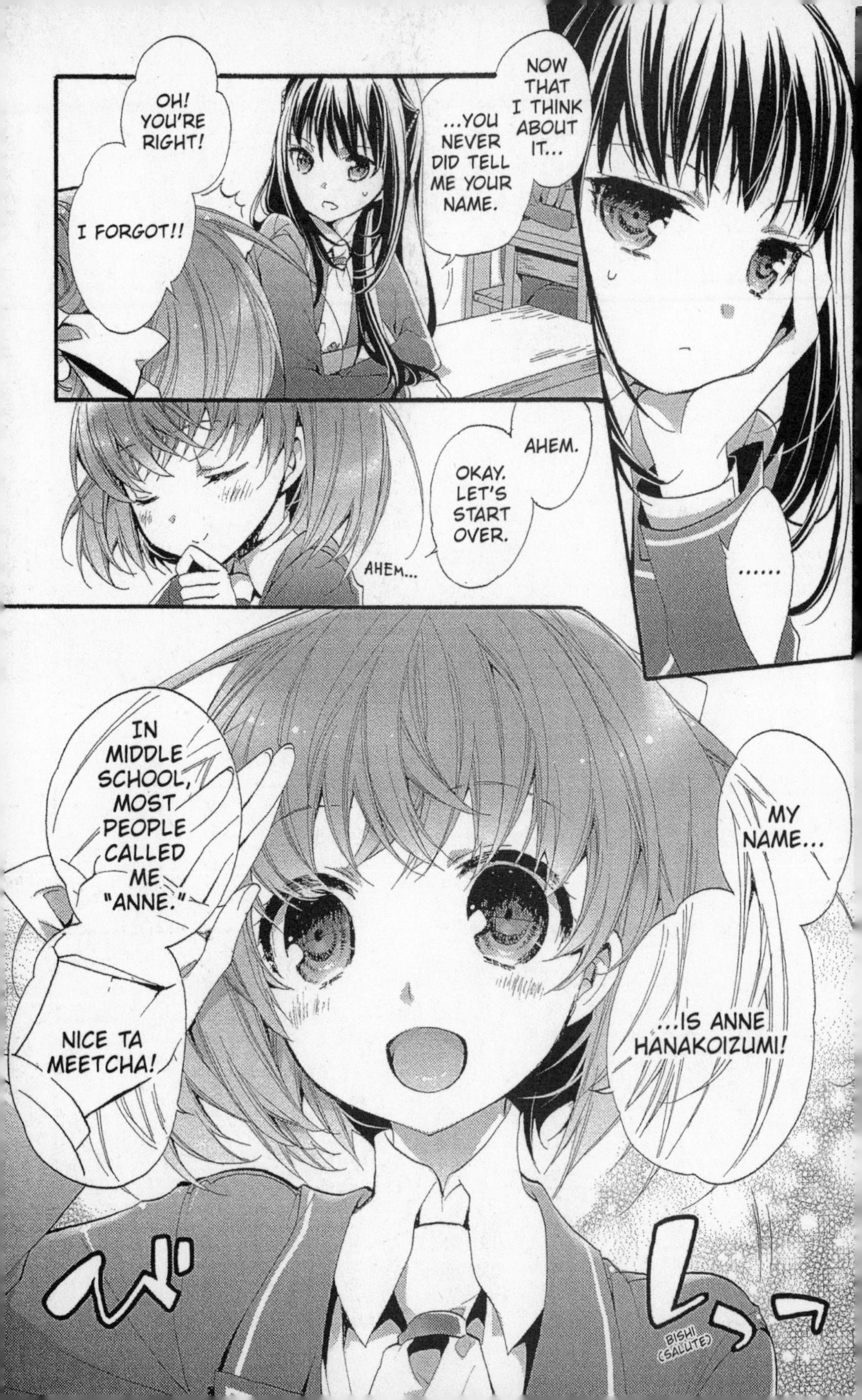
NOW THAT I THINK ABOUT IT...
......
...YOU NEVER DID TELL ME YOUR NAME.
OH! YOU'RE RIGHT!
I FORGOT!!
AHEM.
OKAY. LET'S START OVER.
AHEM...
MY NAME...
...IS ANNE HANAKOIZUMI!
IN MIDDLE SCHOOL, MOST PEOPLE CALLED ME "ANNE."
NICE TA MEETCHA!
BISHI (SALUTE)

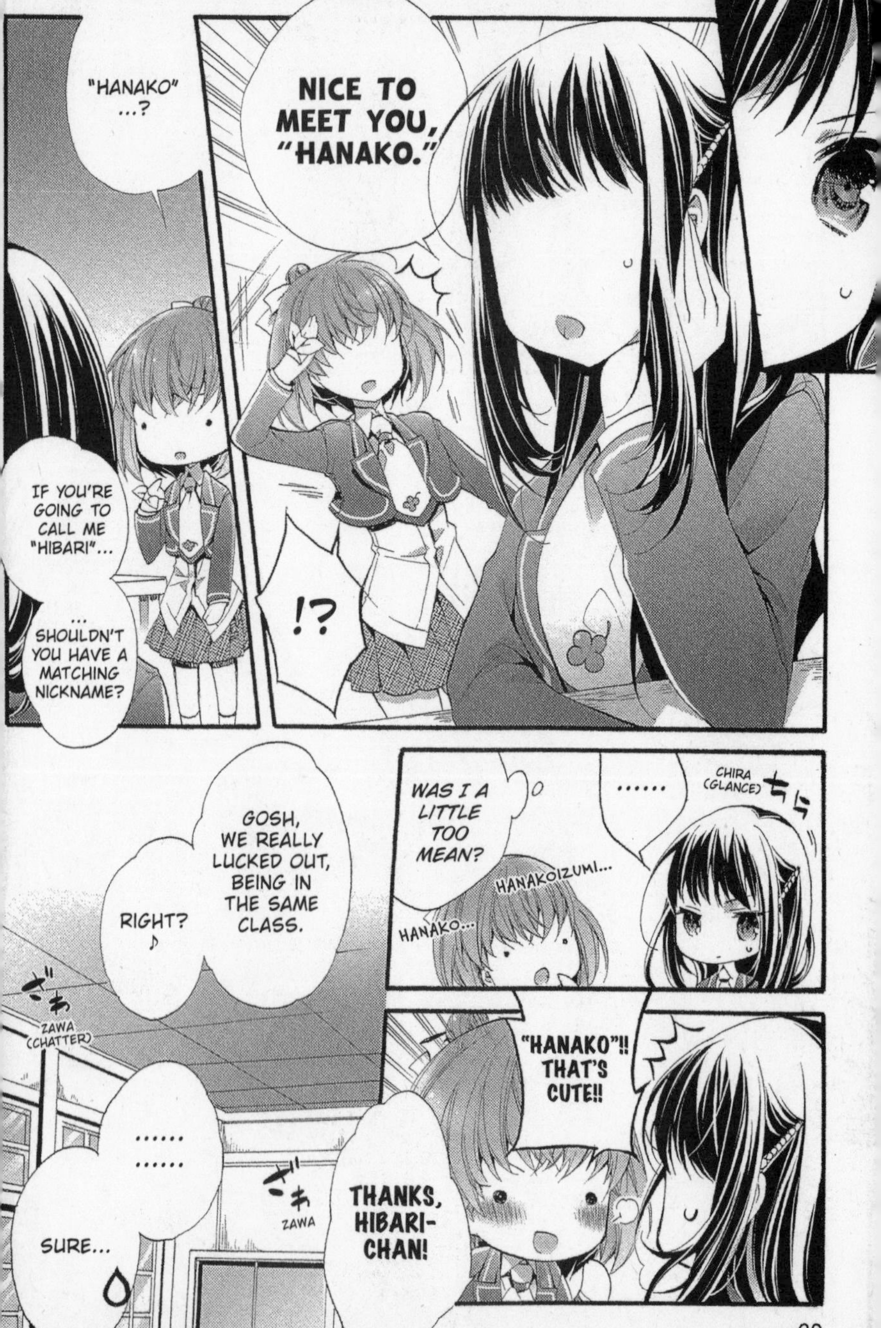
NICE TO MEET YOU, "HANAKO."
!?
"HANAKO" ...?
IF YOU'RE GOING TO CALL ME "HIBARI"...
...SHOULDN'T YOU HAVE A MATCHING NICKNAME?
CHIRA (GLANCE)
......
WAS I A LITTLE TOO MEAN?
HANAKOIZUMI...
HANAKO...
"HANAKO"!! THAT'S CUTE!!
THANKS, HIBARI-CHAN!
ZAWA
GOSH, WE REALLY LUCKED OUT, BEING IN THE SAME CLASS.
RIGHT? ♪
ZAWA (CHATTER)
....
SURE...

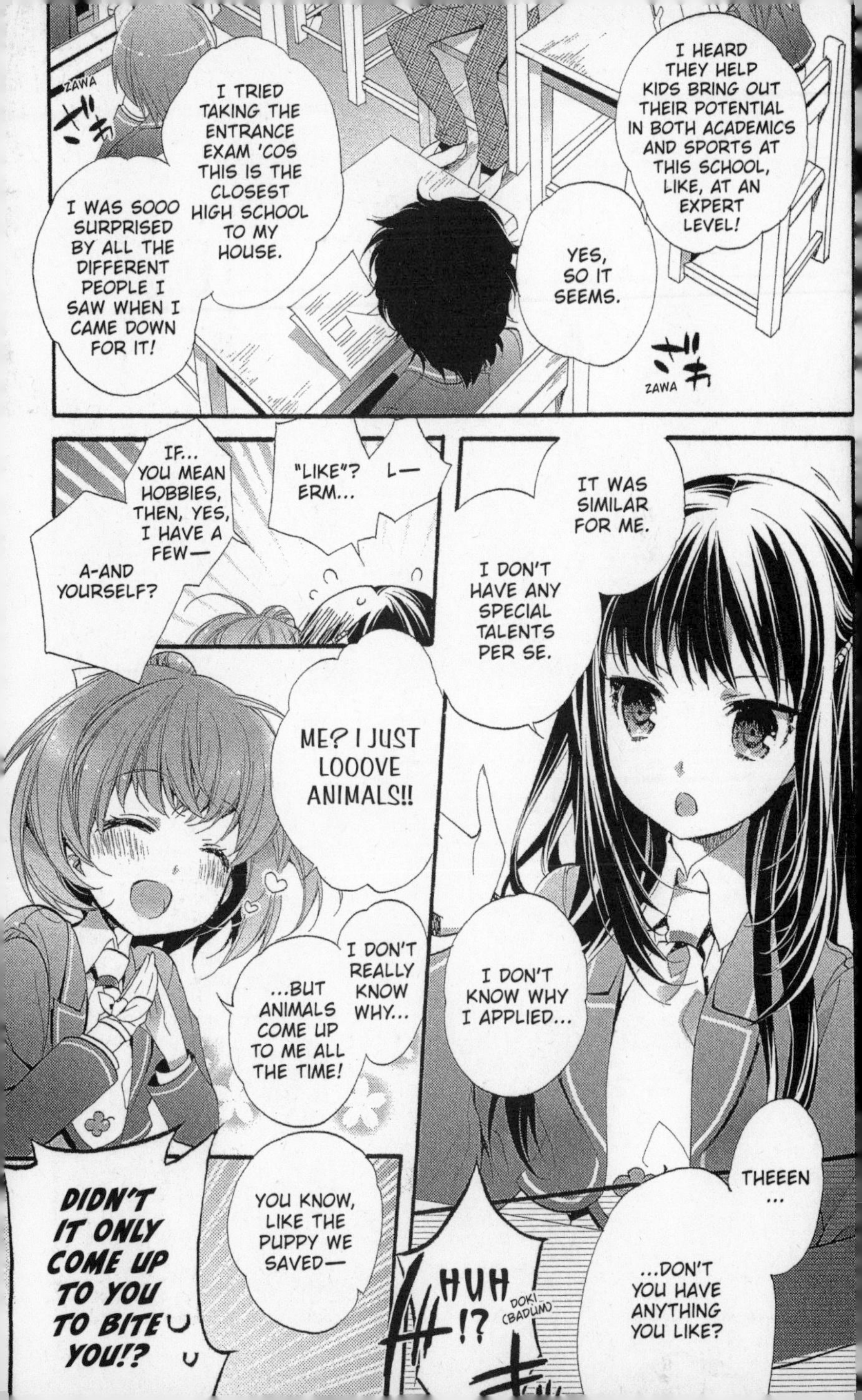
I HEARD THEY HELP KIDS BRING OUT THEIR POTENTIAL IN BOTH ACADEMICS AND SPORTS AT THIS SCHOOL, LIKE, AT AN EXPERT LEVEL!
YES, SO IT SEEMS.
ZAWA
I TRIED TAKING THE ENTRANCE EXAM 'COS THIS IS THE CLOSEST HIGH SCHOOL TO MY HOUSE.
ZAWA
I WAS SOOO SURPRISED BY ALL THE DIFFERENT PEOPLE I SAW WHEN I CAME DOWN FOR IT!
IT WAS SIMILAR FOR ME.
I DON'T HAVE ANY SPECIAL TALENTS PER SE.
I DON'T KNOW WHY I APPLIED...
THEEEN...
...DON'T YOU HAVE ANYTHING YOU LIKE?
DOKI (BADUM)
HUH!?
L— "LIKE"? ERM...
IF... YOU MEAN HOBBIES, THEN, YES, I HAVE A FEW—
A-AND YOURSELF?
ME? I JUST LOOOVE ANIMALS!!
I DON'T REALLY KNOW WHY...
...BUT ANIMALS COME UP TO ME ALL THE TIME!
YOU KNOW, LIKE THE PUPPY WE SAVED—
DIDN'T IT ONLY COME UP TO YOU TO BITE YOU!?

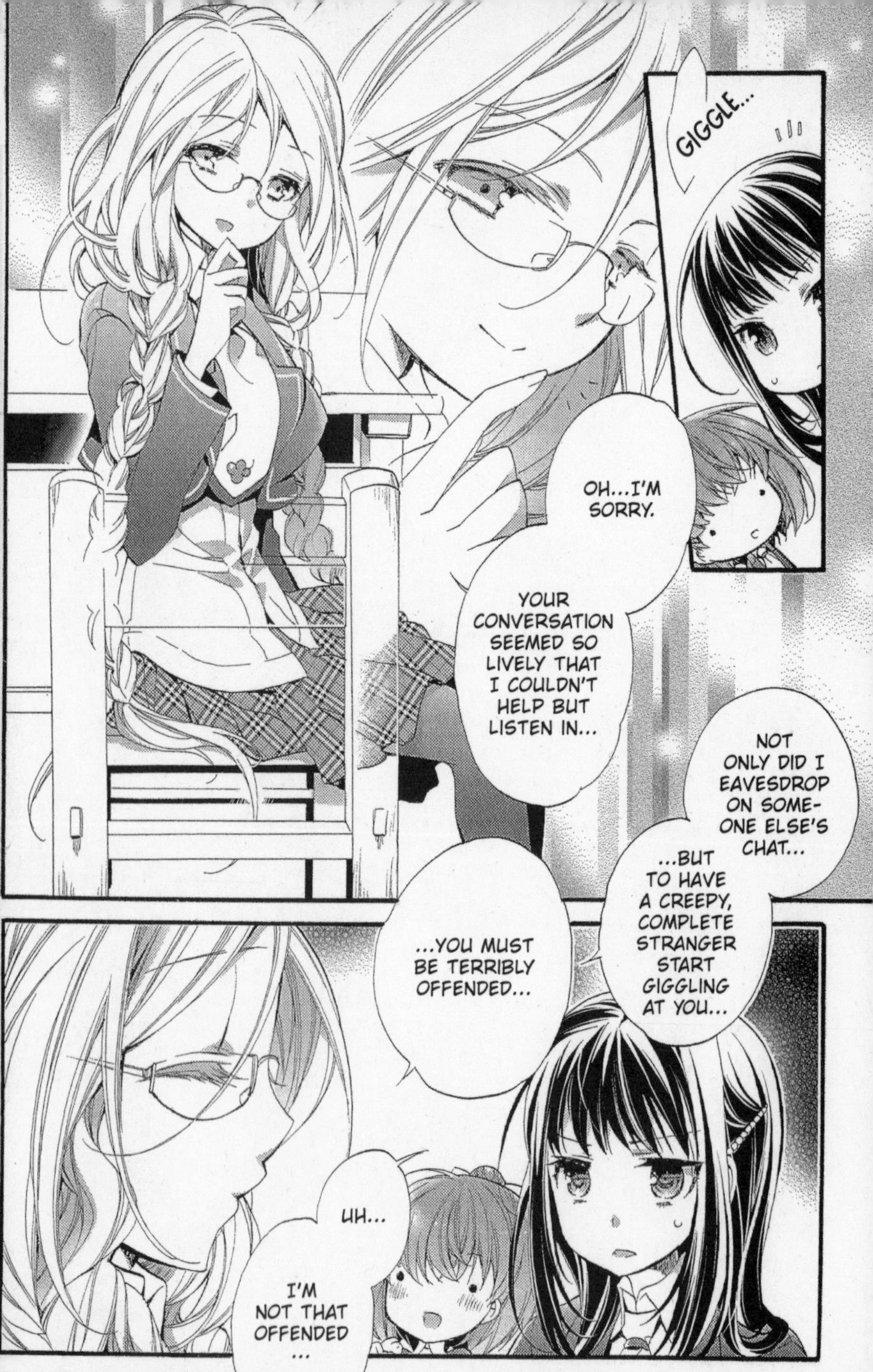
GIGGLE...
OH...I'M SORRY.
YOUR CONVERSATION SEEMED SO LIVELY THAT I COULDN'T HELP BUT LISTEN IN...
NOT ONLY DID I EAVESDROP ON SOME-ONE ELSE'S CHAT...
...BUT TO HAVE A CREEPY, COMPLETE STRANGER START GIGGLING AT YOU...
...YOU MUST BE TERRIBLY OFFENDED...
UH...
I'M NOT THAT OFFENDED ...

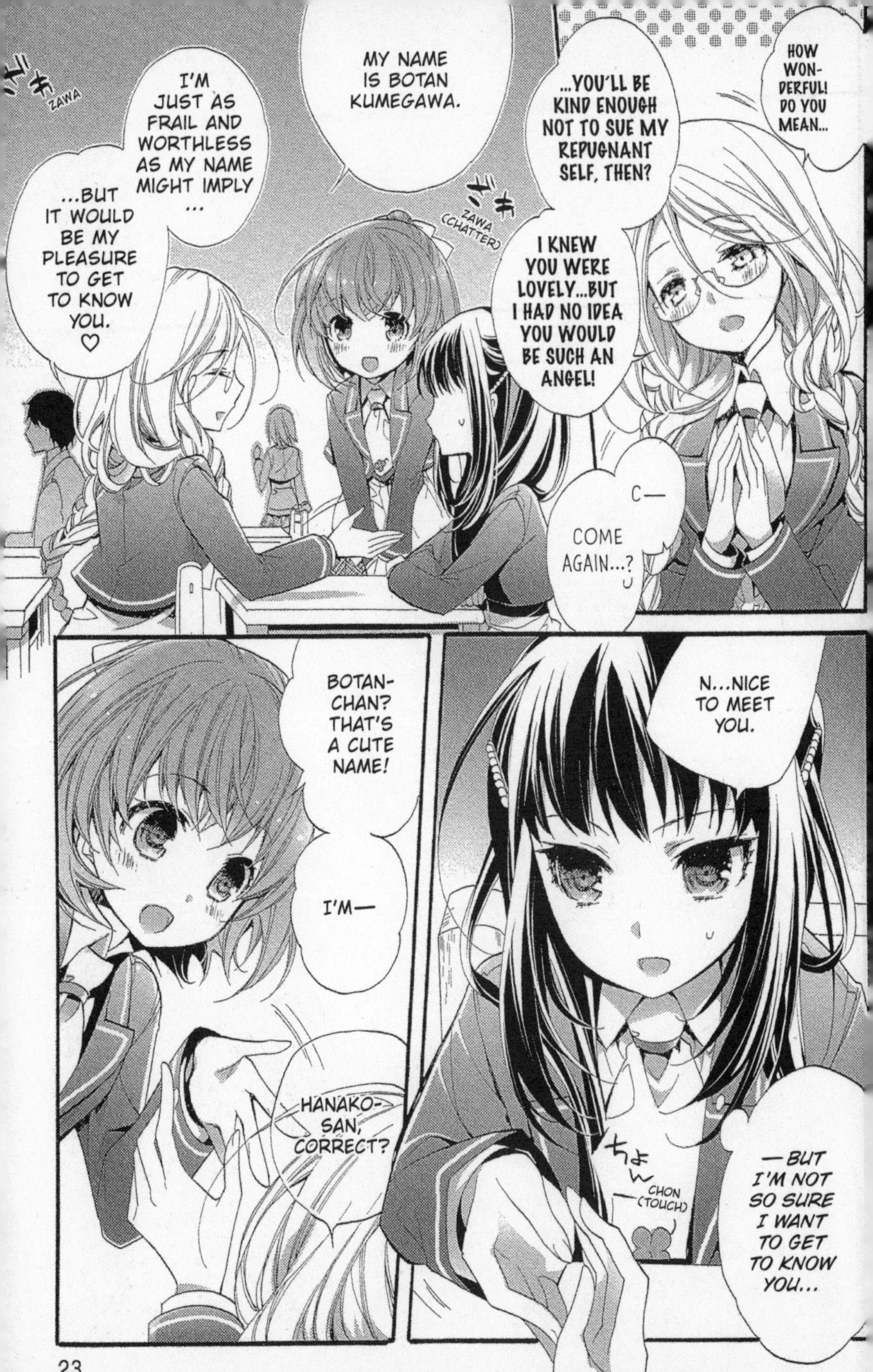
HOW WONDERFUL! DO YOU MEAN...
...YOU'LL BE KIND ENOUGH NOT TO SUE MY REPUGNANT SELF, THEN?
I KNEW YOU WERE LOVELY...BUT I HAD NO IDEA YOU WOULD BE SUCH AN ANGEL!
C— COME AGAIN...?
MY NAME IS BOTAN KUMEGAWA.
ZAWA (CHATTER)
I'M JUST AS FRAIL AND WORTHLESS AS MY NAME MIGHT IMPLY...
...BUT IT WOULD BE MY PLEASURE TO GET TO KNOW YOU. ♡
ZAWA
N...NICE TO MEET YOU.
—BUT I'M NOT SO SURE I WANT TO GET TO KNOW YOU...
ちょん
CHON (TOUCH)
BOTAN-CHAN? THAT'S A CUTE NAME!
I'M—
HANAKO-SAN, CORRECT?

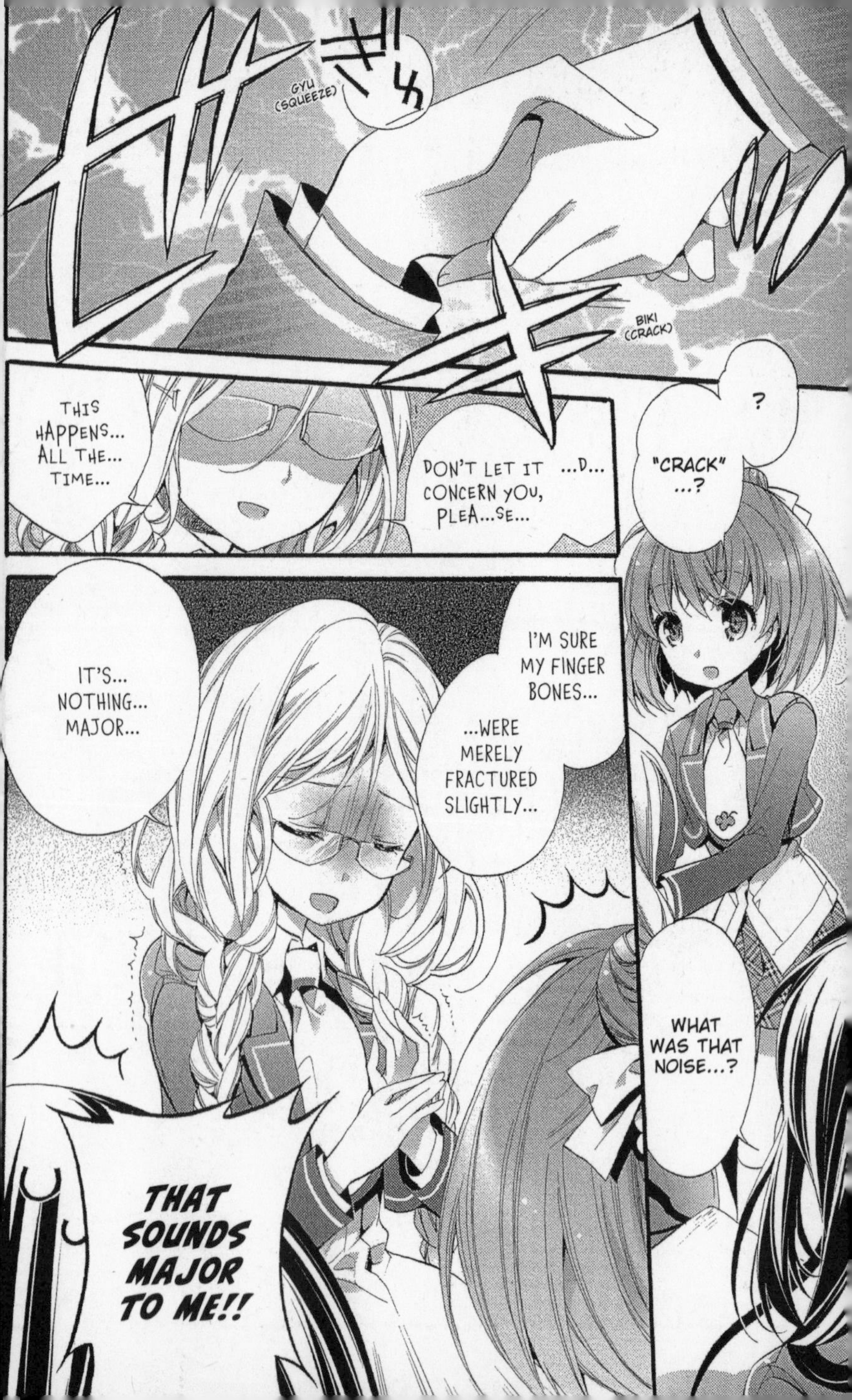
GYU (SQUEEZE)
BIKI (CRACK)
?
"CRACK" ...?
WHAT WAS THAT NOISE...?
...D...
DON'T LET IT CONCERN YOU, PLEA...SE...
THIS HAPPENS... ALL THE... TIME...
I'M SURE MY FINGER BONES...
...WERE MERELY FRACTURED SLIGHTLY...
IT'S... NOTHING... MAJOR...
THAT SOUNDS MAJOR TO ME!!

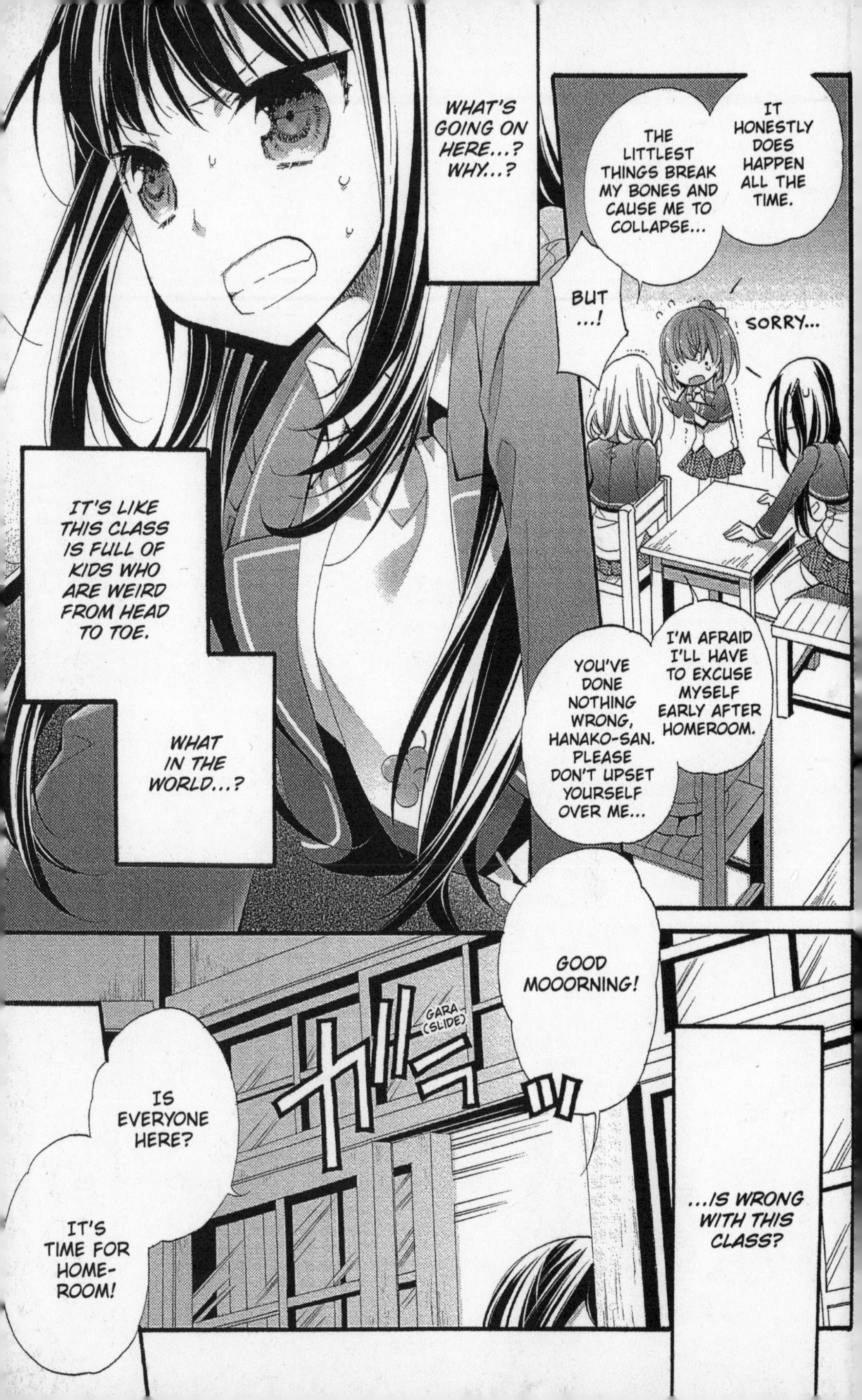
IT HONESTLY DOES HAPPEN ALL THE TIME.
THE LITTLEST THINGS BREAK MY BONES AND CAUSE ME TO COLLAPSE...
BUT ...!
SORRY...
I'M AFRAID I'LL HAVE TO EXCUSE MYSELF EARLY AFTER HOMEROOM.
YOU'VE DONE NOTHING WRONG, HANAKO-SAN. PLEASE DON'T UPSET YOURSELF OVER ME...
WHAT'S GOING ON HERE...? WHY...?
IT'S LIKE THIS CLASS IS FULL OF KIDS WHO ARE WEIRD FROM HEAD TO TOE.
WHAT IN THE WORLD...?
...IS WRONG WITH THIS CLASS?
GOOD MOOORNING!
GARA (SLIDE)
IS EVERYONE HERE?
IT'S TIME FOR HOME-ROOM!

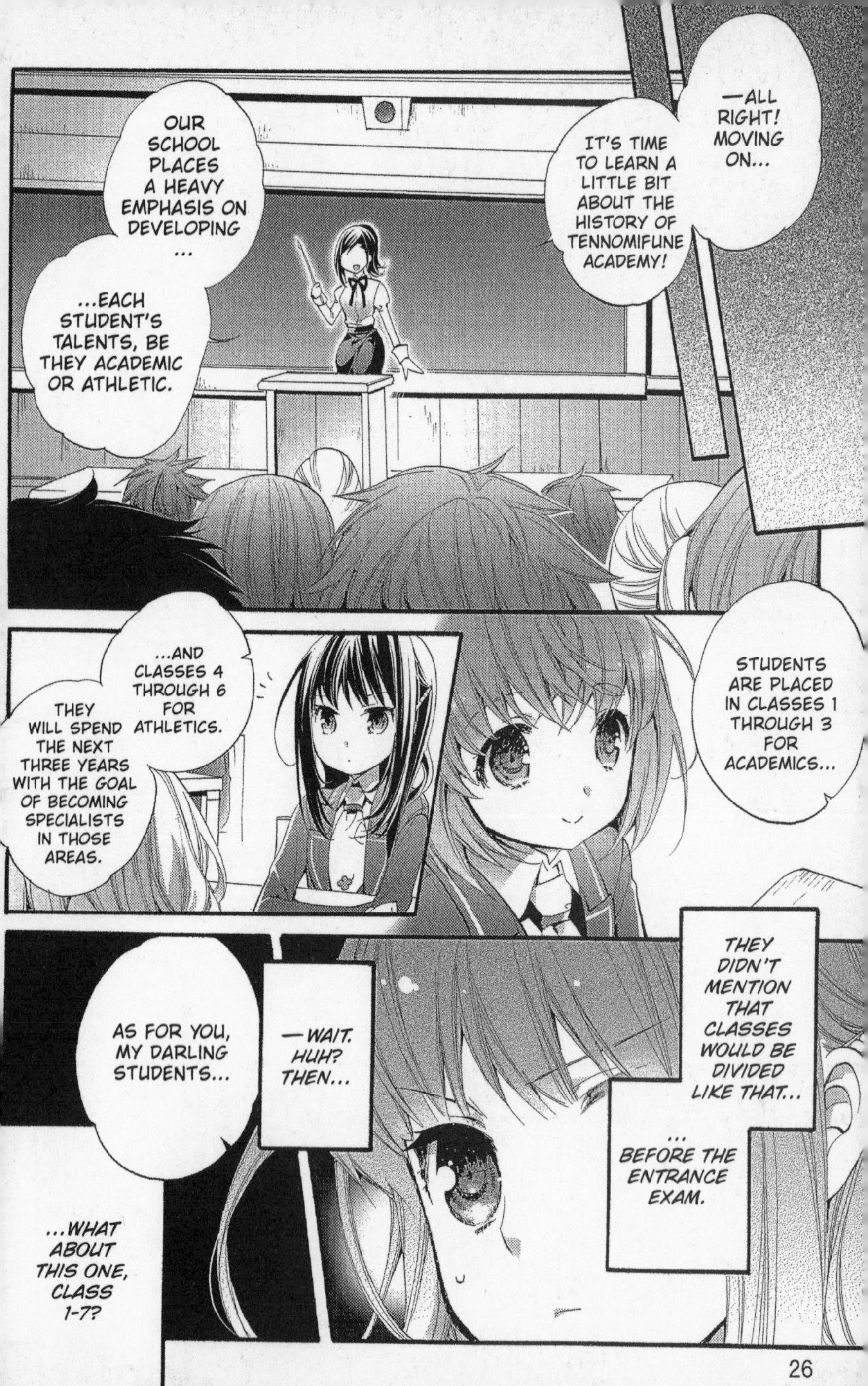
—ALL RIGHT! MOVING ON...
IT'S TIME TO LEARN A LITTLE BIT ABOUT THE HISTORY OF TENNOMIFUNE ACADEMY!
OUR SCHOOL PLACES A HEAVY EMPHASIS ON DEVELOPING ...
...EACH STUDENT'S TALENTS, BE THEY ACADEMIC OR ATHLETIC.
STUDENTS ARE PLACED IN CLASSES 1 THROUGH 3 FOR ACADEMICS...
...AND CLASSES 4 THROUGH 6 FOR ATHLETICS.
THEY WILL SPEND THE NEXT THREE YEARS WITH THE GOAL OF BECOMING SPECIALISTS IN THOSE AREAS.
THEY DIDN'T MENTION THAT CLASSES WOULD BE DIVIDED LIKE THAT...
... BEFORE THE ENTRANCE EXAM.
—WAIT. HUH? THEN...
AS FOR YOU, MY DARLING STUDENTS...
...WHAT ABOUT THIS ONE, CLASS 1-7?

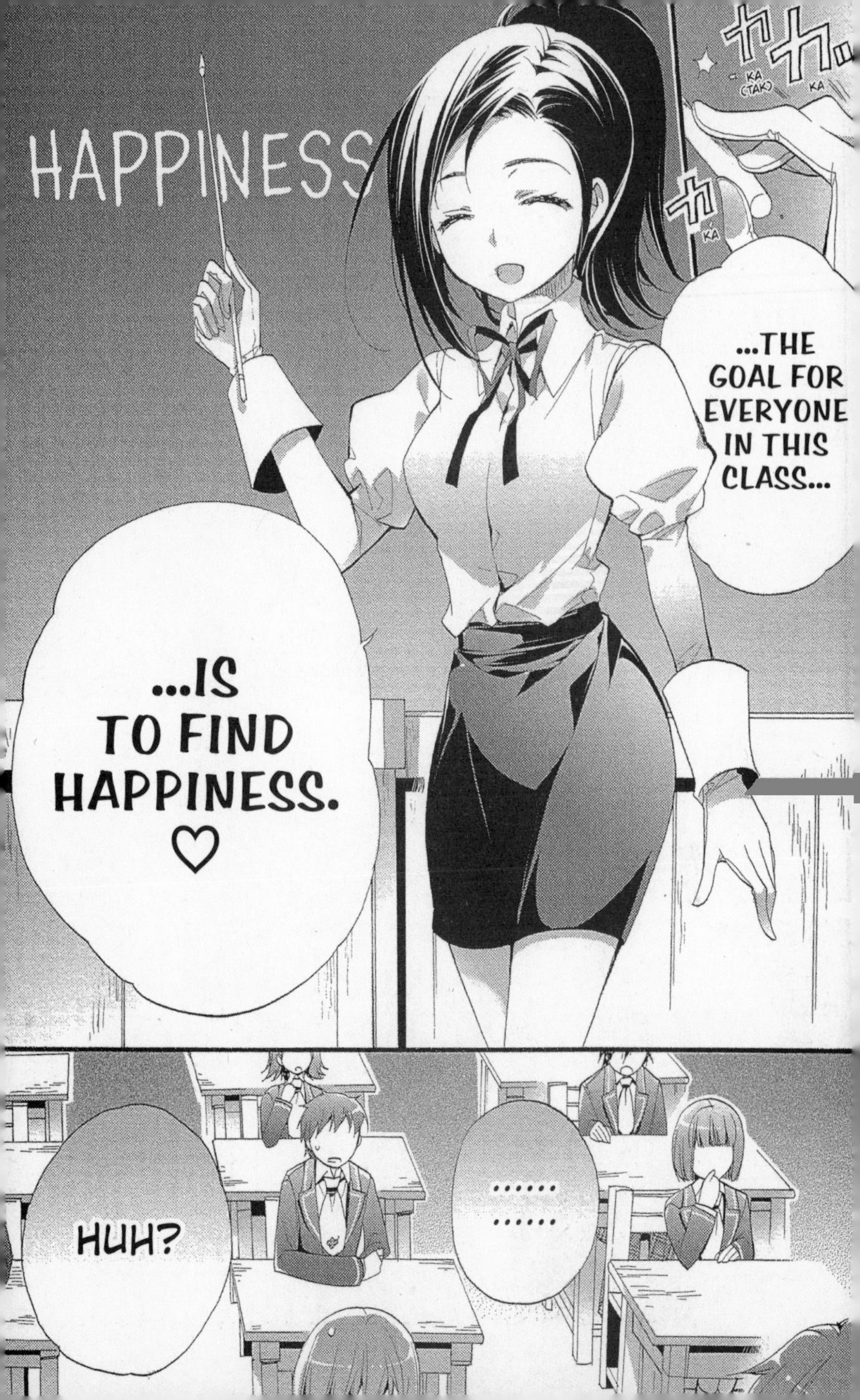
KA (TAK) KA
KA
HAPPINESS
...THE GOAL FOR EVERYONE IN THIS CLASS...
...IS TO FIND HAPPINESS. ♡
......
......
HUH?

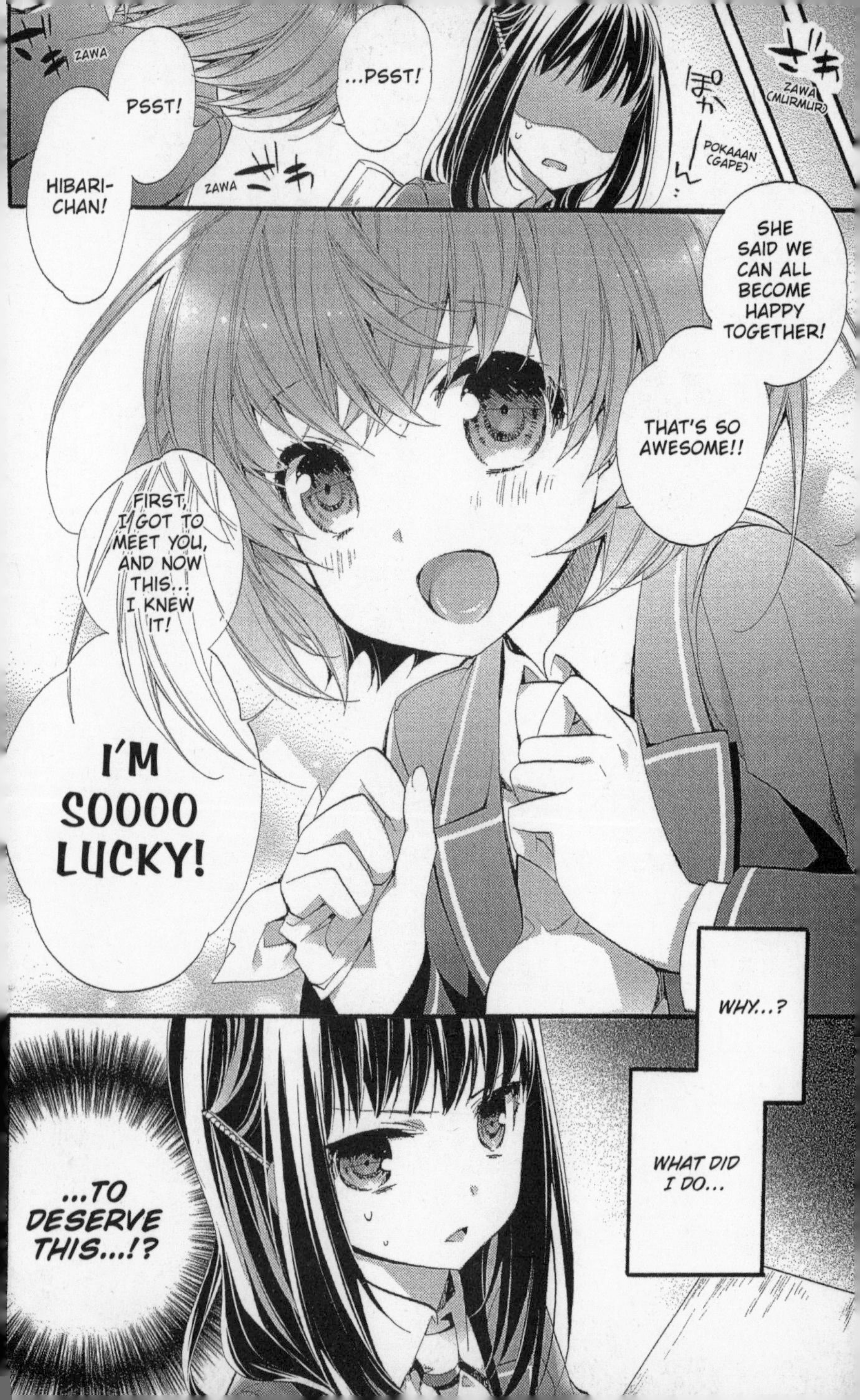
ZAWA (MURMUR)
POKAAAN (GAPE)
...PSST!
ZAWA
PSST!
HIBARI-CHAN!
ZAWA
SHE SAID WE CAN ALL BECOME HAPPY TOGETHER!
THAT'S SO AWESOME!!
FIRST, I GOT TO MEET YOU, AND NOW THIS... I KNEW IT!
I'M SOOOO LUCKY!
WHY...?
WHAT DID I DO...
...TO DESERVE THIS...!?

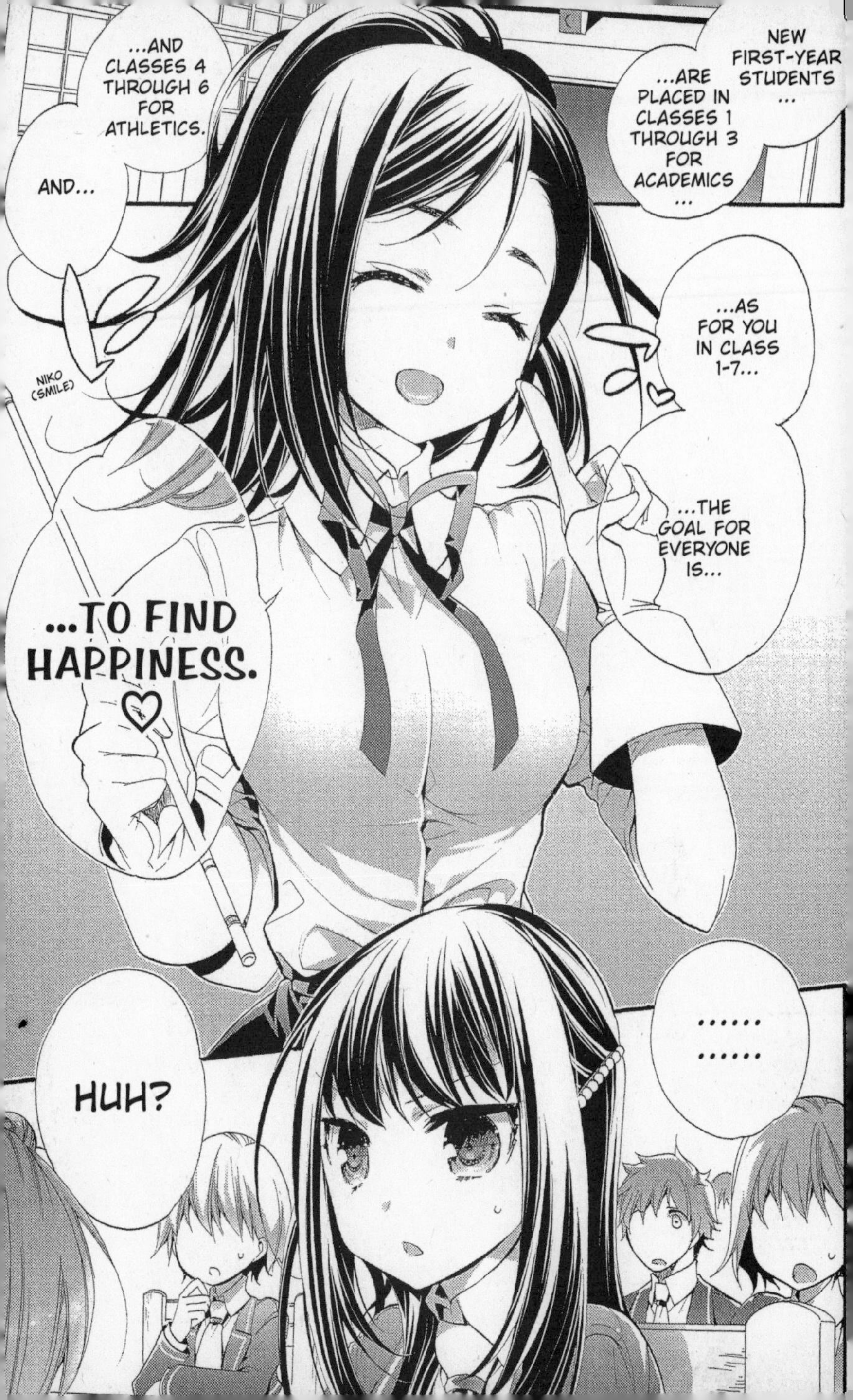
NEW FIRST-YEAR STUDENTS...
...ARE PLACED IN CLASSES 1 THROUGH 3 FOR ACADEMICS...
...AND CLASSES 4 THROUGH 6 FOR ATHLETICS.
AND...
NIKO (SMILE)
...AS FOR YOU IN CLASS 1-7...
...THE GOAL FOR EVERYONE IS...
...TO FIND HAPPINESS. ♡
......
......
HUH?

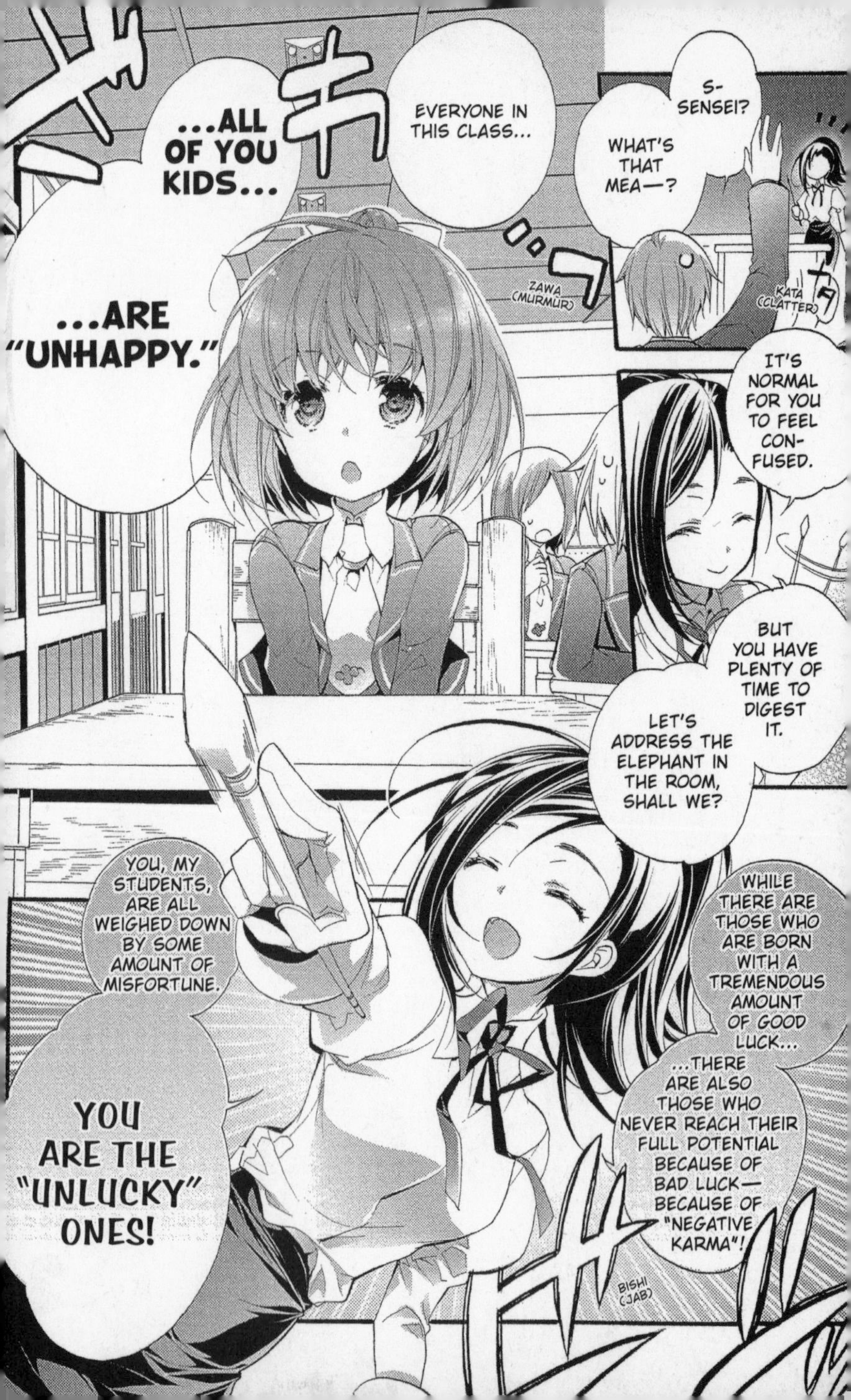
EVERYONE IN THIS CLASS...
...ALL OF YOU KIDS...
...ARE "UNHAPPY."
ZAWA (MURMUR)
S-SENSEI?
WHAT'S THAT MEA—?
KATA (CLATTER)
IT'S NORMAL FOR YOU TO FEEL CON-FUSED.
BUT YOU HAVE PLENTY OF TIME TO DIGEST IT.
LET'S ADDRESS THE ELEPHANT IN THE ROOM, SHALL WE?
WHILE THERE ARE THOSE WHO ARE BORN WITH A TREMENDOUS AMOUNT OF GOOD LUCK...
...THERE ARE ALSO THOSE WHO NEVER REACH THEIR FULL POTENTIAL BECAUSE OF BAD LUCK— BECAUSE OF "NEGATIVE KARMA"!
YOU, MY STUDENTS, ARE ALL WEIGHED DOWN BY SOME AMOUNT OF MISFORTUNE.
YOU ARE THE "UNLUCKY" ONES!
BISHI (JAB)

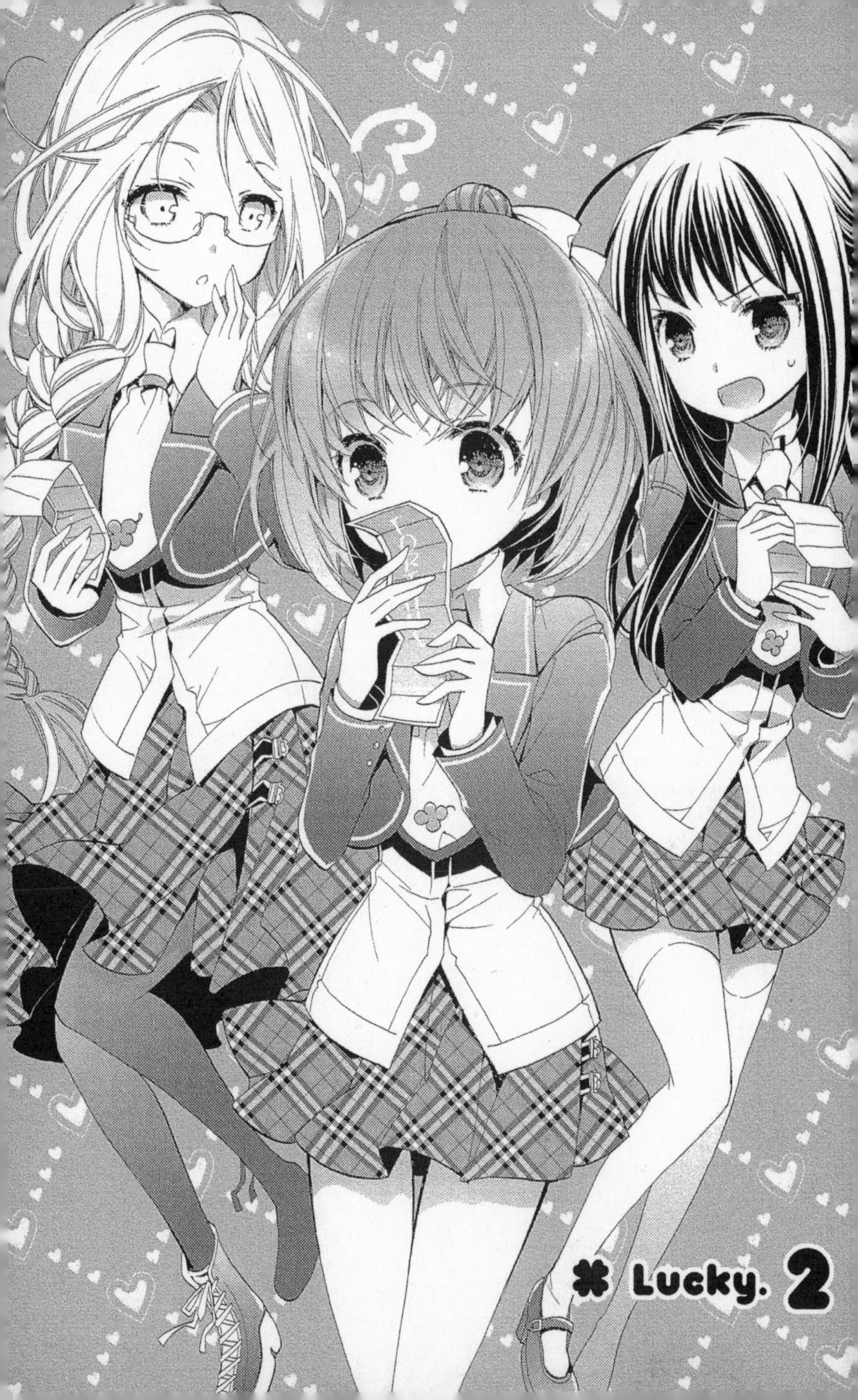
Lucky. 2

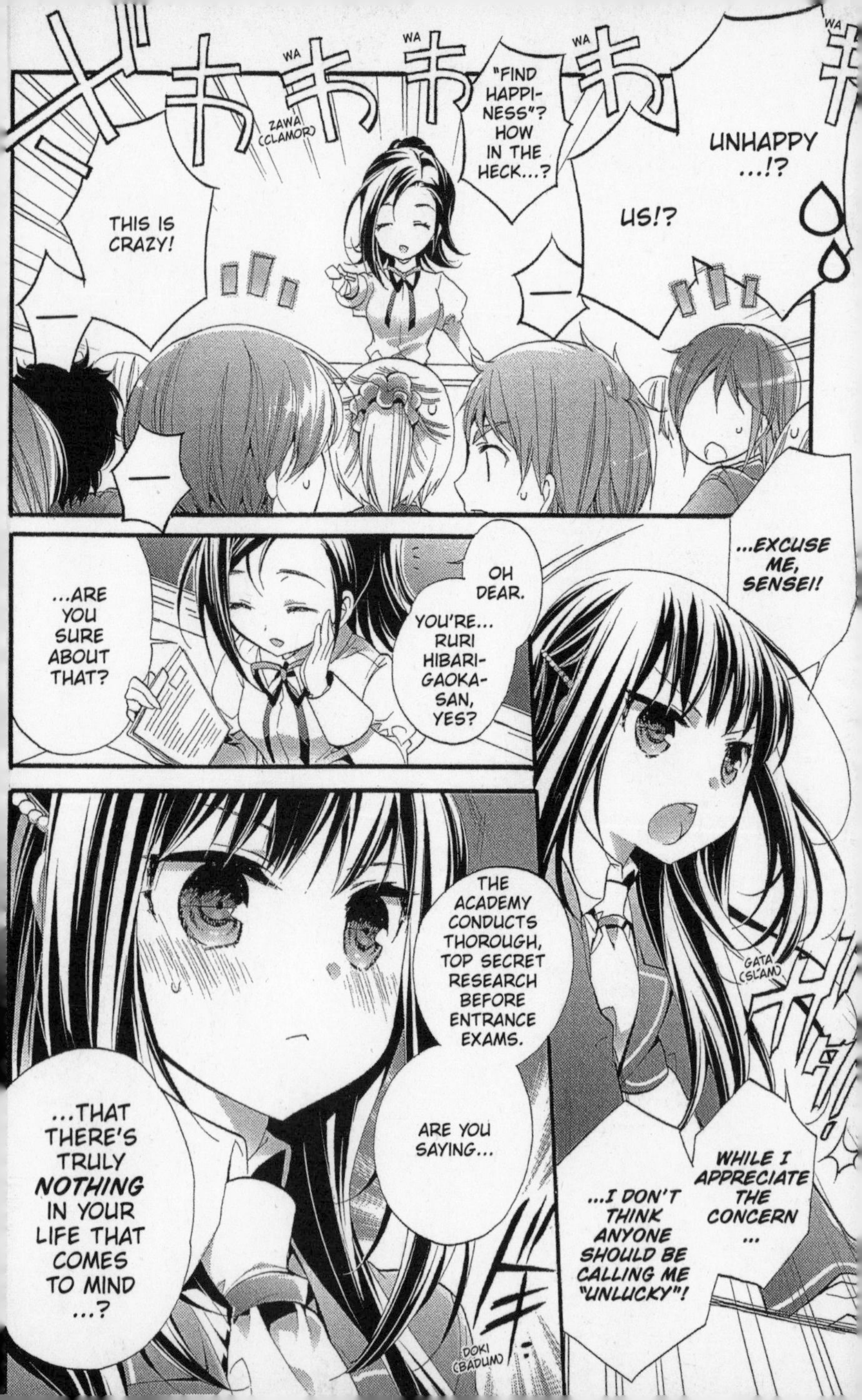
WA
WA
WA
WA
UNHAPPY ...!?
US!?
—
"FIND HAPPINESS"? HOW IN THE HECK...?
ZAWA (CLAMOR)
THIS IS CRAZY!
—
—
...EXCUSE ME, SENSEI!
GATA (SLAM)
WHILE I APPRECIATE THE CONCERN ...
...I DON'T THINK ANYONE SHOULD BE CALLING ME "UNLUCKY"!
OH DEAR. YOU'RE... RURI HIBARI-GAOKA-SAN, YES?
...ARE YOU SURE ABOUT THAT?
THE ACADEMY CONDUCTS THOROUGH, TOP SECRET RESEARCH BEFORE ENTRANCE EXAMS.
ARE YOU SAYING...
...THAT THERE'S TRULY NOTHING IN YOUR LIFE THAT COMES TO MIND ...?
DOKI (BADUM)

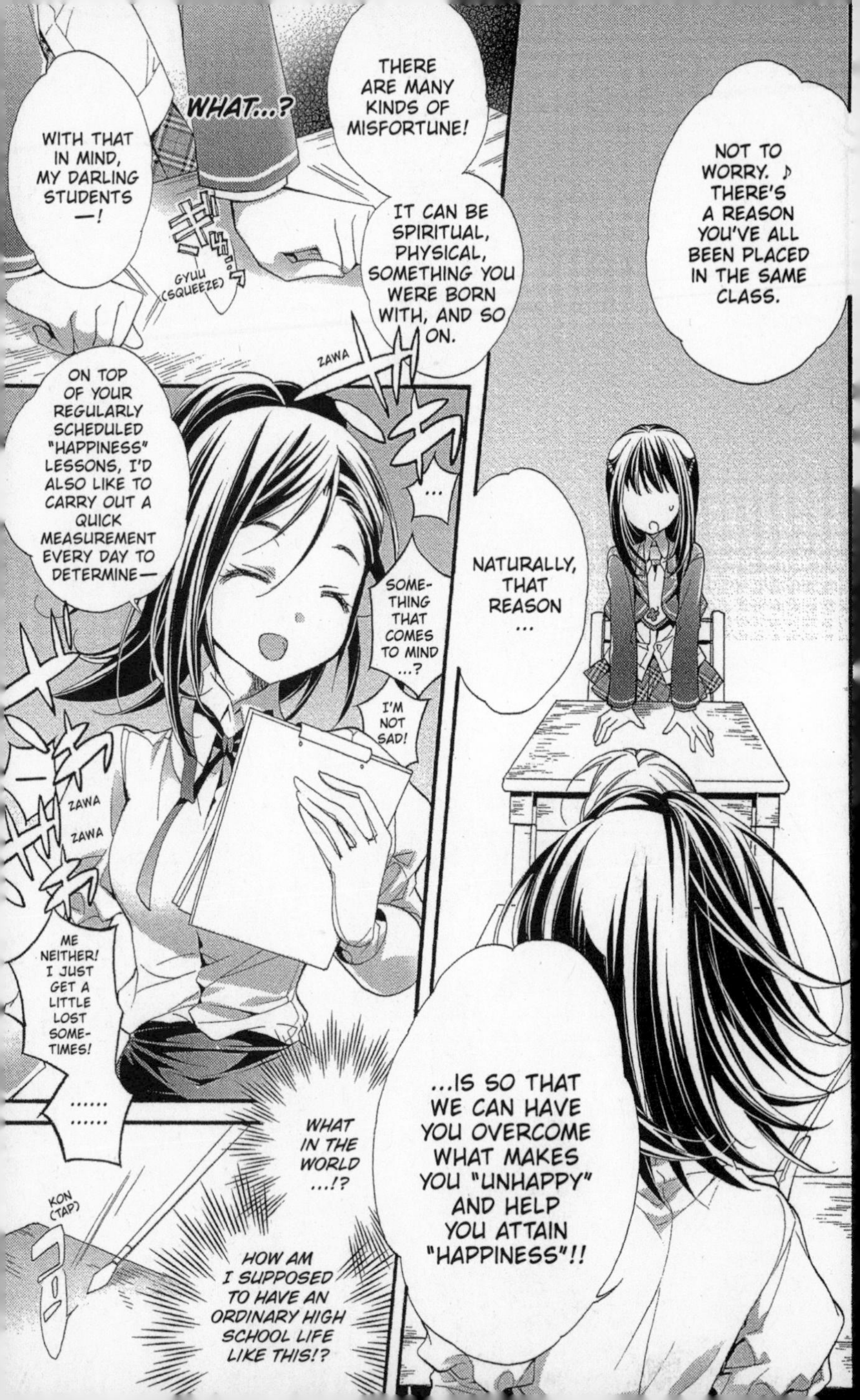
NOT TO WORRY. ♪ THERE'S A REASON YOU'VE ALL BEEN PLACED IN THE SAME CLASS.
NATURALLY, THAT REASON ...
...IS SO THAT WE CAN HAVE YOU OVERCOME WHAT MAKES YOU "UNHAPPY" AND HELP YOU ATTAIN "HAPPINESS"!!
THERE ARE MANY KINDS OF MISFORTUNE!
IT CAN BE SPIRITUAL, PHYSICAL, SOMETHING YOU WERE BORN WITH, AND SO ON.
WHAT...?
GYUU (SQUEEZE)
WITH THAT IN MIND, MY DARLING STUDENTS —!
ZAWA
...
ON TOP OF YOUR REGULARLY SCHEDULED "HAPPINESS" LESSONS, I'D ALSO LIKE TO CARRY OUT A QUICK MEASUREMENT EVERY DAY TO DETERMINE—
SOME-THING THAT COMES TO MIND ...?
I'M NOT SAD!
ZAWA
ZAWA
ME NEITHER! I JUST GET A LITTLE LOST SOME-TIMES!
......
......
WHAT IN THE WORLD ...!?
KON (TAP)
HOW AM I SUPPOSED TO HAVE AN ORDINARY HIGH SCHOOL LIFE LIKE THIS!?

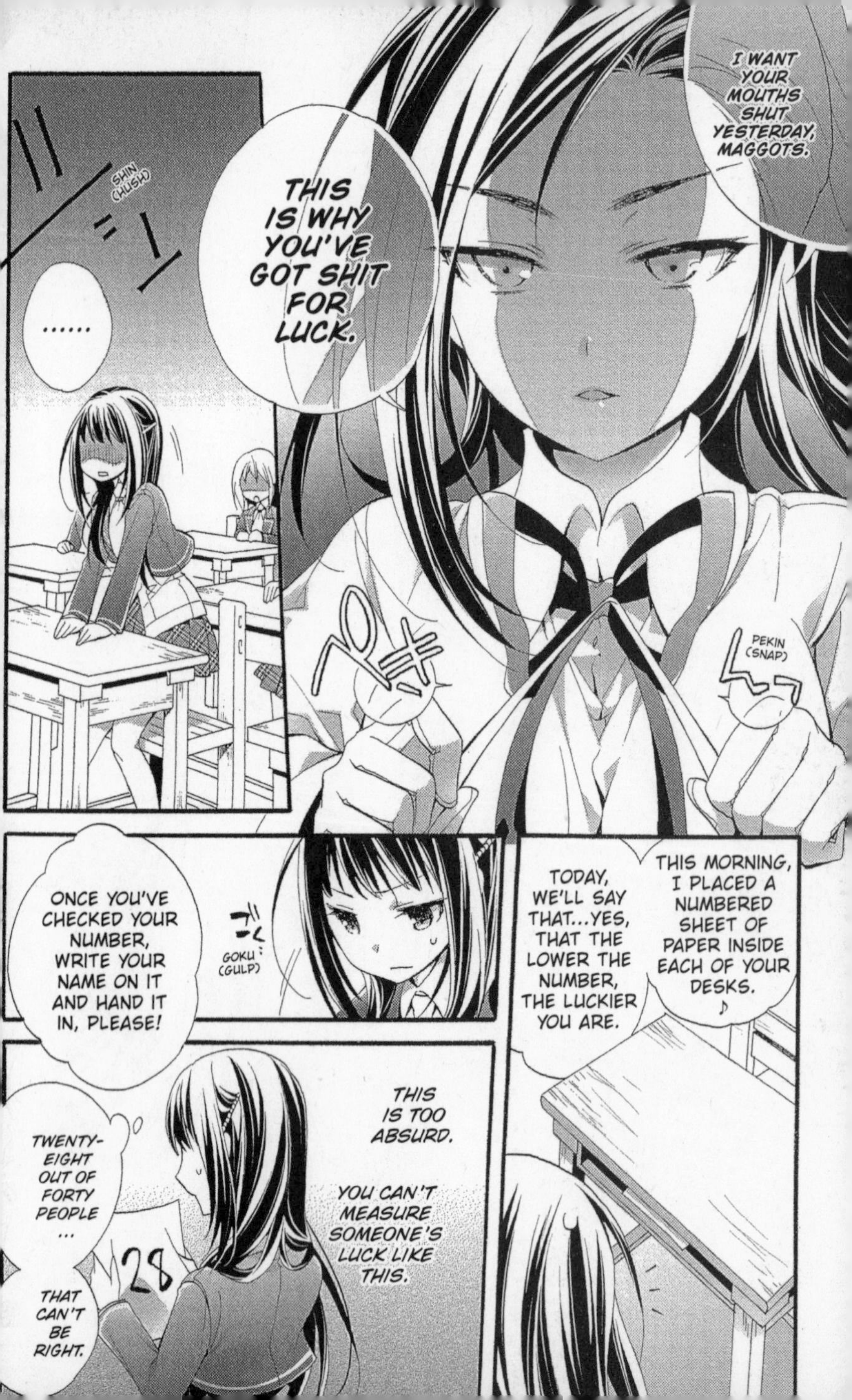
I WANT YOUR MOUTHS SHUT YESTERDAY, MAGGOTS.
THIS IS WHY YOU'VE GOT SHIT FOR LUCK.
PEKIN (SNAP)
SHIN (HUSH)
......
THIS MORNING, I PLACED A NUMBERED SHEET OF PAPER INSIDE EACH OF YOUR DESKS. ♪
TODAY, WE'LL SAY THAT...YES, THAT THE LOWER THE NUMBER, THE LUCKIER YOU ARE.
GOKU (GULP)
ONCE YOU'VE CHECKED YOUR NUMBER, WRITE YOUR NAME ON IT AND HAND IT IN, PLEASE!
THIS IS TOO ABSURD.
YOU CAN'T MEASURE SOMEONE'S LUCK LIKE THIS.
TWENTY-EIGHT OUT OF FORTY PEOPLE ...
28
THAT CAN'T BE RIGHT.

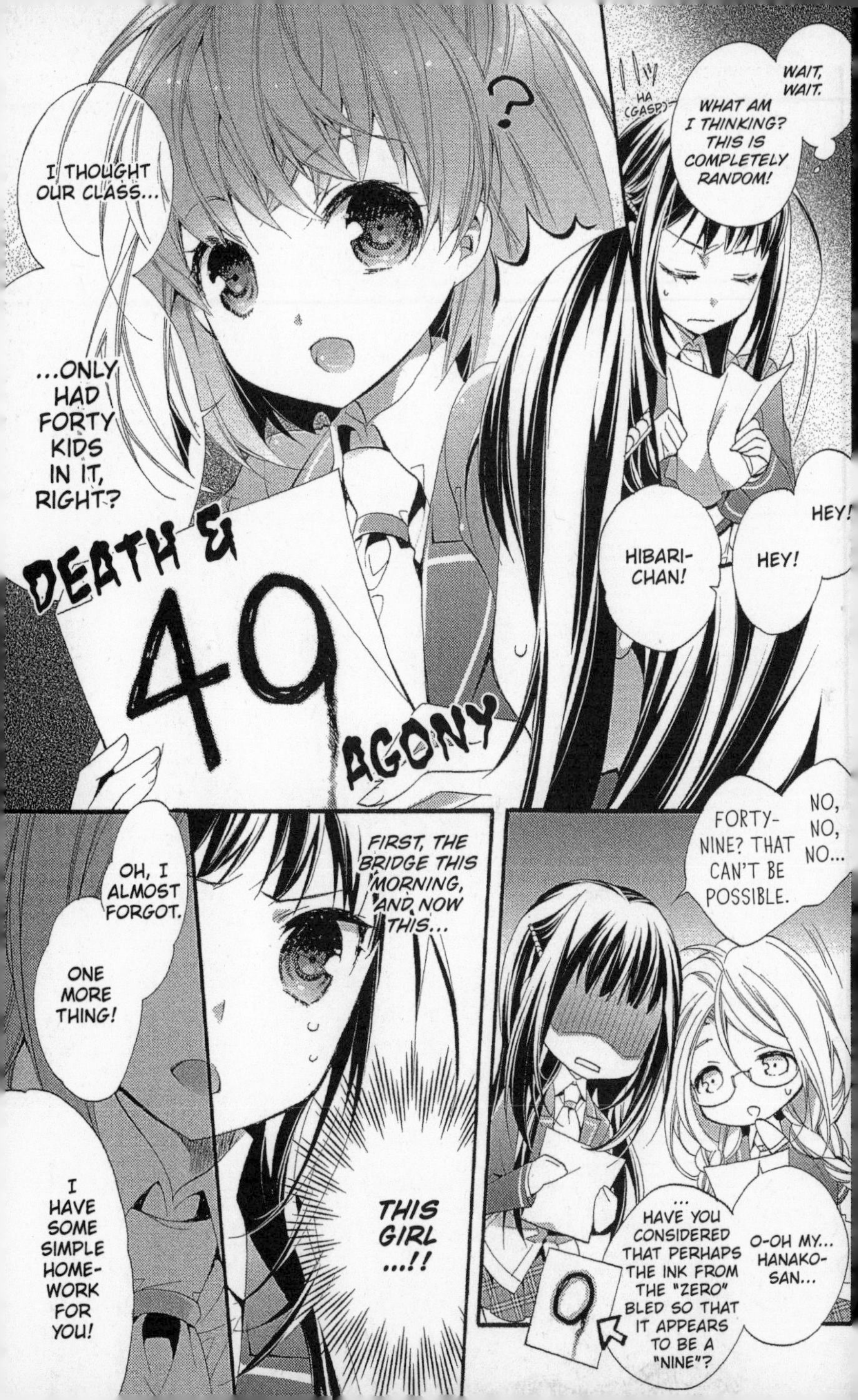
HA (GASP)
WAIT, WAIT.
WHAT AM I THINKING? THIS IS COMPLETELY RANDOM!
HEY!
HEY!
HIBARI-CHAN!
I THOUGHT OUR CLASS...
...ONLY HAD FORTY KIDS IN IT, RIGHT?
DEATH &
49
AGONY
NO, NO, NO...
FORTY-NINE? THAT CAN'T BE POSSIBLE.
O-OH MY... HANAKO-SAN...
...HAVE YOU CONSIDERED THAT PERHAPS THE INK FROM THE "ZERO" BLED SO THAT IT APPEARS TO BE A "NINE"?
9
FIRST, THE BRIDGE THIS MORNING, AND NOW THIS...
THIS GIRL...!!
OH, I ALMOST FORGOT.
ONE MORE THING!
I HAVE SOME SIMPLE HOMEWORK FOR YOU!

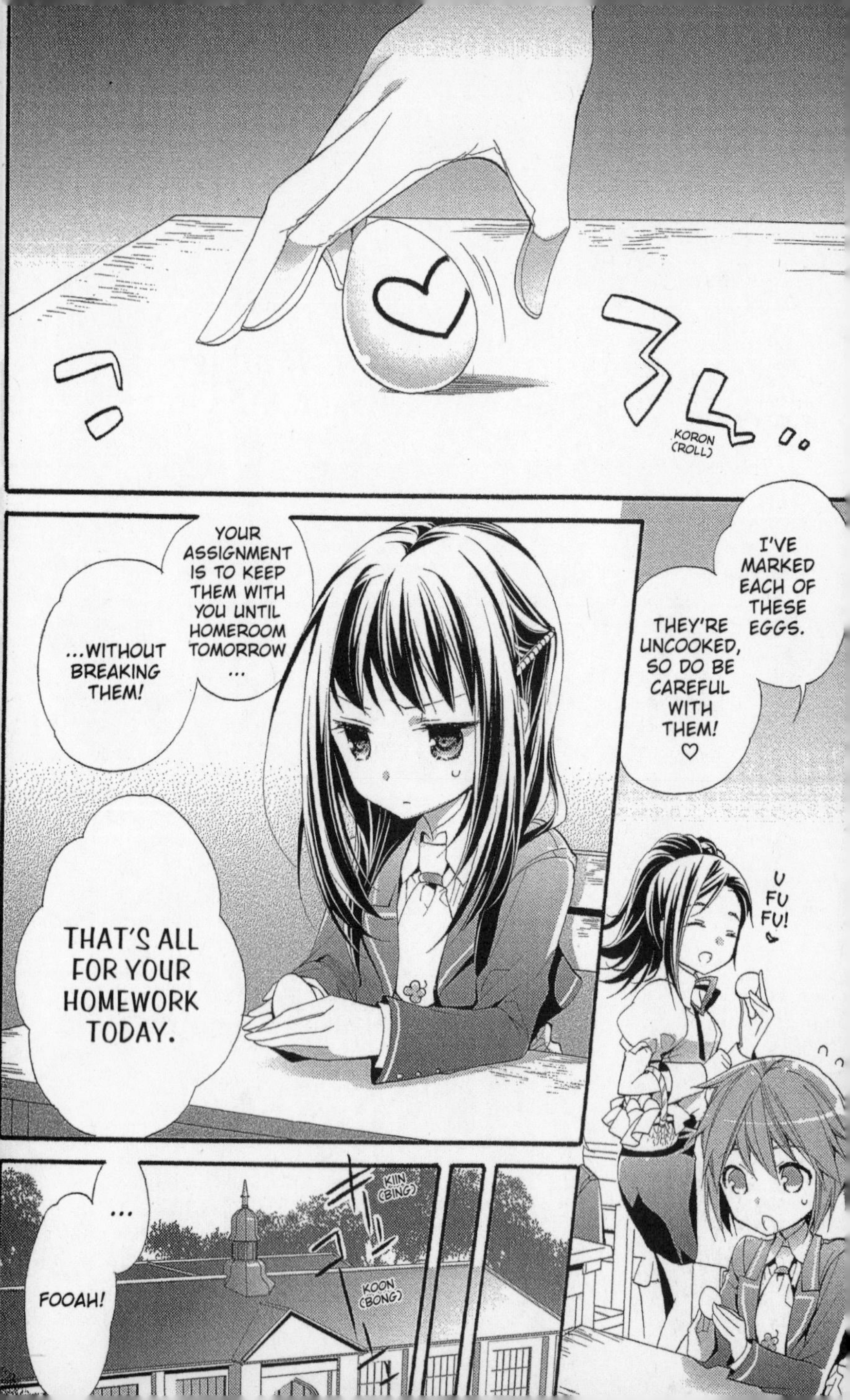
KORON (ROLL)
I'VE MARKED EACH OF THESE EGGS.
THEY'RE UNCOOKED, SO DO BE CAREFUL WITH THEM! ♡
YOUR ASSIGNMENT IS TO KEEP THEM WITH YOU UNTIL HOMEROOM TOMORROW ...
...WITHOUT BREAKING THEM!
THAT'S ALL FOR YOUR HOMEWORK TODAY.
U FU FU!
KIIN (BING)
KOON (BONG)
...
FOOAH!

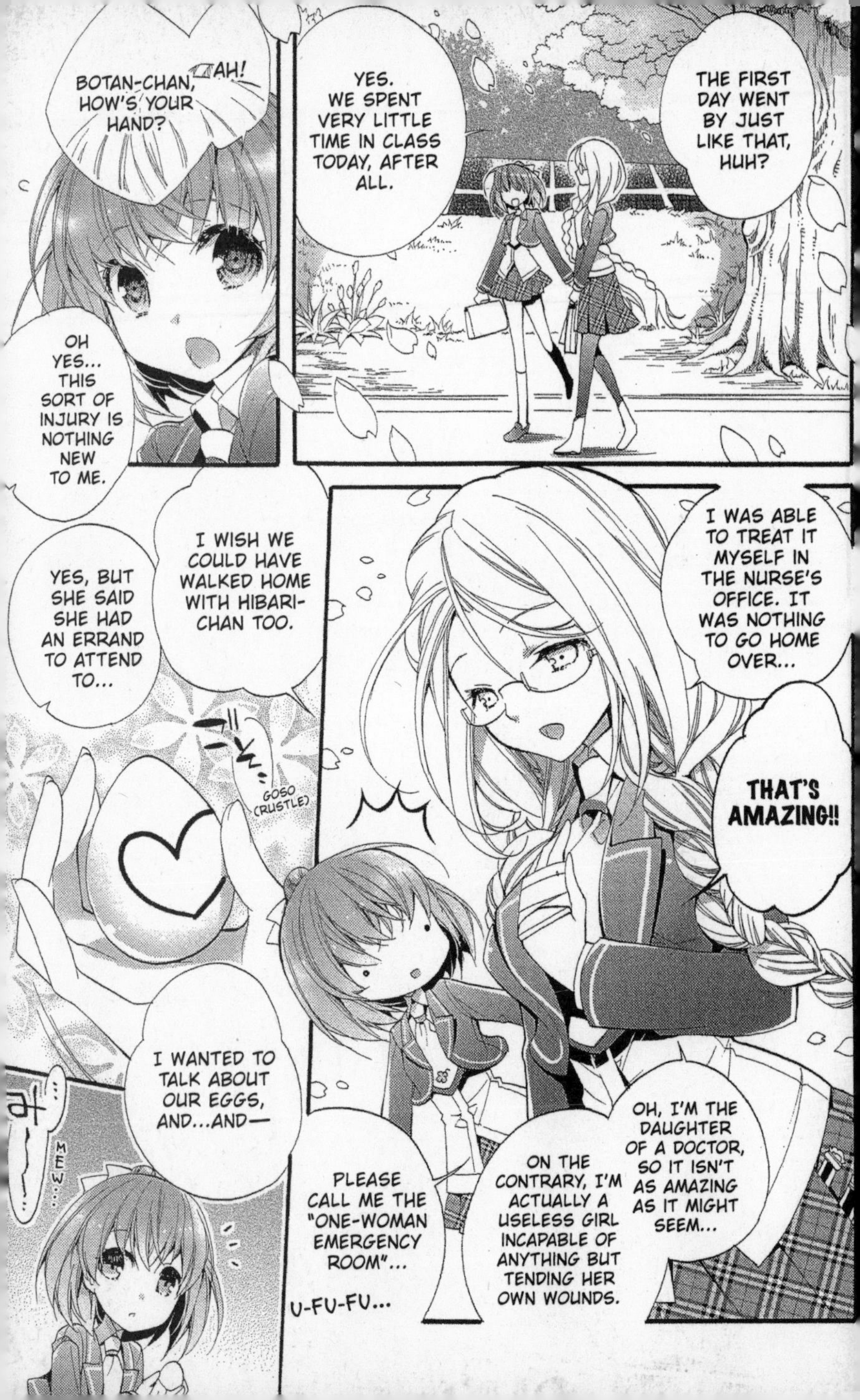
THE FIRST DAY WENT BY JUST LIKE THAT, HUH?
YES. WE SPENT VERY LITTLE TIME IN CLASS TODAY, AFTER ALL.
AH!
BOTAN-CHAN, HOW'S YOUR HAND?
OH YES... THIS SORT OF INJURY IS NOTHING NEW TO ME.
I WAS ABLE TO TREAT IT MYSELF IN THE NURSE'S OFFICE. IT WAS NOTHING TO GO HOME OVER...
THAT'S AMAZING!!
OH, I'M THE DAUGHTER OF A DOCTOR, SO IT ISN'T AS AMAZING AS IT MIGHT SEEM...
ON THE CONTRARY, I'M ACTUALLY A USELESS GIRL INCAPABLE OF ANYTHING BUT TENDING HER OWN WOUNDS.
PLEASE CALL ME THE "ONE-WOMAN EMERGENCY ROOM"...
U-FU-FU...
I WISH WE COULD HAVE WALKED HOME WITH HIBARI-CHAN TOO.
YES, BUT SHE SAID SHE HAD AN ERRAND TO ATTEND TO...
GOSO (RUSTLE)
I WANTED TO TALK ABOUT OUR EGGS, AND...AND—
MEW...

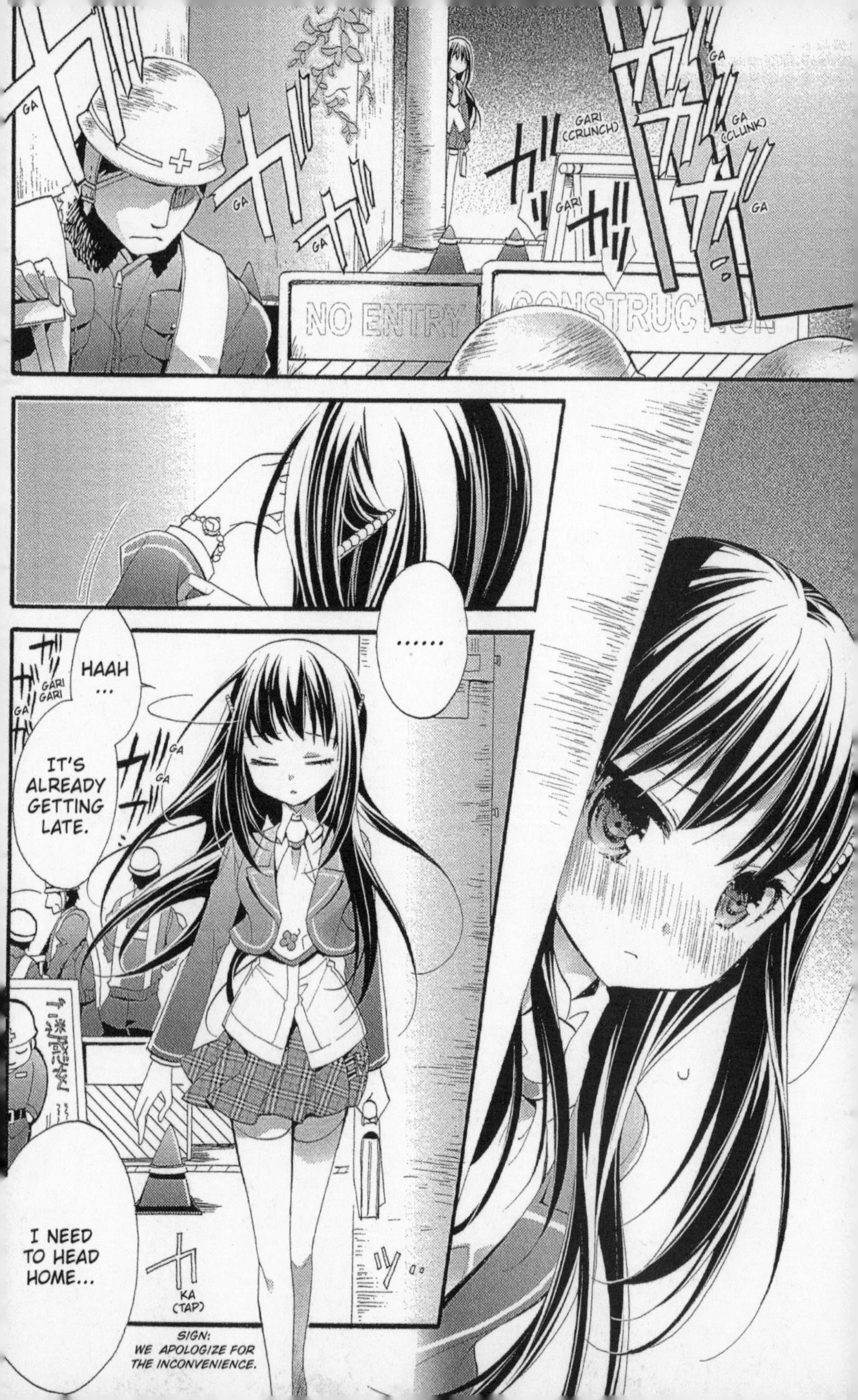
GA
GARI (CRUNCH)
GA (CLUNK)
GA
GARI
CONSTRUCTION
NO ENTRY
GA
GA
GA
GA
......
HAAH ...
GARI GARI
GA
GA
GA
IT'S ALREADY GETTING LATE.
I NEED TO HEAD HOME...
KA (TAP)
SIGN: WE APOLOGIZE FOR THE INCONVENIENCE.

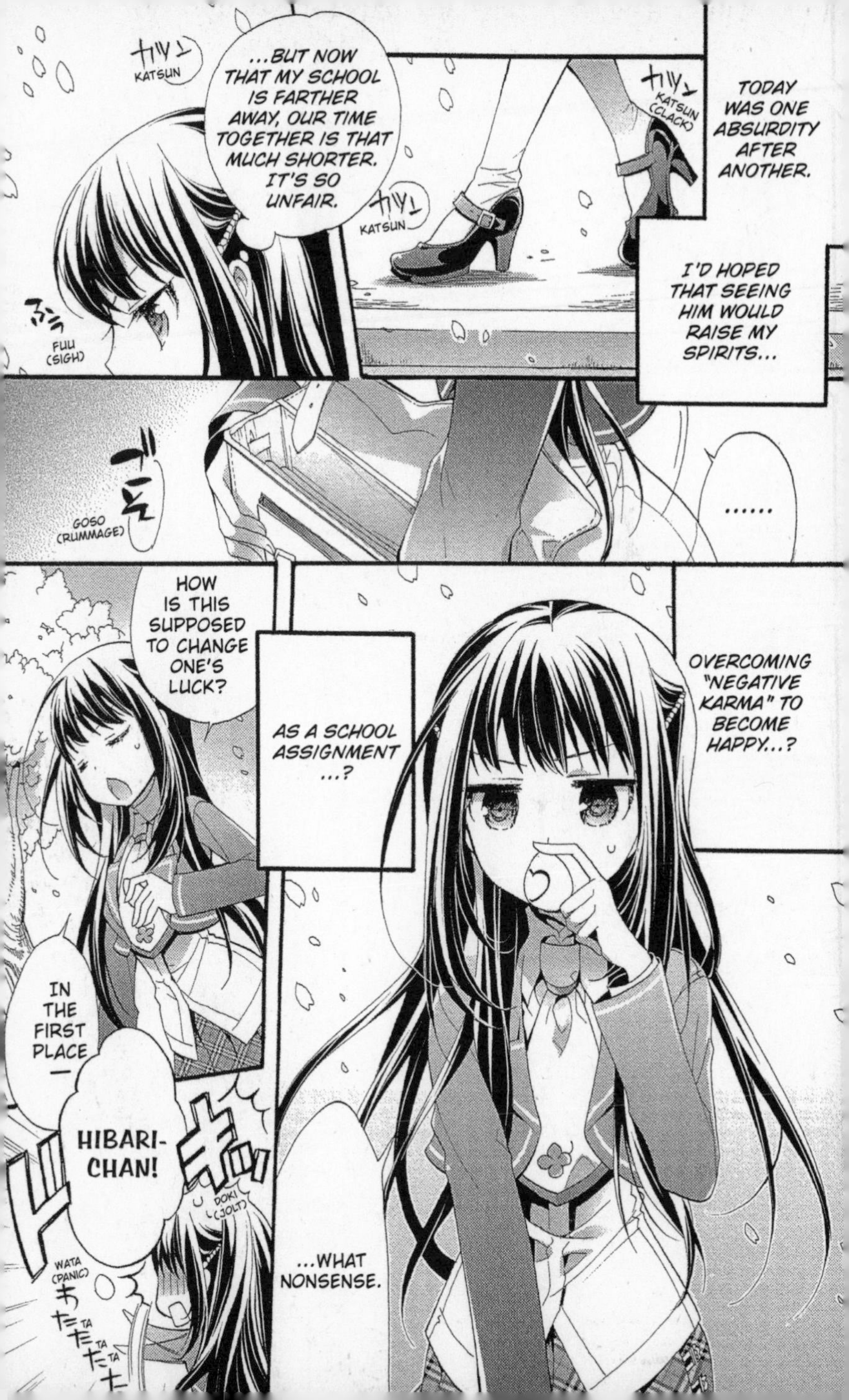

TODAY WAS ONE ABSURDITY AFTER ANOTHER.
KATSUN (CLACK)
KATSUN
I'D HOPED THAT SEEING HIM WOULD RAISE MY SPIRITS...
KATSUN
...BUT NOW THAT MY SCHOOL IS FARTHER AWAY, OUR TIME TOGETHER IS THAT MUCH SHORTER. IT'S SO UNFAIR.
FUU (SIGH)
......
GOSO (RUMMAGE)
OVERCOMING "NEGATIVE KARMA" TO BECOME HAPPY...?
AS A SCHOOL ASSIGNMENT ...?
...WHAT NONSENSE.
HOW IS THIS SUPPOSED TO CHANGE ONE'S LUCK?
IN THE FIRST PLACE—
HIBARI-CHAN!
DOKI (JOLT)
WATA (PANIC)

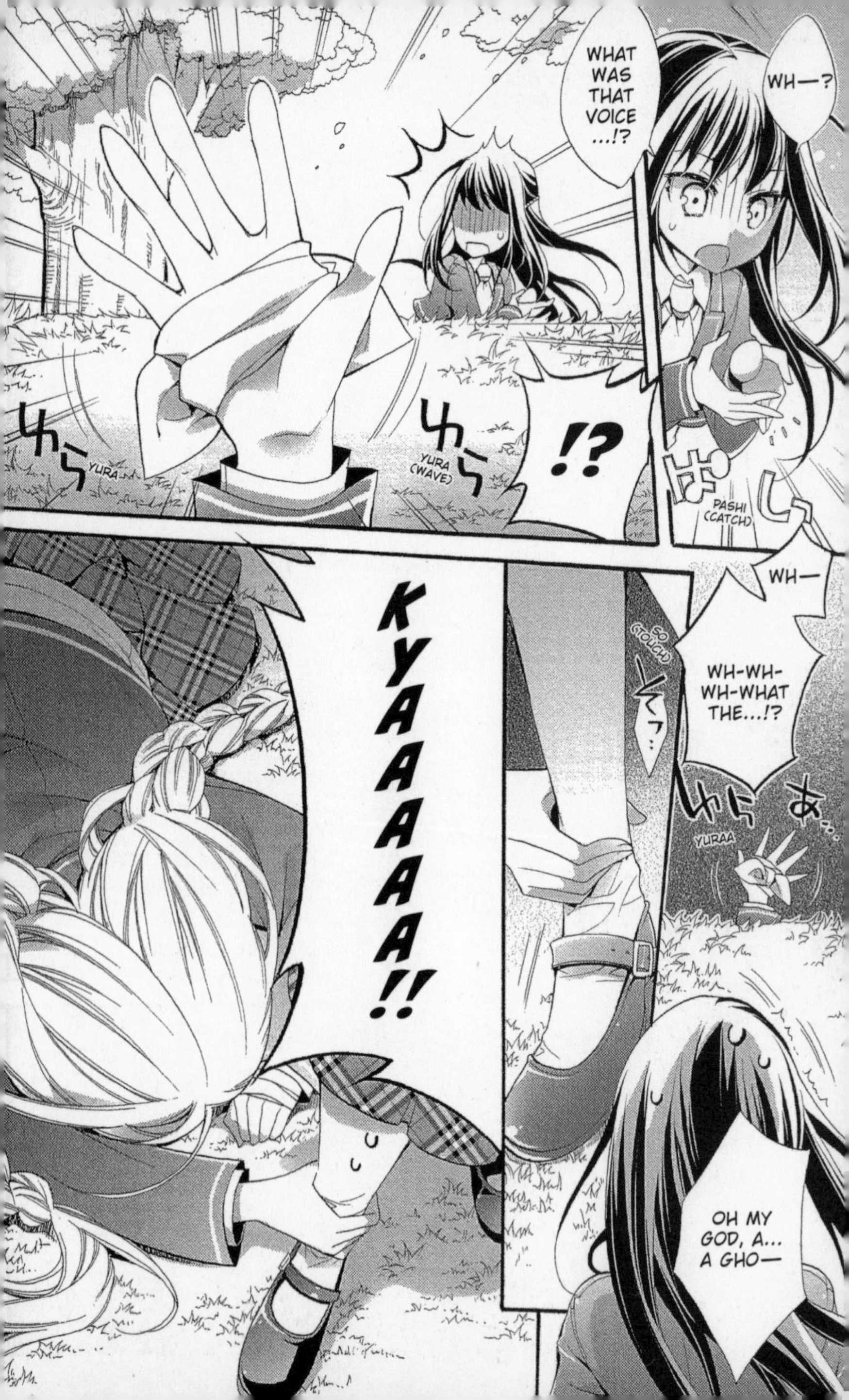
WH—?
WHAT WAS THAT VOICE ...!?
PASHI (CATCH)
!?
YURA (WAVE)
YURA
WH—
WH-WH-WH-WHAT THE...!?
YURAA
SO (TOUCH)
OH MY GOD, A... A GHO—
KYAAAAAA!!

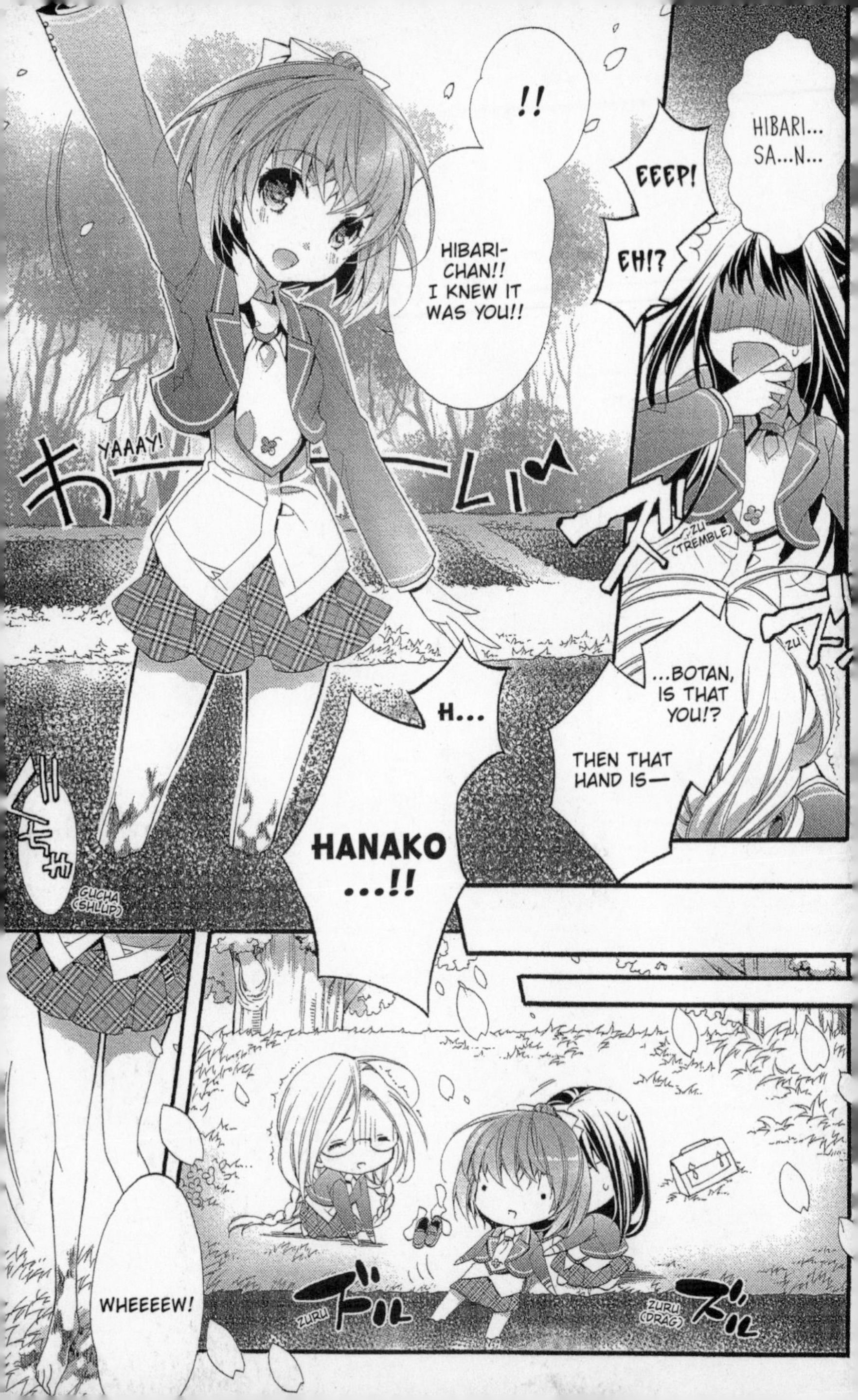
HIBARI... SA...N...
EEEP!
EH!?
ZU (TREMBLE)
ZU
...BOTAN, IS THAT YOU!?
THEN THAT HAND IS—
H...
HANAKO ...!!
!!
HIBARI-CHAN!! I KNEW IT WAS YOU!!
YAAAY!
GUCHA (SHLUP)
ZURU (DRAG)
ZURU
WHEEEEW!

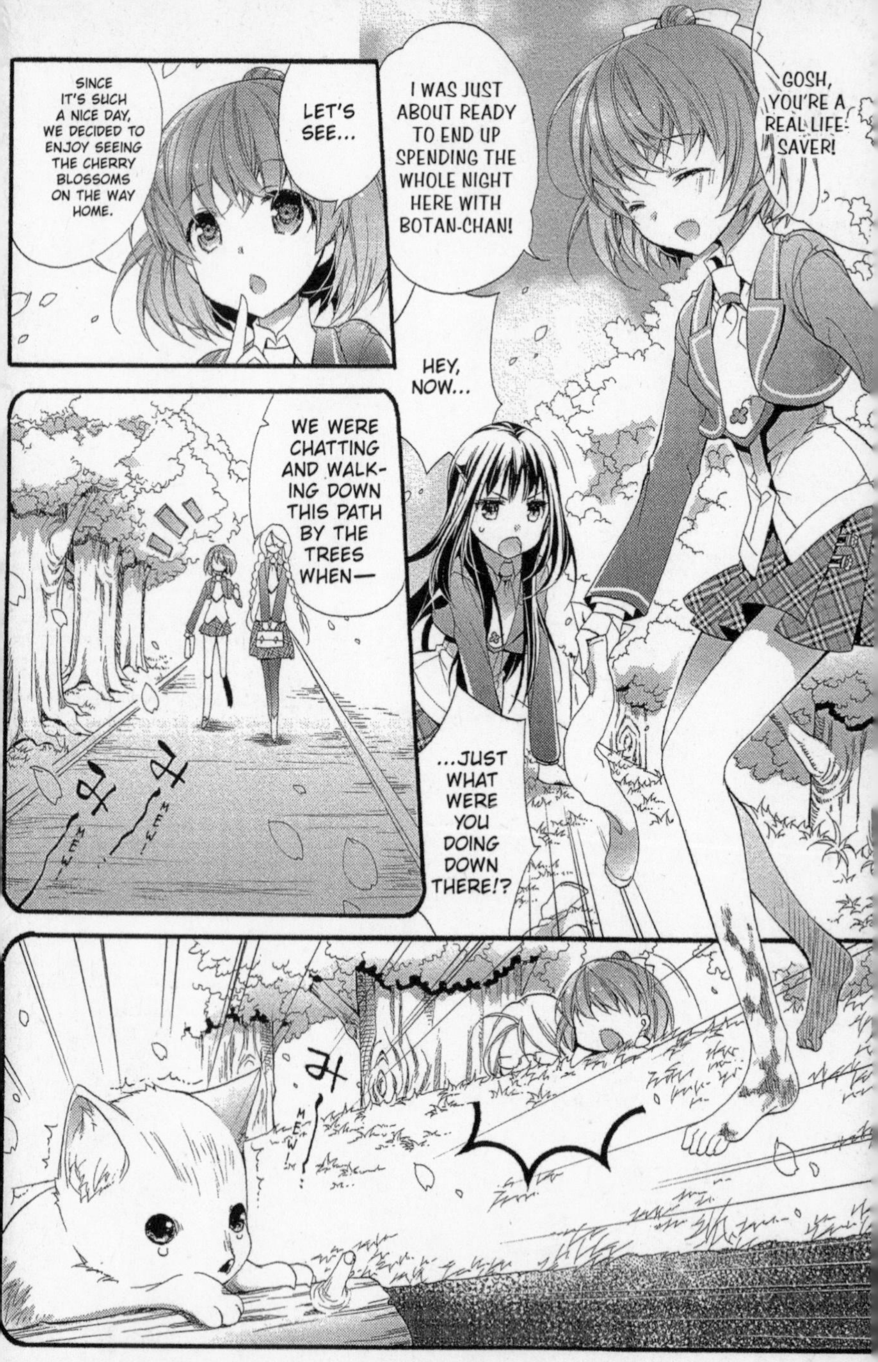
GOSH, YOU'RE A REAL LIFE-SAVER!
I WAS JUST ABOUT READY TO END UP SPENDING THE WHOLE NIGHT HERE WITH BOTAN-CHAN!
HEY, NOW...
...JUST WHAT WERE YOU DOING DOWN THERE!?
LET'S SEE...
SINCE IT'S SUCH A NICE DAY, WE DECIDED TO ENJOY SEEING THE CHERRY BLOSSOMS ON THE WAY HOME.
WE WERE CHATTING AND WALKING DOWN THIS PATH BY THE TREES WHEN—
MEW!
MEW!
MEW!

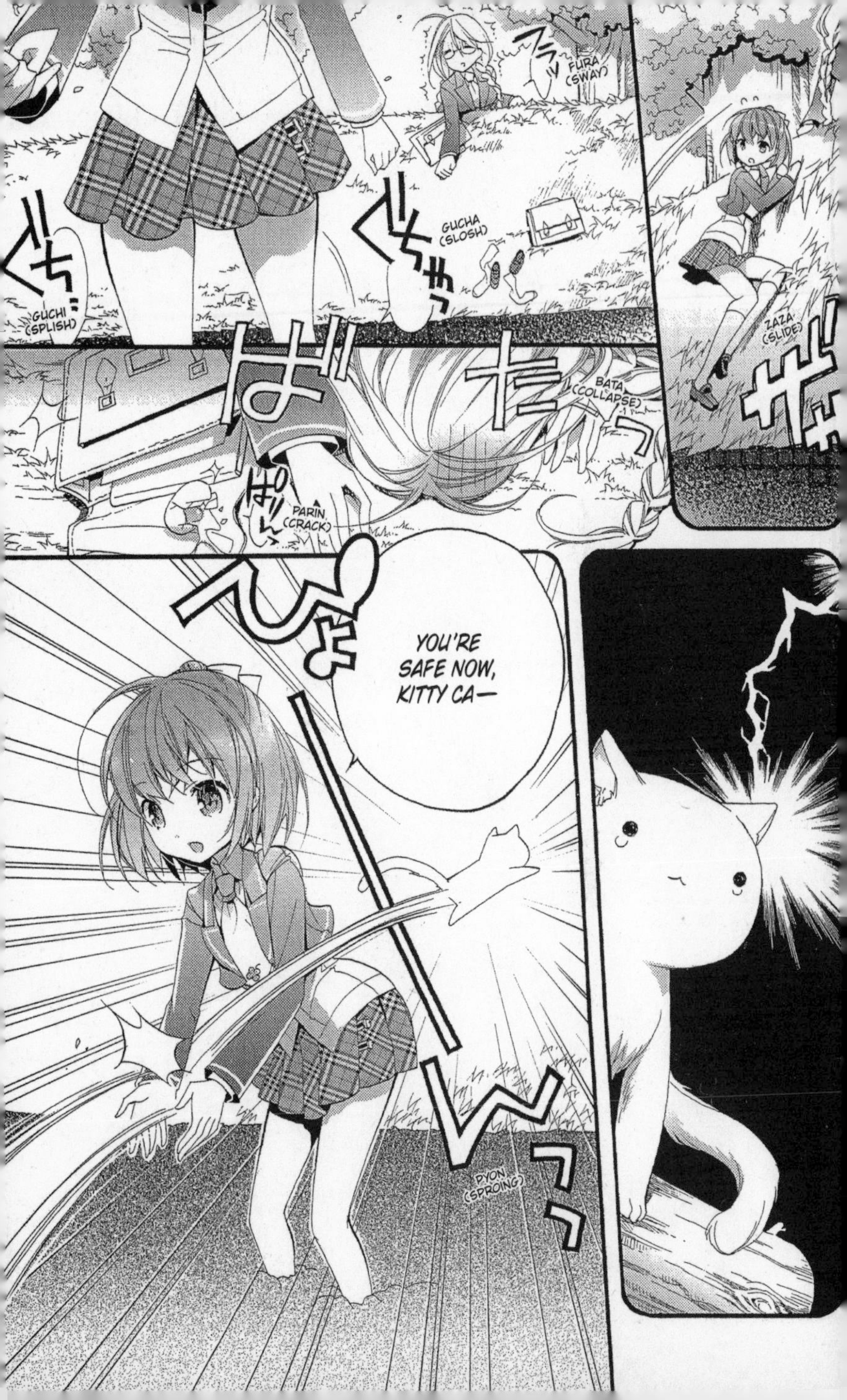
ZAZA (SLIDE)
FURA (SWAY)
GUCHA (SLOSH)
GUCHI (SPLISH)
BATA (COLLAPSE)
PARIN (CRACK)
YOU'RE SAFE NOW, KITTY CA—
PYON (SPROING)

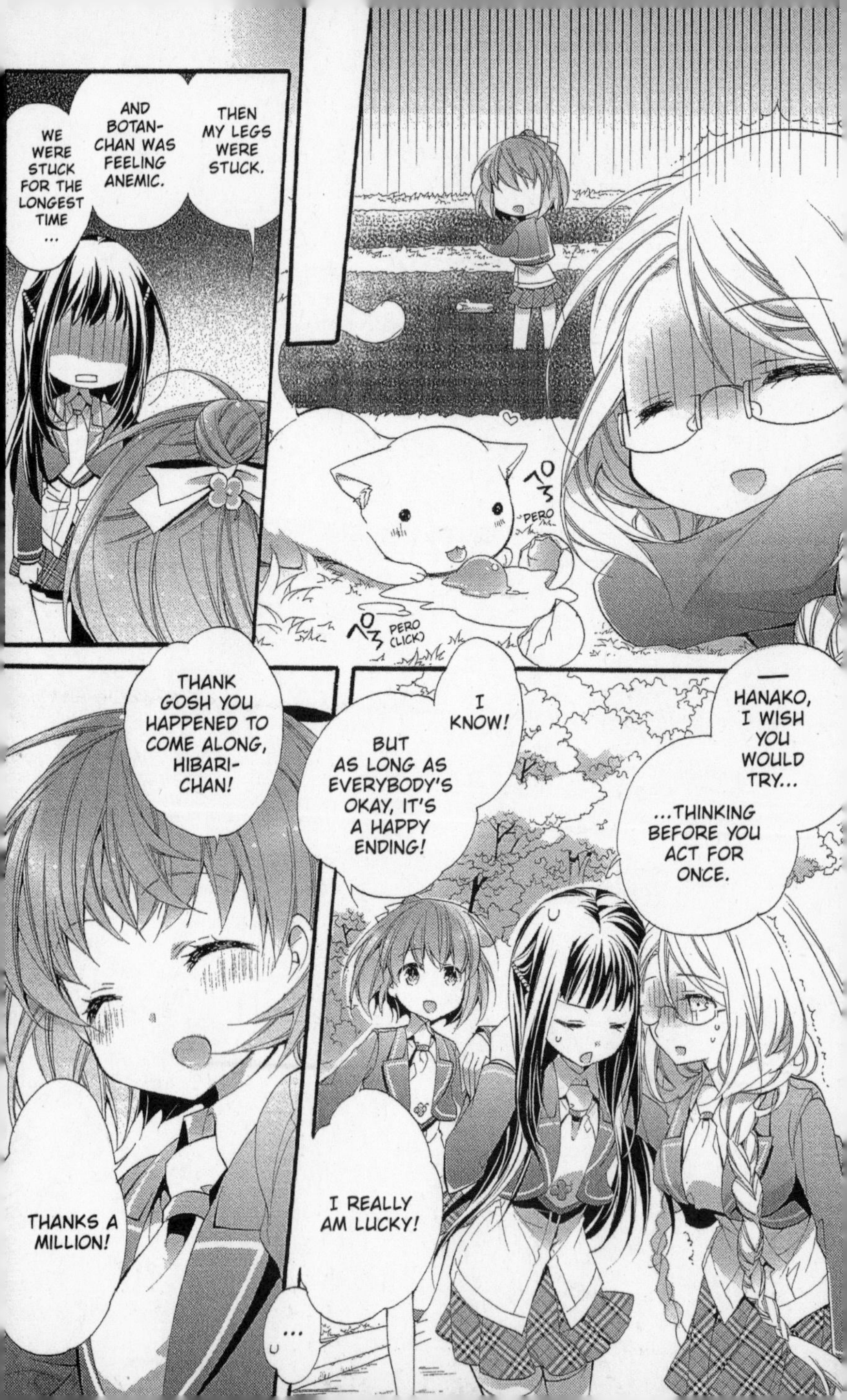
ぺろ PERO
ぺろ PERO (LICK)
THEN MY LEGS WERE STUCK.
AND BOTAN-CHAN WAS FEELING ANEMIC.
WE WERE STUCK FOR THE LONGEST TIME ...
—HANAKO, I WISH YOU WOULD TRY...
...THINKING BEFORE YOU ACT FOR ONCE.
I KNOW!
BUT AS LONG AS EVERYBODY'S OKAY, IT'S A HAPPY ENDING!
I REALLY AM LUCKY!
...
THANK GOSH YOU HAPPENED TO COME ALONG, HIBARI-CHAN!
THANKS A MILLION!

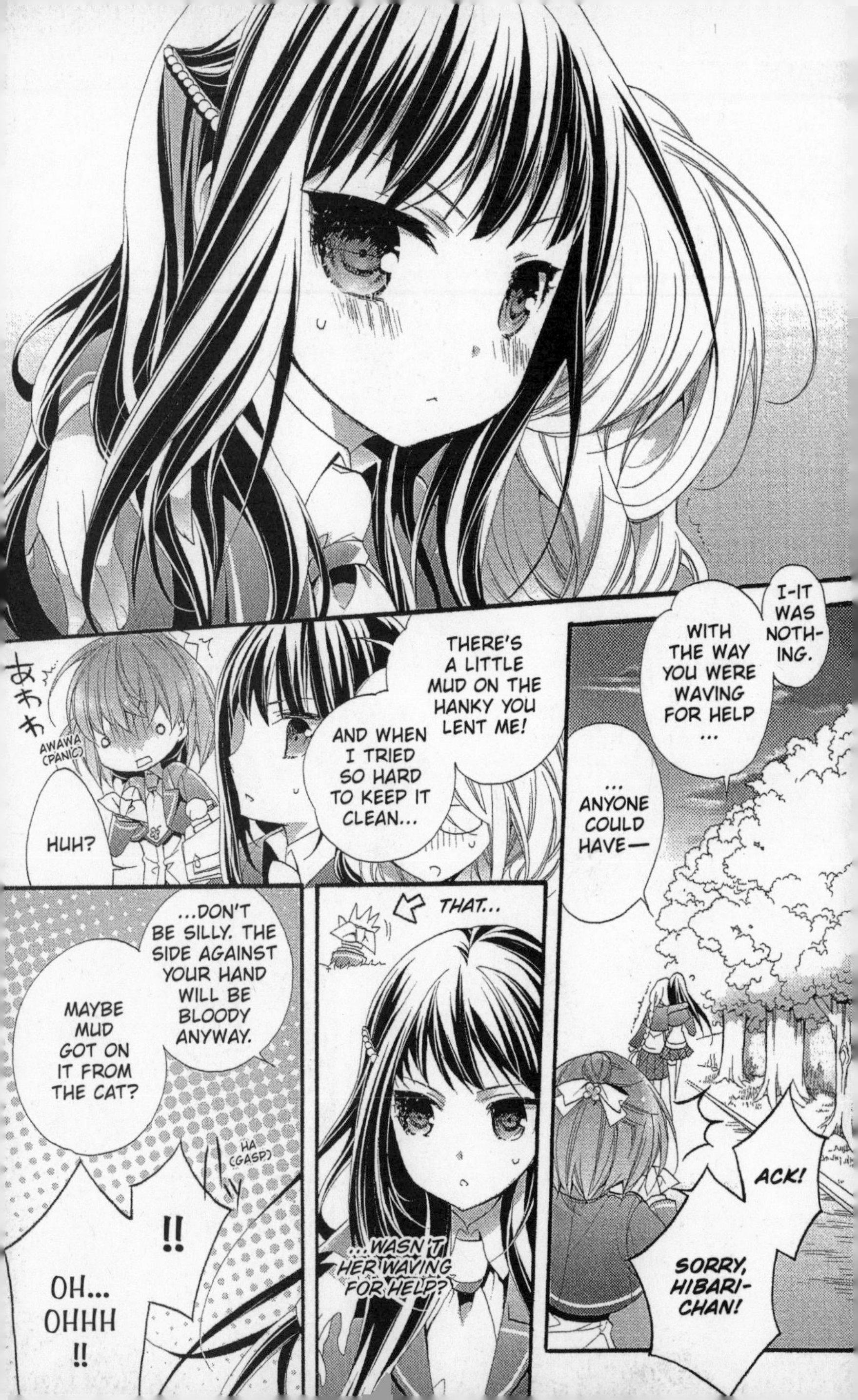
I-IT WAS NOTHING.
WITH THE WAY YOU WERE WAVING FOR HELP ...
... ANYONE COULD HAVE—
ACK!
SORRY, HIBARI-CHAN!
THERE'S A LITTLE MUD ON THE HANKY YOU LENT ME!
AND WHEN I TRIED SO HARD TO KEEP IT CLEAN...
あわわ
AWAWA (PANIC)
HUH?
THAT...
...WASN'T HER WAVING FOR HELP?
...DON'T BE SILLY. THE SIDE AGAINST YOUR HAND WILL BE BLOODY ANYWAY.
MAYBE MUD GOT ON IT FROM THE CAT?
HA (GASP)
!!
OH... OHHH !!

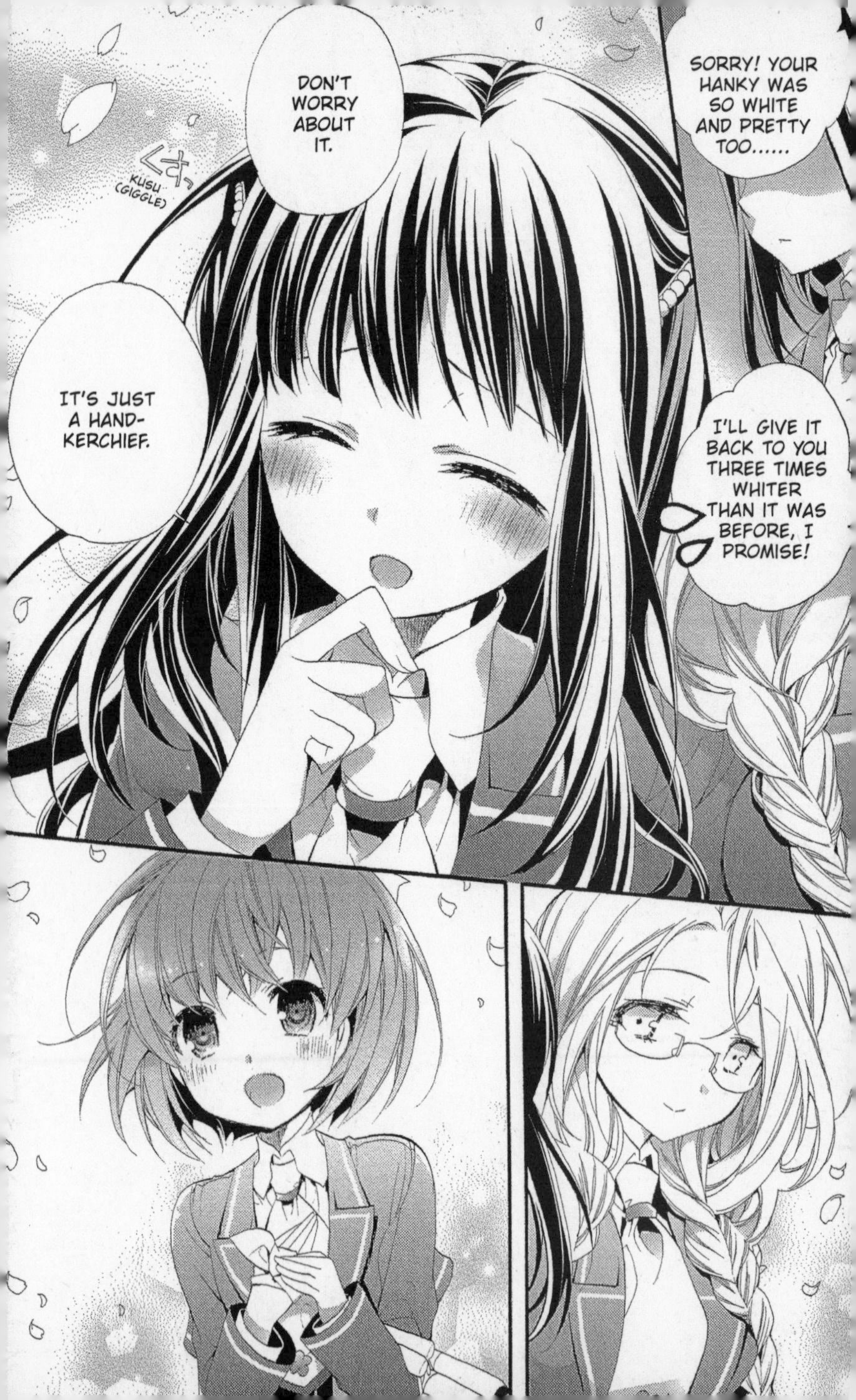
SORRY! YOUR HANKY WAS SO WHITE AND PRETTY TOO......
DON'T WORRY ABOUT IT.
くすっ
KUSU (GIGGLE)
IT'S JUST A HAND-KERCHIEF.
I'LL GIVE IT BACK TO YOU THREE TIMES WHITER THAN IT WAS BEFORE, I PROMISE!

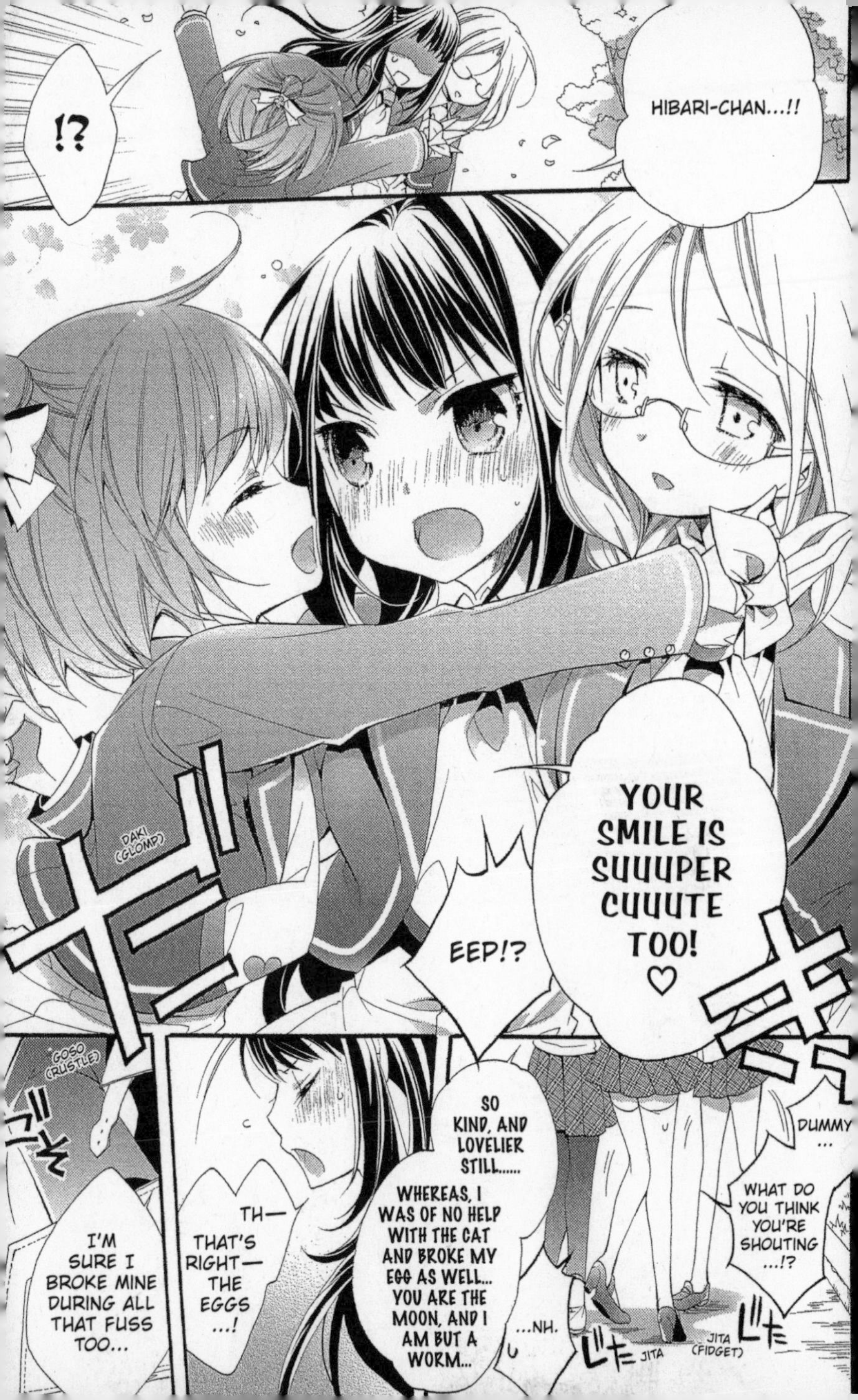
HIBARI-CHAN...!!
!?
YOUR SMILE IS SUUUPER CUUUTE TOO! ♡
EEP!?
DAKI (GLOMP)
DUMMY...
WHAT DO YOU THINK YOU'RE SHOUTING...!?
JITA (FIDGET)
JITA
SO KIND, AND LOVELIER STILL......
WHEREAS, I WAS OF NO HELP WITH THE CAT AND BROKE MY EGG AS WELL... YOU ARE THE MOON, AND I AM BUT A WORM...
...NH.
TH— THAT'S RIGHT— THE EGGS...!
I'M SURE I BROKE MINE DURING ALL THAT FUSS TOO...
GOSO (RUSTLE)

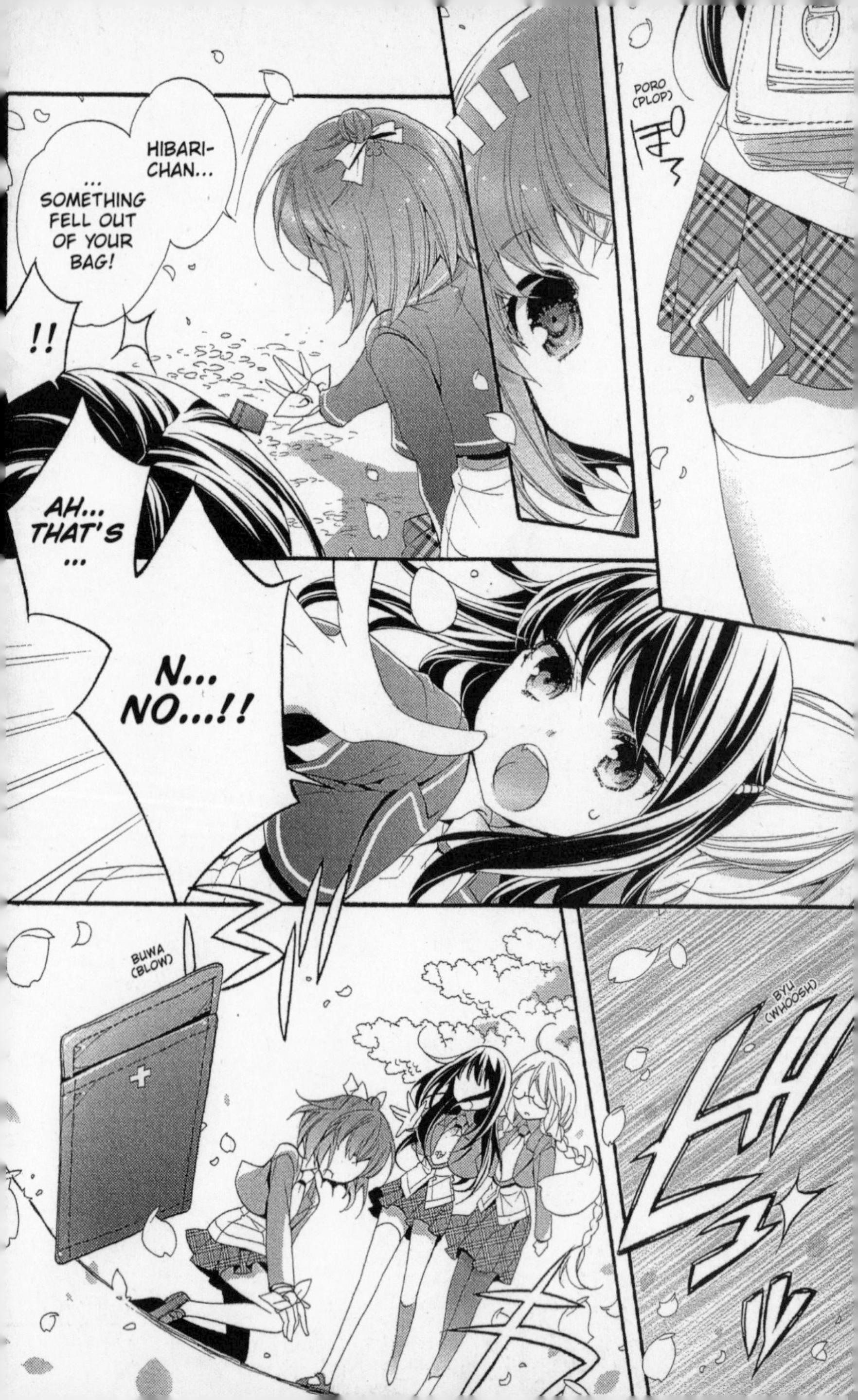
PORO (PLOP)
ぽろ
HIBARI-CHAN...
... SOMETHING FELL OUT OF YOUR BAG!
!!
AH... THAT'S ...
N... NO...!!
BYU (WHOOSH)
BUWA (BLOW)

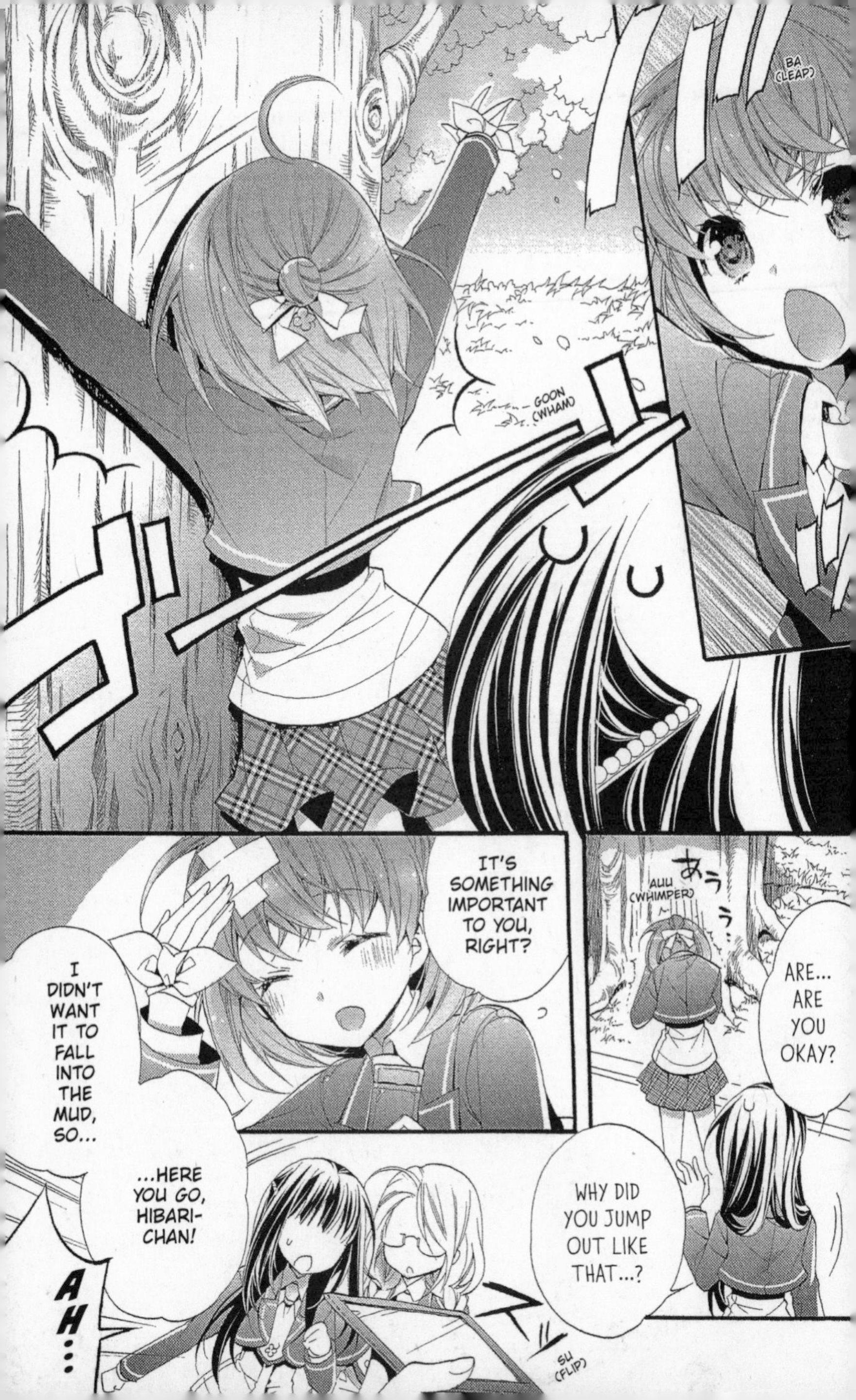
BA (LEAP)
GOON (WHAM)
AUU (WHIMPER)
ARE... ARE YOU OKAY?
WHY DID YOU JUMP OUT LIKE THAT...?
IT'S SOMETHING IMPORTANT TO YOU, RIGHT?
I DIDN'T WANT IT TO FALL INTO THE MUD, SO...
...HERE YOU GO, HIBARI-CHAN!
AH...
SU (FLIP)

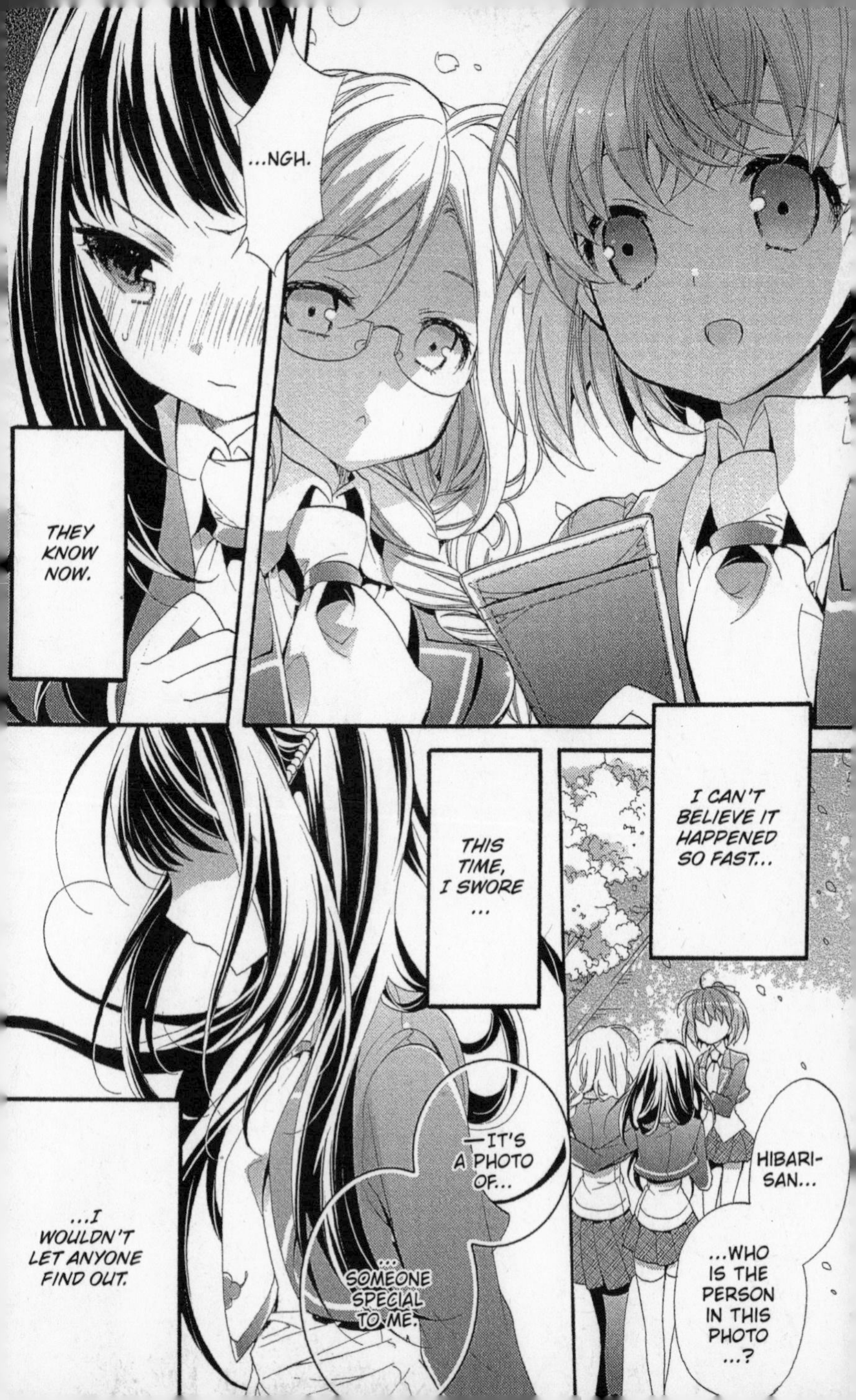
...NGH.
THEY KNOW NOW.
I CAN'T BELIEVE IT HAPPENED SO FAST...
HIBARI-SAN...
...WHO IS THE PERSON IN THIS PHOTO ...?
THIS TIME, I SWORE ...
—IT'S A PHOTO OF...
...SOMEONE SPECIAL TO ME.
...I WOULDN'T LET ANYONE FIND OUT.

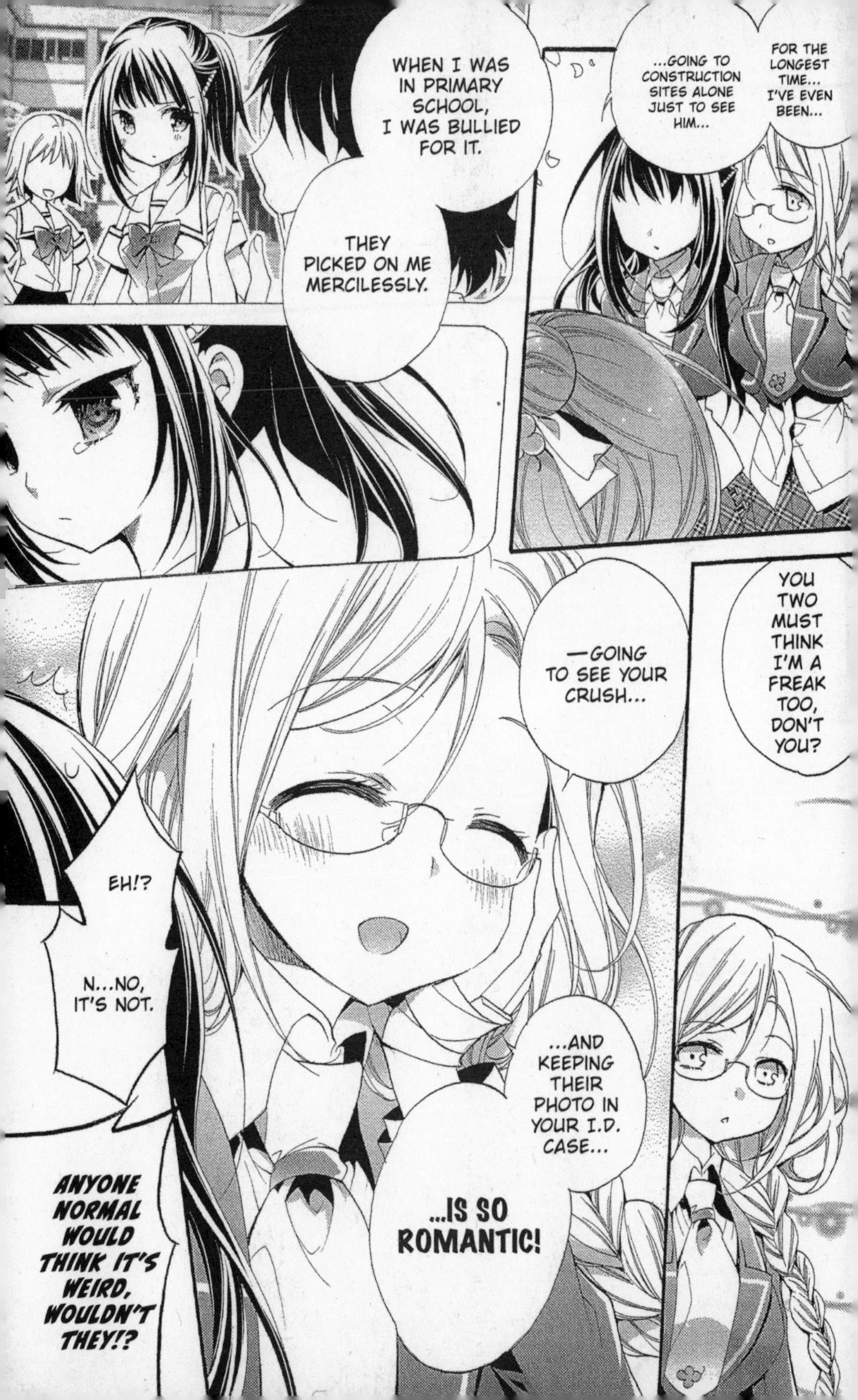
FOR THE LONGEST TIME... I'VE EVEN BEEN...
...GOING TO CONSTRUCTION SITES ALONE JUST TO SEE HIM...
WHEN I WAS IN PRIMARY SCHOOL, I WAS BULLIED FOR IT.
THEY PICKED ON ME MERCILESSLY.
YOU TWO MUST THINK I'M A FREAK TOO, DON'T YOU?
—GOING TO SEE YOUR CRUSH...
...AND KEEPING THEIR PHOTO IN YOUR I.D. CASE...
...IS SO ROMANTIC!
EH!?
N...NO, IT'S NOT.
ANYONE NORMAL WOULD THINK IT'S WEIRD, WOULDN'T THEY!?

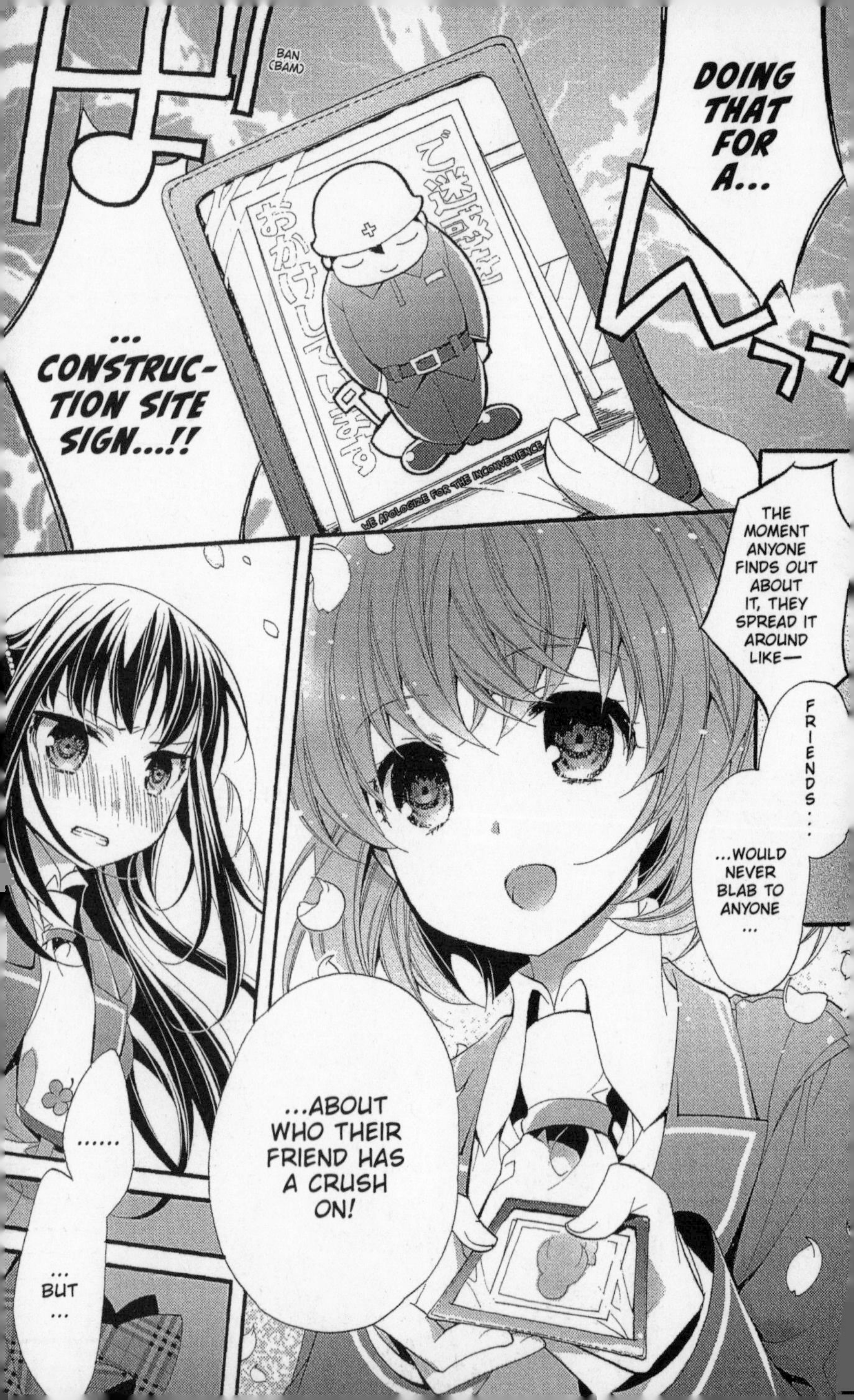
DOING THAT FOR A...
BAN (BAM)
ご迷惑をおかけしております
WE APOLOGIZE FOR THE INCONVENIENCE
...CONSTRUCTION SITE SIGN...!!
THE MOMENT ANYONE FINDS OUT ABOUT IT, THEY SPREAD IT AROUND LIKE—
FRIENDS...
...WOULD NEVER BLAB TO ANYONE...
...ABOUT WHO THEIR FRIEND HAS A CRUSH ON!
......
...BUT...

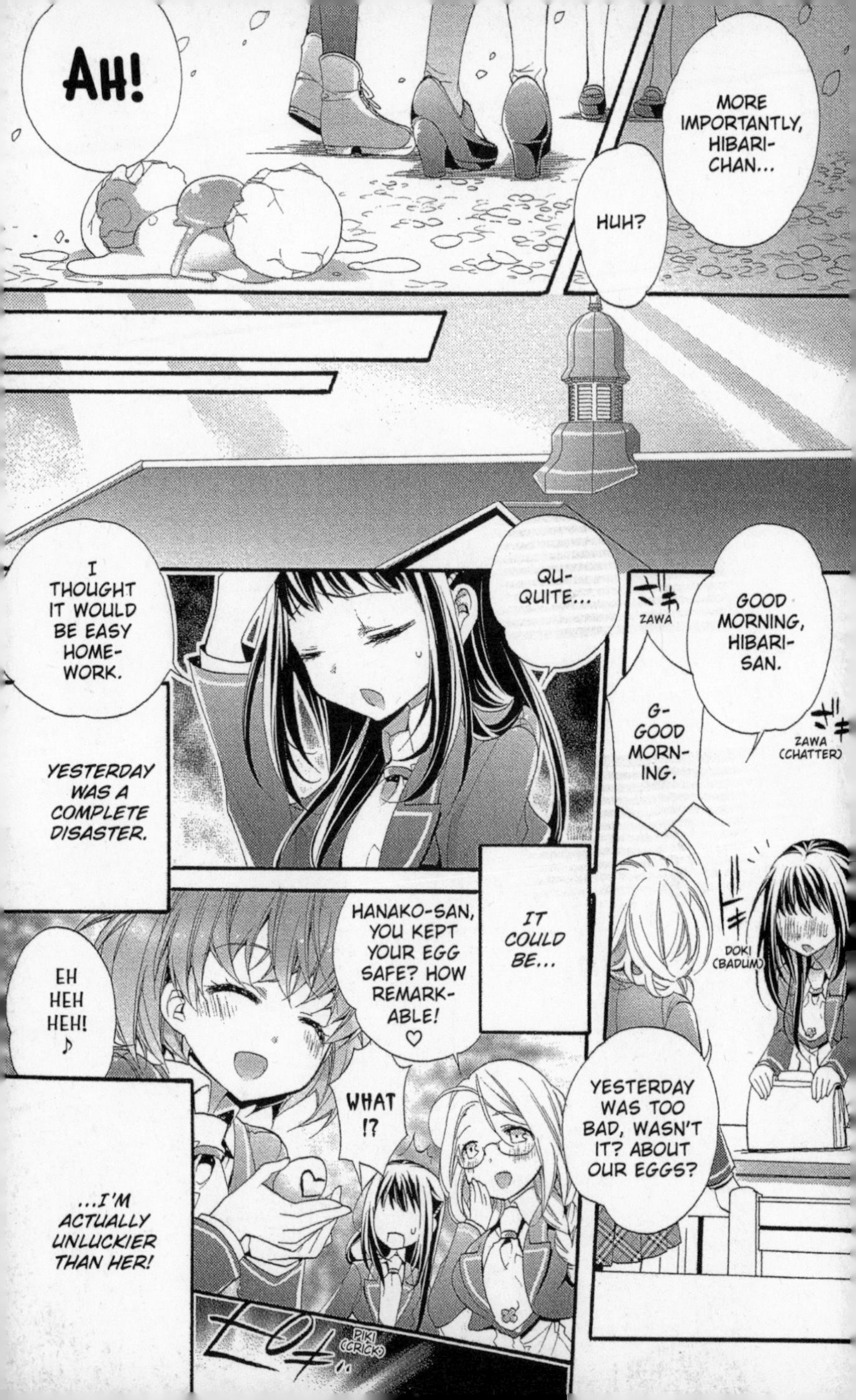
MORE IMPORTANTLY, HIBARI-CHAN...
HUH?
AH!
GOOD MORNING, HIBARI-SAN.
ZAWA
ZAWA (CHATTER)
G-GOOD MORNING.
DOKI (BADUM)
YESTERDAY WAS TOO BAD, WASN'T IT? ABOUT OUR EGGS?
QU-QUITE...
I THOUGHT IT WOULD BE EASY HOMEWORK.
YESTERDAY WAS A COMPLETE DISASTER.
IT COULD BE...
HANAKO-SAN, YOU KEPT YOUR EGG SAFE? HOW REMARKABLE! ♡
WHAT!?
EH HEH HEH! ♪
PIKI (CRICK)
...I'M ACTUALLY UNLUCKIER THAN HER!

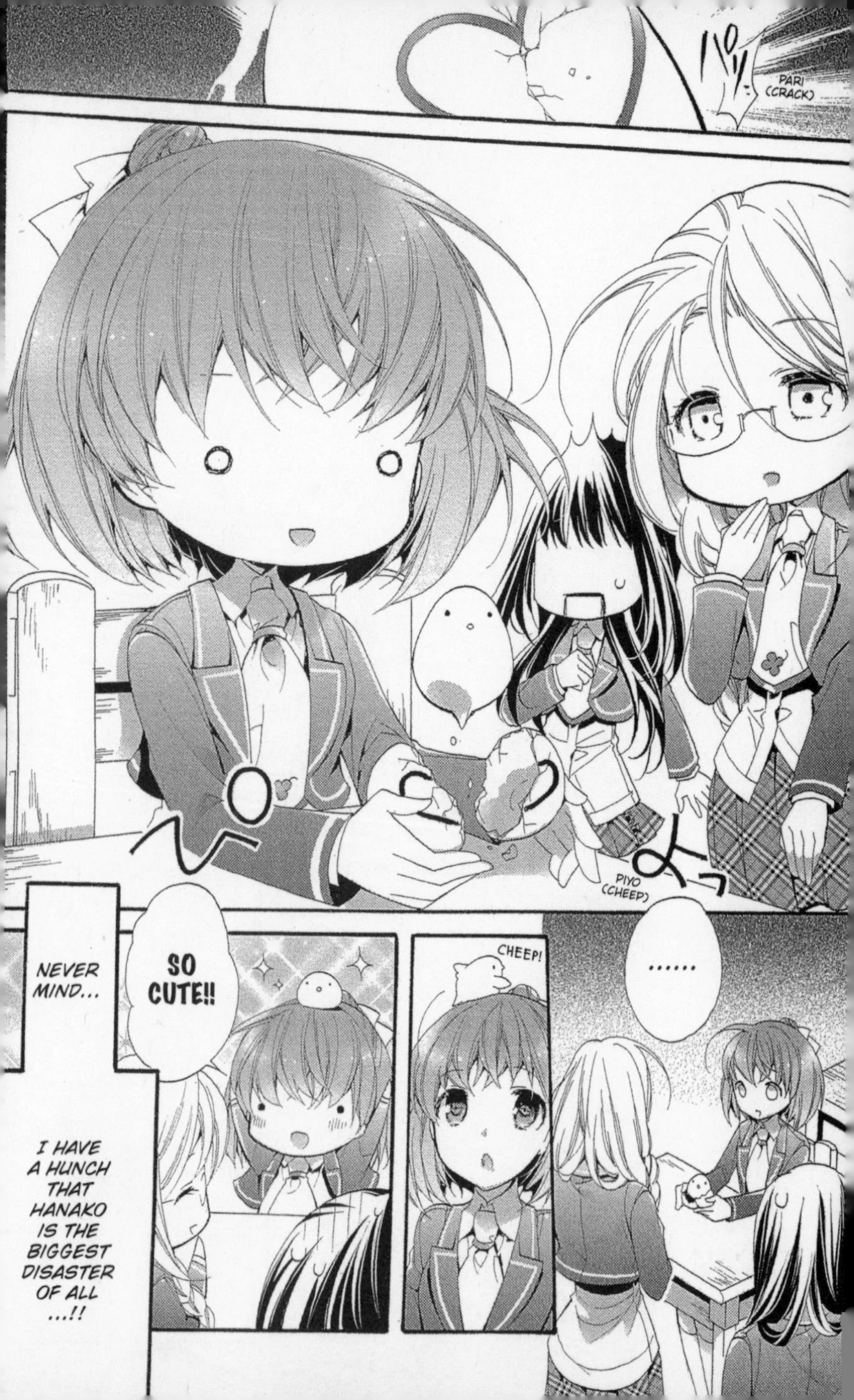

PARI (CRACK)
PIYO (CHEEP)
......
CHEEP!
SO CUTE!!
NEVER MIND...
I HAVE A HUNCH THAT HANAKO IS THE BIGGEST DISASTER OF ALL ...!!

AnneHappy
unhappy go lucky!

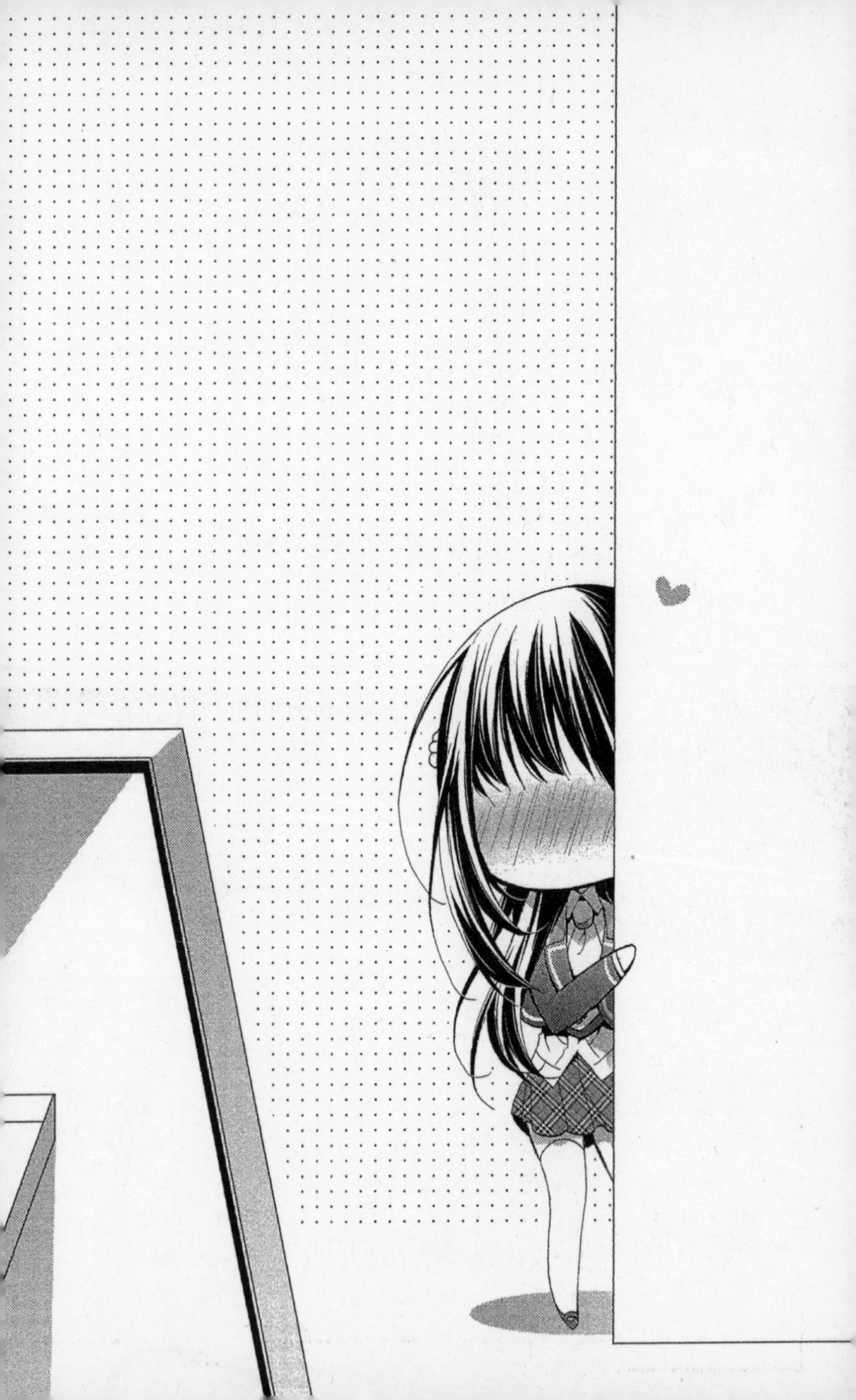

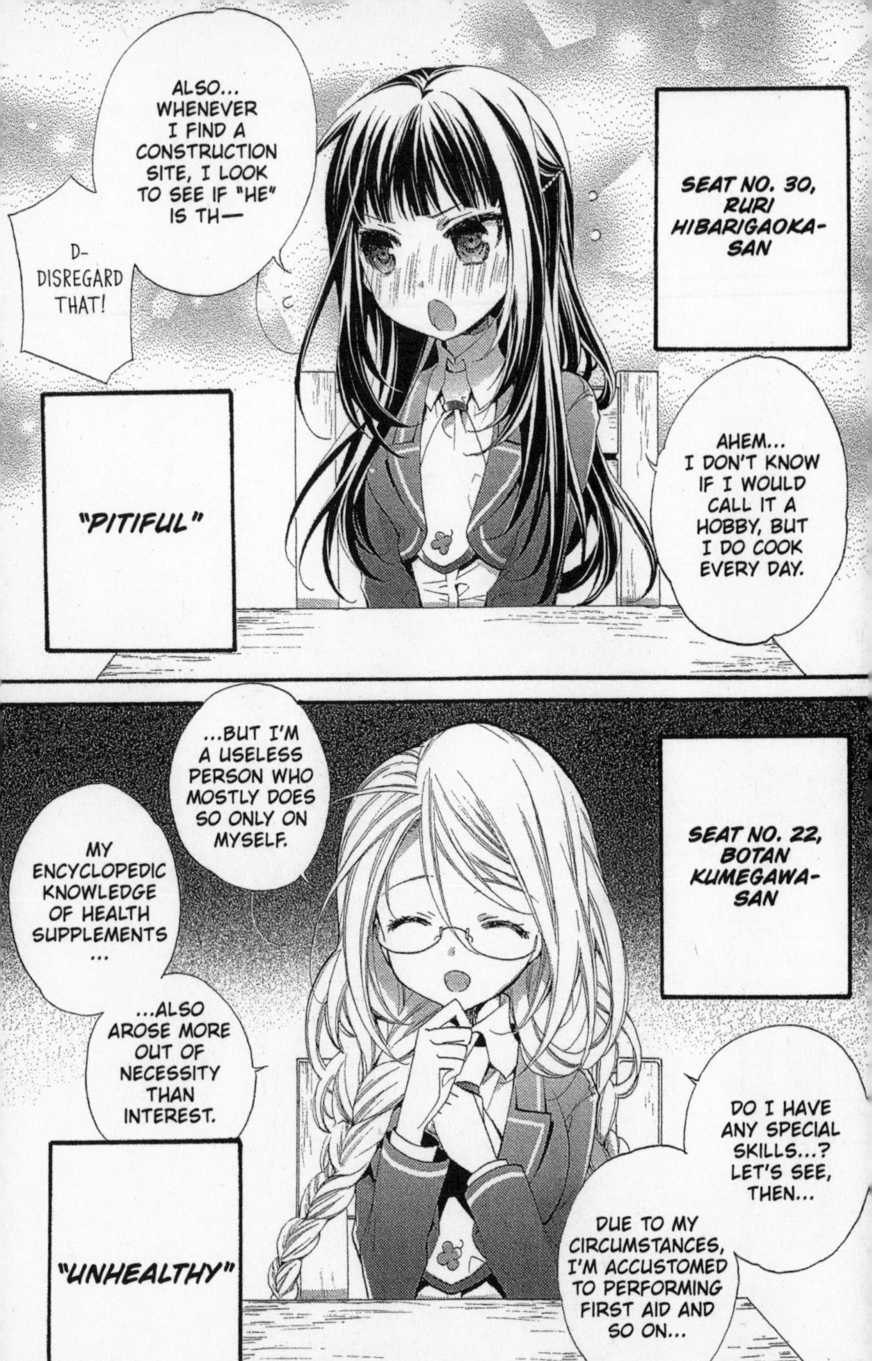
SEAT NO. 30, RURI HIBARIGAOKA-SAN
AHEM... I DON'T KNOW IF I WOULD CALL IT A HOBBY, BUT I DO COOK EVERY DAY.
ALSO... WHENEVER I FIND A CONSTRUCTION SITE, I LOOK TO SEE IF "HE" IS TH—
D-DISREGARD THAT!
"PITIFUL"
SEAT NO. 22, BOTAN KUMEGAWA-SAN
DO I HAVE ANY SPECIAL SKILLS...? LET'S SEE, THEN...
DUE TO MY CIRCUMSTANCES, I'M ACCUSTOMED TO PERFORMING FIRST AID AND SO ON...
...BUT I'M A USELESS PERSON WHO MOSTLY DOES SO ONLY ON MYSELF.
MY ENCYCLOPEDIC KNOWLEDGE OF HEALTH SUPPLEMENTS ...
...ALSO AROSE MORE OUT OF NECESSITY THAN INTEREST.
"UNHEALTHY"

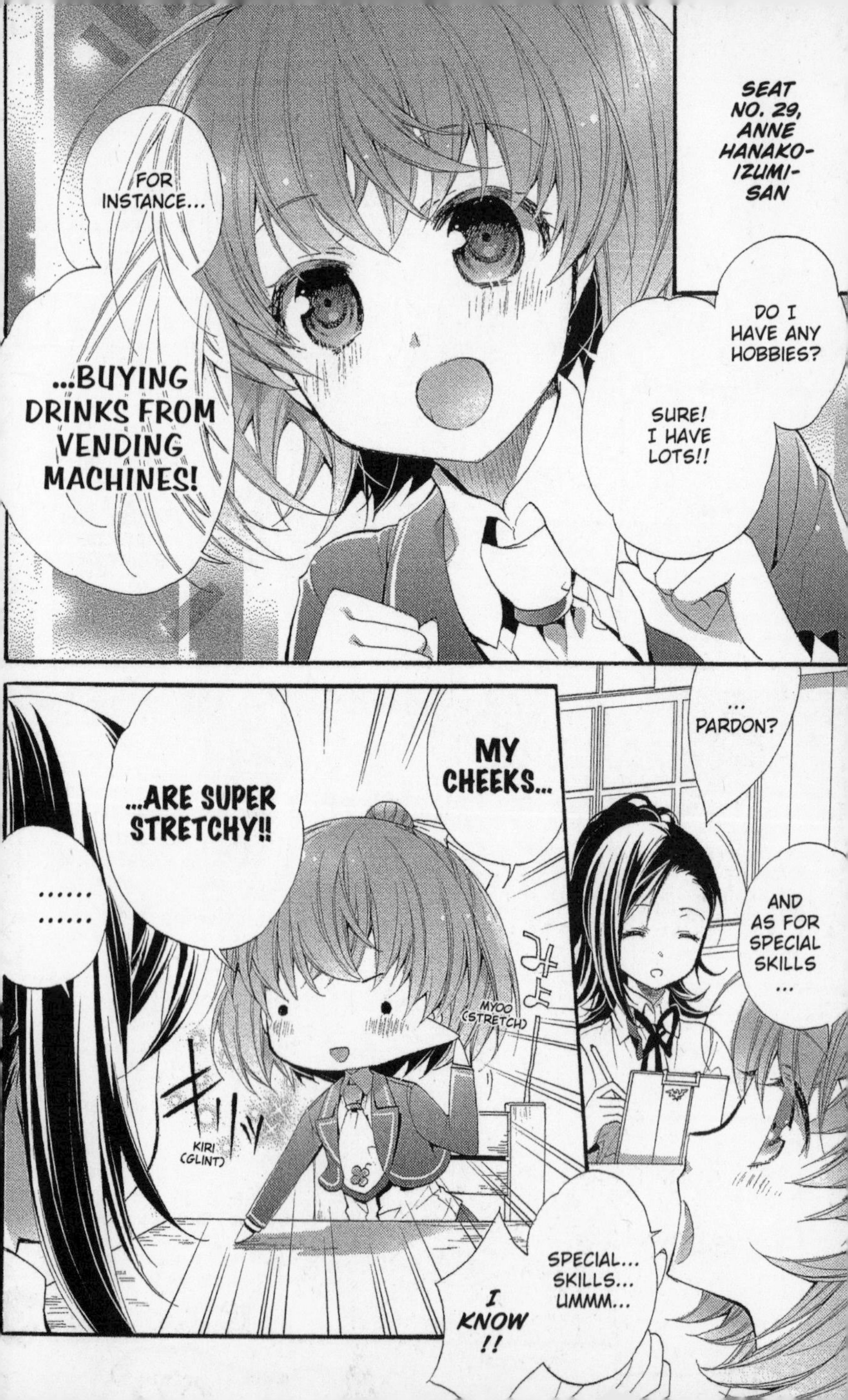
SEAT NO. 29, ANNE HANAKO-IZUMI-SAN
DO I HAVE ANY HOBBIES?
SURE! I HAVE LOTS!!
FOR INSTANCE...
...BUYING DRINKS FROM VENDING MACHINES!
... PARDON?
AND AS FOR SPECIAL SKILLS ...
SPECIAL... SKILLS... UMMM...
I KNOW!!
MY CHEEKS...
MYOO (STRETCH)
...ARE SUPER STRETCHY!!
KIRI (GLINT)
....

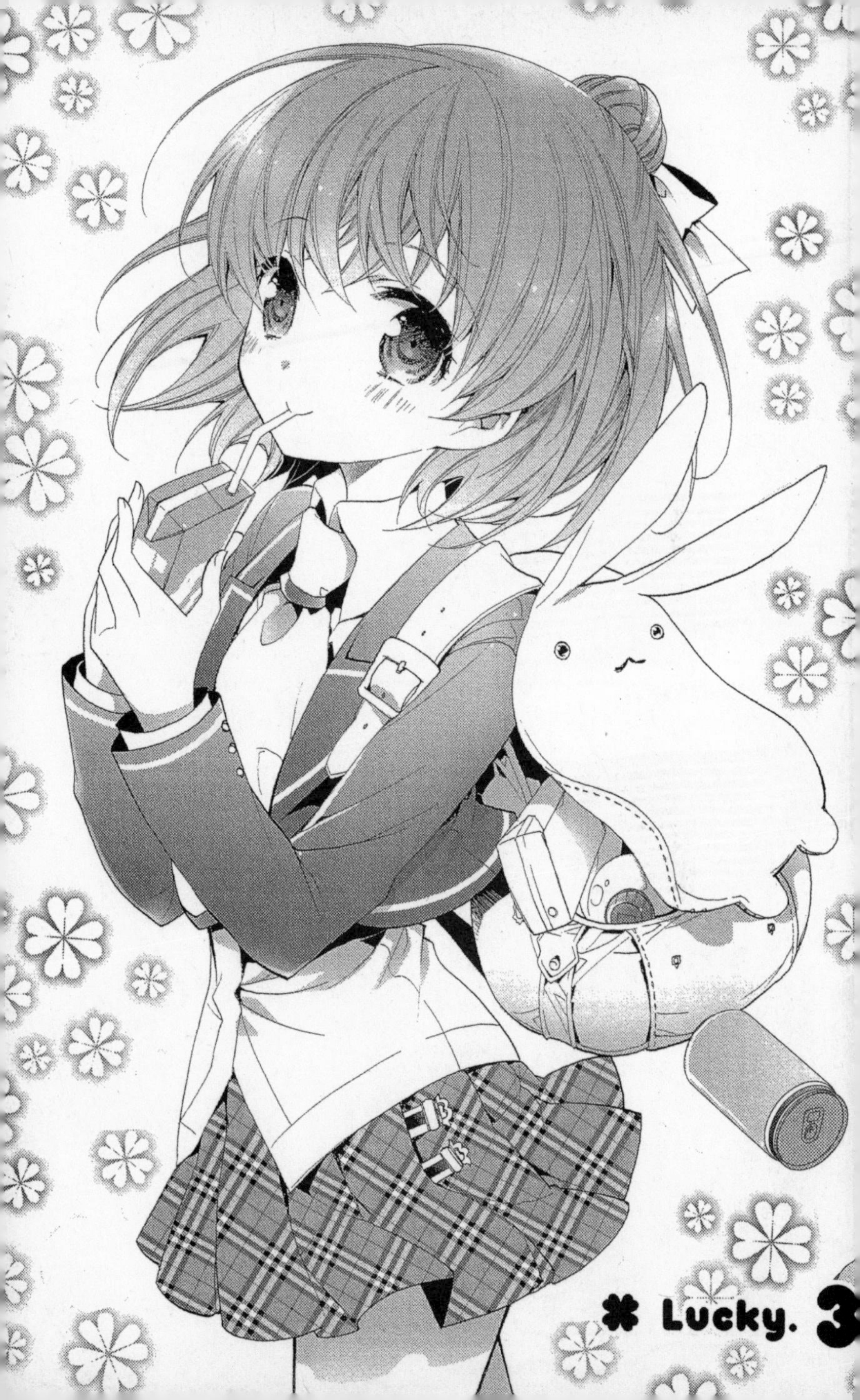
Lucky. 3

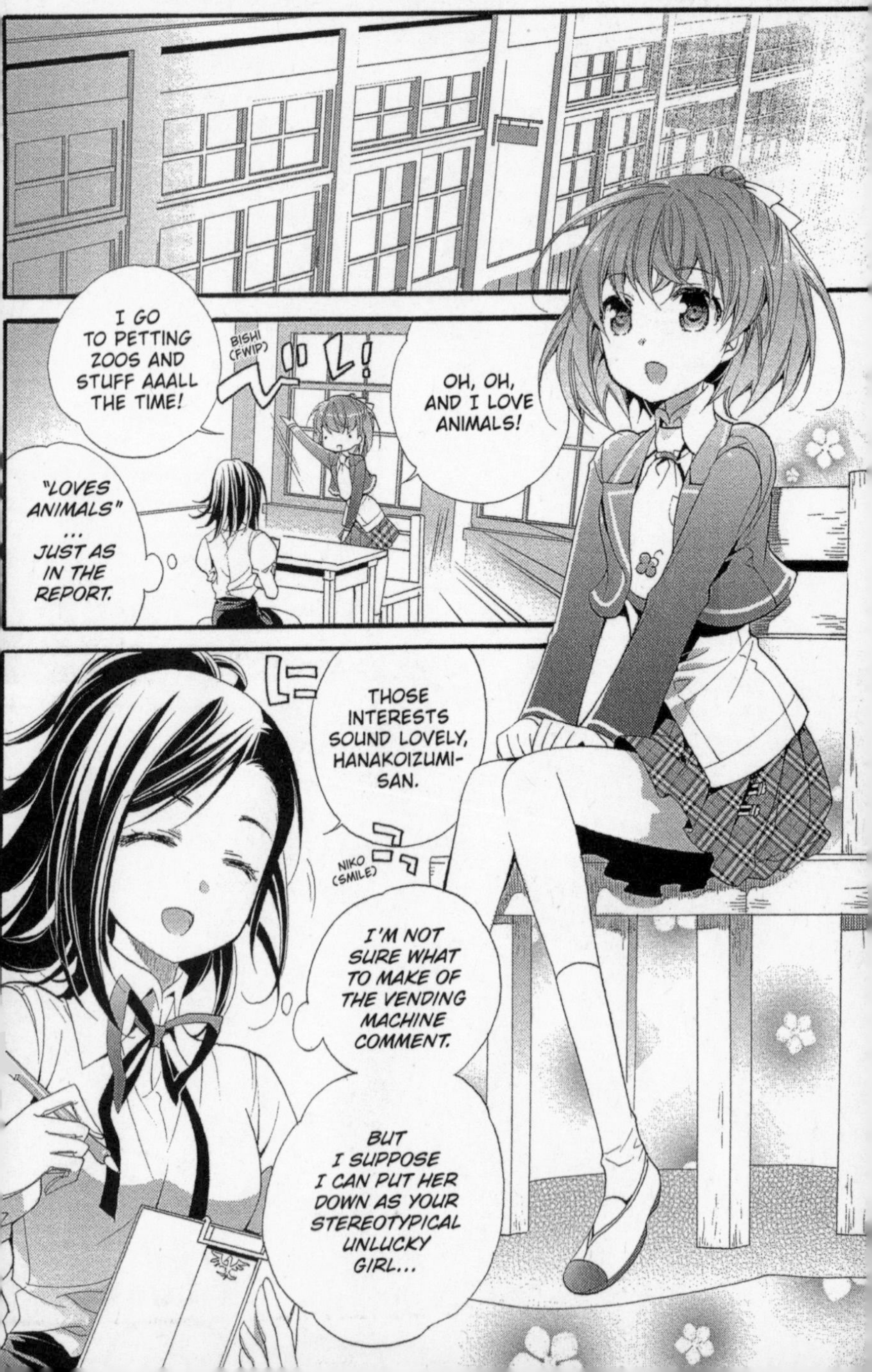
OH, OH, AND I LOVE ANIMALS!
BISHI (FWIP)
I GO TO PETTING ZOOS AND STUFF AAALL THE TIME!
"LOVES ANIMALS" ... JUST AS IN THE REPORT.
THOSE INTERESTS SOUND LOVELY, HANAKOIZUMI-SAN.
NIKO (SMILE)
I'M NOT SURE WHAT TO MAKE OF THE VENDING MACHINE COMMENT.
BUT I SUPPOSE I CAN PUT HER DOWN AS YOUR STEREOTYPICAL UNLUCKY GIRL...

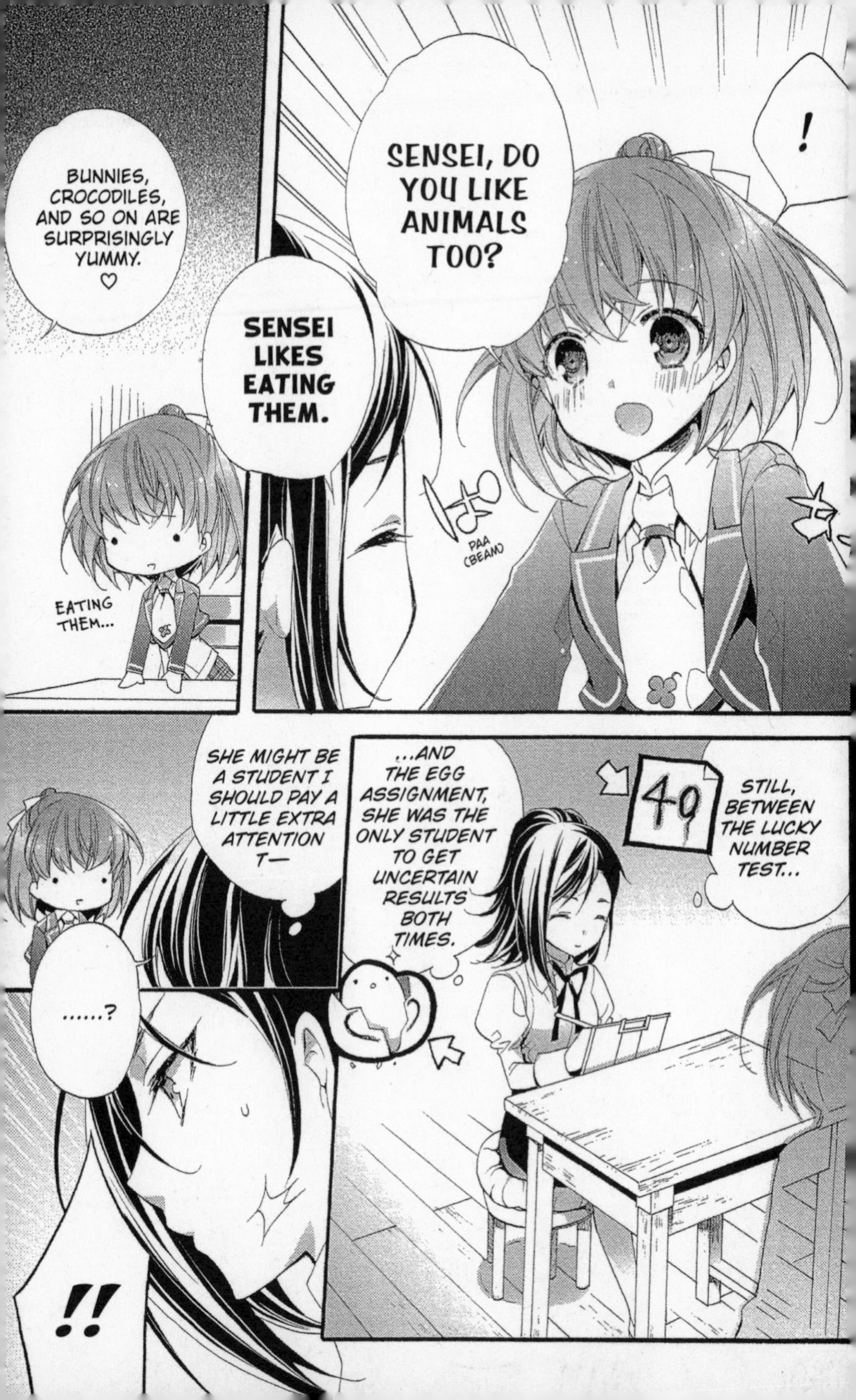
!
SENSEI, DO YOU LIKE ANIMALS TOO?
PAA (BEAM)
SENSEI LIKES EATING THEM.
BUNNIES, CROCODILES, AND SO ON ARE SURPRISINGLY YUMMY. ♡
EATING THEM...
STILL, BETWEEN THE LUCKY NUMBER TEST...
49
...AND THE EGG ASSIGNMENT, SHE WAS THE ONLY STUDENT TO GET UNCERTAIN RESULTS BOTH TIMES.
SHE MIGHT BE A STUDENT I SHOULD PAY A LITTLE EXTRA ATTENTION T—
......?
!!

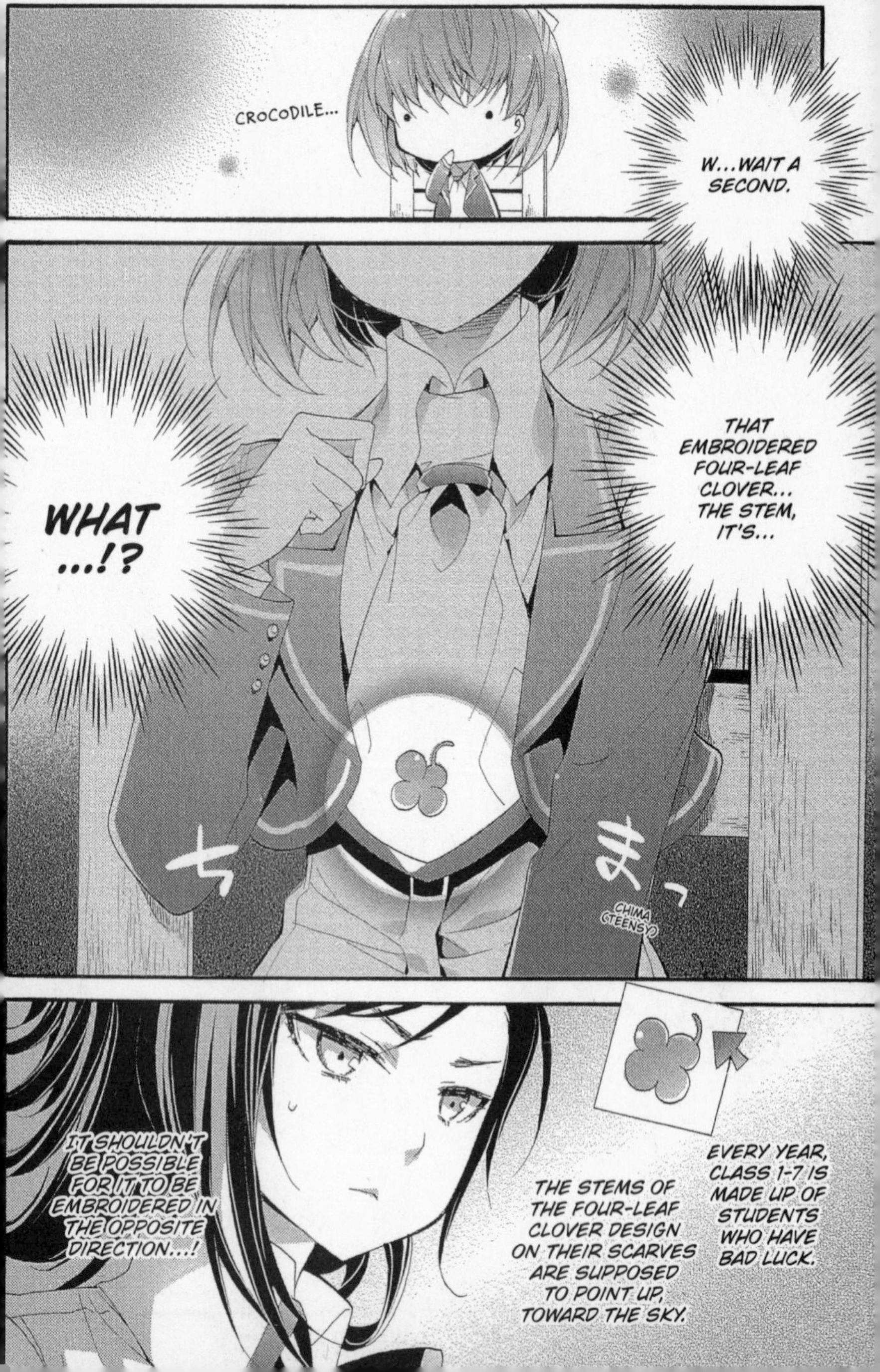
CROCODILE...
W...WAIT A SECOND.
THAT EMBROIDERED FOUR-LEAF CLOVER... THE STEM, IT'S...
WHAT ...!?
ちまっ
CHIMA (TEENSY)
EVERY YEAR, CLASS 1-7 IS MADE UP OF STUDENTS WHO HAVE BAD LUCK.
THE STEMS OF THE FOUR-LEAF CLOVER DESIGN ON THEIR SCARVES ARE SUPPOSED TO POINT UP, TOWARD THE SKY.
IT SHOULDN'T BE POSSIBLE FOR IT TO BE EMBROIDERED IN THE OPPOSITE DIRECTION...!

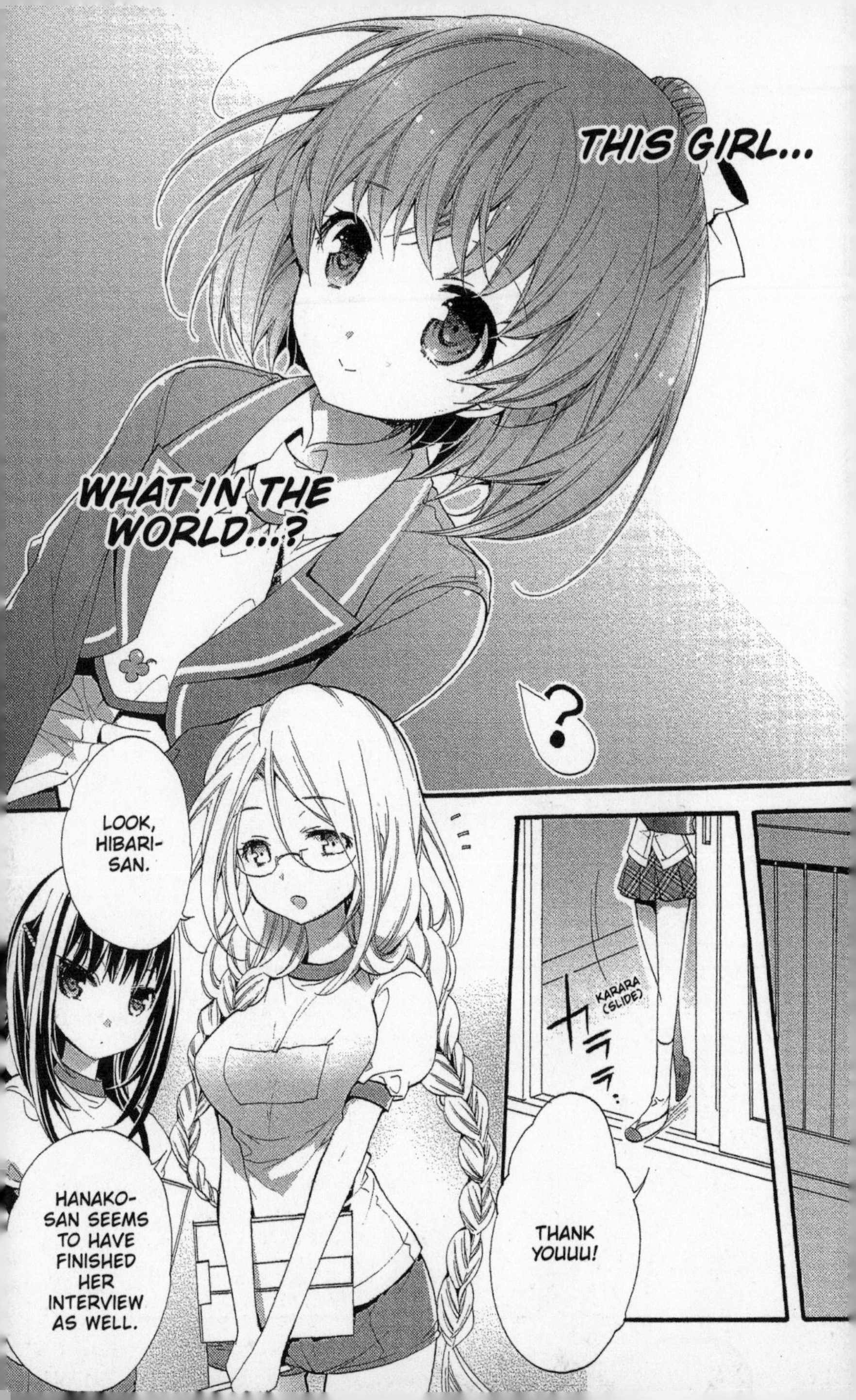
THIS GIRL...
WHAT IN THE WORLD...?
?
KARARA (SLIDE)
THANK YOUUU!
LOOK, HIBARI-SAN.
HANAKO-SAN SEEMS TO HAVE FINISHED HER INTERVIEW AS WELL.

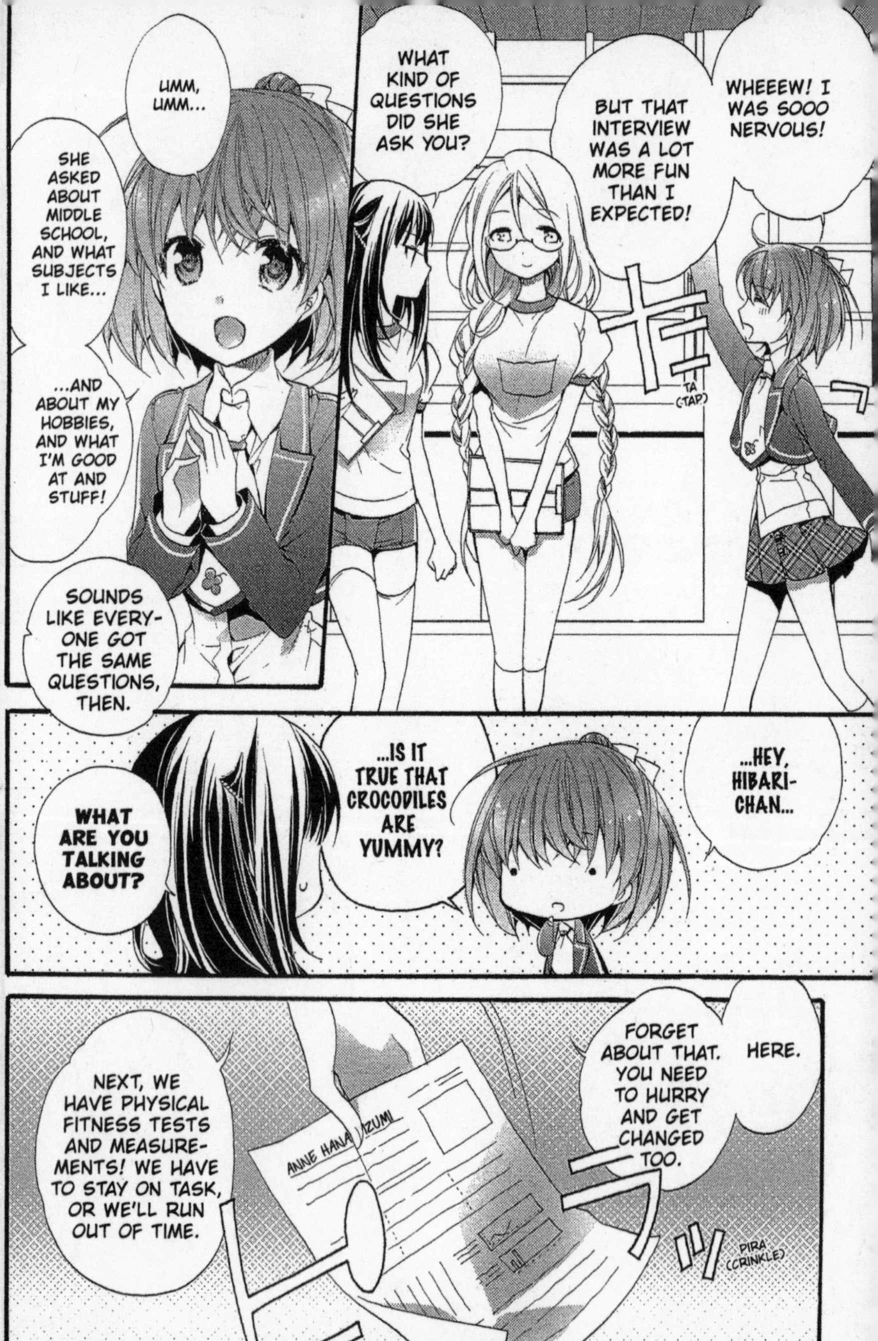
WHEEEW! I WAS SOOO NERVOUS!
BUT THAT INTERVIEW WAS A LOT MORE FUN THAN I EXPECTED!
TA (TAP)
WHAT KIND OF QUESTIONS DID SHE ASK YOU?
UMM, UMM...
SHE ASKED ABOUT MIDDLE SCHOOL, AND WHAT SUBJECTS I LIKE...
...AND ABOUT MY HOBBIES, AND WHAT I'M GOOD AT AND STUFF!
SOUNDS LIKE EVERY-ONE GOT THE SAME QUESTIONS, THEN.
...HEY, HIBARI-CHAN...
...IS IT TRUE THAT CROCODILES ARE YUMMY?
WHAT ARE YOU TALKING ABOUT?
HERE.
FORGET ABOUT THAT. YOU NEED TO HURRY AND GET CHANGED TOO.
PIRA (CRINKLE)
ANNE HANA IZUMI
NEXT, WE HAVE PHYSICAL FITNESS TESTS AND MEASURE-MENTS! WE HAVE TO STAY ON TASK, OR WE'LL RUN OUT OF TIME.

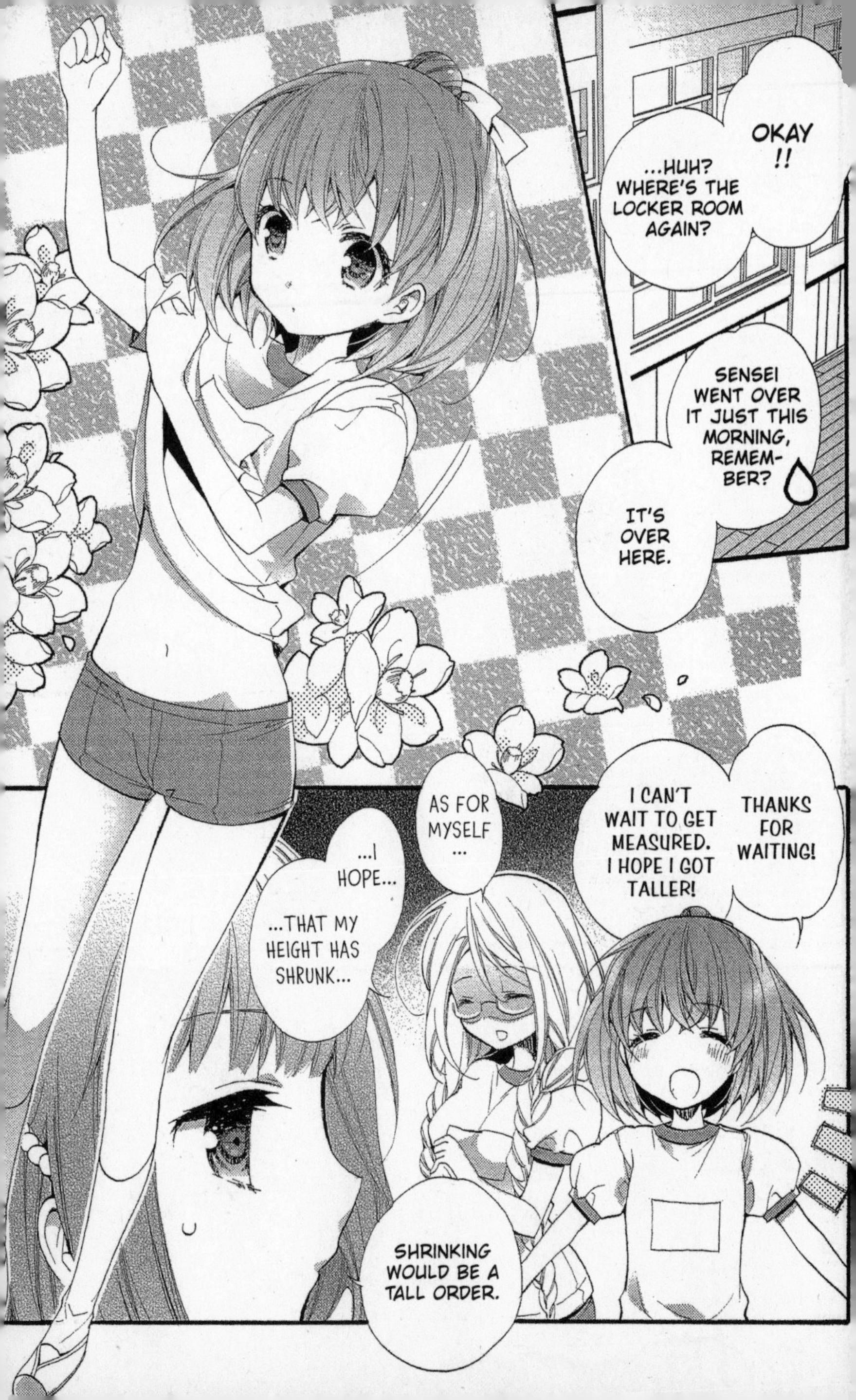
OKAY!!
...HUH? WHERE'S THE LOCKER ROOM AGAIN?
SENSEI WENT OVER IT JUST THIS MORNING, REMEMBER?
IT'S OVER HERE.
THANKS FOR WAITING!
I CAN'T WAIT TO GET MEASURED. I HOPE I GOT TALLER!
AS FOR MYSELF...
...I HOPE...
...THAT MY HEIGHT HAS SHRUNK...
SHRINKING WOULD BE A TALL ORDER.

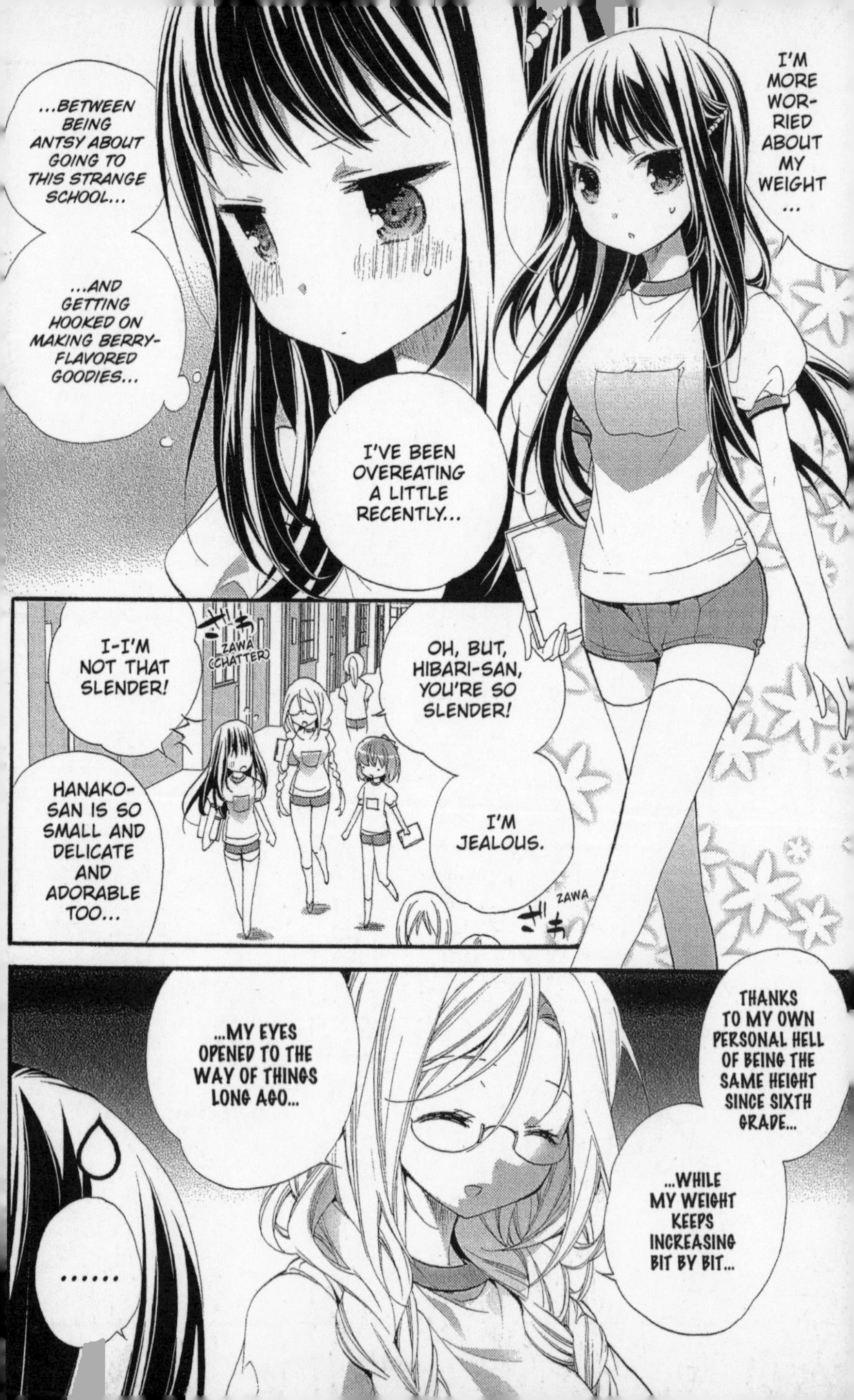
I'M MORE WORRIED ABOUT MY WEIGHT...
...BETWEEN BEING ANTSY ABOUT GOING TO THIS STRANGE SCHOOL...
...AND GETTING HOOKED ON MAKING BERRY-FLAVORED GOODIES...
I'VE BEEN OVEREATING A LITTLE RECENTLY...
OH, BUT, HIBARI-SAN, YOU'RE SO SLENDER!
I'M JEALOUS.
ZAWA
ZAWA (CHATTER)
I-I'M NOT THAT SLENDER!
HANAKO-SAN IS SO SMALL AND DELICATE AND ADORABLE TOO...
THANKS TO MY OWN PERSONAL HELL OF BEING THE SAME HEIGHT SINCE SIXTH GRADE...
...WHILE MY WEIGHT KEEPS INCREASING BIT BY BIT...
...MY EYES OPENED TO THE WAY OF THINGS LONG AGO...
......

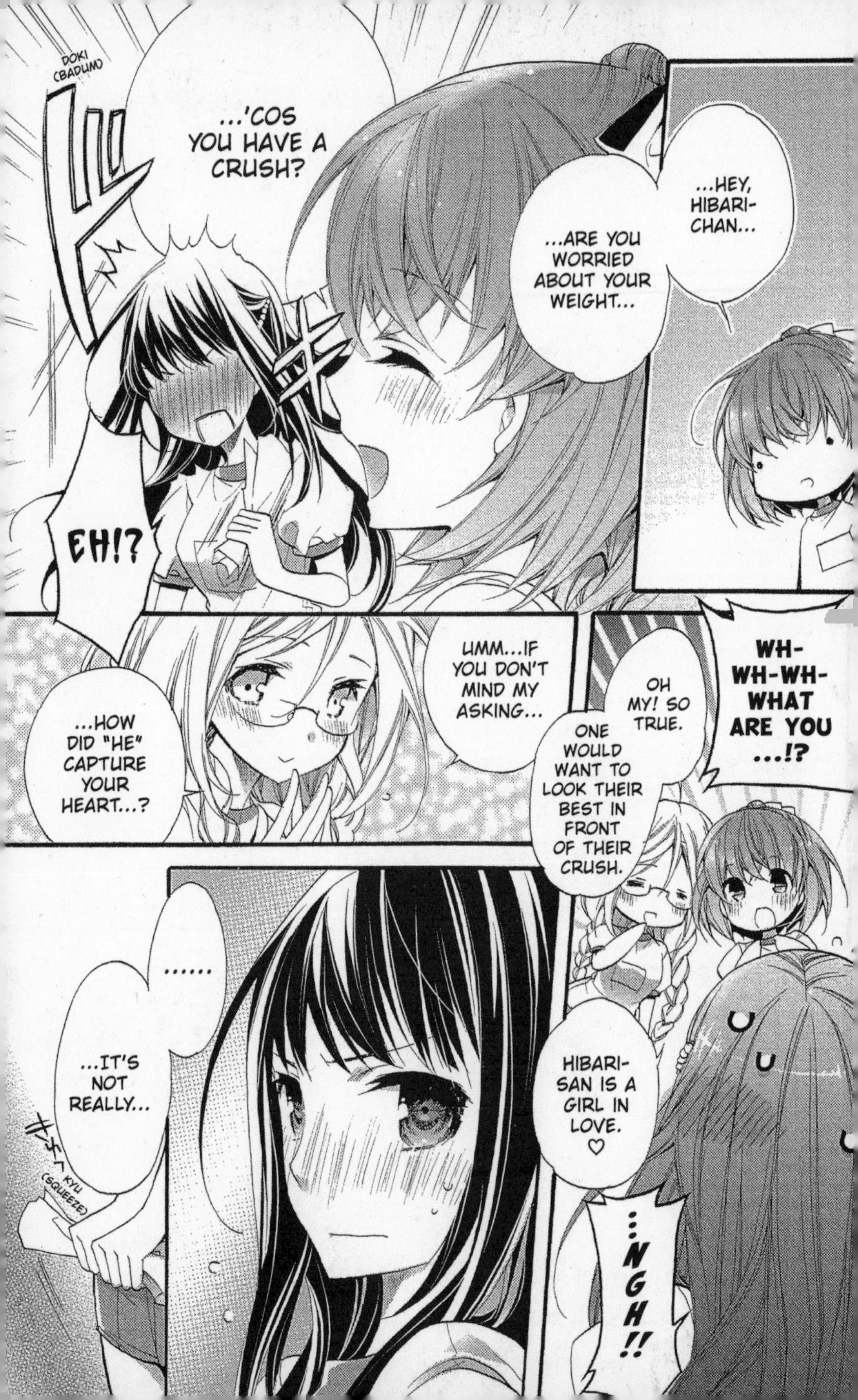
...HEY, HIBARI-CHAN...
...ARE YOU WORRIED ABOUT YOUR WEIGHT...
...'COS YOU HAVE A CRUSH?
DOKI (BADUM)
EH!?
WH-WH-WH-WHAT ARE YOU ...!?
OH MY! SO TRUE.
ONE WOULD WANT TO LOOK THEIR BEST IN FRONT OF THEIR CRUSH.
UMM...IF YOU DON'T MIND MY ASKING...
...HOW DID "HE" CAPTURE YOUR HEART...?
HIBARI-SAN IS A GIRL IN LOVE. ♡
...NGH!!
......
...IT'S NOT REALLY...
KYU (SQUEEZE)

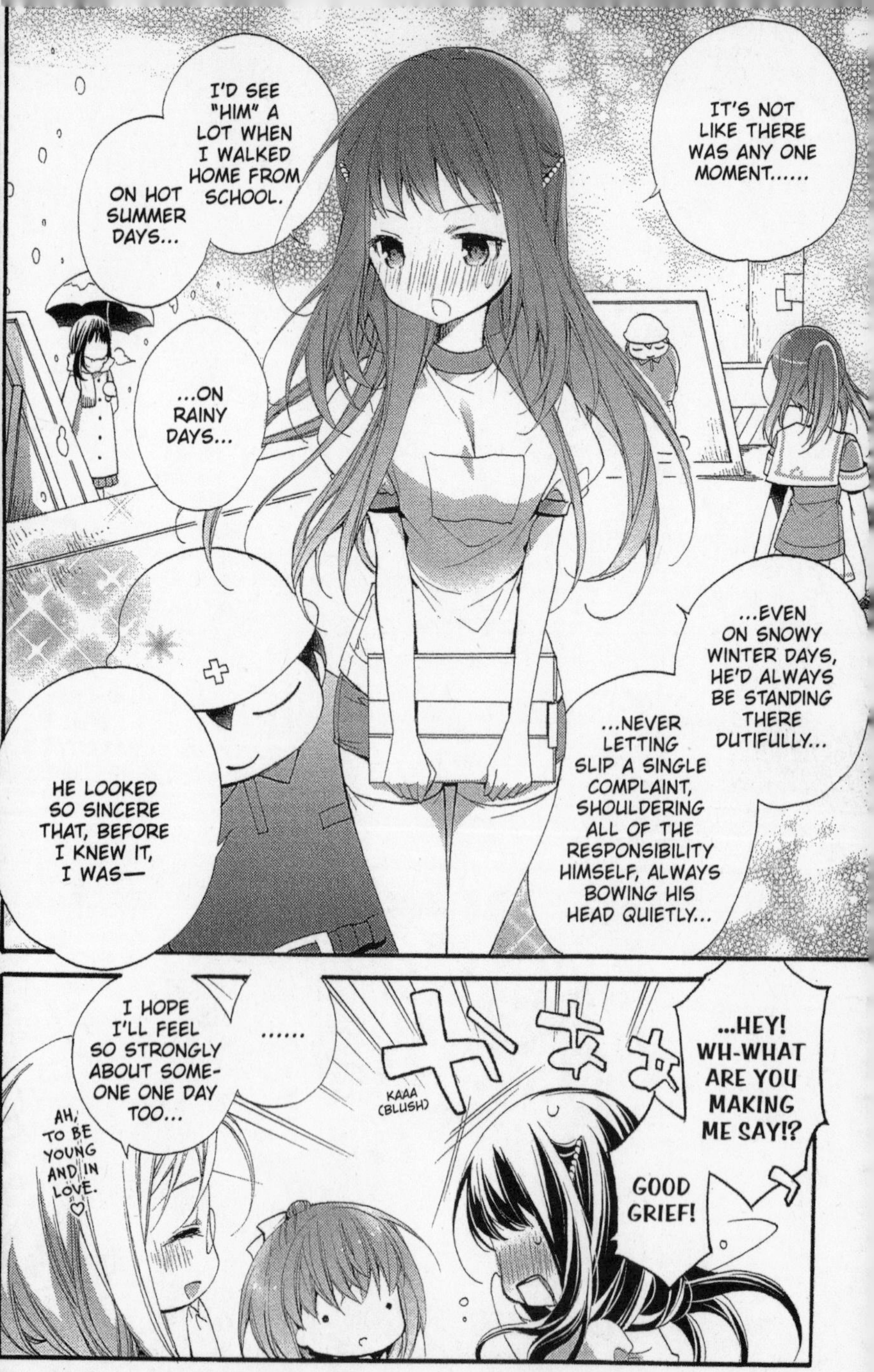
IT'S NOT LIKE THERE WAS ANY ONE MOMENT......
I'D SEE "HIM" A LOT WHEN I WALKED HOME FROM SCHOOL.
ON HOT SUMMER DAYS...
...ON RAINY DAYS...
...EVEN ON SNOWY WINTER DAYS, HE'D ALWAYS BE STANDING THERE DUTIFULLY...
...NEVER LETTING SLIP A SINGLE COMPLAINT, SHOULDERING ALL OF THE RESPONSIBILITY HIMSELF, ALWAYS BOWING HIS HEAD QUIETLY...
HE LOOKED SO SINCERE THAT, BEFORE I KNEW IT, I WAS—
...HEY! WH-WHAT ARE YOU MAKING ME SAY!?
GOOD GRIEF!
KAAA (BLUSH)
......
I HOPE I'LL FEEL SO STRONGLY ABOUT SOME-ONE ONE DAY TOO...
AH, TO BE YOUNG AND IN LOVE. ♡

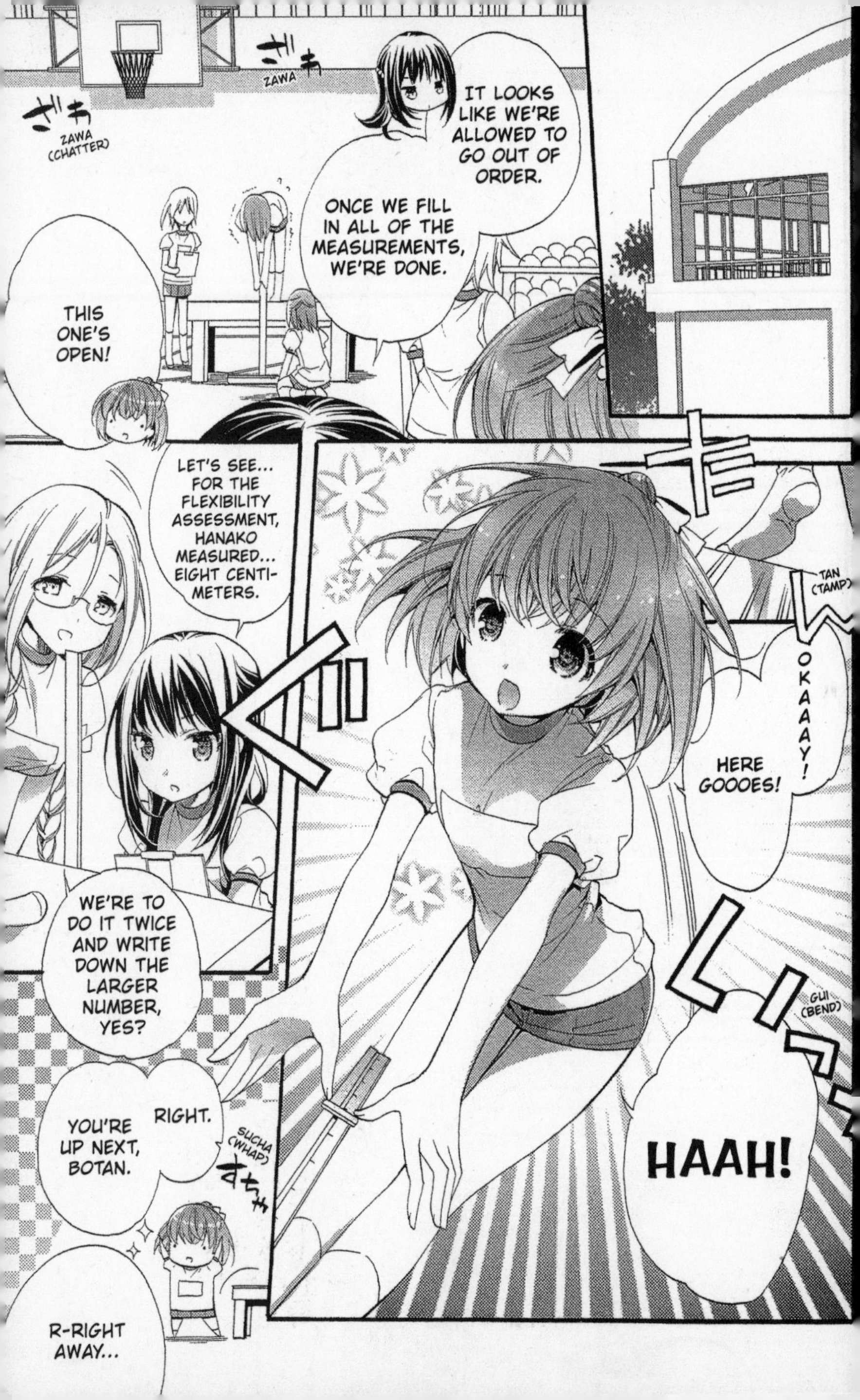
ZAWA
IT LOOKS LIKE WE'RE ALLOWED TO GO OUT OF ORDER.
ONCE WE FILL IN ALL OF THE MEASUREMENTS, WE'RE DONE.
ZAWA (CHATTER)
THIS ONE'S OPEN!
TAN (TAMP)
OKAAAY!
HERE GOOOES!
GUI (BEND)
HAAH!
LET'S SEE... FOR THE FLEXIBILITY ASSESSMENT, HANAKO MEASURED... EIGHT CENTI-METERS.
WE'RE TO DO IT TWICE AND WRITE DOWN THE LARGER NUMBER, YES?
RIGHT.
YOU'RE UP NEXT, BOTAN.
SUCHA (WHAP)
R-RIGHT AWAY...

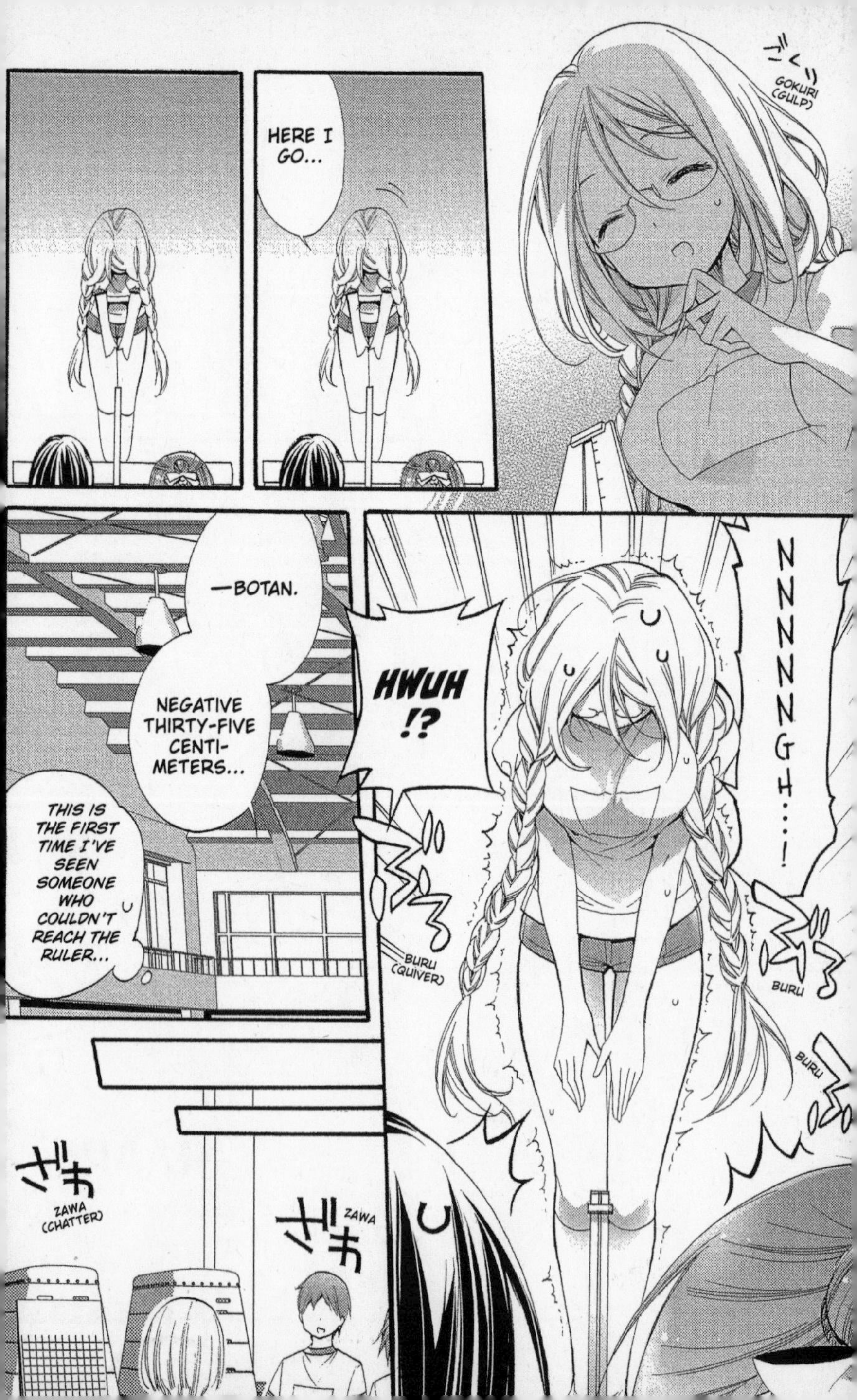
ごくり
GOKURI (GULP)
HERE I GO...
NNNNNGH...!
ぶる
BURU
BURU
HWUH !?
ぶる
BURU (QUIVER)
—BOTAN.
NEGATIVE THIRTY-FIVE CENTI-METERS...
THIS IS THE FIRST TIME I'VE SEEN SOMEONE WHO COULDN'T REACH THE RULER...
ざわ
ZAWA (CHATTER)
ざわ
ZAWA

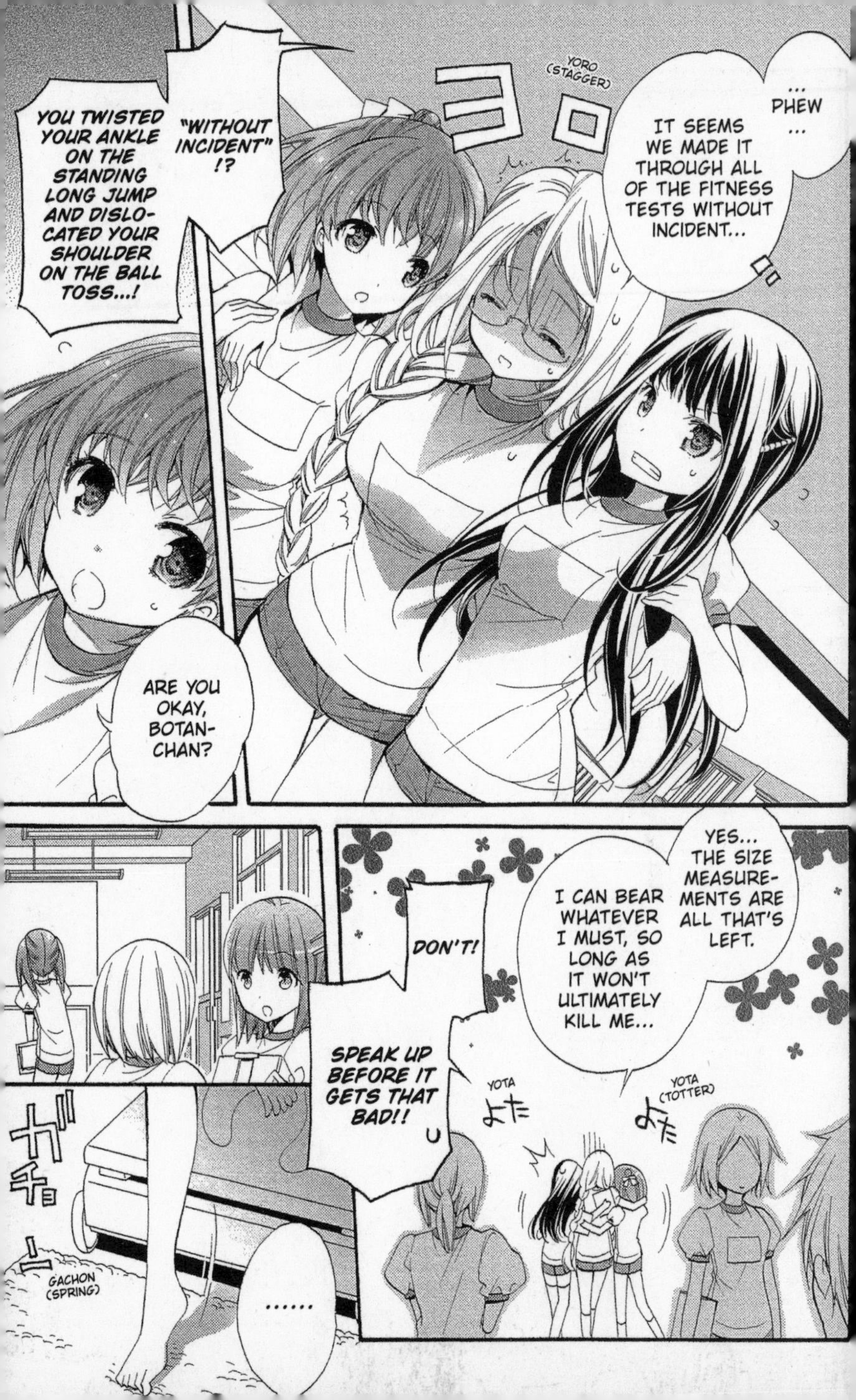
... PHEW ...
IT SEEMS WE MADE IT THROUGH ALL OF THE FITNESS TESTS WITHOUT INCIDENT...
YORO (STAGGER)
"WITHOUT INCIDENT" !?
YOU TWISTED YOUR ANKLE ON THE STANDING LONG JUMP AND DISLOCATED YOUR SHOULDER ON THE BALL TOSS...!
ARE YOU OKAY, BOTAN-CHAN?
YES... THE SIZE MEASUREMENTS ARE ALL THAT'S LEFT.
I CAN BEAR WHATEVER I MUST, SO LONG AS IT WON'T ULTIMATELY KILL ME...
DON'T!
SPEAK UP BEFORE IT GETS THAT BAD!!
YOTA (TOTTER)
YOTA
GACHON (SPRING)
......

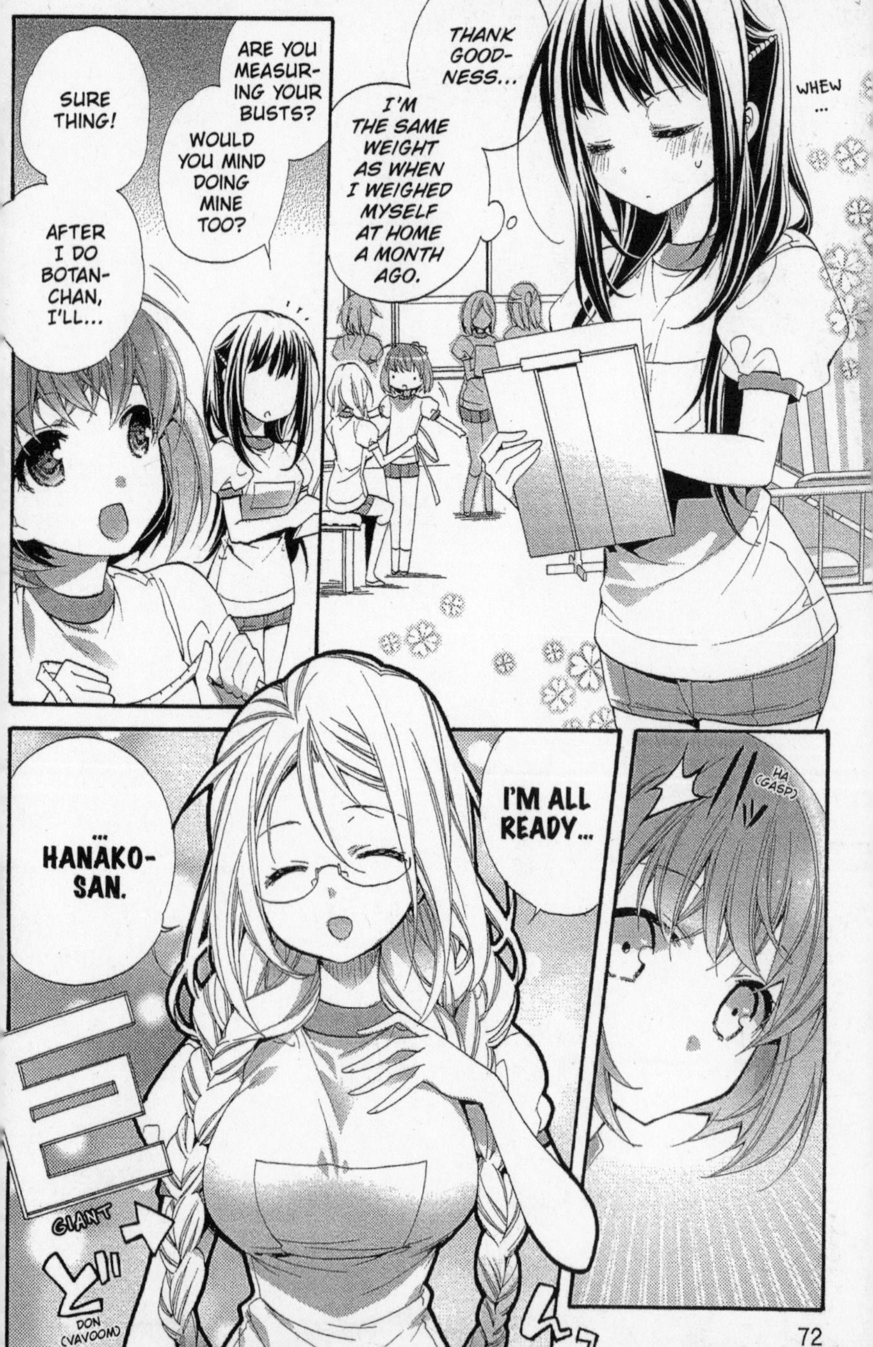
THANK GOODNESS...
I'M THE SAME WEIGHT AS WHEN I WEIGHED MYSELF AT HOME A MONTH AGO.
WHEW ...
ARE YOU MEASURING YOUR BUSTS?
WOULD YOU MIND DOING MINE TOO?
SURE THING!
AFTER I DO BOTAN-CHAN, I'LL...
HA (GASP)
I'M ALL READY...
... HANAKO-SAN.
GIANT
DON (VAVOOM)

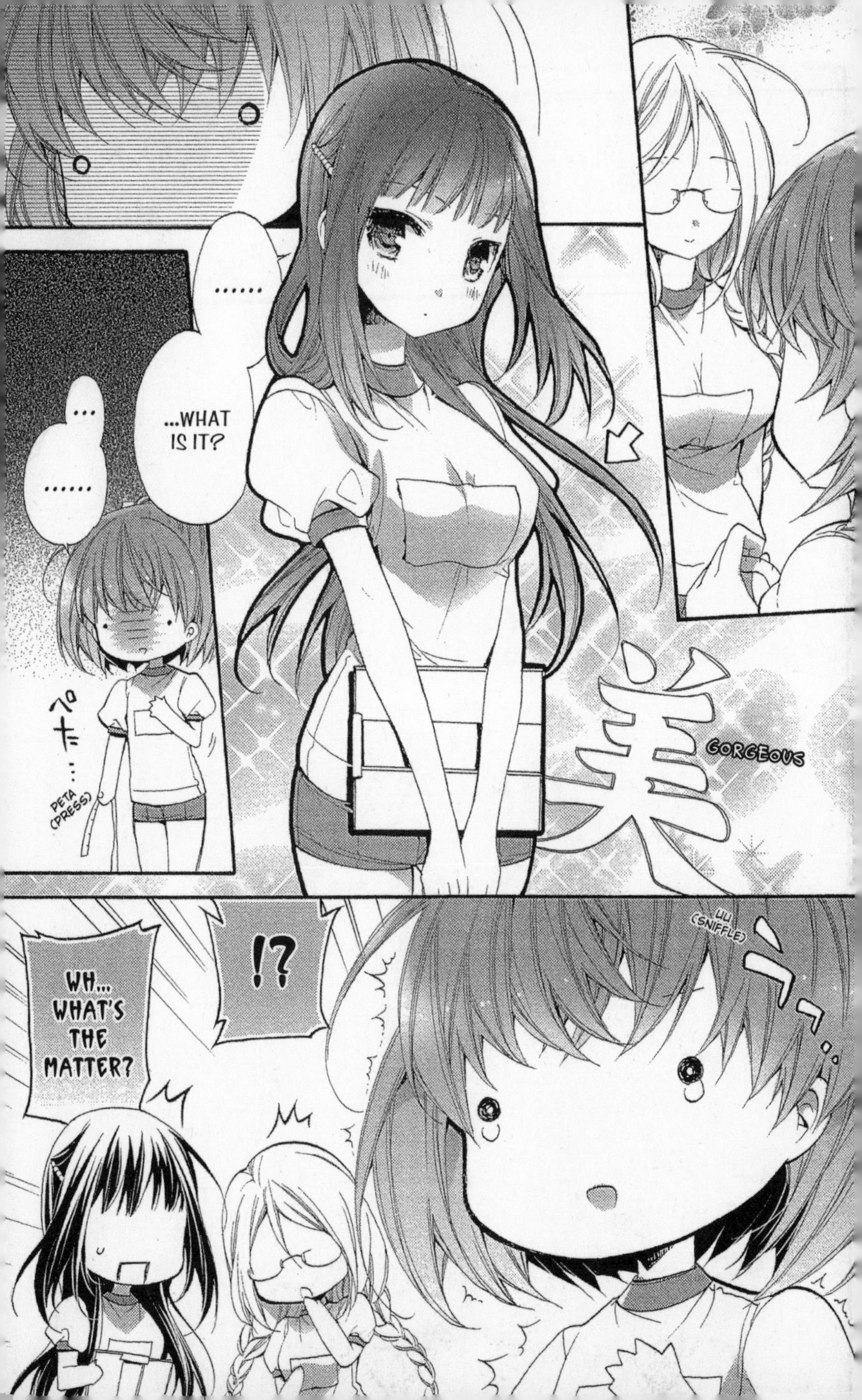

美
GORGEOUS
......
...WHAT IS IT?
...
......
ぺた…
PETA (PRESS)
うぅ…
UU (SNIFFLE)
!?
WH... WHAT'S THE MATTER?

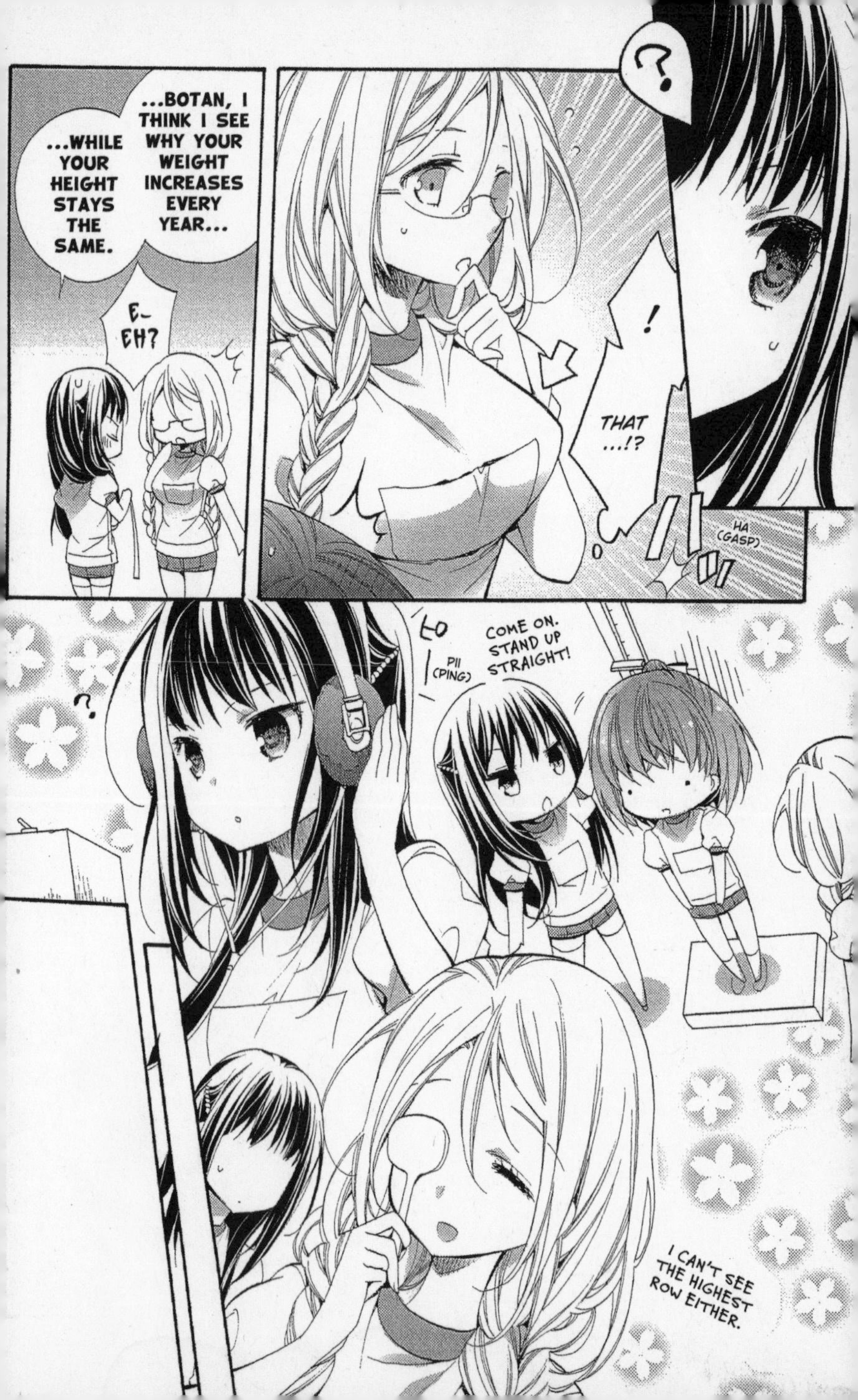
?
!
THAT ...!?
HA (GASP)
...BOTAN, I THINK I SEE WHY YOUR WEIGHT INCREASES EVERY YEAR...
...WHILE YOUR HEIGHT STAYS THE SAME.
E-EH?
COME ON. STAND UP STRAIGHT!
ピロ
PII (PING)
?
I CAN'T SEE THE HIGHEST ROW EITHER.

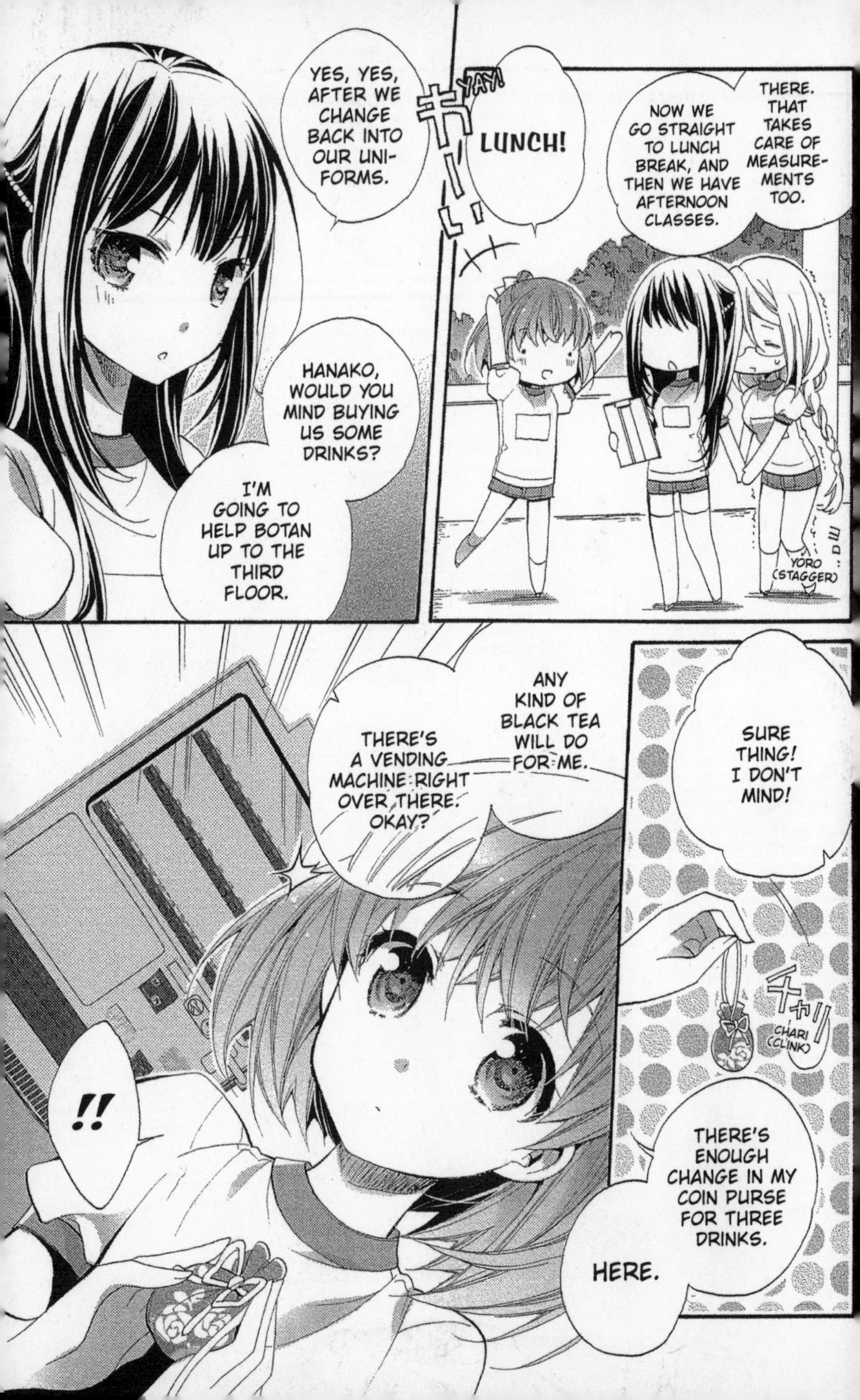
THERE. THAT TAKES CARE OF MEASUREMENTS TOO.
NOW WE GO STRAIGHT TO LUNCH BREAK, AND THEN WE HAVE AFTERNOON CLASSES.
YAY!
LUNCH!
YORO (STAGGER)
YES, YES, AFTER WE CHANGE BACK INTO OUR UNIFORMS.
HANAKO, WOULD YOU MIND BUYING US SOME DRINKS?
I'M GOING TO HELP BOTAN UP TO THE THIRD FLOOR.
SURE THING! I DON'T MIND!
CHARI (CL'INK)
THERE'S ENOUGH CHANGE IN MY COIN PURSE FOR THREE DRINKS.
HERE.
ANY KIND OF BLACK TEA WILL DO FOR ME.
THERE'S A VENDING MACHINE RIGHT OVER THERE. OKAY?
!!

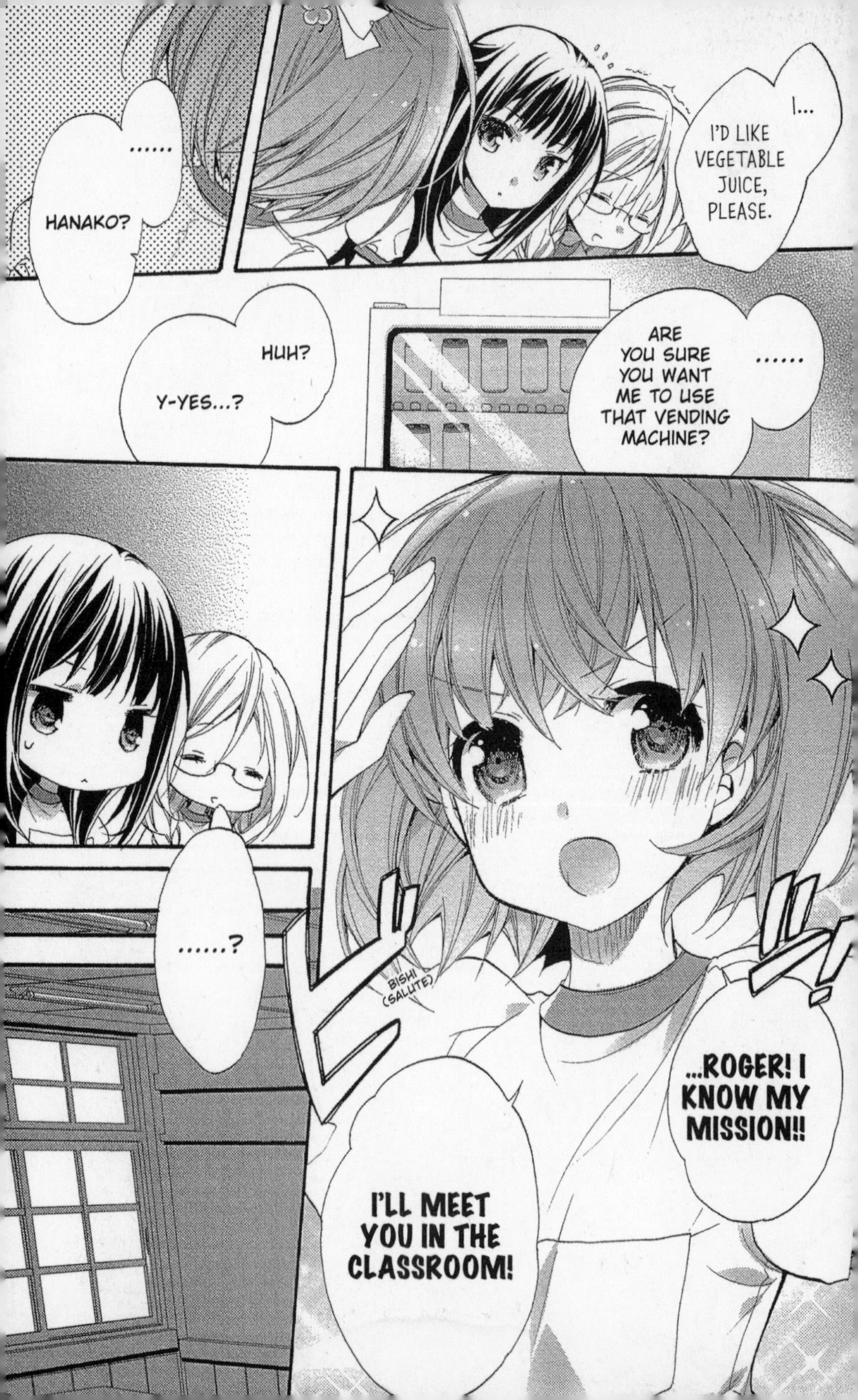
I...
I'D LIKE VEGETABLE JUICE, PLEASE.
......
HANAKO?
......
ARE YOU SURE YOU WANT ME TO USE THAT VENDING MACHINE?
HUH?
Y-YES...?
BISHI (SALUTE)
...ROGER! I KNOW MY MISSION!!
I'LL MEET YOU IN THE CLASSROOM!
......?

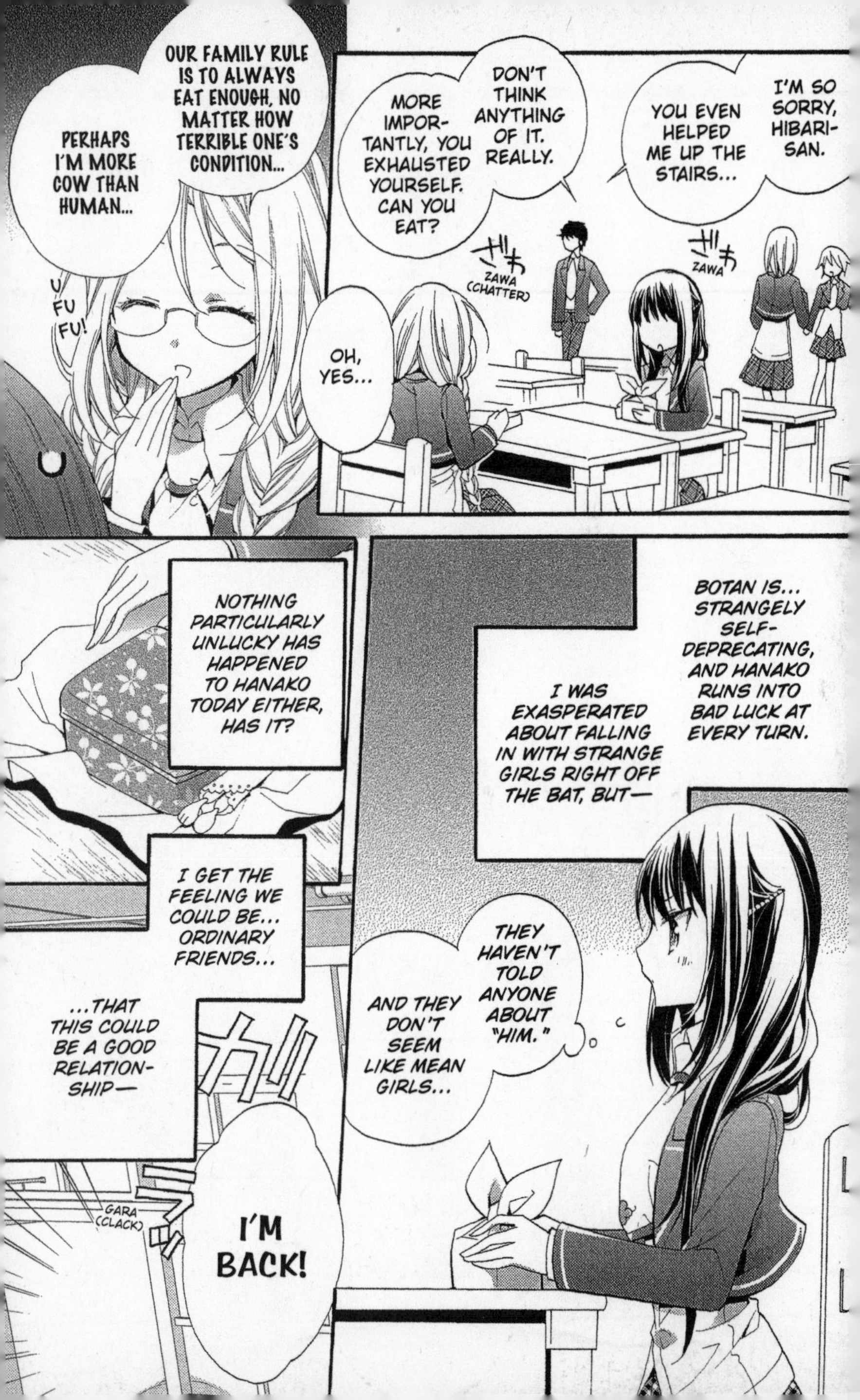
I'M SO SORRY, HIBARI-SAN.
YOU EVEN HELPED ME UP THE STAIRS...
DON'T THINK ANYTHING OF IT. REALLY.
MORE IMPORTANTLY, YOU EXHAUSTED YOURSELF. CAN YOU EAT?
ZAWA
ZAWA (CHATTER)
OH, YES...
OUR FAMILY RULE IS TO ALWAYS EAT ENOUGH, NO MATTER HOW TERRIBLE ONE'S CONDITION...
PERHAPS I'M MORE COW THAN HUMAN...
U FU FU!
BOTAN IS... STRANGELY SELF-DEPRECATING, AND HANAKO RUNS INTO BAD LUCK AT EVERY TURN.
I WAS EXASPERATED ABOUT FALLING IN WITH STRANGE GIRLS RIGHT OFF THE BAT, BUT—
THEY HAVEN'T TOLD ANYONE ABOUT "HIM."
AND THEY DON'T SEEM LIKE MEAN GIRLS...
NOTHING PARTICULARLY UNLUCKY HAS HAPPENED TO HANAKO TODAY EITHER, HAS IT?
I GET THE FEELING WE COULD BE... ORDINARY FRIENDS...
...THAT THIS COULD BE A GOOD RELATIONSHIP—
GARA (CLACK)
I'M BACK!

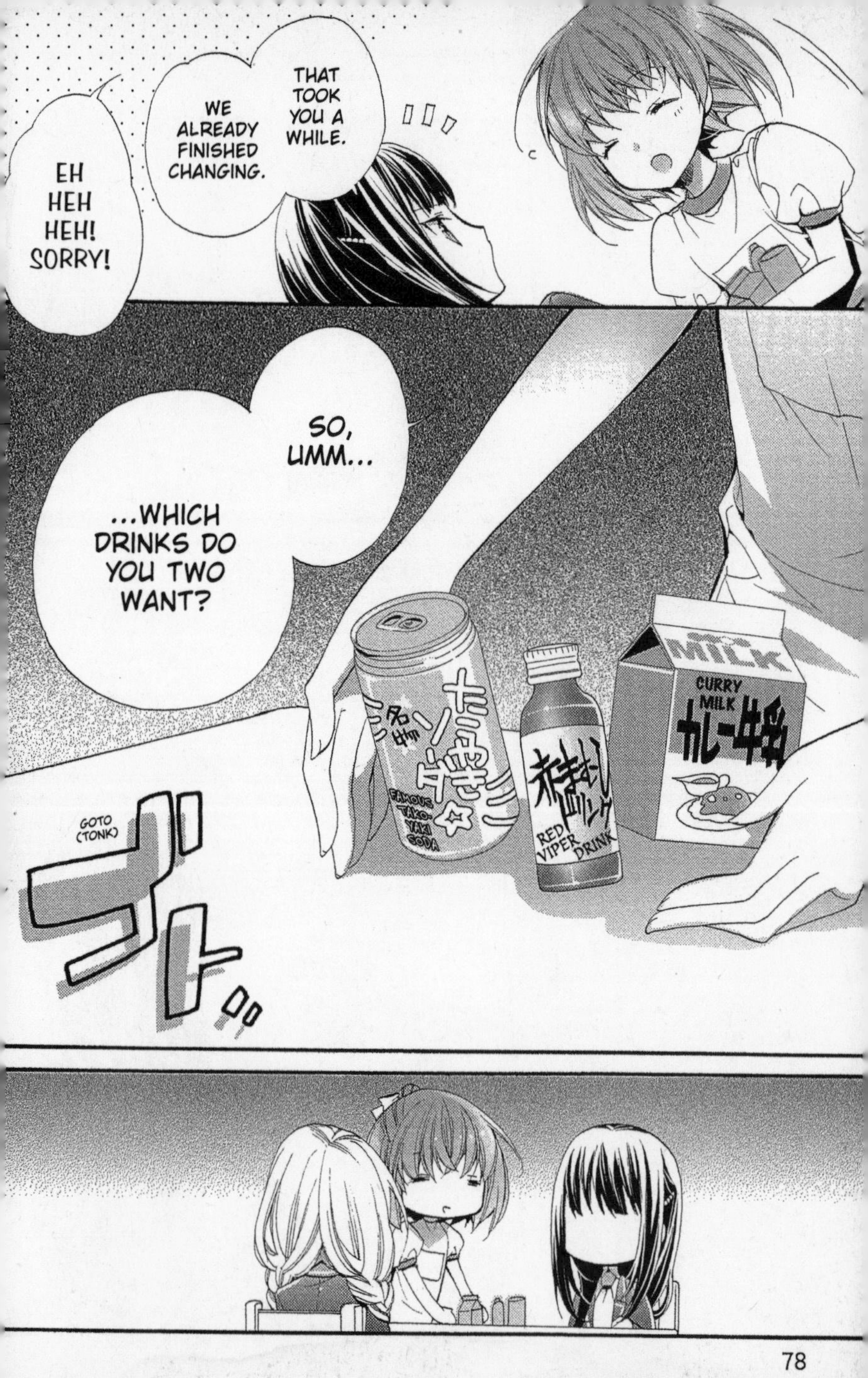
THAT TOOK YOU A WHILE.
WE ALREADY FINISHED CHANGING.
EH HEH HEH! SORRY!
SO, UMM...
...WHICH DRINKS DO YOU TWO WANT?
MILK
CURRY MILK
カレー牛乳
RED VIPER DRINK
FAMOUS TAKO-YAKI SODA
GOTO (TONK)

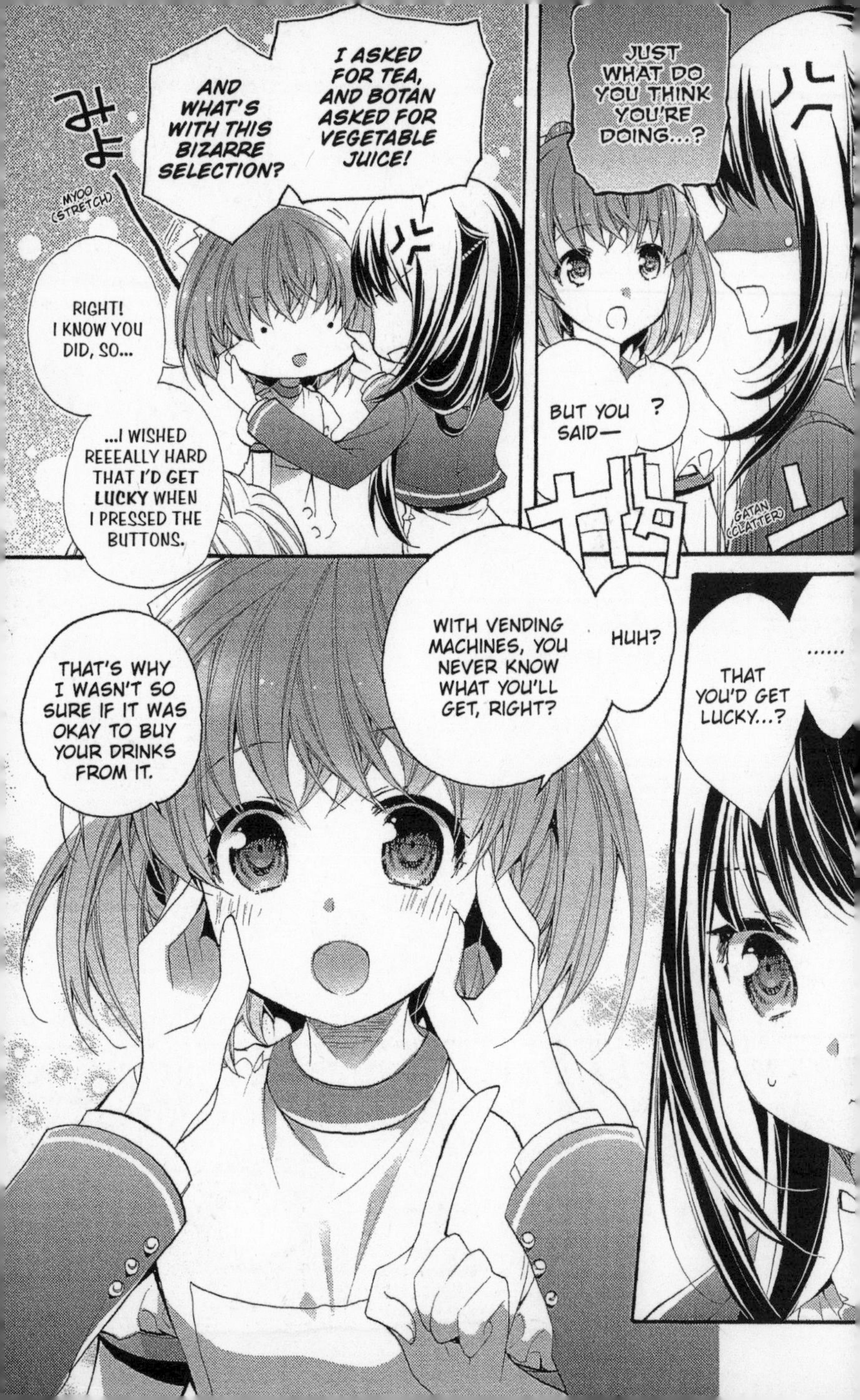
JUST WHAT DO YOU THINK YOU'RE DOING...?
BUT YOU SAID— ?
ガタン
GATAN (CLATTER)
I ASKED FOR TEA, AND BOTAN ASKED FOR VEGETABLE JUICE!
AND WHAT'S WITH THIS BIZARRE SELECTION?
みょ
MYOO (STRETCH)
RIGHT! I KNOW YOU DID, SO...
...I WISHED REEEALLY HARD THAT **I'D GET LUCKY** WHEN I PRESSED THE BUTTONS.
......
THAT YOU'D GET LUCKY...?
HUH?
WITH VENDING MACHINES, YOU NEVER KNOW WHAT YOU'LL GET, RIGHT?
THAT'S WHY I WASN'T SO SURE IF IT WAS OKAY TO BUY YOUR DRINKS FROM IT.

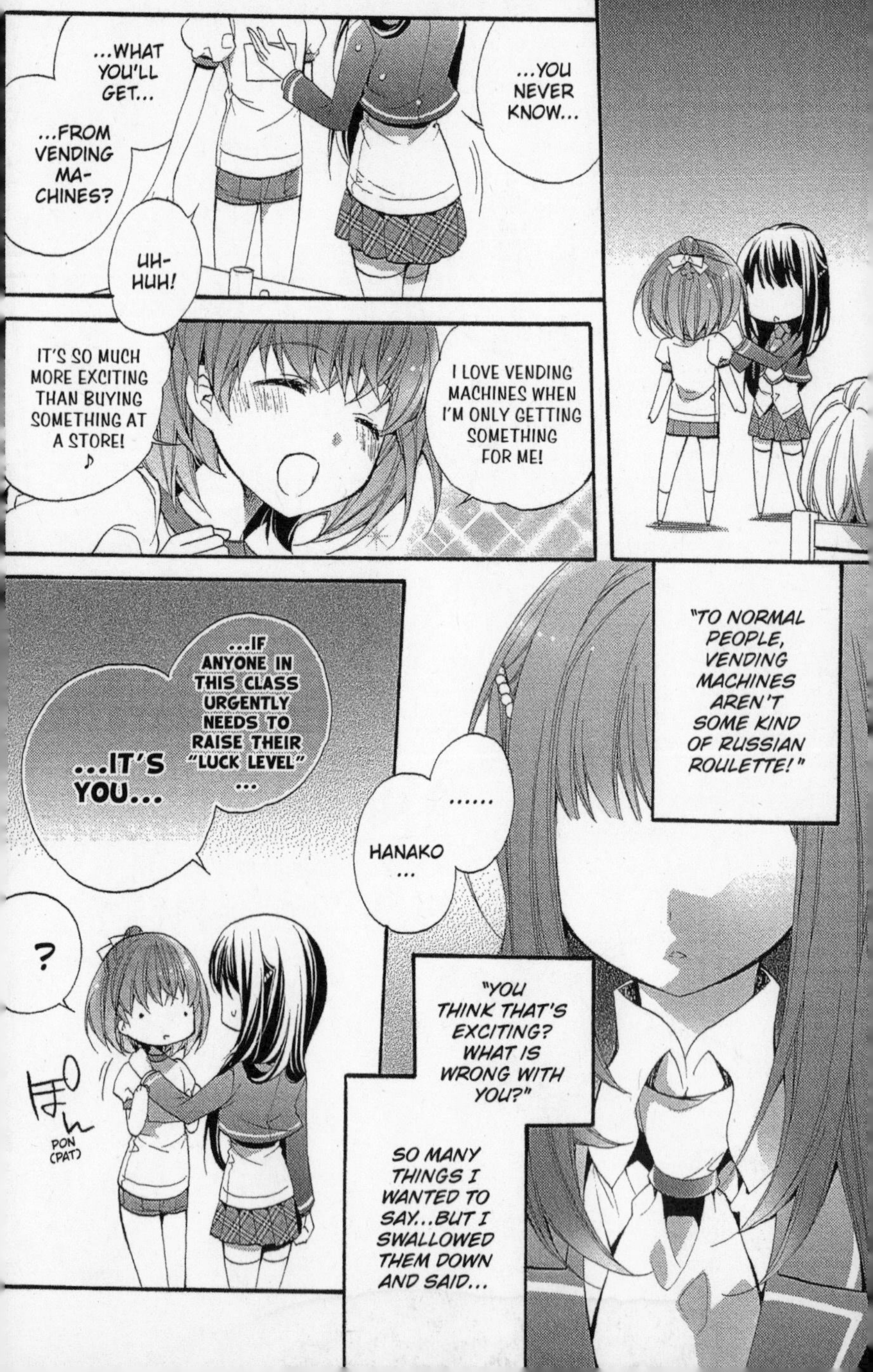
...YOU NEVER KNOW...
...WHAT YOU'LL GET...
...FROM VENDING MA-CHINES?
UH-HUH!
I LOVE VENDING MACHINES WHEN I'M ONLY GETTING SOMETHING FOR ME!
IT'S SO MUCH MORE EXCITING THAN BUYING SOMETHING AT A STORE! ♪
"TO NORMAL PEOPLE, VENDING MACHINES AREN'T SOME KIND OF RUSSIAN ROULETTE!"
......
HANAKO ...
"YOU THINK THAT'S EXCITING? WHAT IS WRONG WITH YOU?"
SO MANY THINGS I WANTED TO SAY...BUT I SWALLOWED THEM DOWN AND SAID...
...IF ANYONE IN THIS CLASS URGENTLY NEEDS TO RAISE THEIR "LUCK LEVEL" ... ...IT'S YOU...
?
ぽん
PON (PAT)

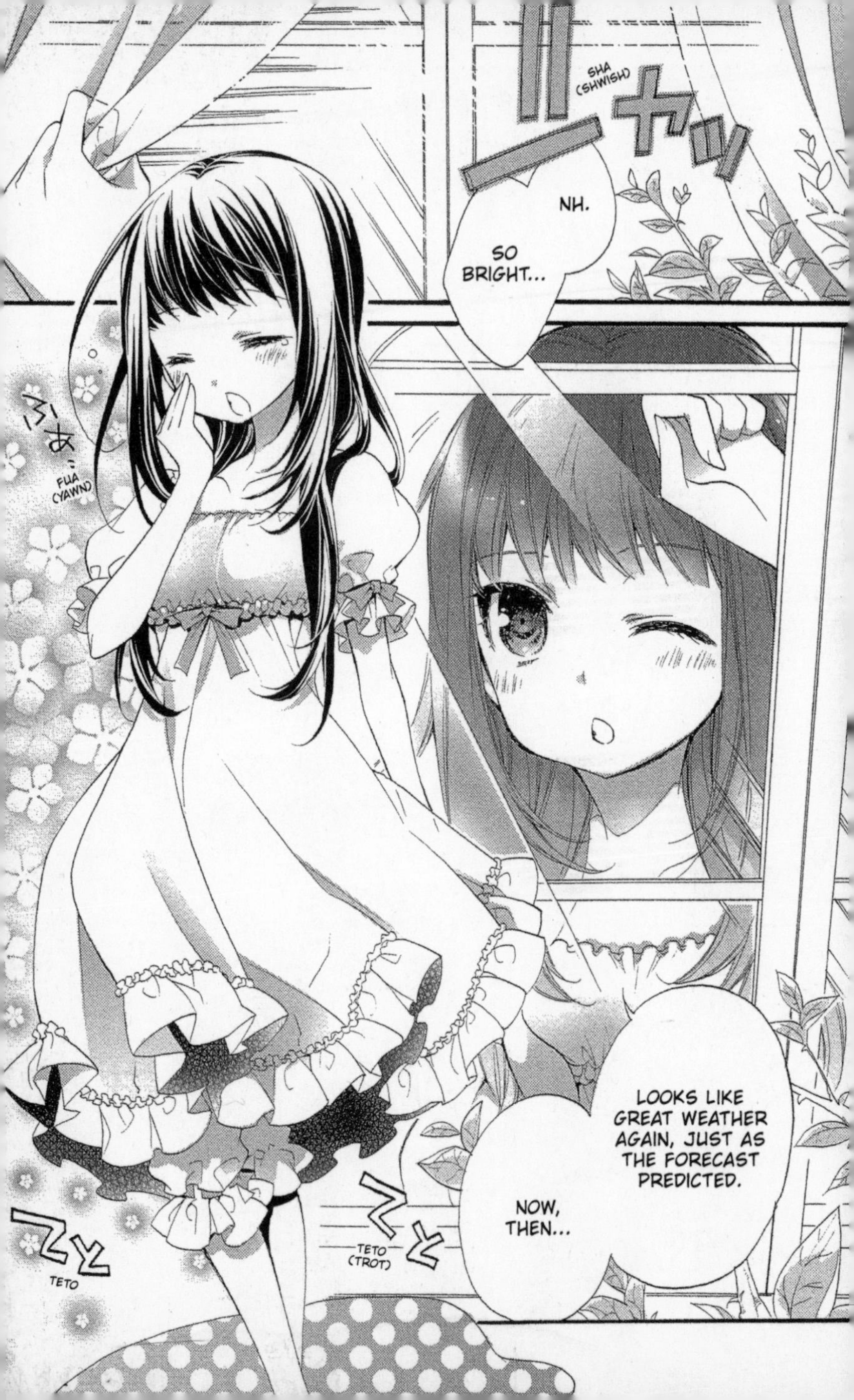
SHA (SHWISH)
NH.
SO BRIGHT...
LOOKS LIKE GREAT WEATHER AGAIN, JUST AS THE FORECAST PREDICTED.
NOW, THEN...
FUA (YAWN)
TETO (TROT)
TETO

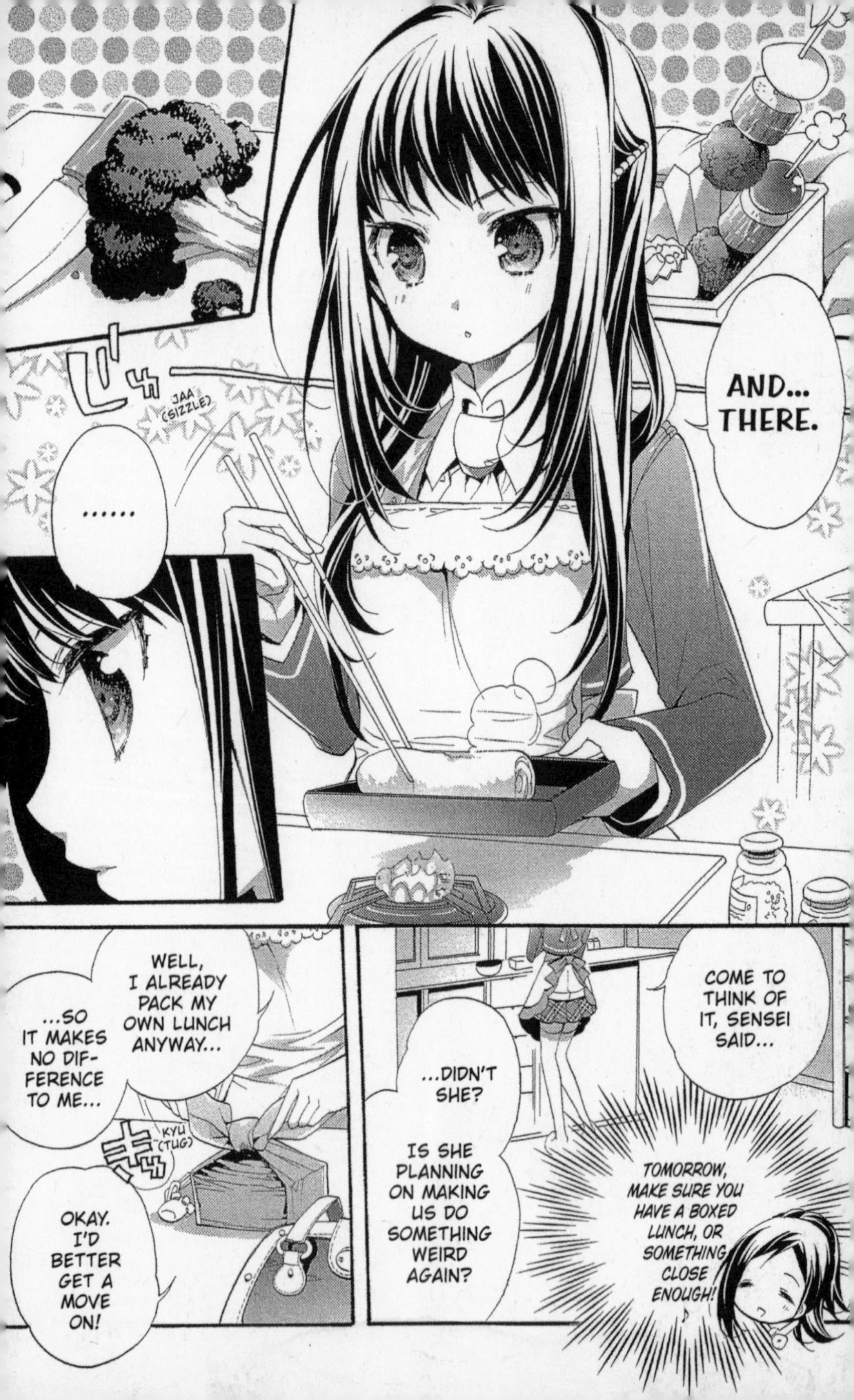
AND... THERE.
JAA (SIZZLE)
......
COME TO THINK OF IT, SENSEI SAID...
TOMORROW, MAKE SURE YOU HAVE A BOXED LUNCH, OR SOMETHING CLOSE ENOUGH!
...DIDN'T SHE?
IS SHE PLANNING ON MAKING US DO SOMETHING WEIRD AGAIN?
WELL, I ALREADY PACK MY OWN LUNCH ANYWAY...
...SO IT MAKES NO DIF-FERENCE TO ME...
KYU (TUG)
OKAY. I'D BETTER GET A MOVE ON!

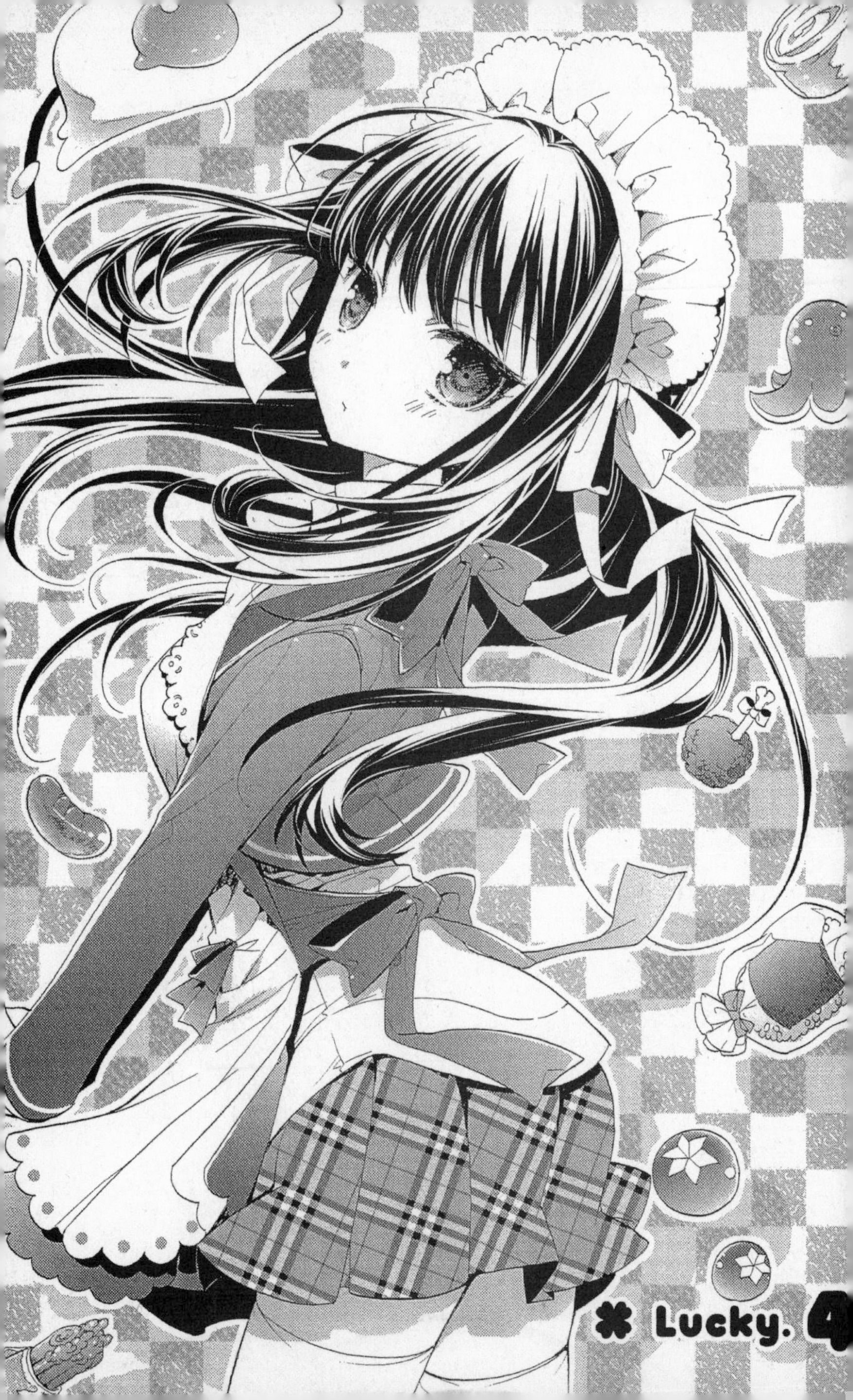
Lucky. 4

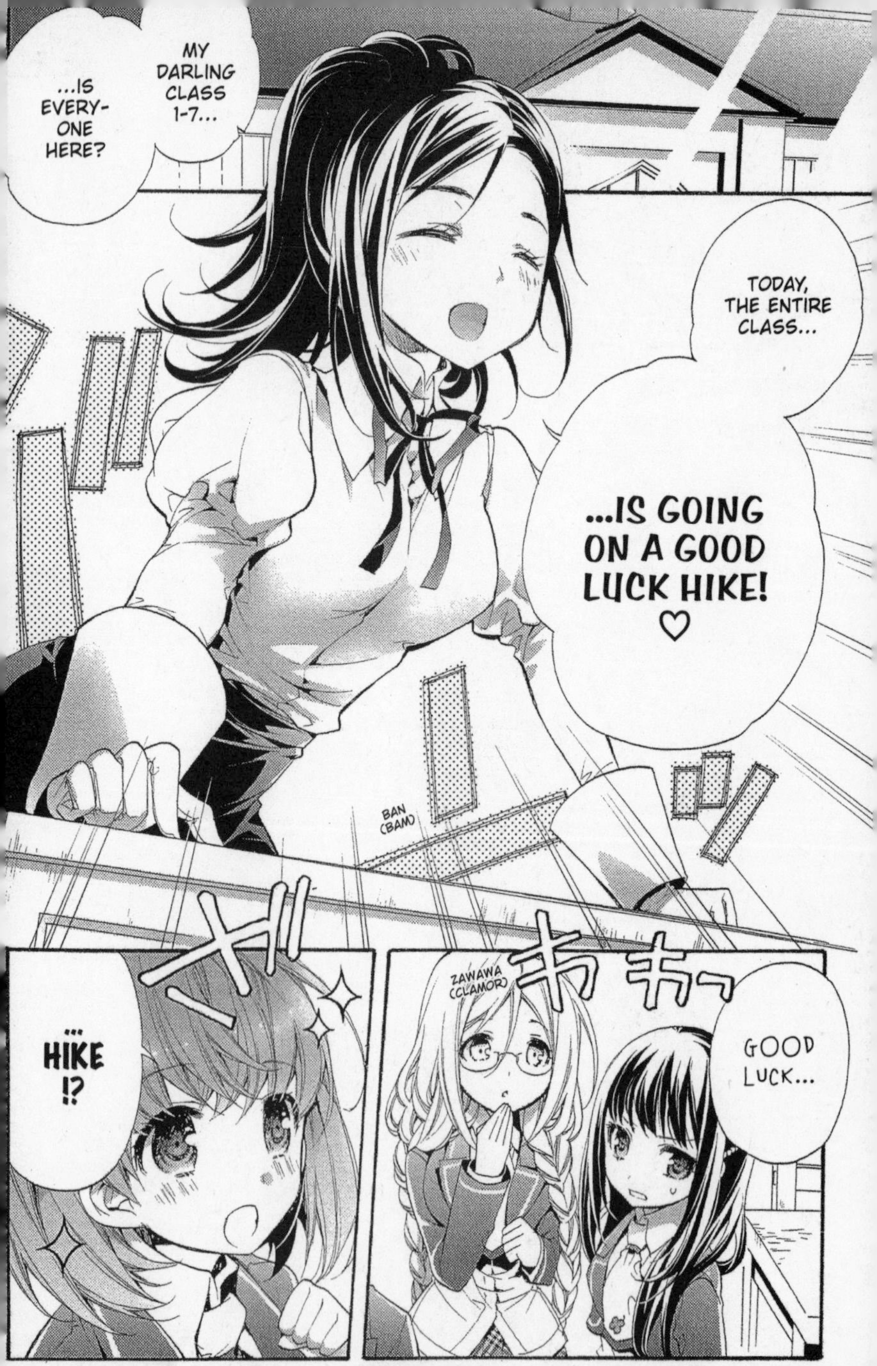
MY DARLING CLASS 1-7...
...IS EVERY-ONE HERE?
TODAY, THE ENTIRE CLASS...
...IS GOING ON A GOOD LUCK HIKE! ♡
BAN (BAM)
GOOD LUCK...
ZAWAWA (CLAMOR)
...HIKE!?

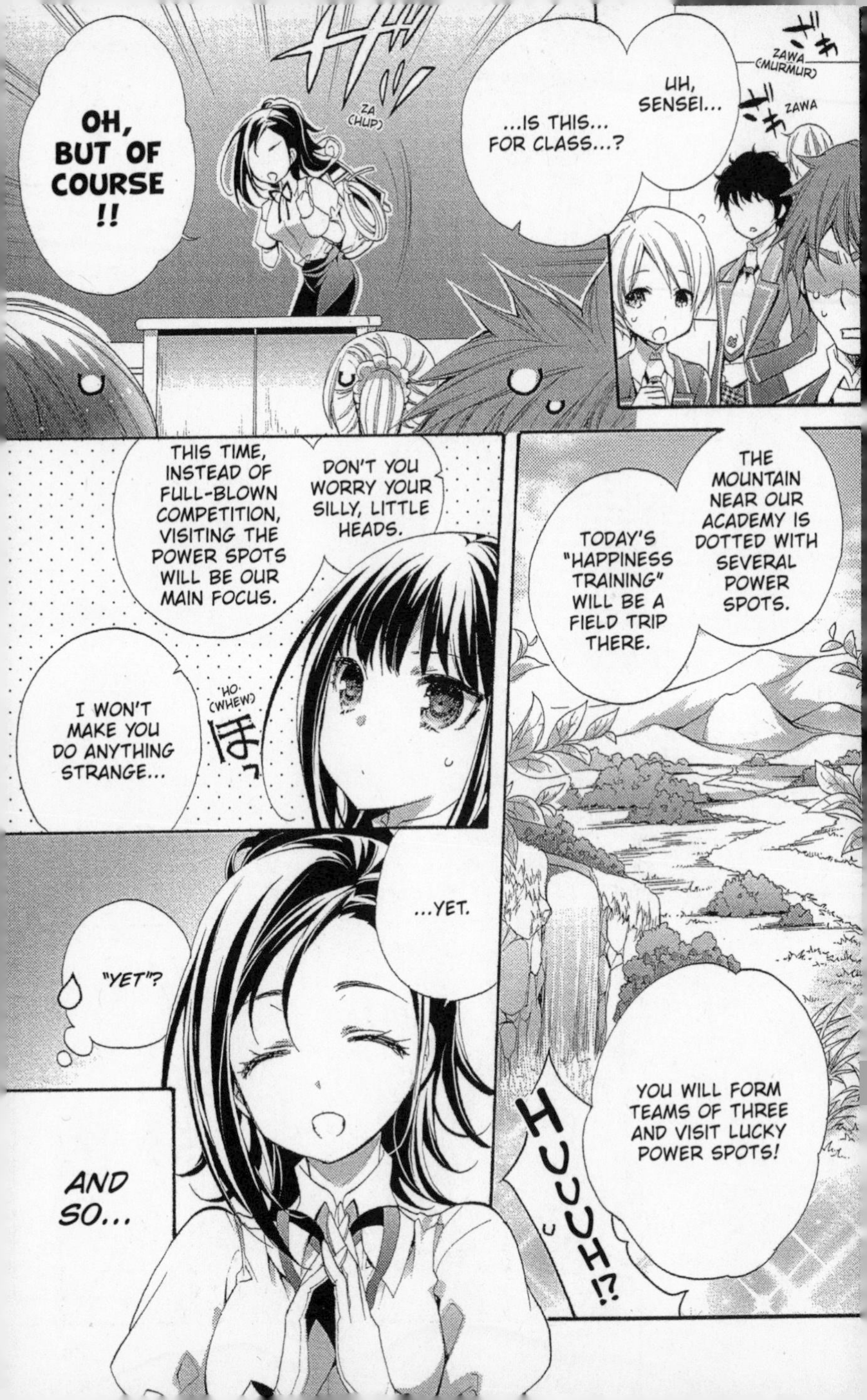
ZAWA (MURMUR)
ZAWA
UH, SENSEI...
...IS THIS... FOR CLASS...?
ZA (HUP)
OH, BUT OF COURSE!!
THE MOUNTAIN NEAR OUR ACADEMY IS DOTTED WITH SEVERAL POWER SPOTS.
TODAY'S "HAPPINESS TRAINING" WILL BE A FIELD TRIP THERE.
YOU WILL FORM TEAMS OF THREE AND VISIT LUCKY POWER SPOTS!
HUUUH!?
DON'T YOU WORRY YOUR SILLY, LITTLE HEADS.
THIS TIME, INSTEAD OF FULL-BLOWN COMPETITION, VISITING THE POWER SPOTS WILL BE OUR MAIN FOCUS.
HO (WHEW)
I WON'T MAKE YOU DO ANYTHING STRANGE...
...YET.
"YET"?
AND SO...

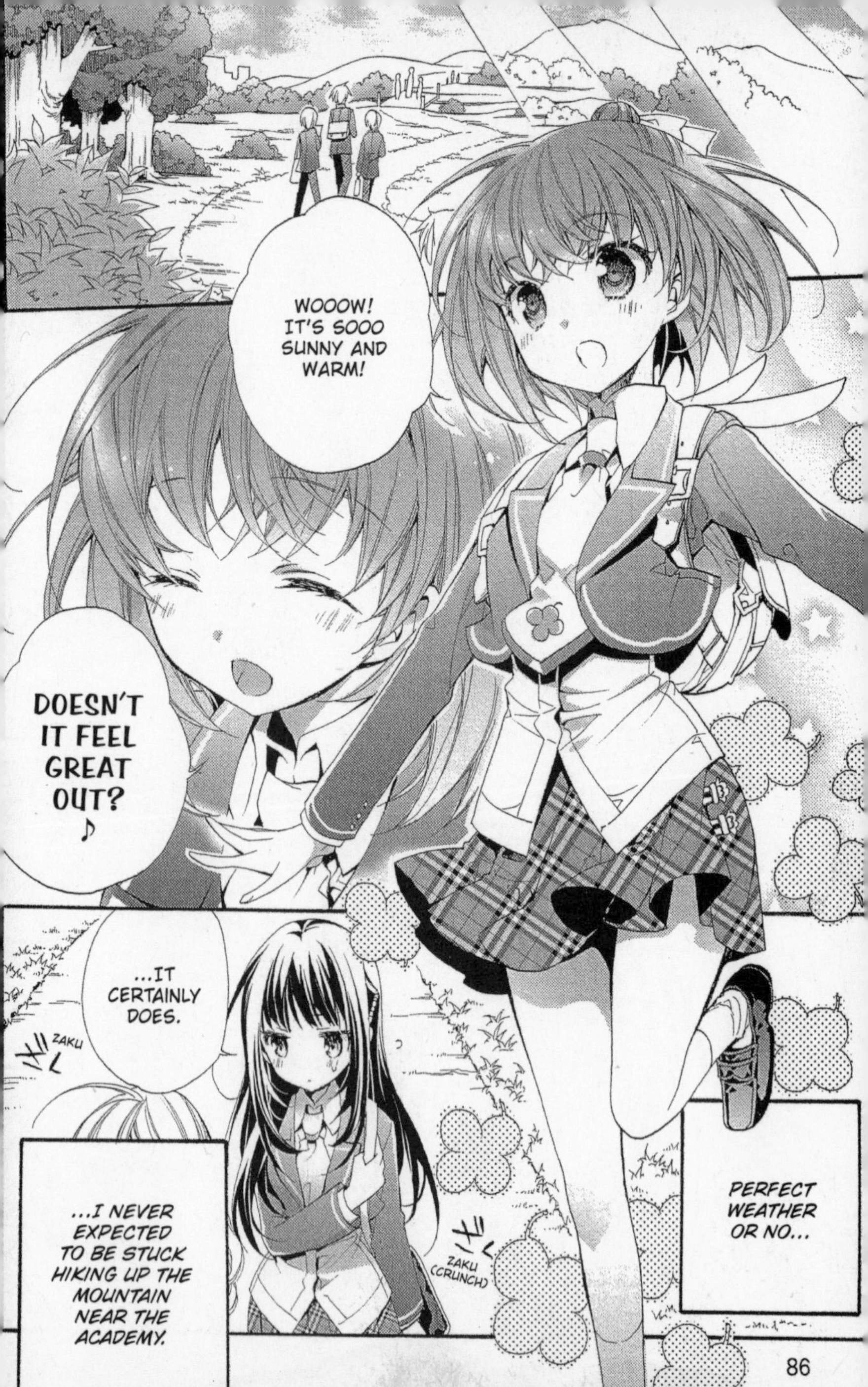
WOOOW! IT'S SOOO SUNNY AND WARM!
DOESN'T IT FEEL GREAT OUT? ♪
PERFECT WEATHER OR NO...
ZAKU (CRUNCH)
...IT CERTAINLY DOES.
ZAKU
...I NEVER EXPECTED TO BE STUCK HIKING UP THE MOUNTAIN NEAR THE ACADEMY.

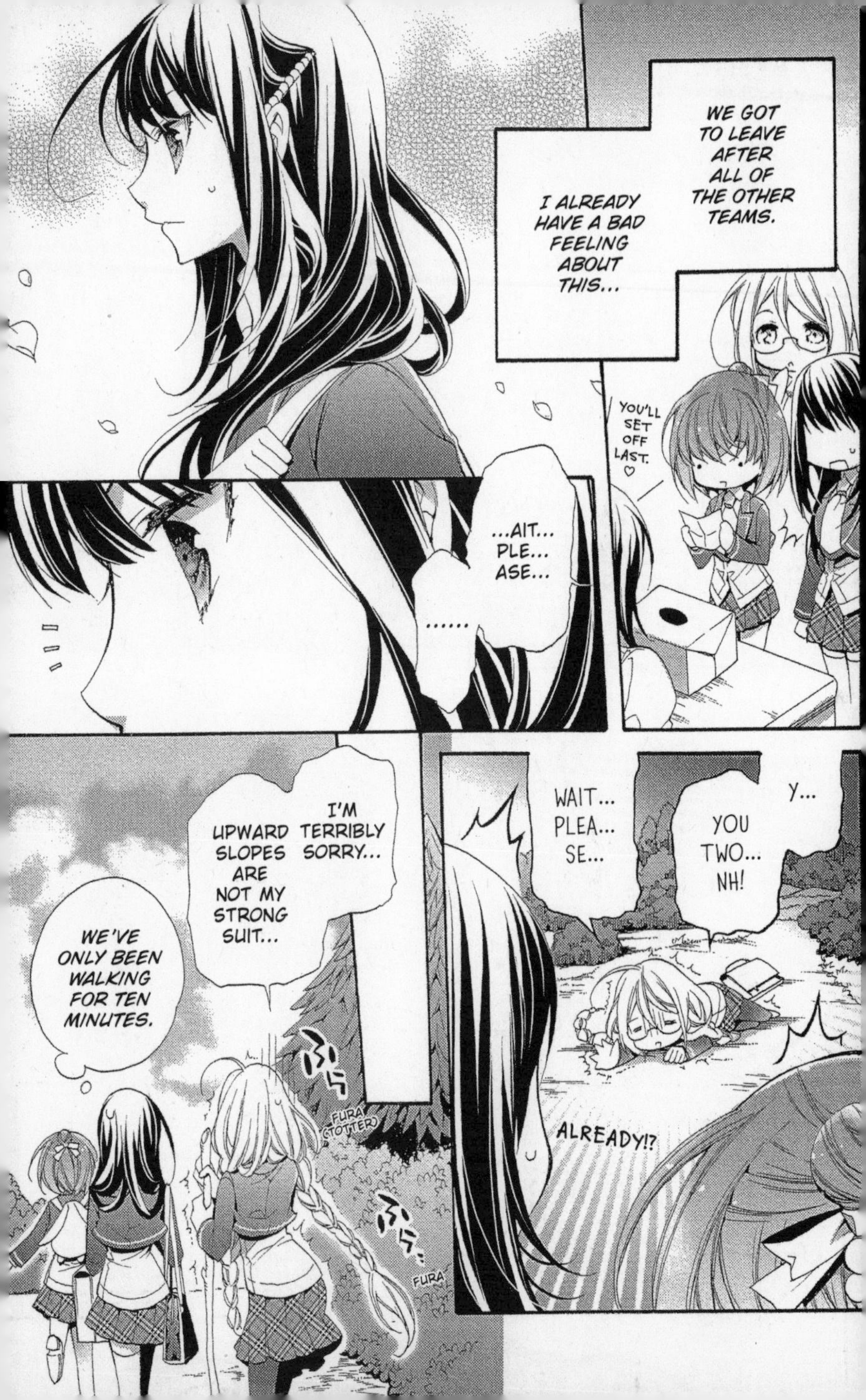
WE GOT TO LEAVE AFTER ALL OF THE OTHER TEAMS.
I ALREADY HAVE A BAD FEELING ABOUT THIS...
YOU'LL SET OFF LAST. ♡
...AIT... PLE... ASE...
......
Y... YOU TWO... NH!
WAIT... PLEA... SE...
ALREADY!?
I'M TERRIBLY SORRY... UPWARD SLOPES ARE NOT MY STRONG SUIT...
WE'VE ONLY BEEN WALKING FOR TEN MINUTES.
ふら
FURA (TOTTER)
ふら
FURA

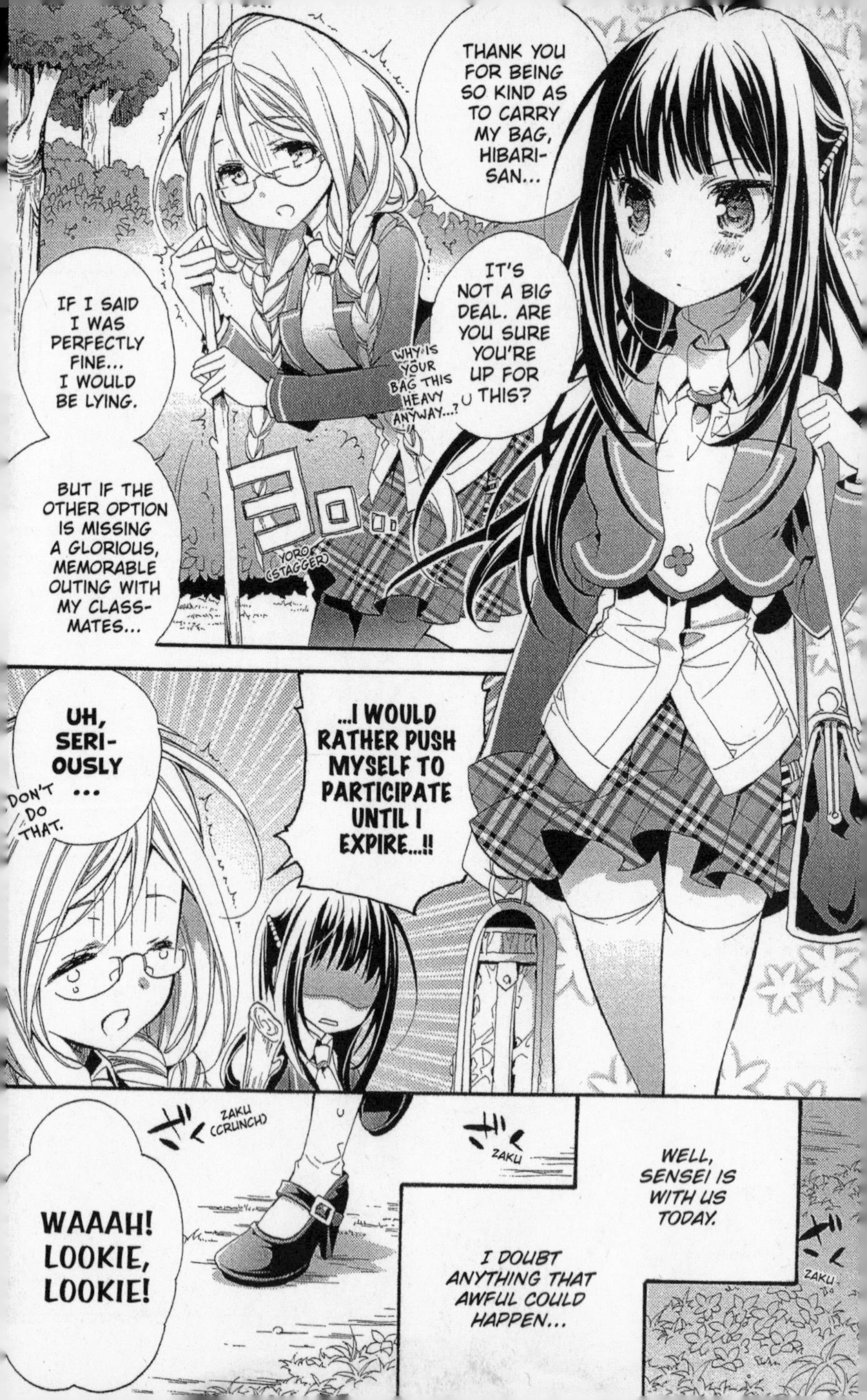

THANK YOU FOR BEING SO KIND AS TO CARRY MY BAG, HIBARI-SAN...
IT'S NOT A BIG DEAL. ARE YOU SURE YOU'RE UP FOR THIS?
WHY IS YOUR BAG THIS HEAVY ANYWAY...?
IF I SAID I WAS PERFECTLY FINE... I WOULD BE LYING.
BUT IF THE OTHER OPTION IS MISSING A GLORIOUS, MEMORABLE OUTING WITH MY CLASSMATES...
YORO (STAGGER)
...I WOULD RATHER PUSH MYSELF TO PARTICIPATE UNTIL I EXPIRE...!!
UH, SERIOUSLY...
DON'T DO THAT.
ZAKU
WELL, SENSEI IS WITH US TODAY.
I DOUBT ANYTHING THAT AWFUL COULD HAPPEN...
ZAKU
ZAKU (CRUNCH)
WAAAH! LOOKIE, LOOKIE!

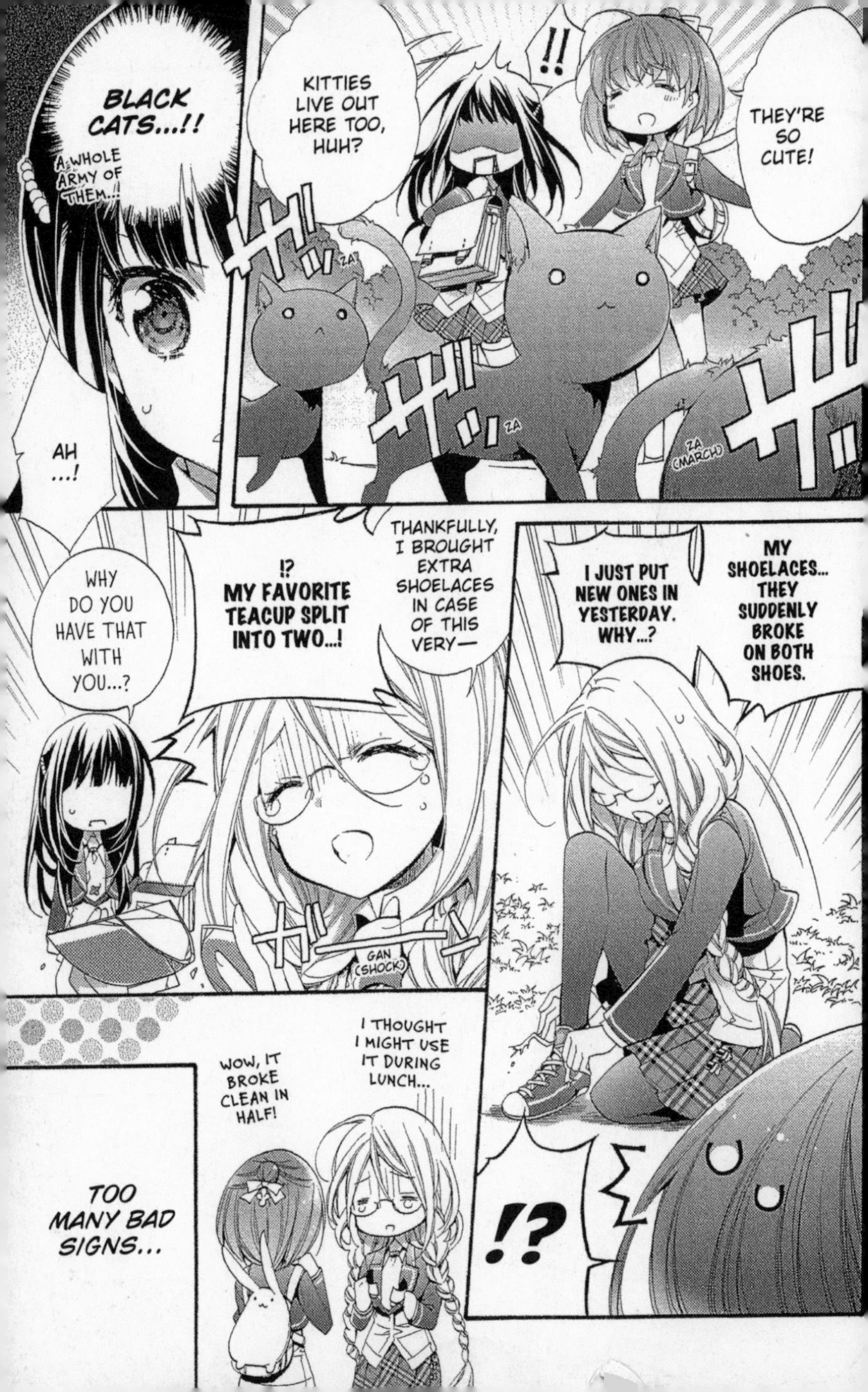
THEY'RE SO CUTE!
!!
KITTIES LIVE OUT HERE TOO, HUH?
ZA
ZA (MARCH)
ZA
BLACK CATS...!!
A WHOLE ARMY OF THEM...!
AH ...!
MY SHOELACES... THEY SUDDENLY BROKE ON BOTH SHOES.
I JUST PUT NEW ONES IN YESTERDAY. WHY...?
!?
THANKFULLY, I BROUGHT EXTRA SHOELACES IN CASE OF THIS VERY—
!? MY FAVORITE TEACUP SPLIT INTO TWO...!
GAN (SHOCK)
WHY DO YOU HAVE THAT WITH YOU...?
I THOUGHT I MIGHT USE IT DURING LUNCH...
WOW, IT BROKE CLEAN IN HALF!
TOO MANY BAD SIGNS...

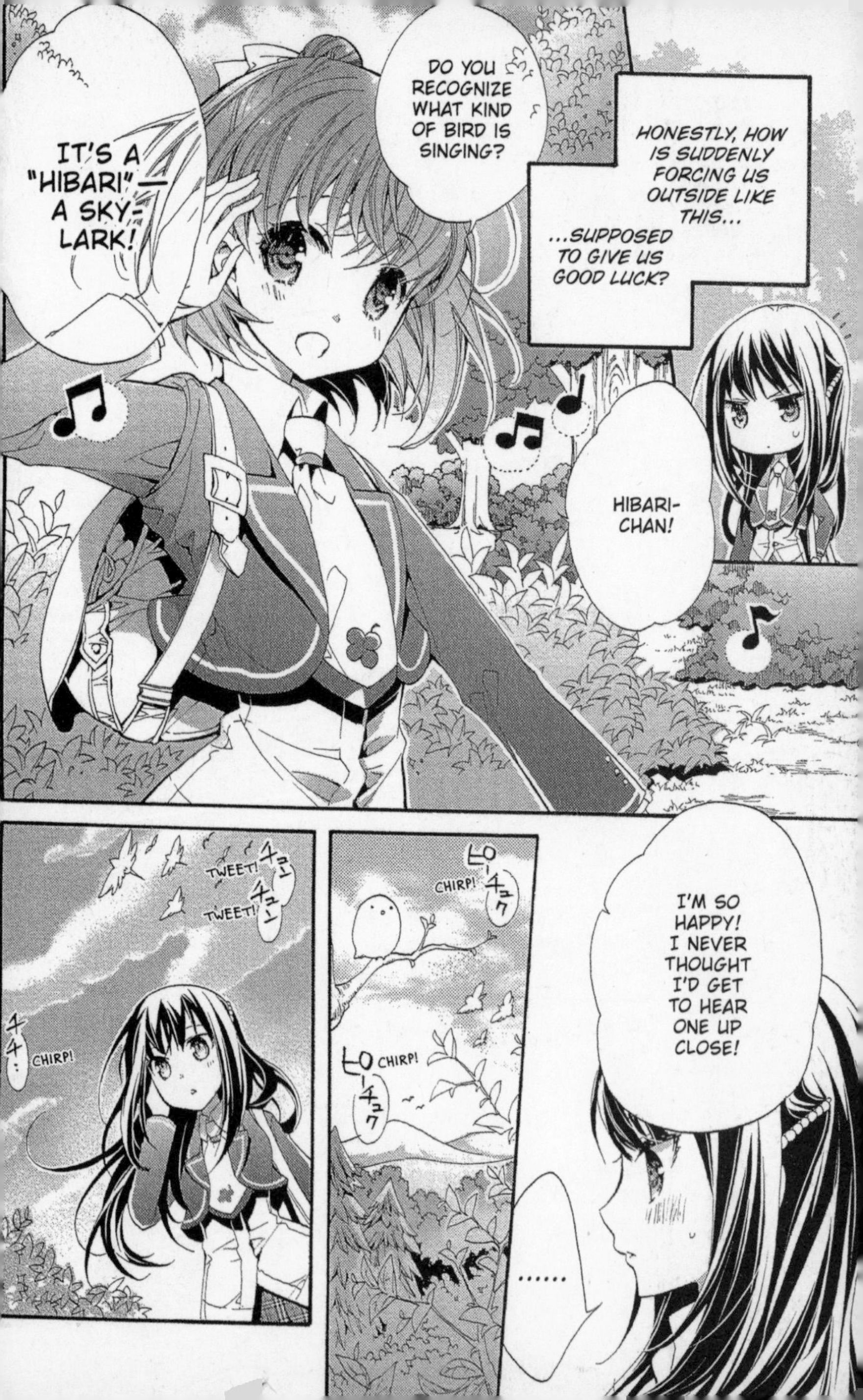
HONESTLY, HOW IS SUDDENLY FORCING US OUTSIDE LIKE THIS...
...SUPPOSED TO GIVE US GOOD LUCK?
DO YOU RECOGNIZE WHAT KIND OF BIRD IS SINGING?
IT'S A "HIBARI"—A SKYLARK!
HIBARI-CHAN!
I'M SO HAPPY! I NEVER THOUGHT I'D GET TO HEAR ONE UP CLOSE!
......
ピーチュク
CHIRP!
ピーチュク
CHIRP!
チュン
TWEET!
チュン
TWEET!
チチ…
CHIRP!

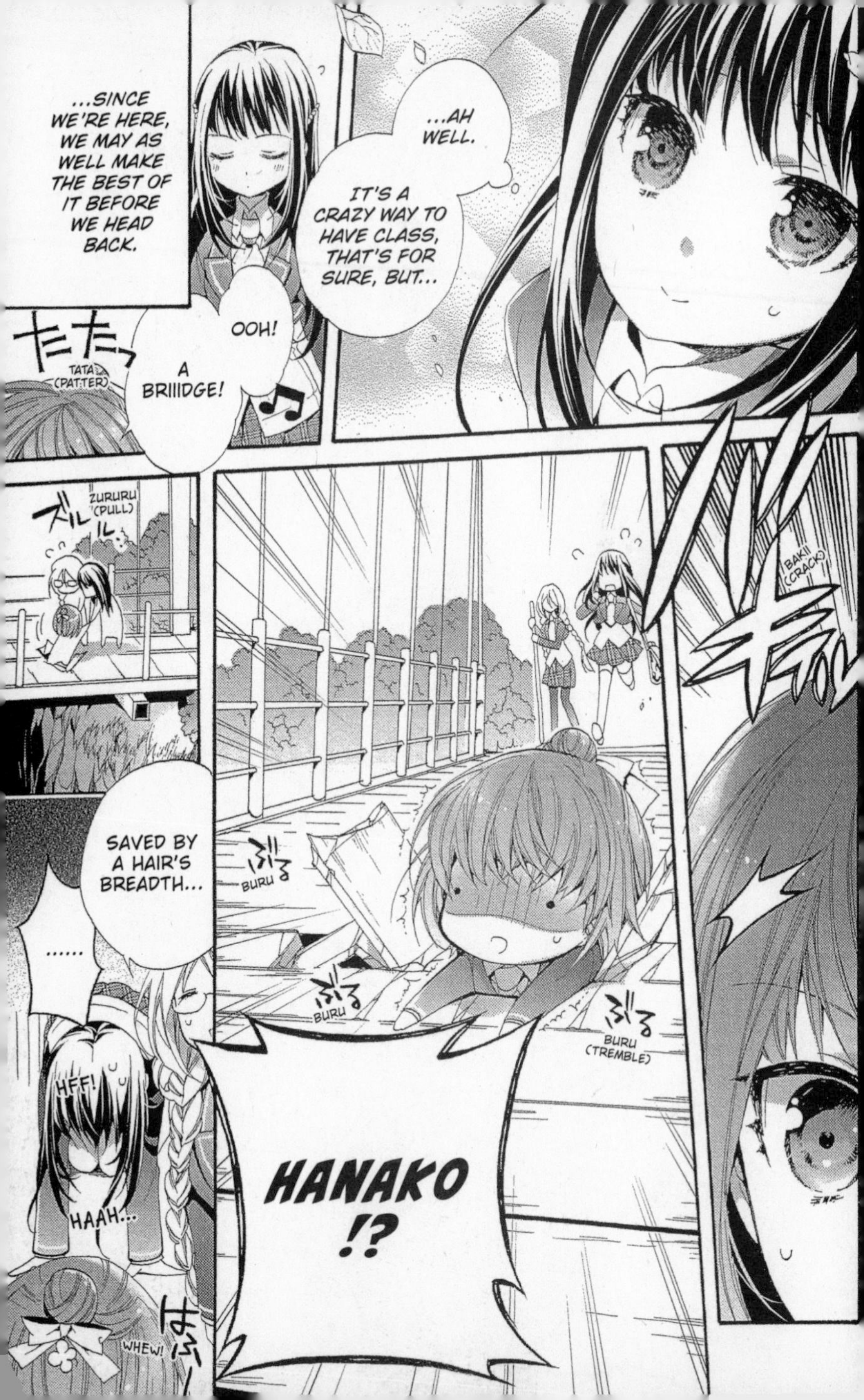
...AH WELL.
IT'S A CRAZY WAY TO HAVE CLASS, THAT'S FOR SURE, BUT...
...SINCE WE'RE HERE, WE MAY AS WELL MAKE THE BEST OF IT BEFORE WE HEAD BACK.
OOH!
A BRIIIDGE!
たたっ
TATA (PATTER)
BAKII (CRACK)
ぶる
BURU (TREMBLE)
ぶる
BURU
ぶる
BURU
ズルル
ZURURU (PULL)
HANAKO !?
SAVED BY A HAIR'S BREADTH...
......
HFF!
HAAH...
WHEW!

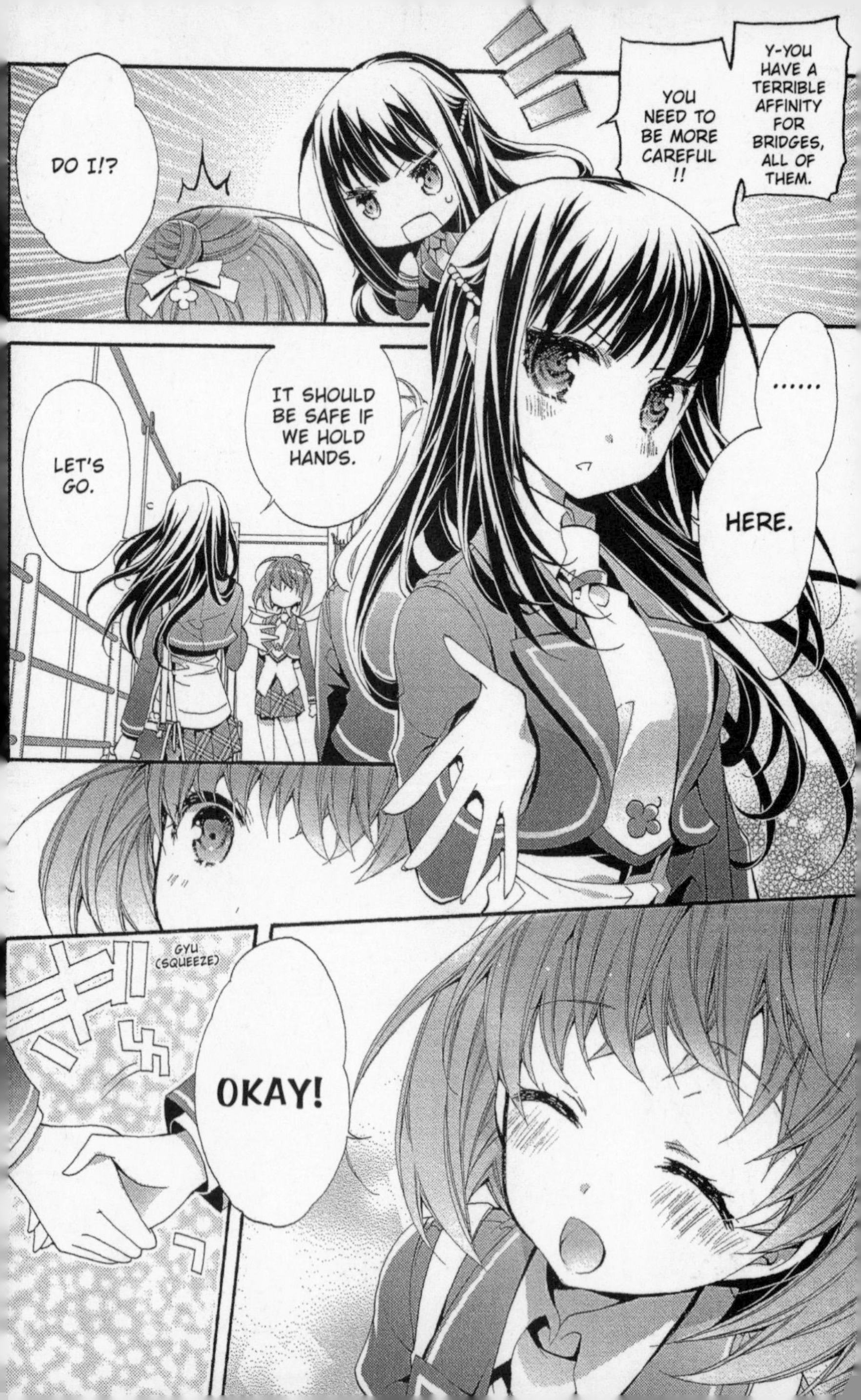
Y-YOU HAVE A TERRIBLE AFFINITY FOR BRIDGES, ALL OF THEM.
YOU NEED TO BE MORE CAREFUL !!
DO I!?
......
HERE.
IT SHOULD BE SAFE IF WE HOLD HANDS.
LET'S GO.
OKAY!
GYU (SQUEEZE)

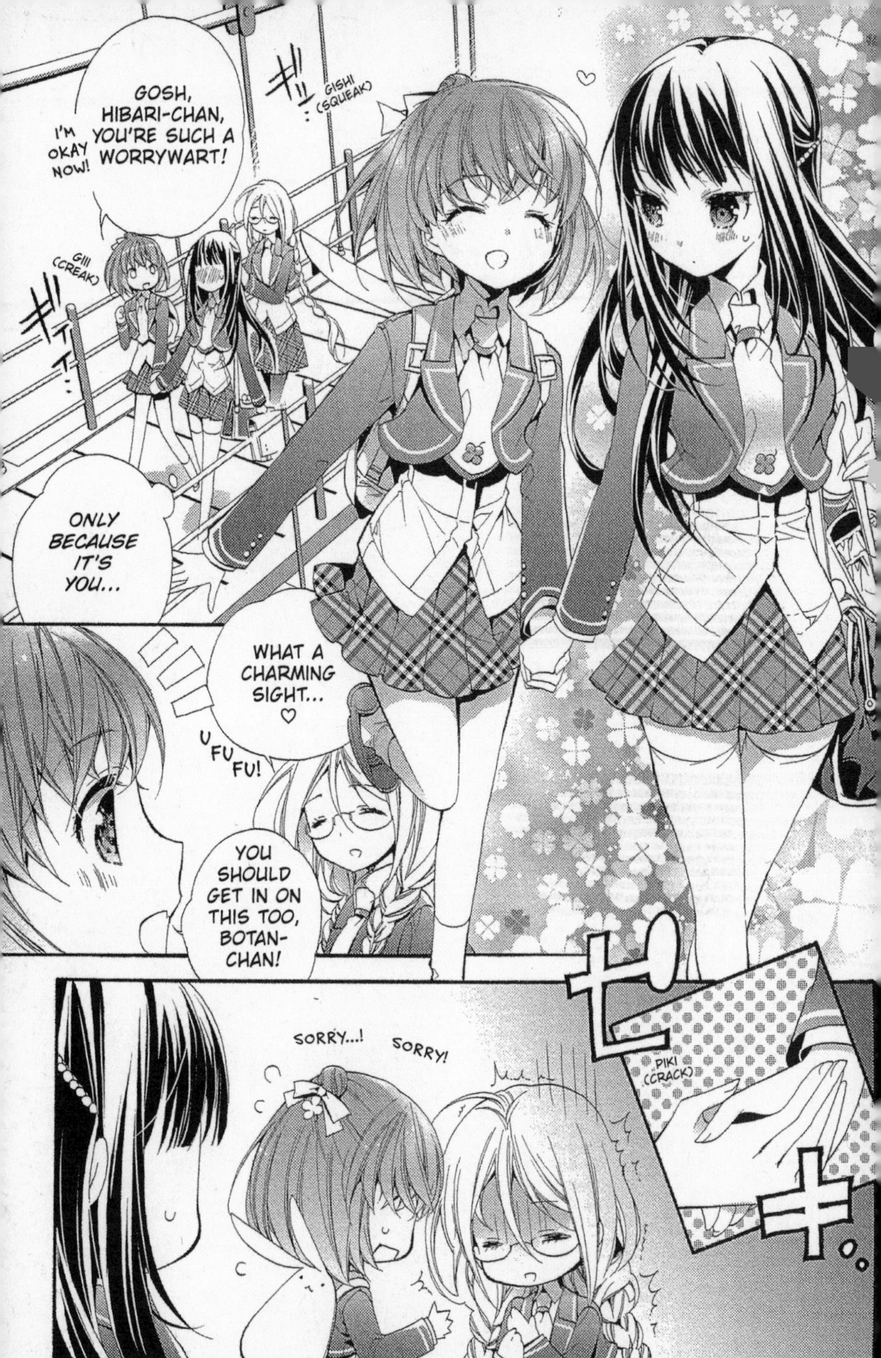
GISHI (SQUEAK)
GOSH, HIBARI-CHAN, YOU'RE SUCH A WORRYWART!
I'M OKAY NOW!
GIII (CREAK)
ONLY BECAUSE IT'S YOU...
WHAT A CHARMING SIGHT... ♡
UFUFU!
YOU SHOULD GET IN ON THIS TOO, BOTAN-CHAN!
PIKI (CRACK)
SORRY!
SORRY...!

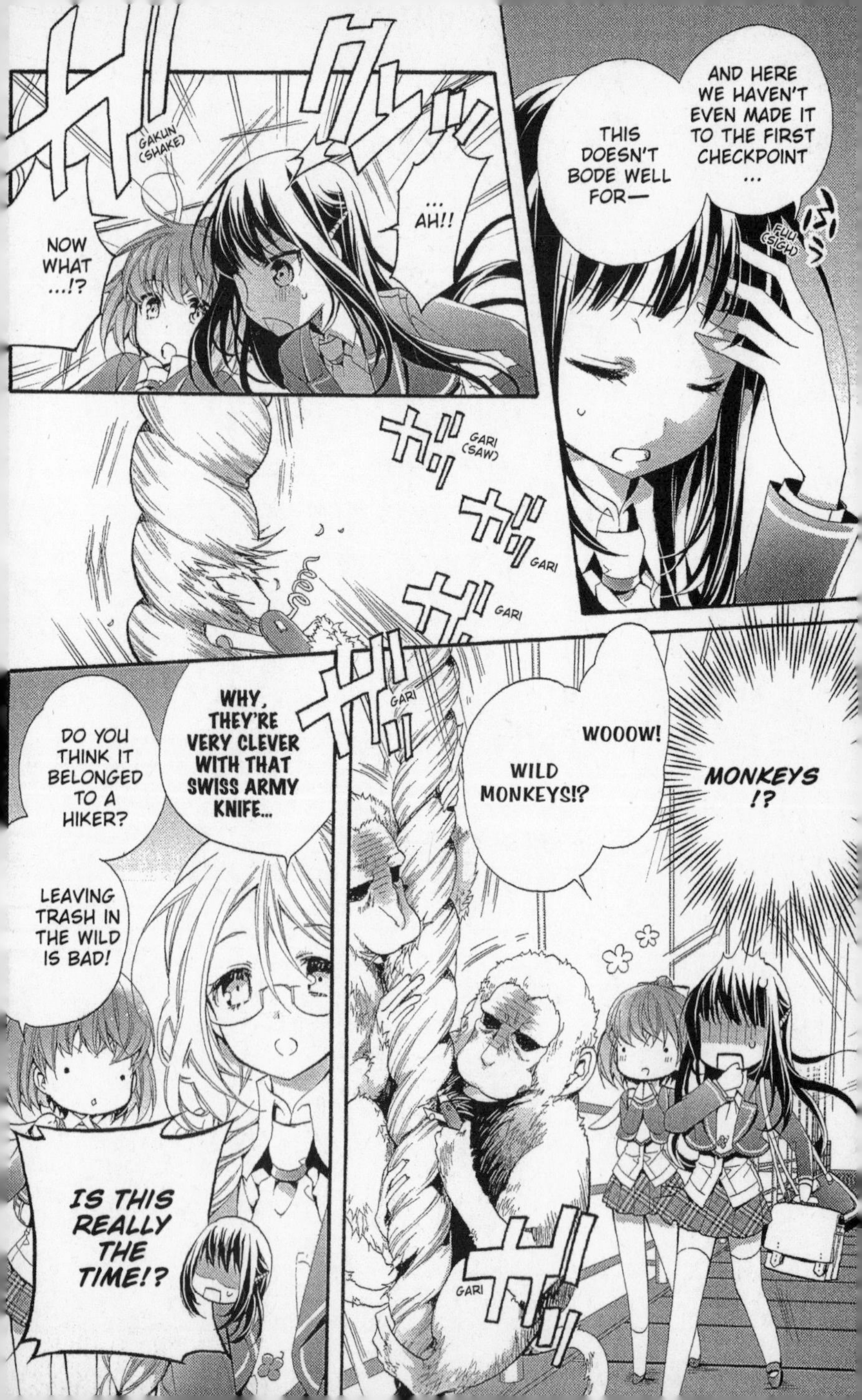

AND HERE WE HAVEN'T EVEN MADE IT TO THE FIRST CHECKPOINT ...
THIS DOESN'T BODE WELL FOR—
FUU (SIGH)
GAKUN (SHAKE)
... AH!!
NOW WHAT ...!?
GARI (SAW)
GARI
GARI
MONKEYS !?
WOOOW!
WILD MONKEYS!?
GARI
GARI
WHY, THEY'RE VERY CLEVER WITH THAT SWISS ARMY KNIFE...
DO YOU THINK IT BELONGED TO A HIKER?
LEAVING TRASH IN THE WILD IS BAD!
IS THIS REALLY THE TIME!?

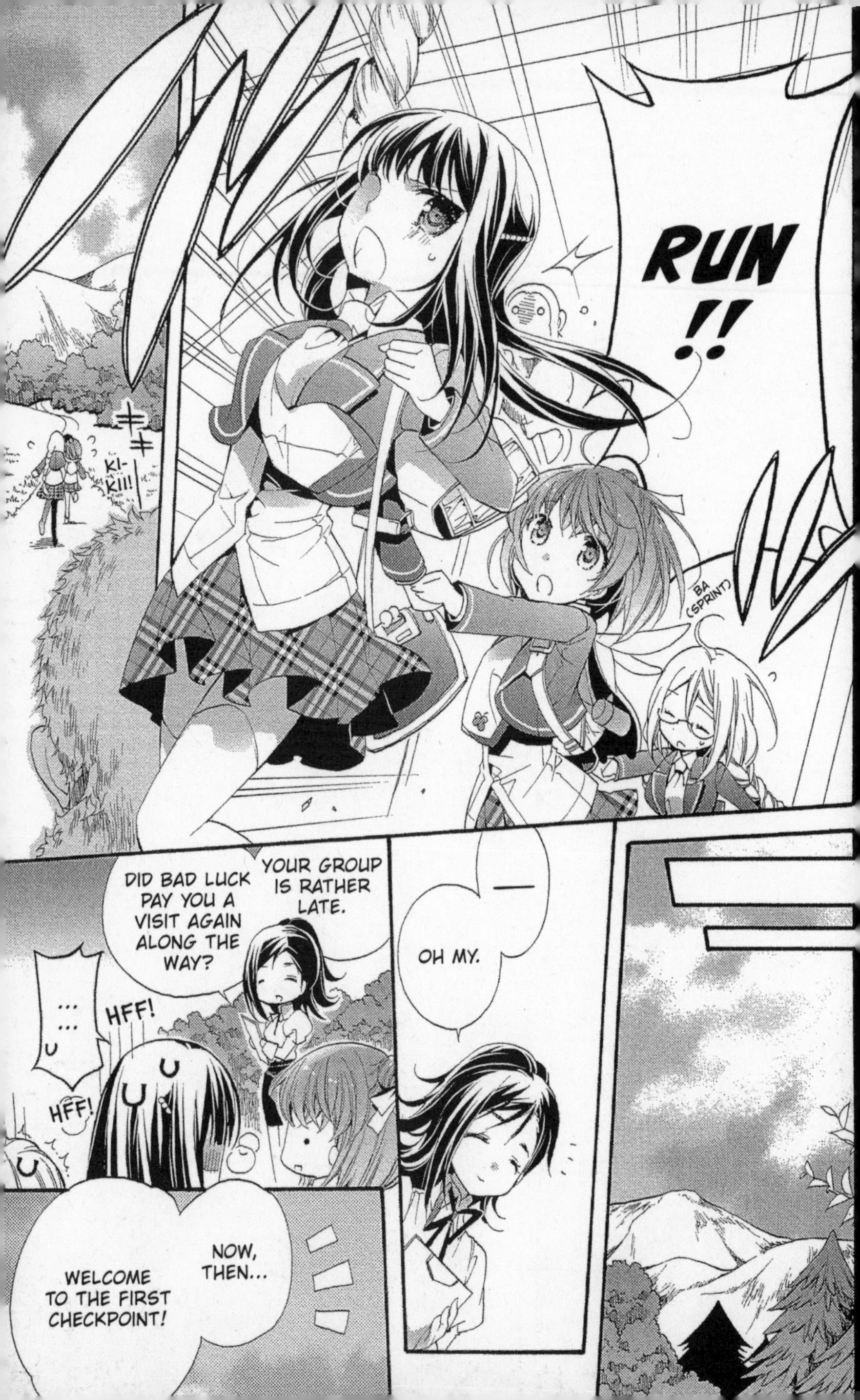
RUN!!
BA (SPRINT)
KI-KII!
—
OH MY.
YOUR GROUP IS RATHER LATE.
DID BAD LUCK PAY YOU A VISIT AGAIN ALONG THE WAY?
HFF!
... ...
HFF!
NOW, THEN...
WELCOME TO THE FIRST CHECKPOINT!

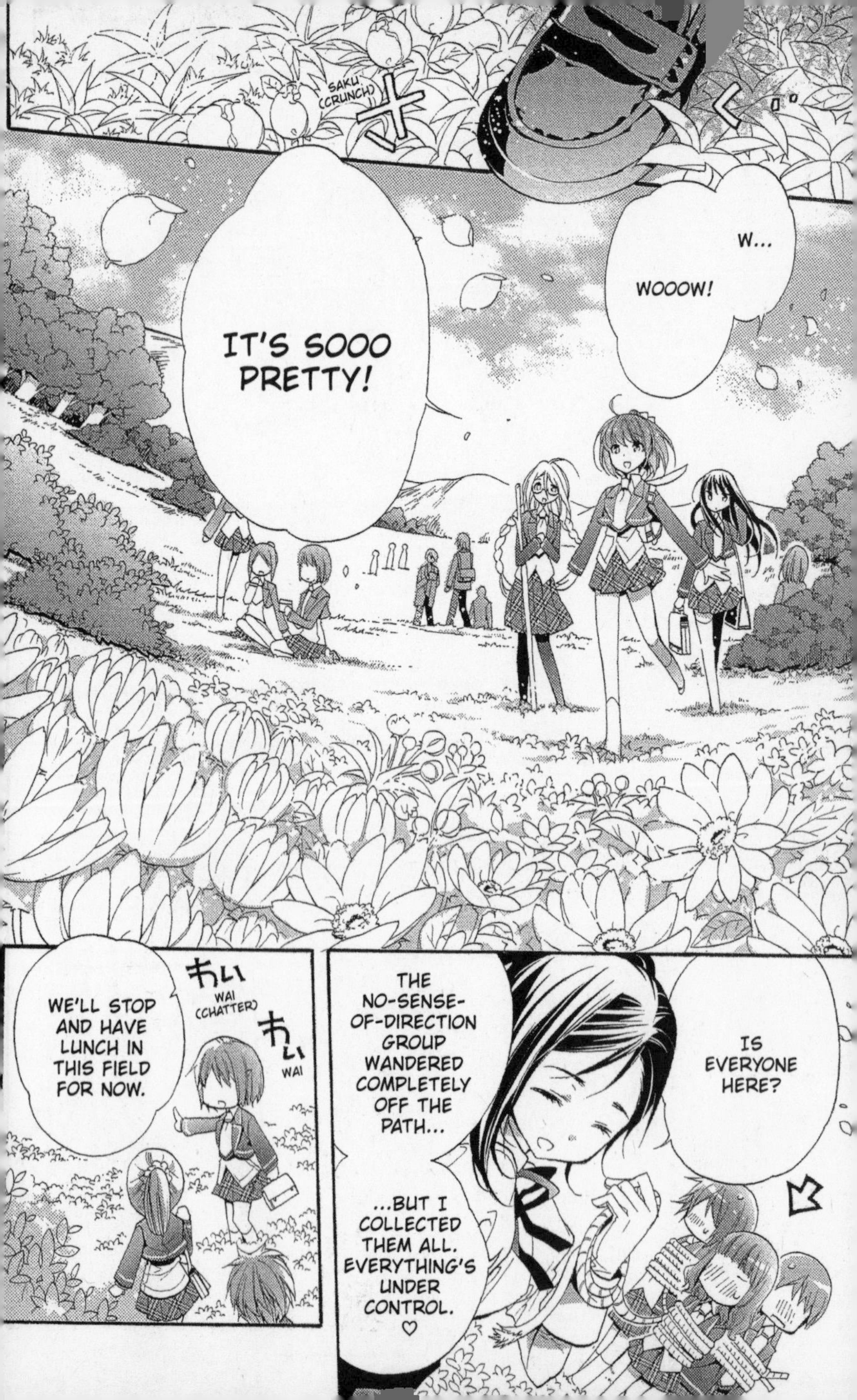
SAKU (CRUNCH)
W... WOOOW!
IT'S SOOO PRETTY!
IS EVERYONE HERE?
THE NO-SENSE-OF-DIRECTION GROUP WANDERED COMPLETELY OFF THE PATH...
...BUT I COLLECTED THEM ALL. EVERYTHING'S UNDER CONTROL. ♡
わい
WAI (CHATTER)
わい
WAI
WE'LL STOP AND HAVE LUNCH IN THIS FIELD FOR NOW.

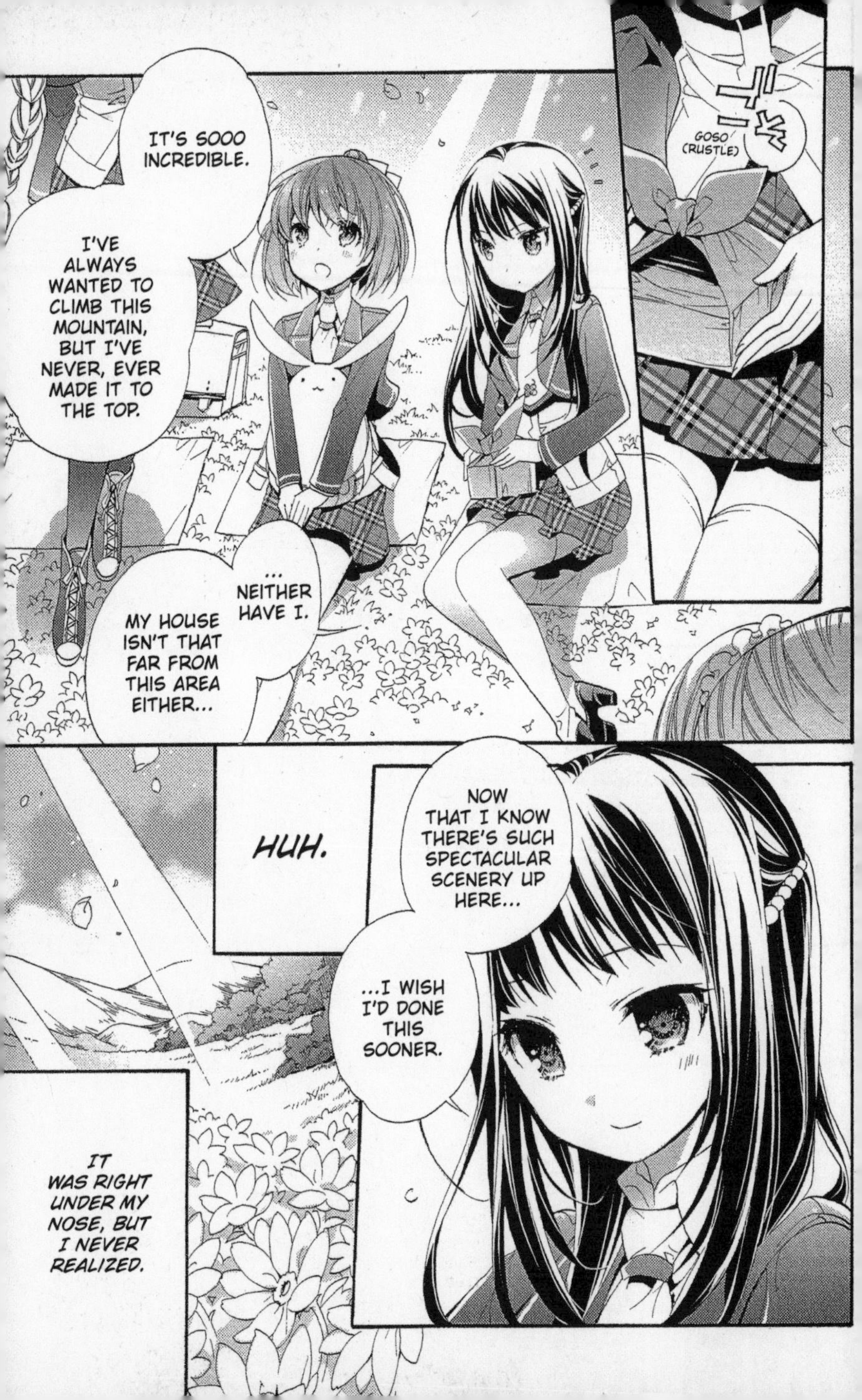
GOSO (RUSTLE)
IT'S SOOO INCREDIBLE.
I'VE ALWAYS WANTED TO CLIMB THIS MOUNTAIN, BUT I'VE NEVER, EVER MADE IT TO THE TOP.
... NEITHER HAVE I.
MY HOUSE ISN'T THAT FAR FROM THIS AREA EITHER...
NOW THAT I KNOW THERE'S SUCH SPECTACULAR SCENERY UP HERE...
...I WISH I'D DONE THIS SOONER.
HUH.
IT WAS RIGHT UNDER MY NOSE, BUT I NEVER REALIZED.

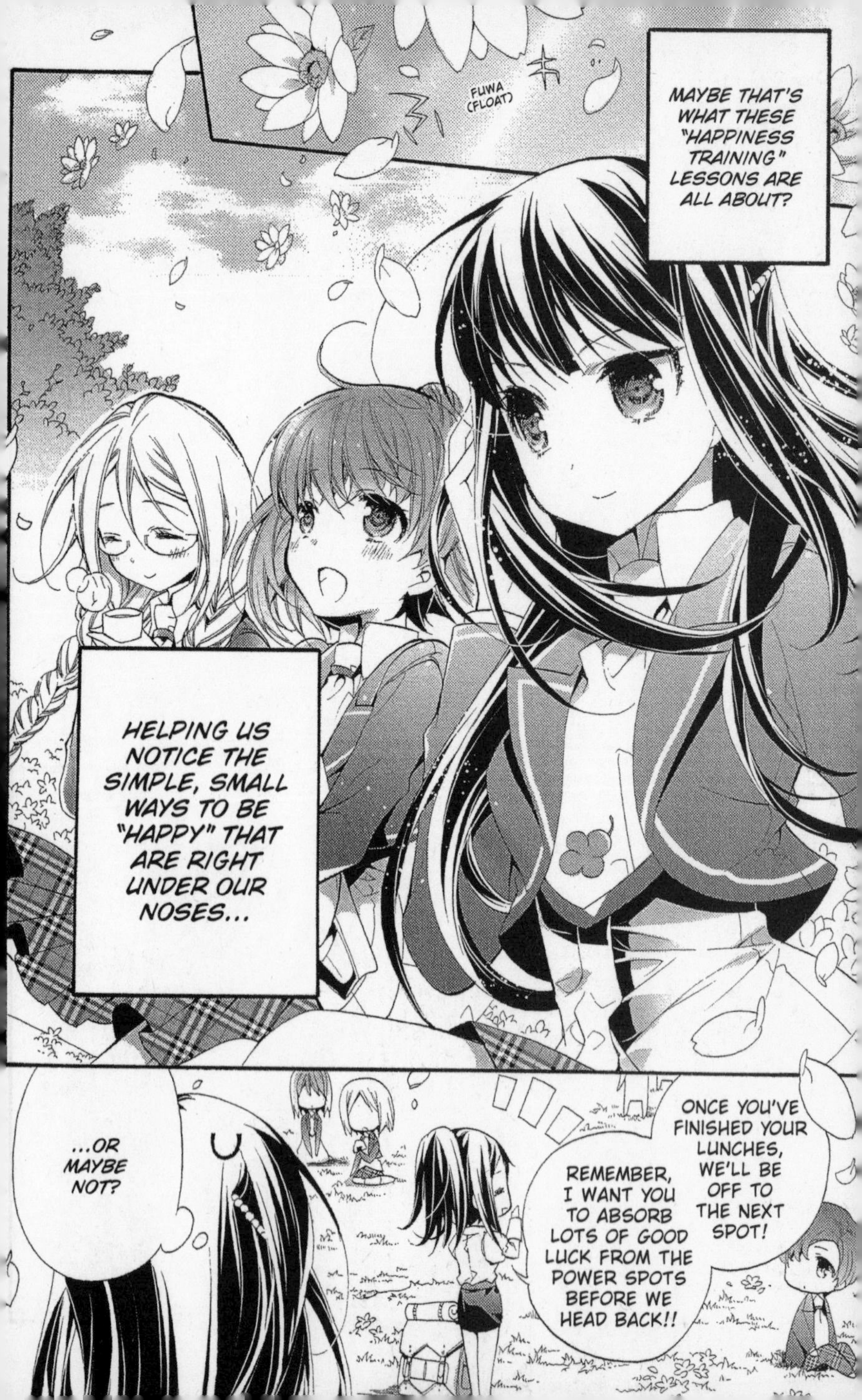
MAYBE THAT'S WHAT THESE "HAPPINESS TRAINING" LESSONS ARE ALL ABOUT?
FUWA (FLOAT)
HELPING US NOTICE THE SIMPLE, SMALL WAYS TO BE "HAPPY" THAT ARE RIGHT UNDER OUR NOSES...
ONCE YOU'VE FINISHED YOUR LUNCHES, WE'LL BE OFF TO THE NEXT SPOT!
REMEMBER, I WANT YOU TO ABSORB LOTS OF GOOD LUCK FROM THE POWER SPOTS BEFORE WE HEAD BACK!!
...OR MAYBE NOT?

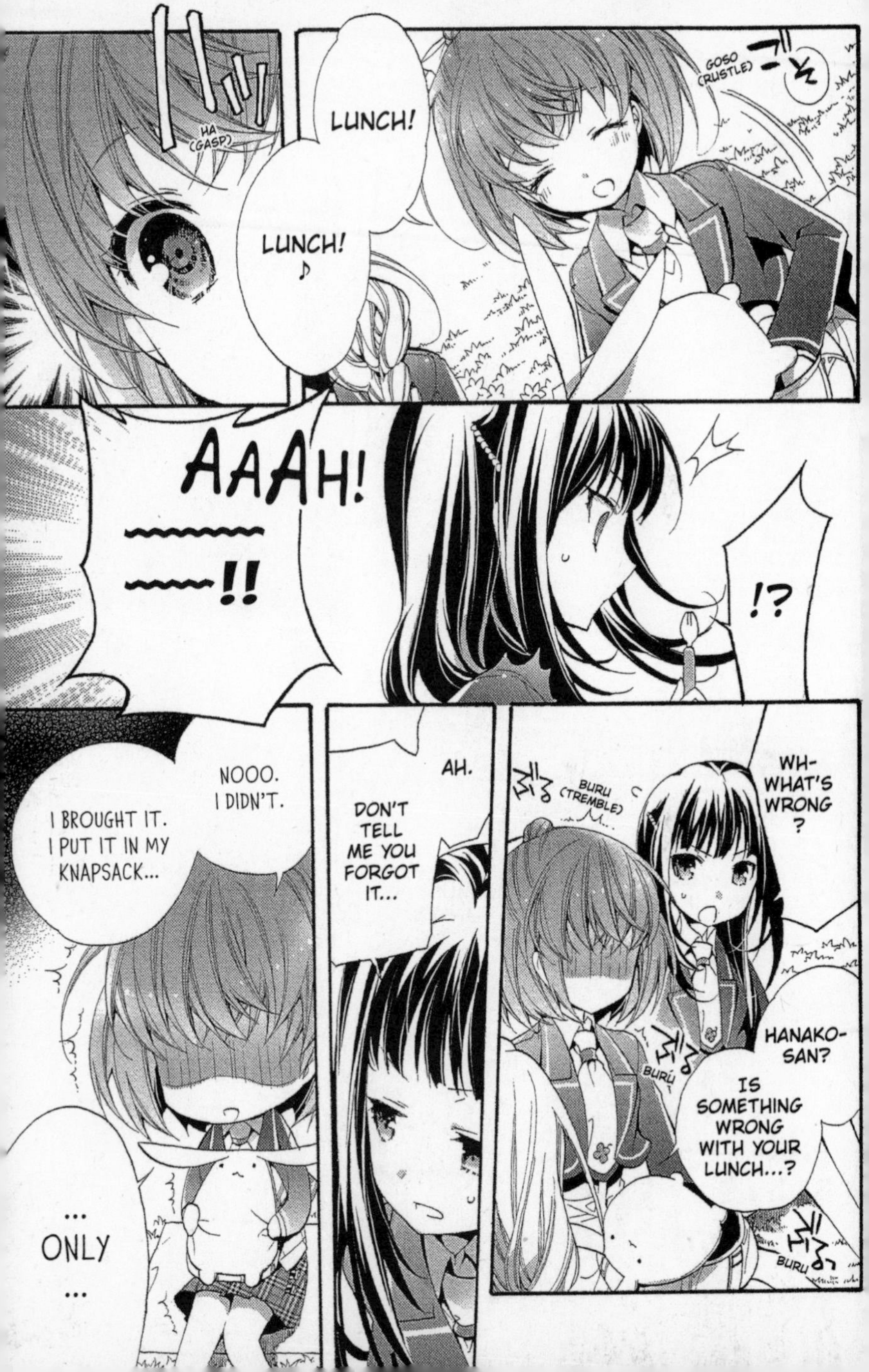
GOSO (RUSTLE)
LUNCH!
LUNCH! ♪
HA (GASP)
!?
AAAH! ———!!
WH-WHAT'S WRONG?
BURU (TREMBLE)
HANAKO-SAN?
IS SOMETHING WRONG WITH YOUR LUNCH...?
BURU
BURU
AH.
DON'T TELL ME YOU FORGOT IT...
NOOO. I DIDN'T.
I BROUGHT IT. I PUT IT IN MY KNAPSACK...
... ONLY ...

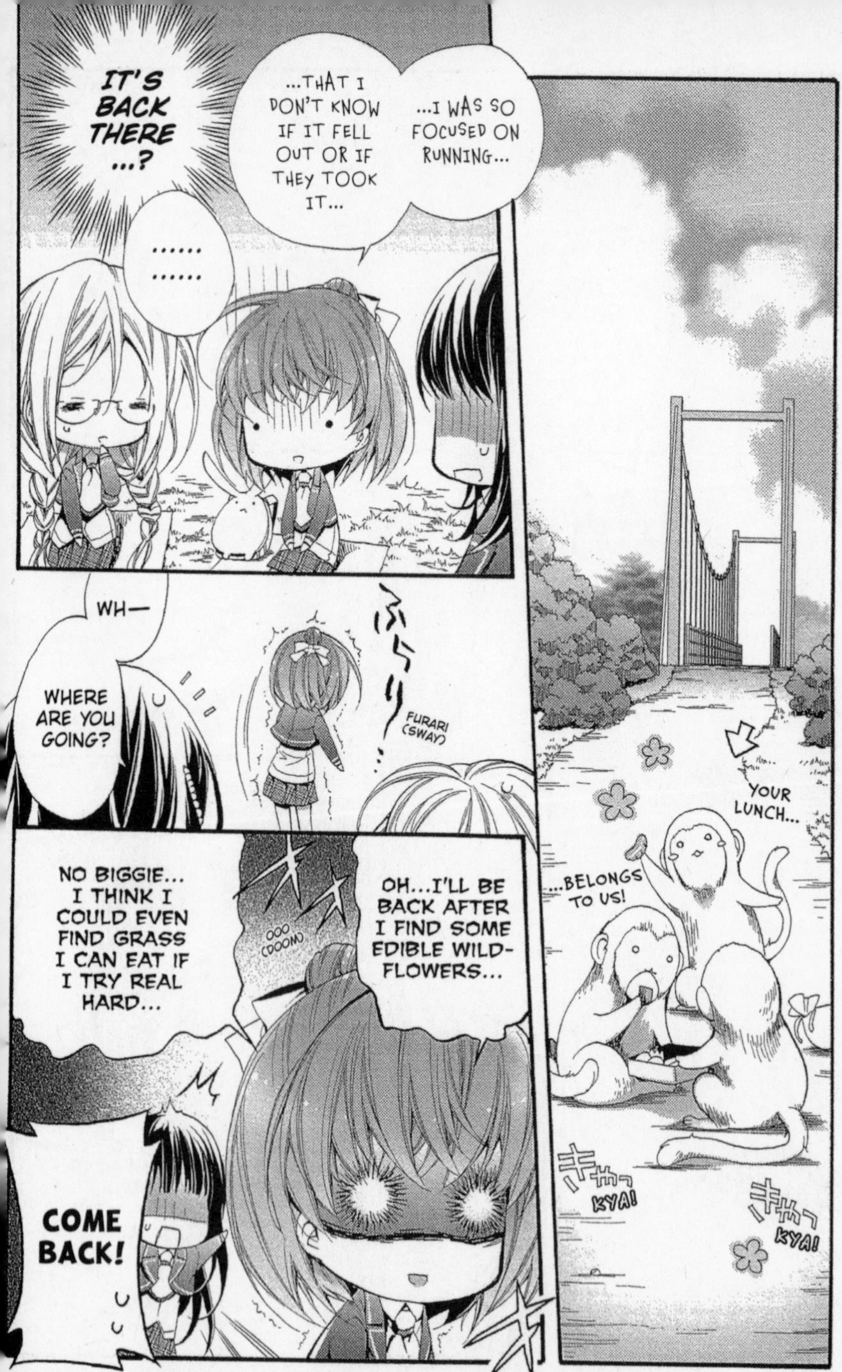
YOUR LUNCH...
...BELONGS TO US!
KYA!
KYA!
...I WAS SO FOCUSED ON RUNNING...
...THAT I DON'T KNOW IF IT FELL OUT OR IF THEY TOOK IT...
IT'S BACK THERE...?
....
ふらり
FURARI (SWAY)
WH—
WHERE ARE YOU GOING?
OH...I'LL BE BACK AFTER I FIND SOME EDIBLE WILD-FLOWERS...
OOO (DOOM)
NO BIGGIE... I THINK I COULD EVEN FIND GRASS I CAN EAT IF I TRY REAL HARD...
COME BACK!

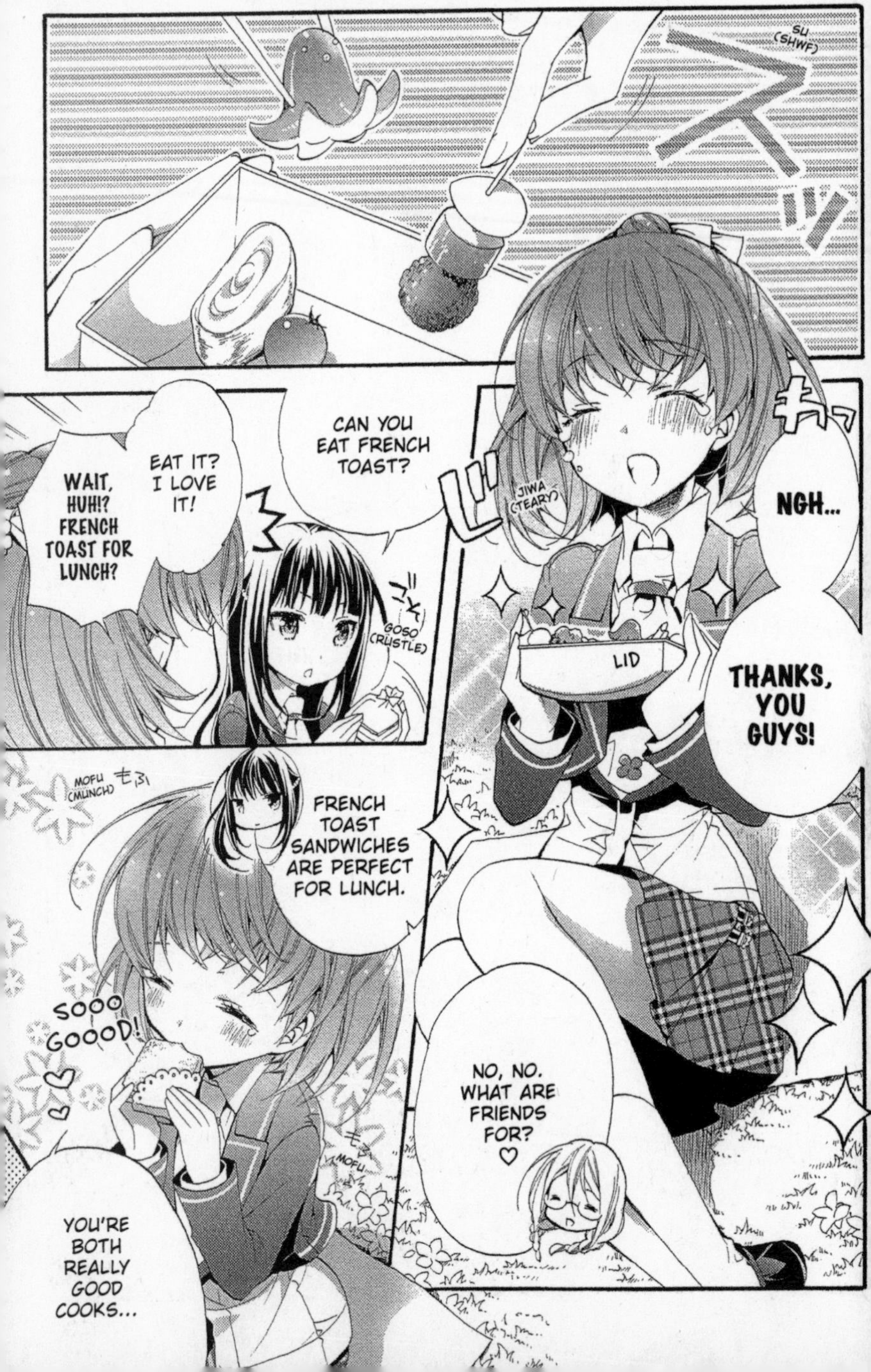
SU (SHWF)
NGH...
JIWA (TEARY)
THANKS, YOU GUYS!
LID
NO, NO. WHAT ARE FRIENDS FOR? ♡
CAN YOU EAT FRENCH TOAST?
GOSO (RUSTLE)
EAT IT? I LOVE IT!
WAIT, HUH!? FRENCH TOAST FOR LUNCH?
FRENCH TOAST SANDWICHES ARE PERFECT FOR LUNCH.
MOFU (MUNCH)
SOOO GOOOD! ♡
MOFU
YOU'RE BOTH REALLY GOOD COOKS...

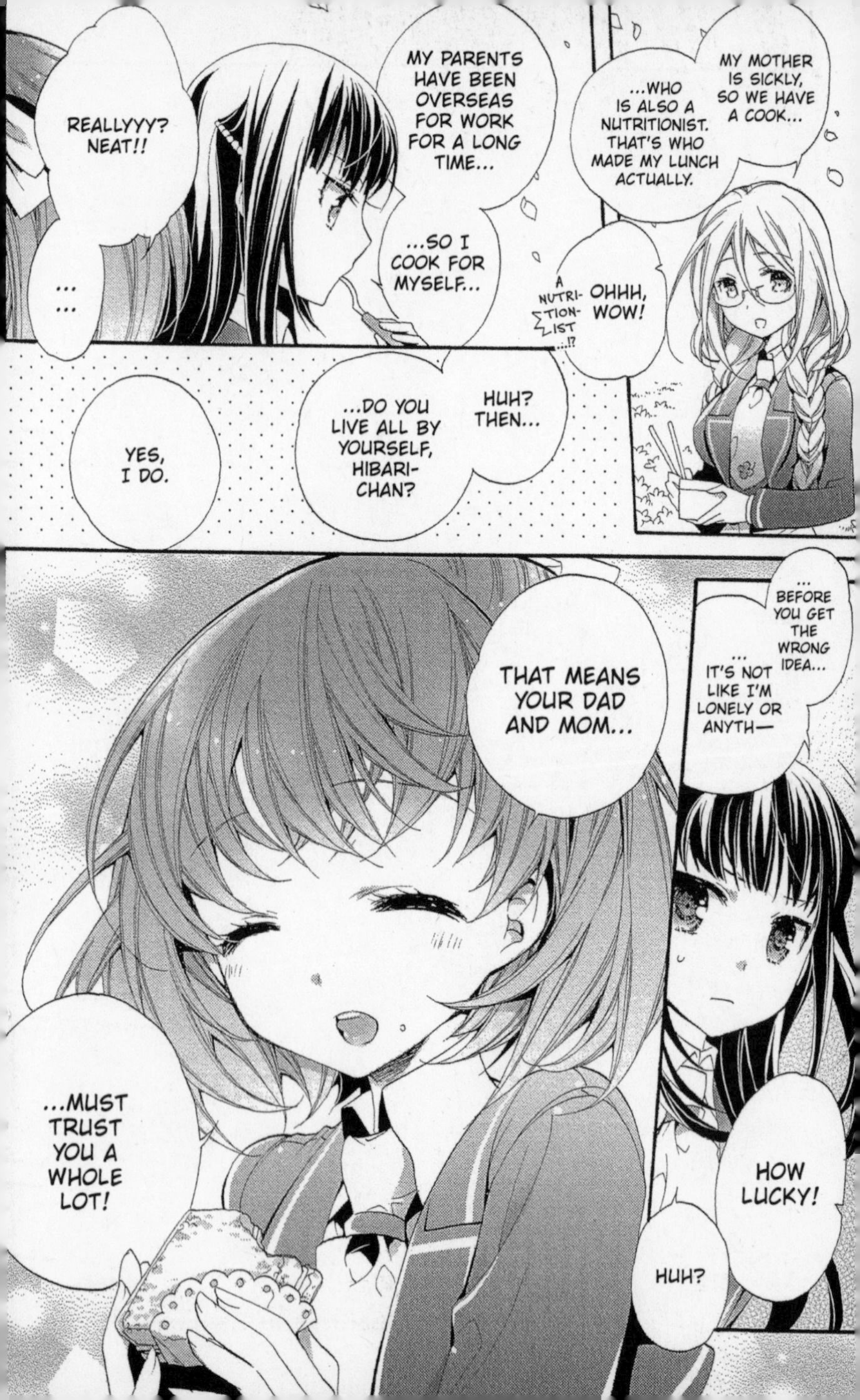
MY MOTHER IS SICKLY, SO WE HAVE A COOK...
...WHO IS ALSO A NUTRITIONIST. THAT'S WHO MADE MY LUNCH ACTUALLY.
OHHH, WOW!
A NUTRI-TION-IST...!?
MY PARENTS HAVE BEEN OVERSEAS FOR WORK FOR A LONG TIME...
...SO I COOK FOR MYSELF...
REALLYYY? NEAT!!
... ...
HUH? THEN...
...DO YOU LIVE ALL BY YOURSELF, HIBARI-CHAN?
YES, I DO.
... BEFORE YOU GET THE WRONG IDEA...
... IT'S NOT LIKE I'M LONELY OR ANYTH—
HOW LUCKY!
HUH?
THAT MEANS YOUR DAD AND MOM...
...MUST TRUST YOU A WHOLE LOT!

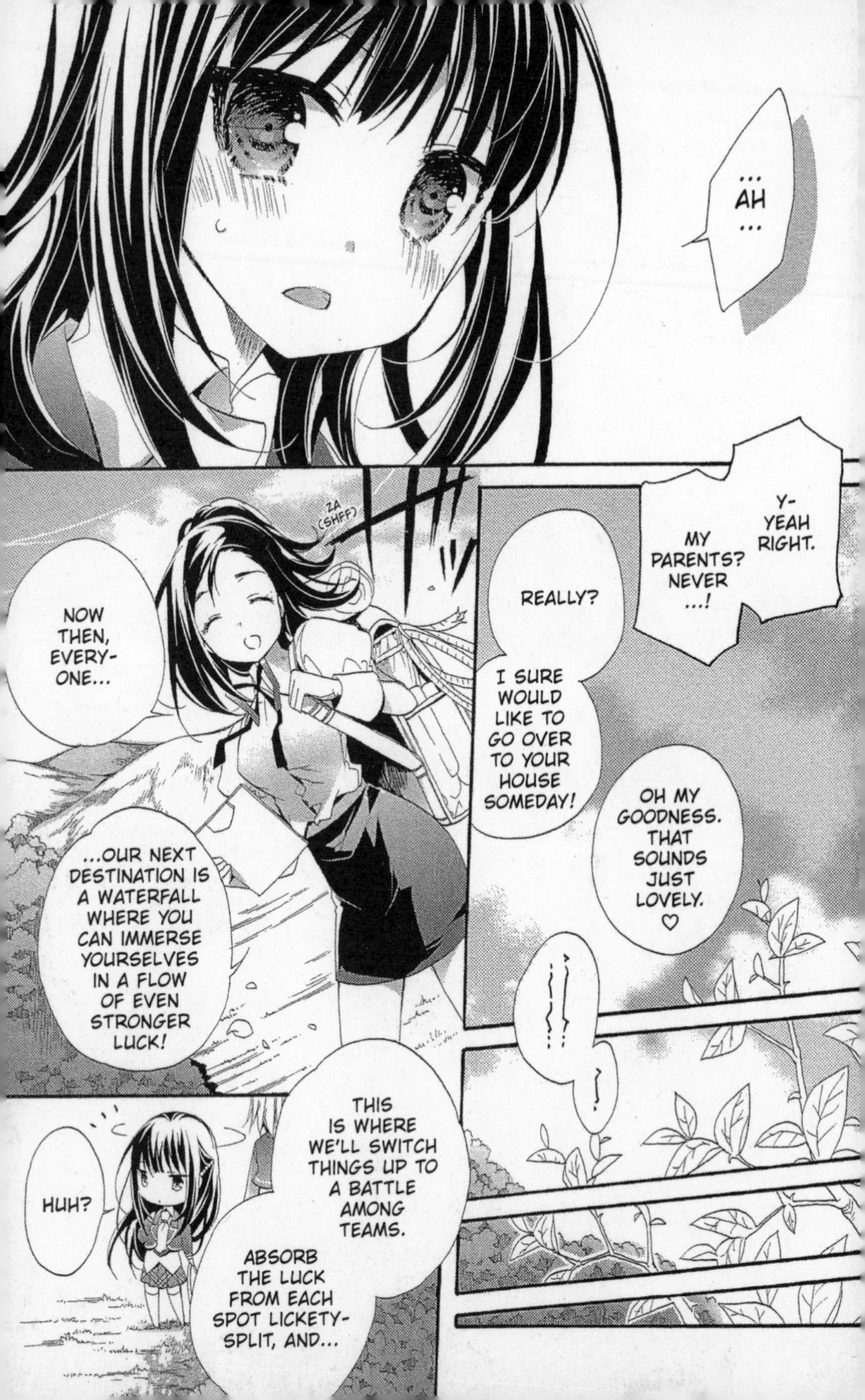
...AH...
Y-YEAH RIGHT.
MY PARENTS? NEVER...!
REALLY?
I SURE WOULD LIKE TO GO OVER TO YOUR HOUSE SOMEDAY!
OH MY GOODNESS. THAT SOUNDS JUST LOVELY. ♡
ZA (SHFF)
NOW THEN, EVERYONE...
...OUR NEXT DESTINATION IS A WATERFALL WHERE YOU CAN IMMERSE YOURSELVES IN A FLOW OF EVEN STRONGER LUCK!
THIS IS WHERE WE'LL SWITCH THINGS UP TO A BATTLE AMONG TEAMS.
ABSORB THE LUCK FROM EACH SPOT LICKETY-SPLIT, AND...
HUH?

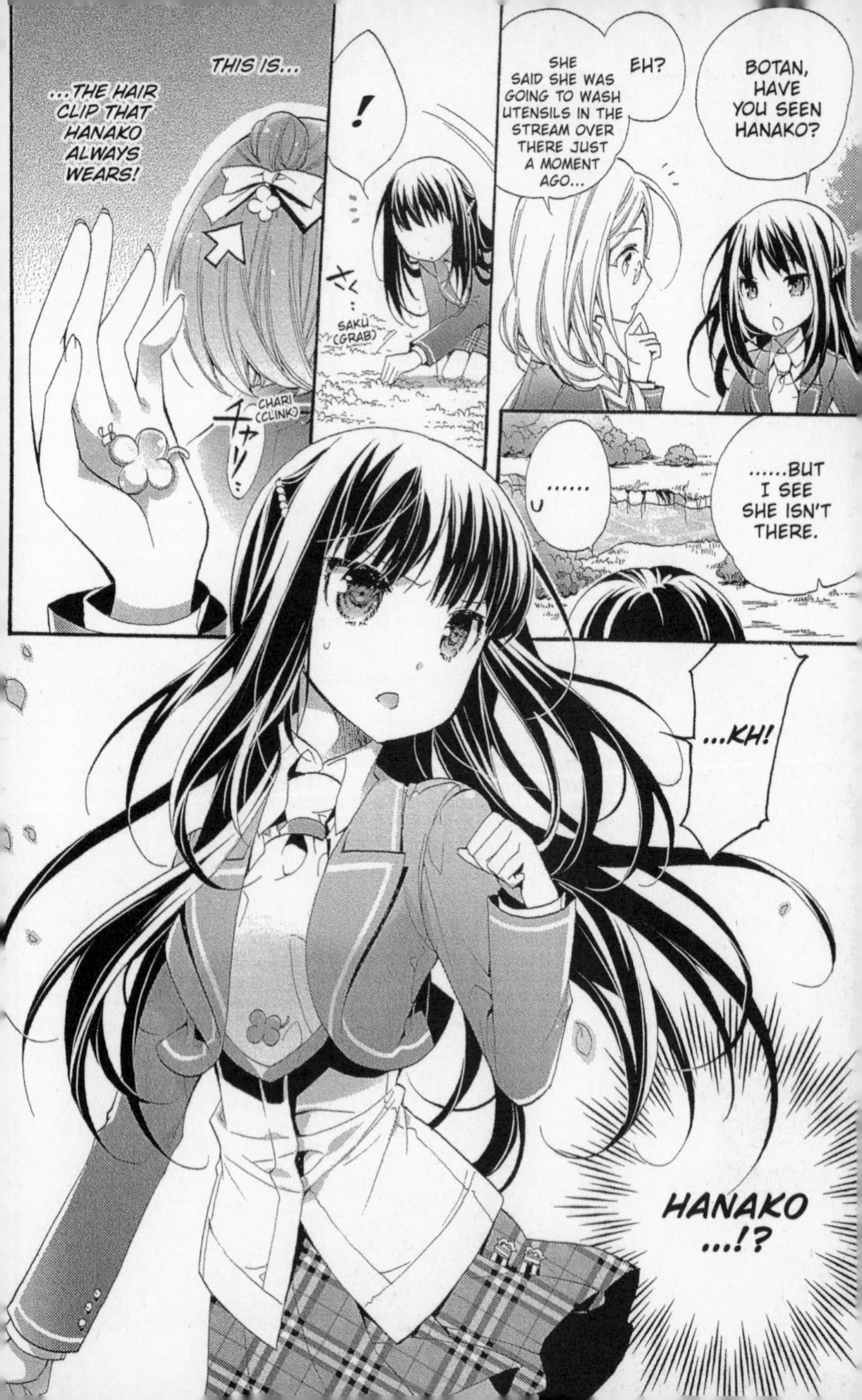

BOTAN, HAVE YOU SEEN HANAKO?
EH?
SHE SAID SHE WAS GOING TO WASH UTENSILS IN THE STREAM OVER THERE JUST A MOMENT AGO...
......BUT I SEE SHE ISN'T THERE.
......
!
SAKU (GRAB)
CHARI (CLINK)
THIS IS...
...THE HAIR CLIP THAT HANAKO ALWAYS WEARS!
...KH!
HANAKO ...!?

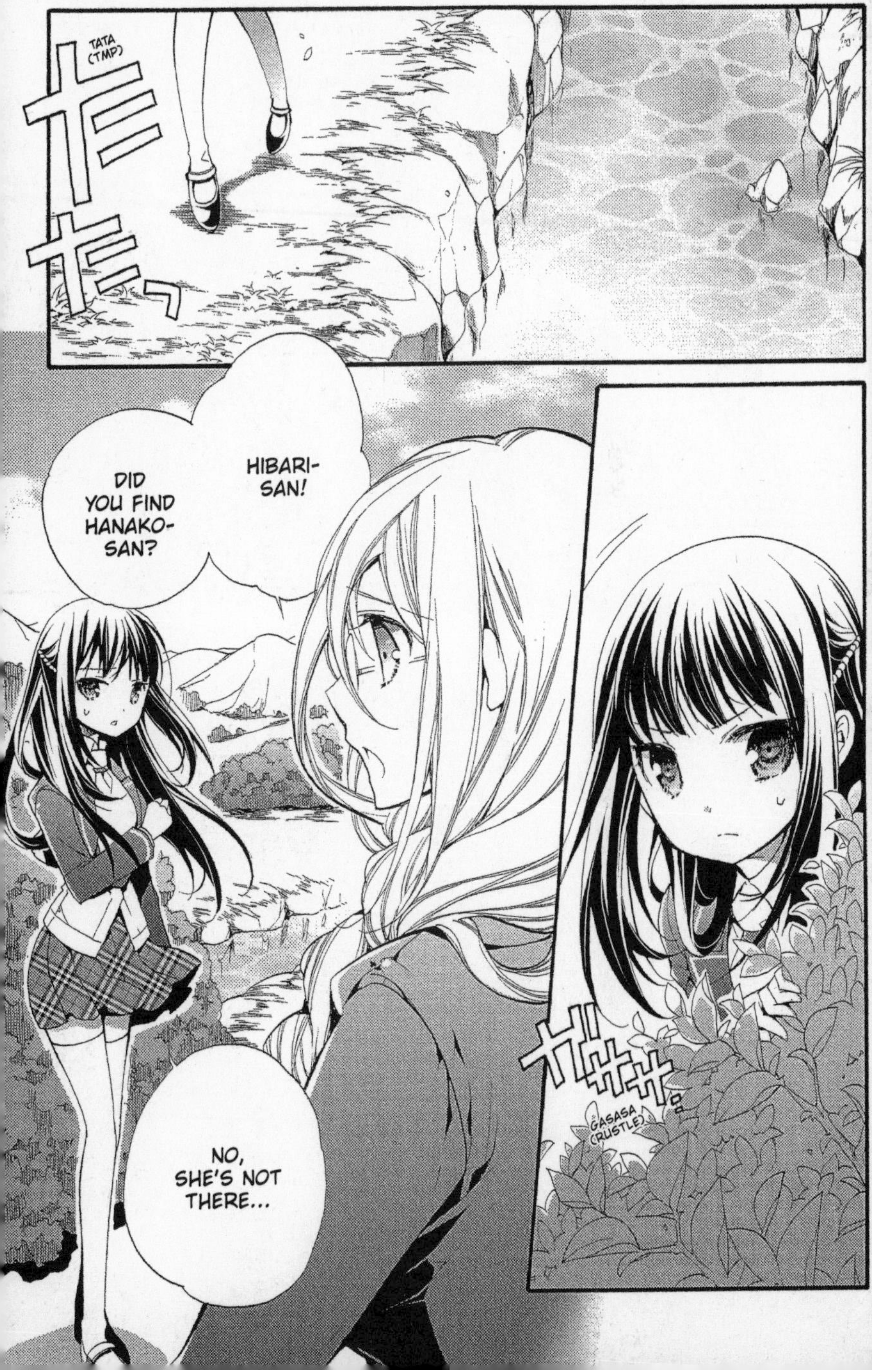
TATA (TMP)
GASASA (RUSTLE)
HIBARI-SAN!
DID YOU FIND HANAKO-SAN?
NO, SHE'S NOT THERE...

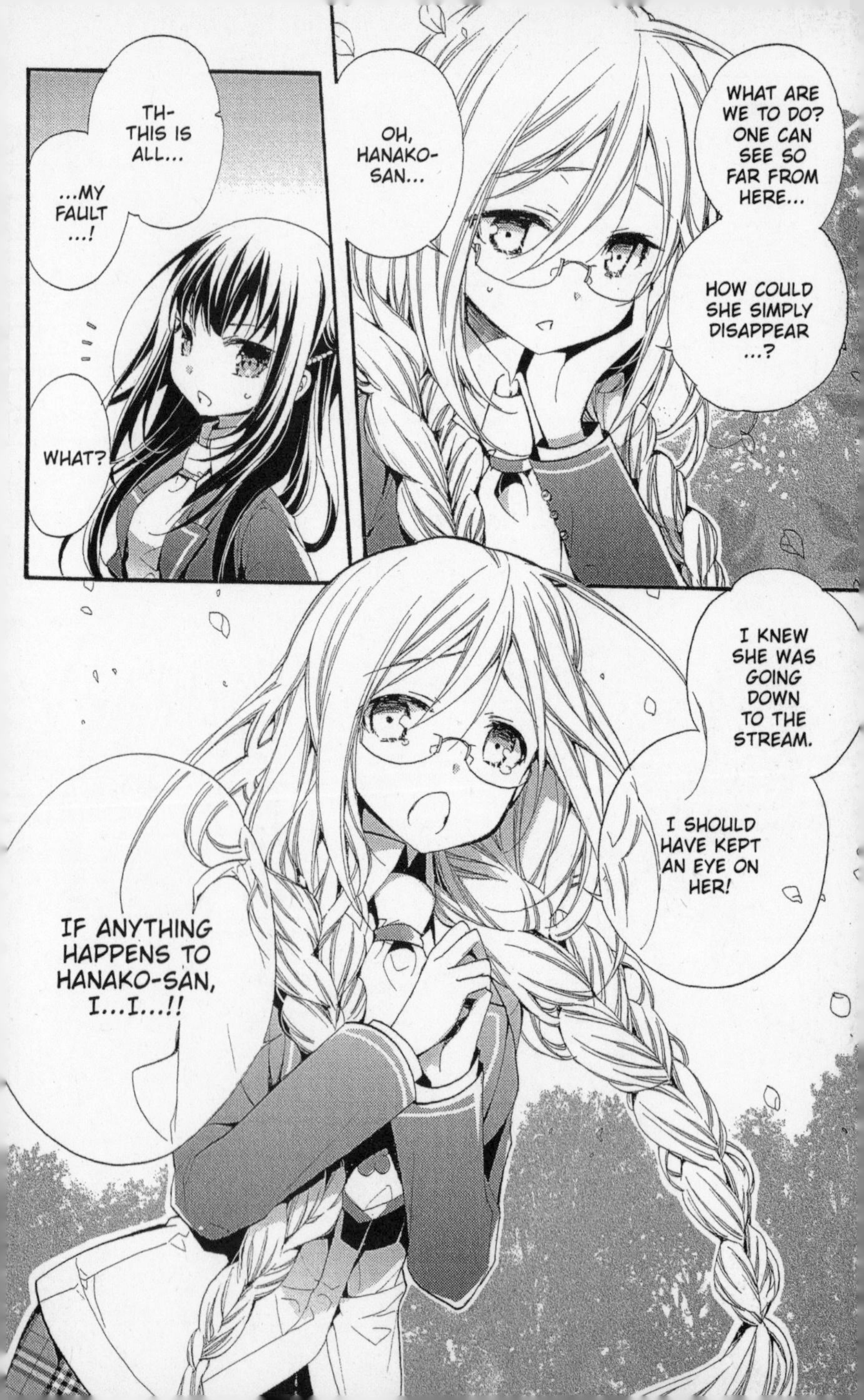
OH, HANAKO-SAN...
WHAT ARE WE TO DO? ONE CAN SEE SO FAR FROM HERE...
HOW COULD SHE SIMPLY DISAPPEAR ...?
TH- THIS IS ALL...
...MY FAULT ...!
WHAT?
I KNEW SHE WAS GOING DOWN TO THE STREAM.
I SHOULD HAVE KEPT AN EYE ON HER!
IF ANYTHING HAPPENS TO HANAKO-SAN, I...I...!!

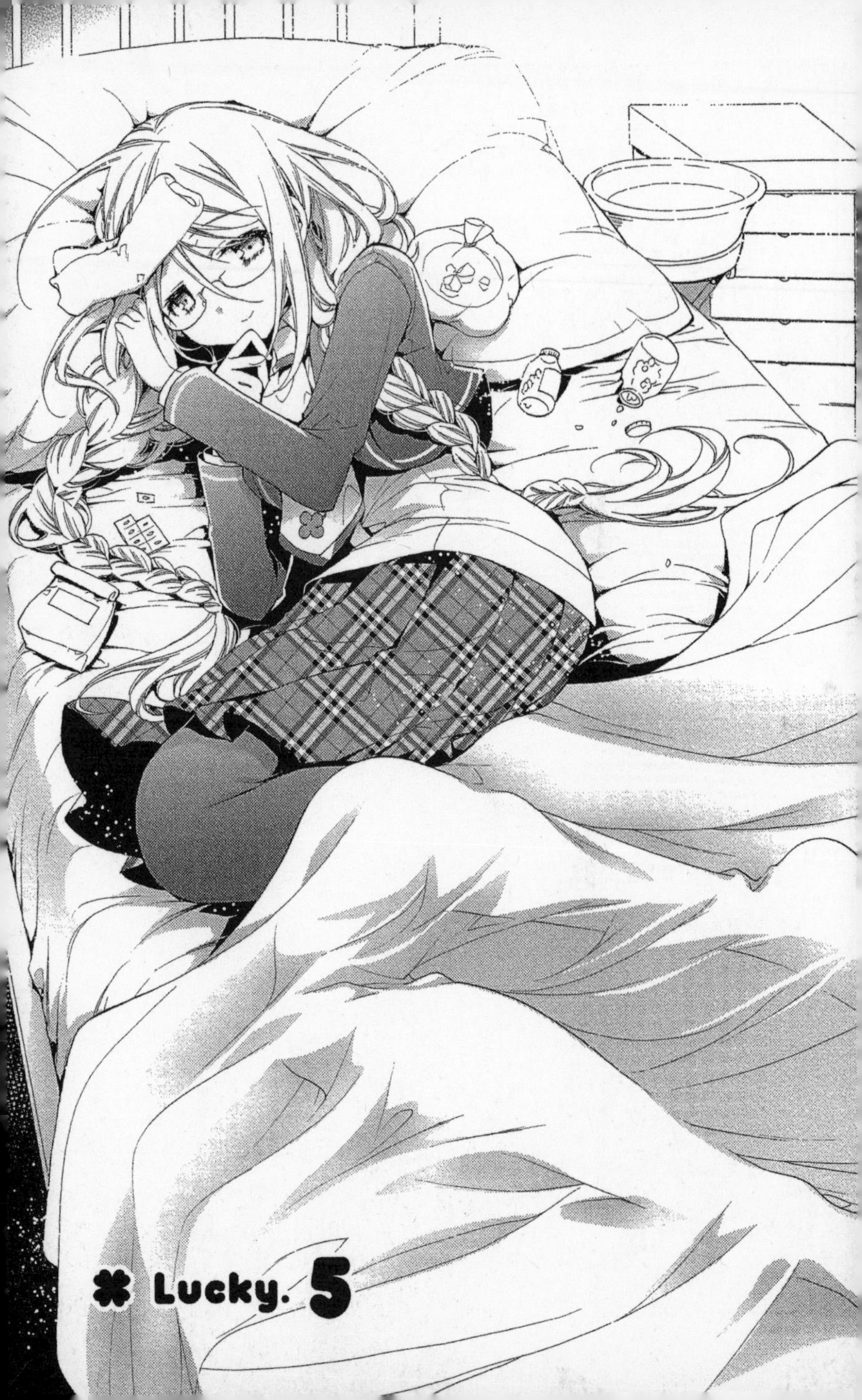
Lucky. 5

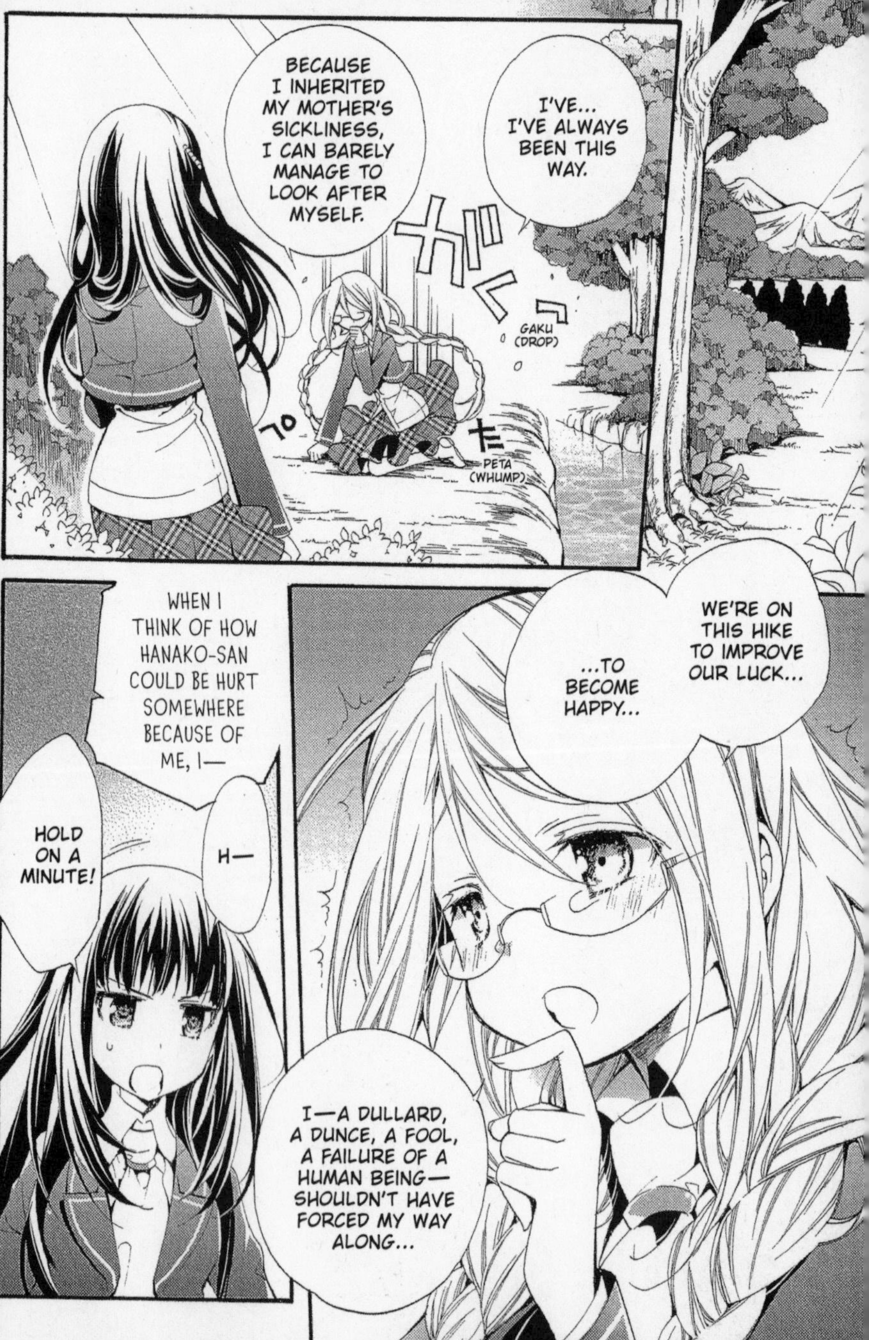
I'VE... I'VE ALWAYS BEEN THIS WAY.
BECAUSE I INHERITED MY MOTHER'S SICKLINESS, I CAN BARELY MANAGE TO LOOK AFTER MYSELF.
GAKU (DROP)
PETA (WHUMP)
WE'RE ON THIS HIKE TO IMPROVE OUR LUCK...
...TO BECOME HAPPY...
I—A DULLARD, A DUNCE, A FOOL, A FAILURE OF A HUMAN BEING—SHOULDN'T HAVE FORCED MY WAY ALONG...
WHEN I THINK OF HOW HANAKO-SAN COULD BE HURT SOMEWHERE BECAUSE OF ME, I—
H—
HOLD ON A MINUTE!

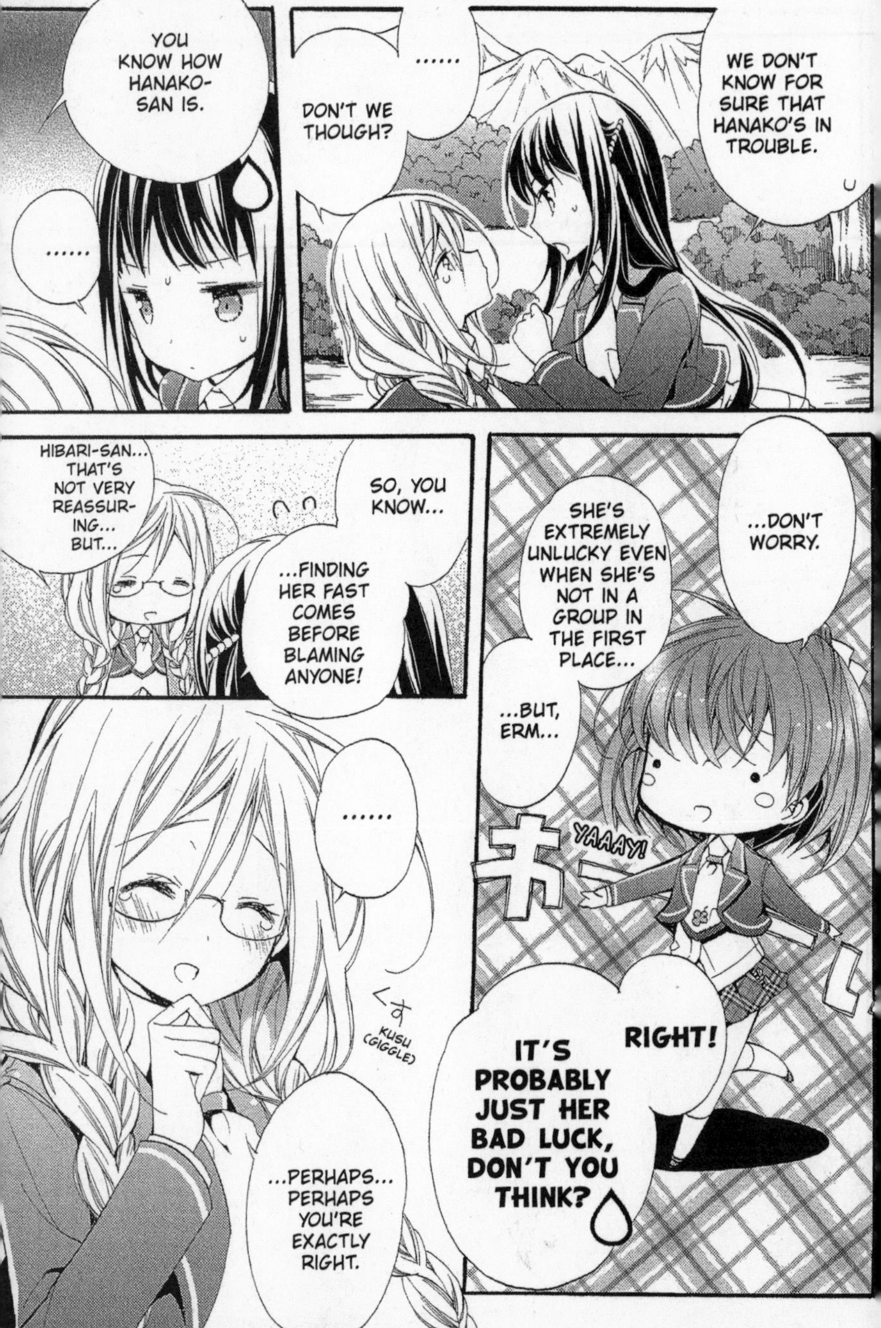
WE DON'T KNOW FOR SURE THAT HANAKO'S IN TROUBLE.
......
DON'T WE THOUGH?
YOU KNOW HOW HANAKO-SAN IS.
......
...DON'T WORRY.
SHE'S EXTREMELY UNLUCKY EVEN WHEN SHE'S NOT IN A GROUP IN THE FIRST PLACE...
...BUT, ERM...
YAAAY!
RIGHT!
IT'S PROBABLY JUST HER BAD LUCK, DON'T YOU THINK?
SO, YOU KNOW...
...FINDING HER FAST COMES BEFORE BLAMING ANYONE!
HIBARI-SAN... THAT'S NOT VERY REASSURING... BUT...
......
くす
KUSU (GIGGLE)
...PERHAPS... PERHAPS YOU'RE EXACTLY RIGHT.

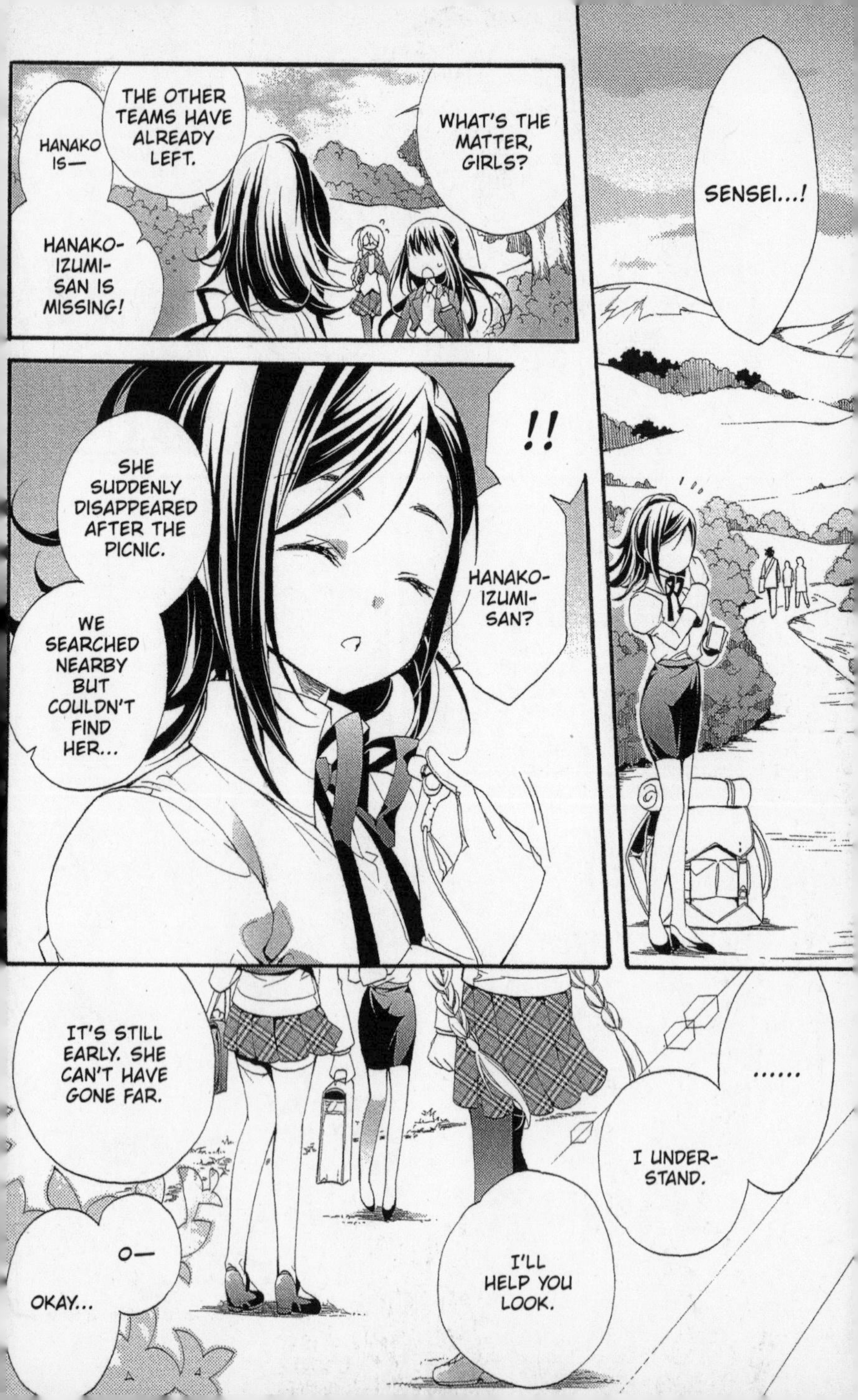
SENSEI...!
WHAT'S THE MATTER, GIRLS?
THE OTHER TEAMS HAVE ALREADY LEFT.
HANAKO IS—
HANAKO-IZUMI-SAN IS MISSING!
!!
HANAKO-IZUMI-SAN?
SHE SUDDENLY DISAPPEARED AFTER THE PICNIC.
WE SEARCHED NEARBY BUT COULDN'T FIND HER...
......
I UNDER-STAND.
I'LL HELP YOU LOOK.
IT'S STILL EARLY. SHE CAN'T HAVE GONE FAR.
O— OKAY...

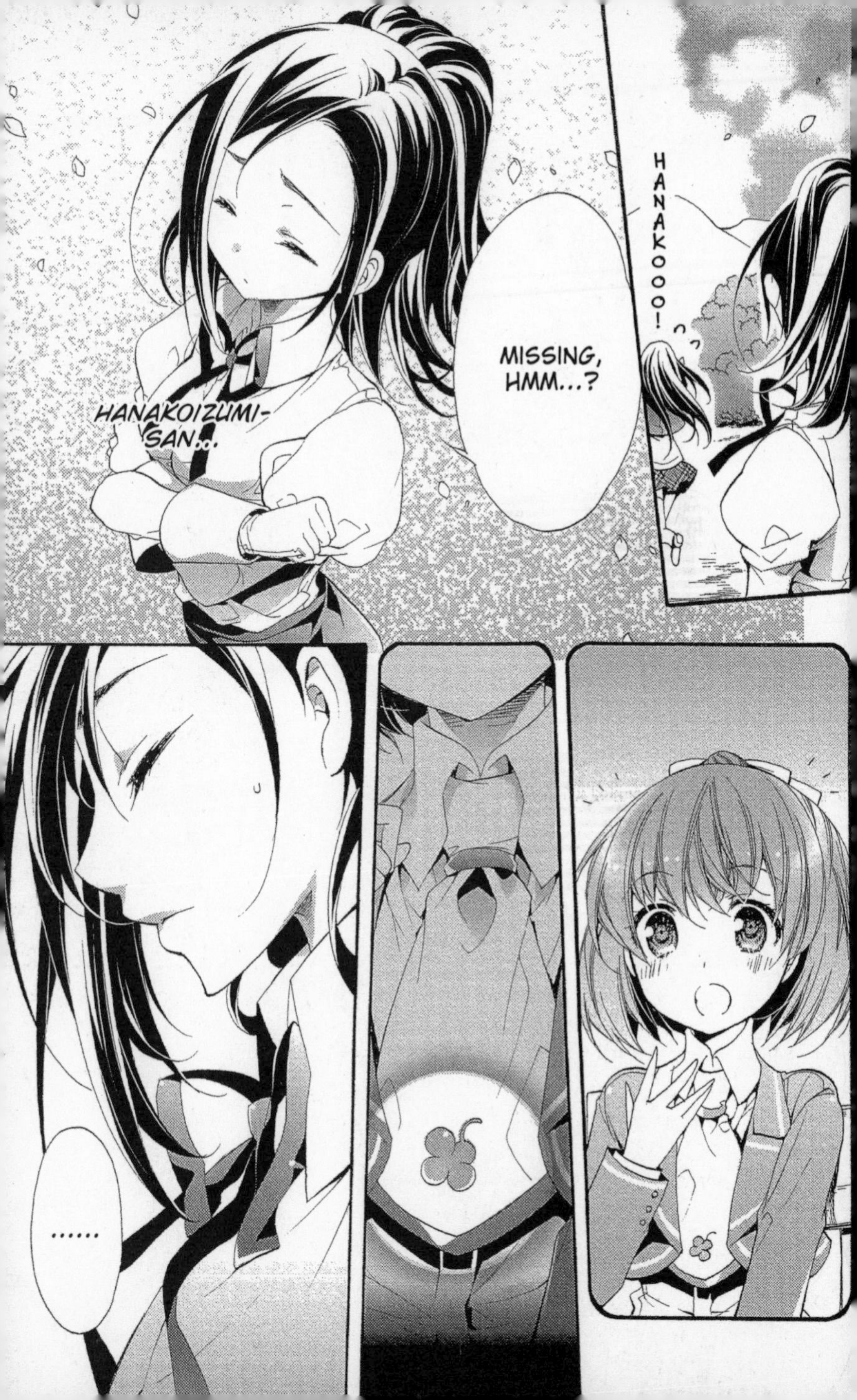
HANAKOOOO!
MISSING, HMM...?
HANAKOIZUMI-SAN...
......

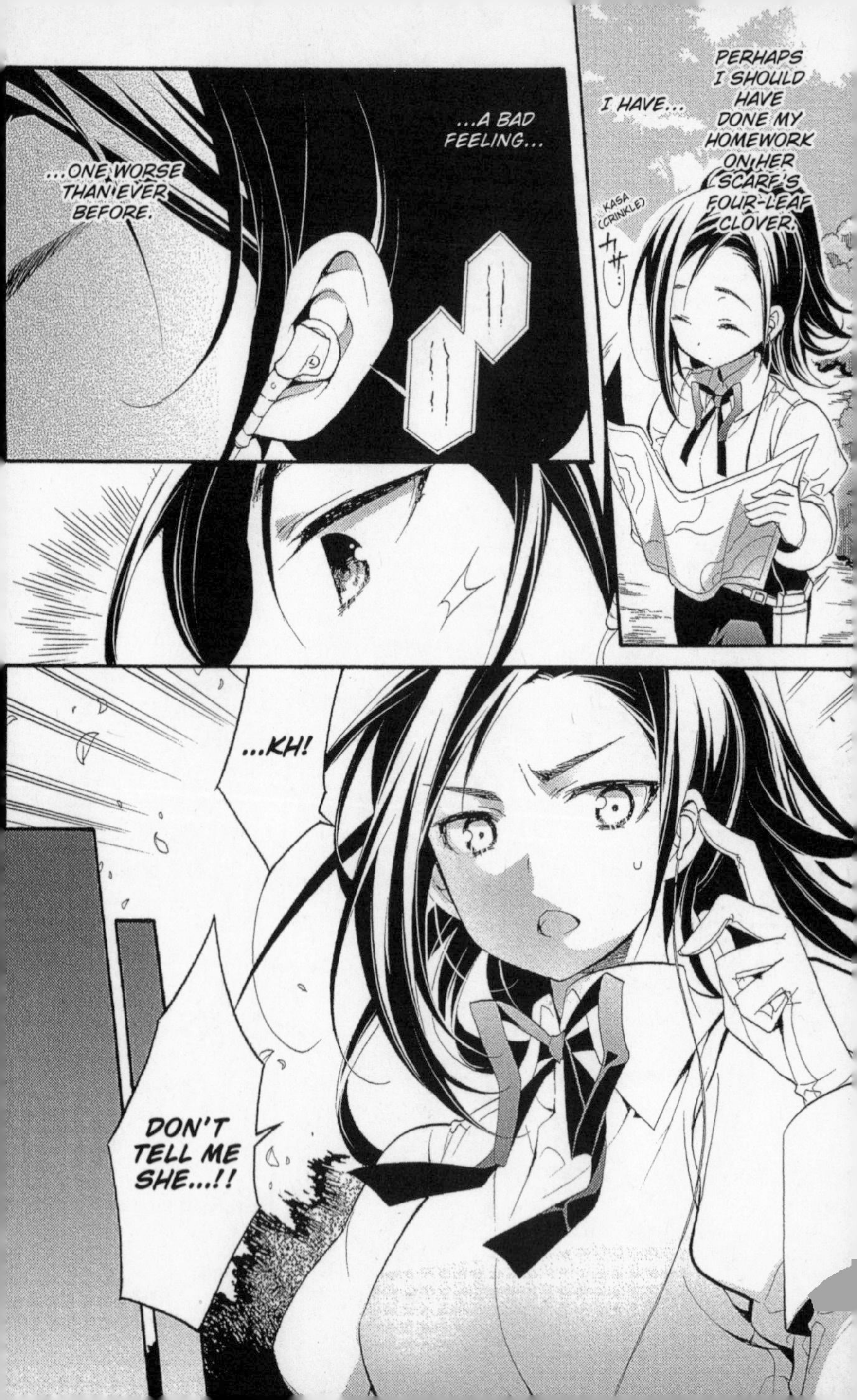
PERHAPS I SHOULD HAVE DONE MY HOMEWORK ON HER SCARF'S FOUR-LEAF CLOVER.
I HAVE...
KASA (CRINKLE)
...A BAD FEELING...
...ONE WORSE THAN EVER BEFORE.
...KH!
DON'T TELL ME SHE...!!

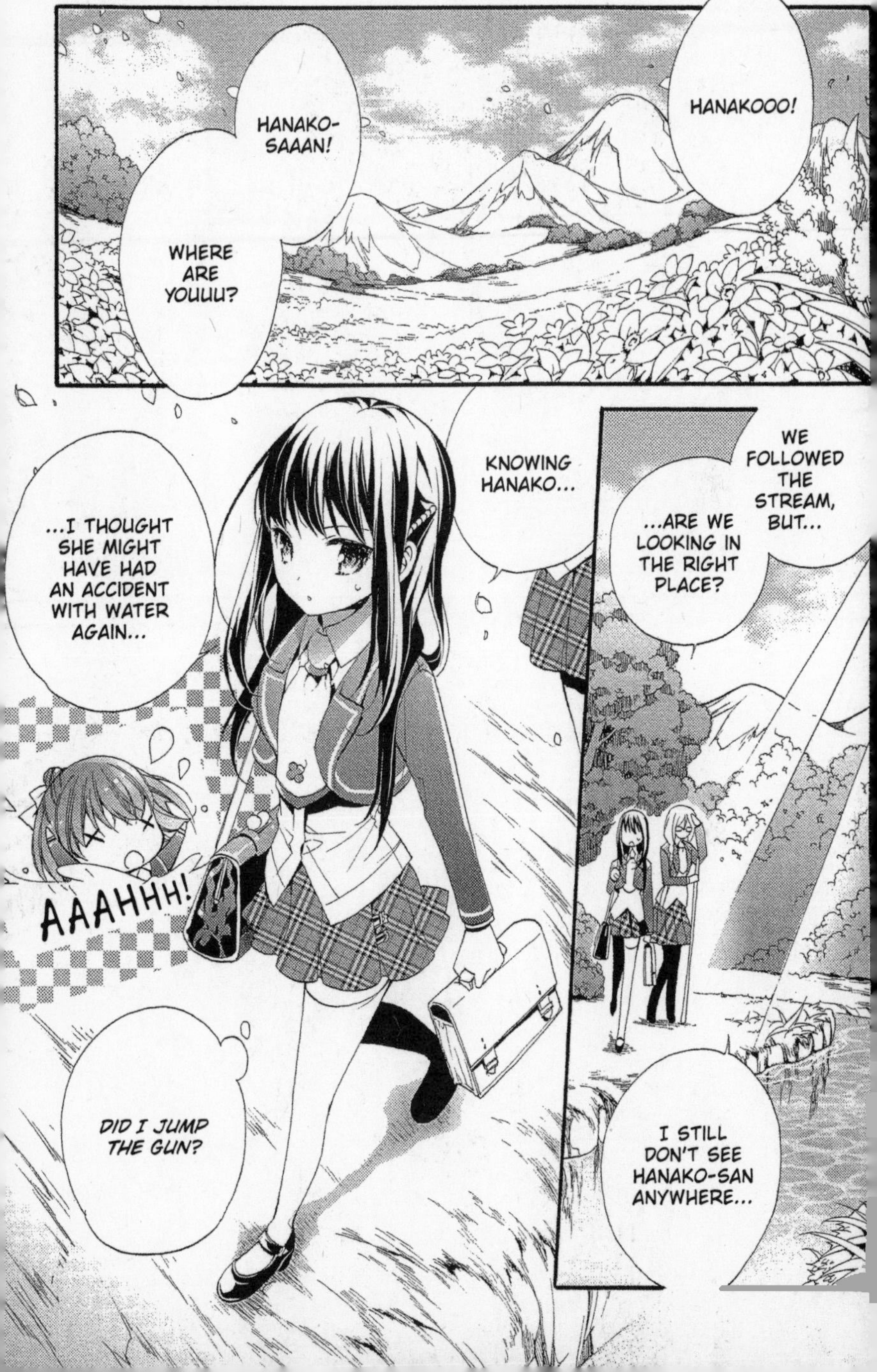
HANAKOOO!
HANAKO-SAAAN!
WHERE ARE YOUUU?
WE FOLLOWED THE STREAM, BUT...
...ARE WE LOOKING IN THE RIGHT PLACE?
I STILL DON'T SEE HANAKO-SAN ANYWHERE...
KNOWING HANAKO...
...I THOUGHT SHE MIGHT HAVE HAD AN ACCIDENT WITH WATER AGAIN...
AAAHHH!
DID I JUMP THE GUN?

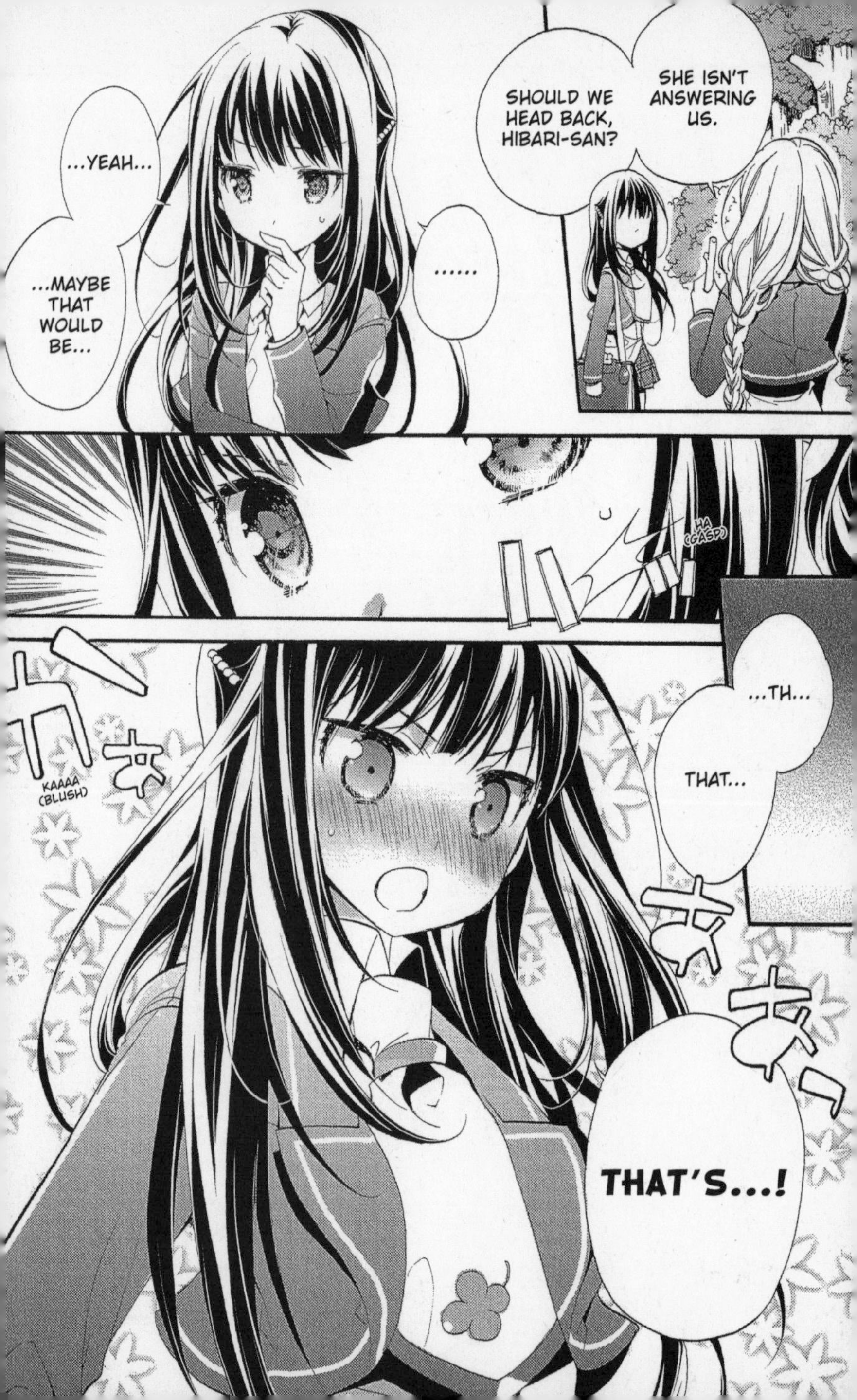
SHE ISN'T ANSWERING US.
SHOULD WE HEAD BACK, HIBARI-SAN?
......
...YEAH...
...MAYBE THAT WOULD BE...
HA (GASP)
...TH...
THAT...
KAAAA (BLUSH)
THAT'S...!

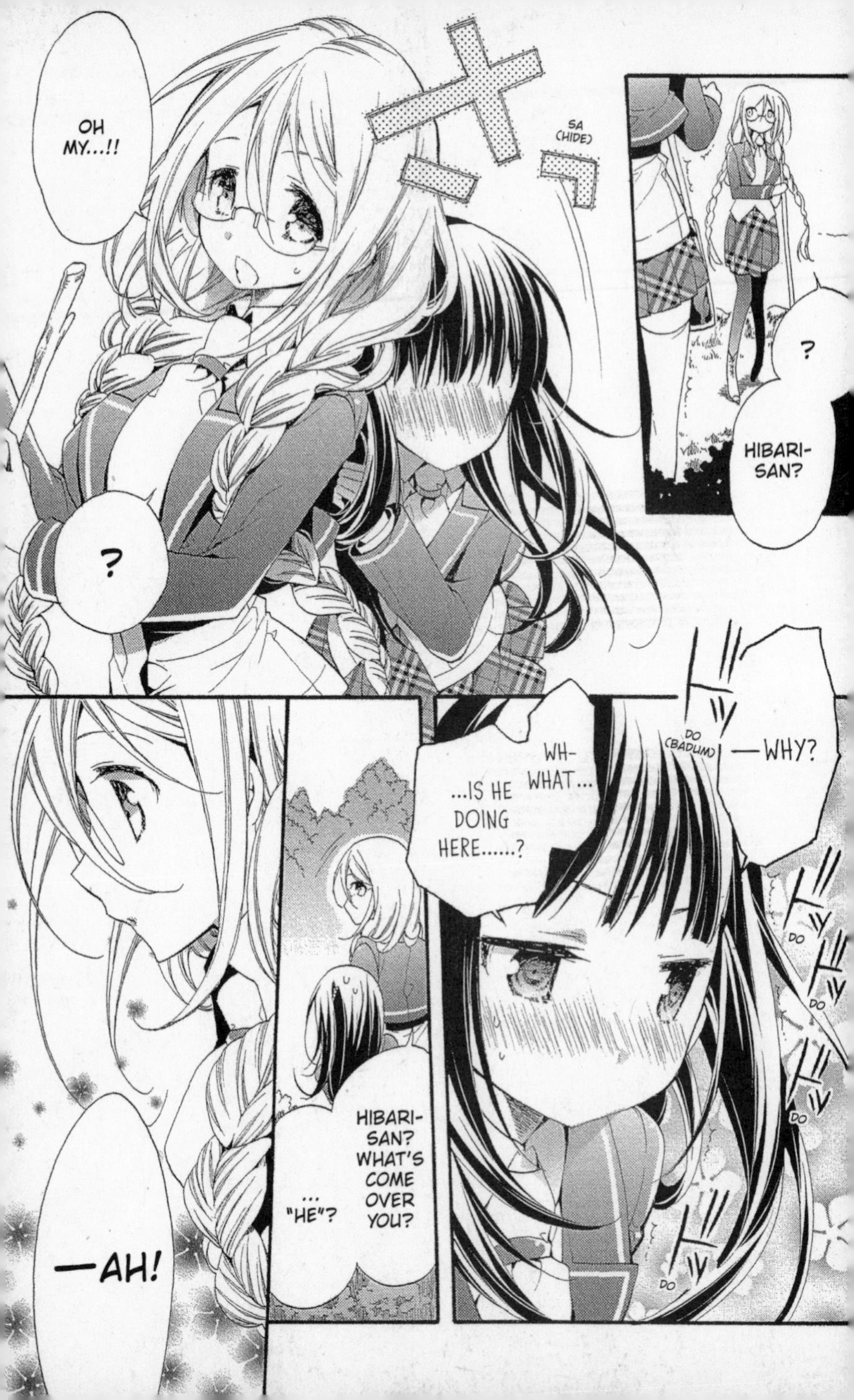
?
HIBARI-SAN?
SA (HIDE)
OH MY...!!
?
DO (BADUM)
—WHY?
WH- WHAT...
...IS HE DOING HERE......?
DO
DO
DO
DO
HIBARI-SAN? WHAT'S COME OVER YOU?
... "HE"?
—AH!

SIGN: ONE WAY

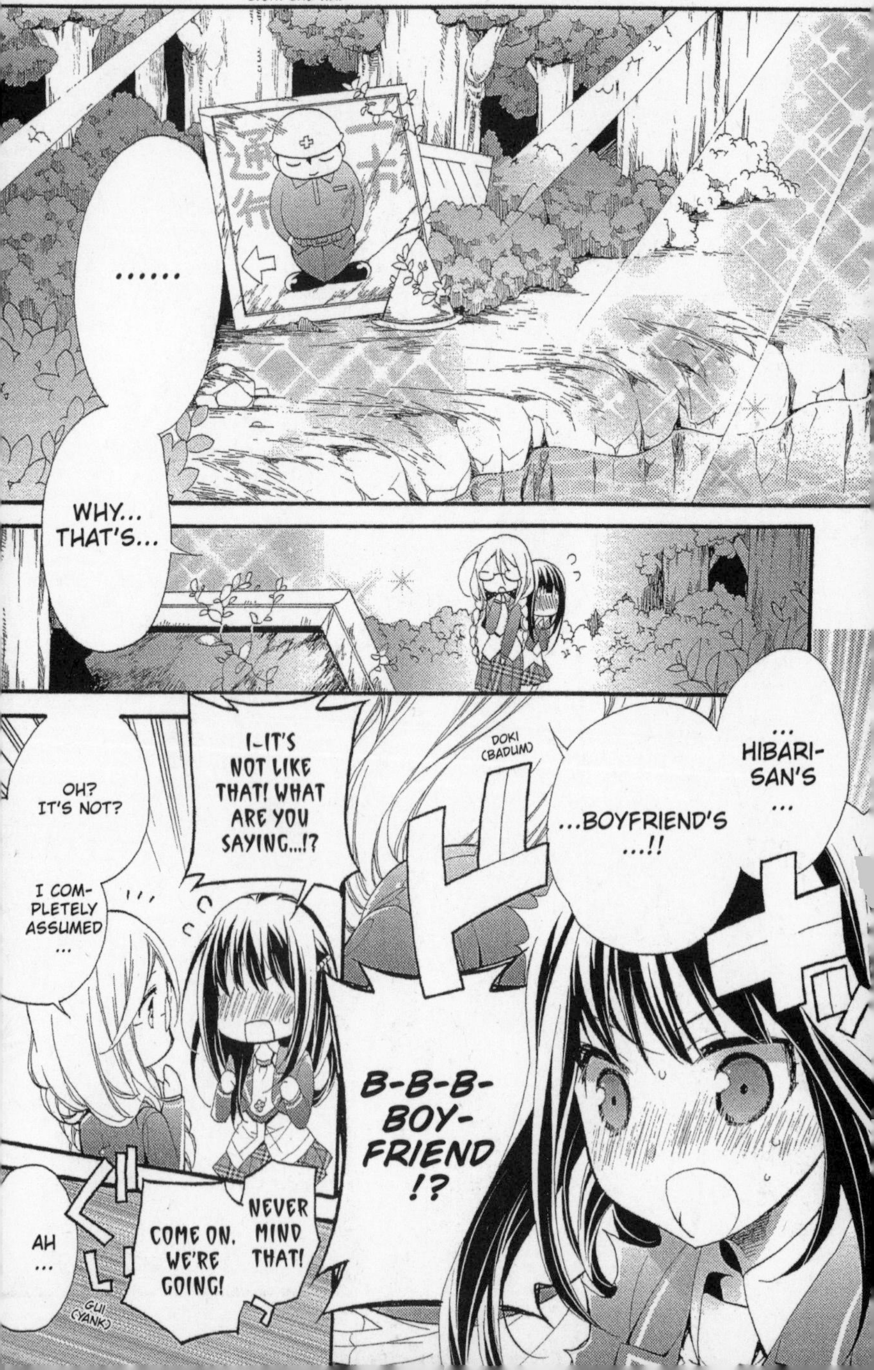
......
WHY... THAT'S...
...HIBARI-SAN'S...
...BOYFRIEND'S...!!
DOKI (BADUM)
B-B-B-BOY-FRIEND!?
I-IT'S NOT LIKE THAT! WHAT ARE YOU SAYING...!?
OH? IT'S NOT?
I COMPLETELY ASSUMED...
NEVER MIND THAT!
COME ON. WE'RE GOING!
AH...
GUI (YANK)

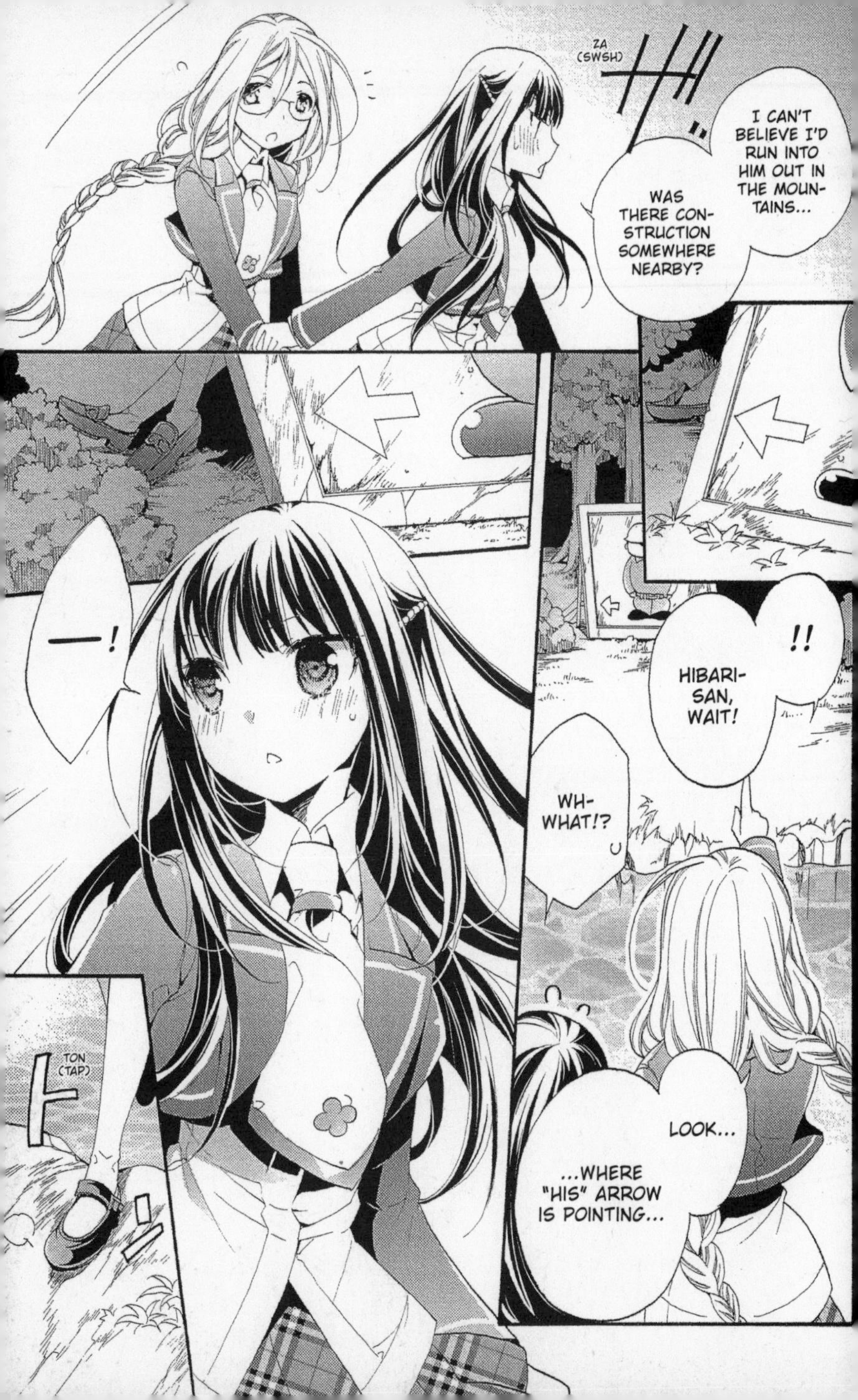
ZA (SWSH)
I CAN'T BELIEVE I'D RUN INTO HIM OUT IN THE MOUNTAINS...
WAS THERE CONSTRUCTION SOMEWHERE NEARBY?
!!
HIBARI-SAN, WAIT!
WH-WHAT!?
—!
TON (TAP)
LOOK...
...WHERE "HIS" ARROW IS POINTING...

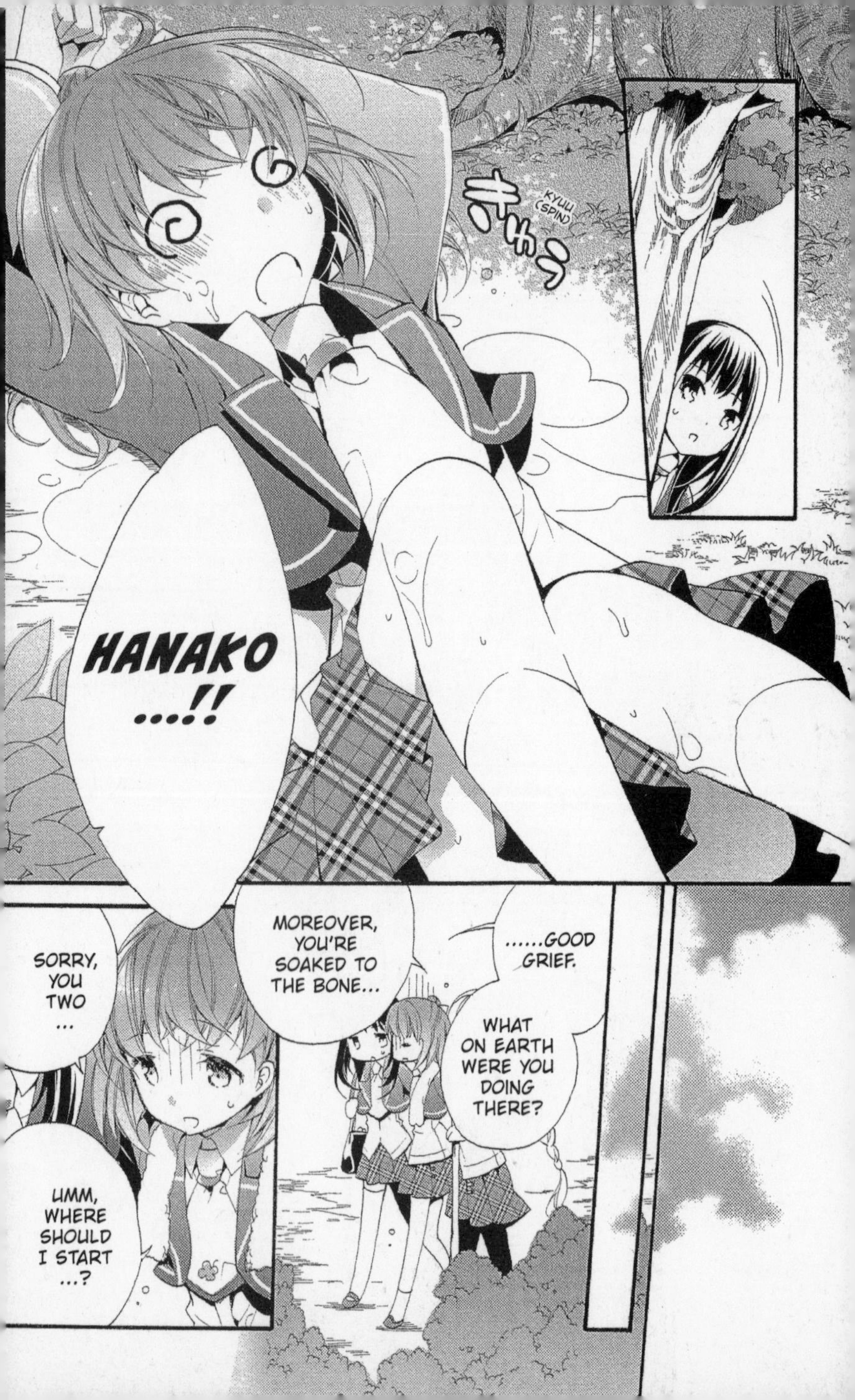
きゅう
KYUU (SPIN)
HANAKO ....!!
......GOOD GRIEF.
MOREOVER, YOU'RE SOAKED TO THE BONE...
WHAT ON EARTH WERE YOU DOING THERE?
SORRY, YOU TWO ...
UMM, WHERE SHOULD I START ...?

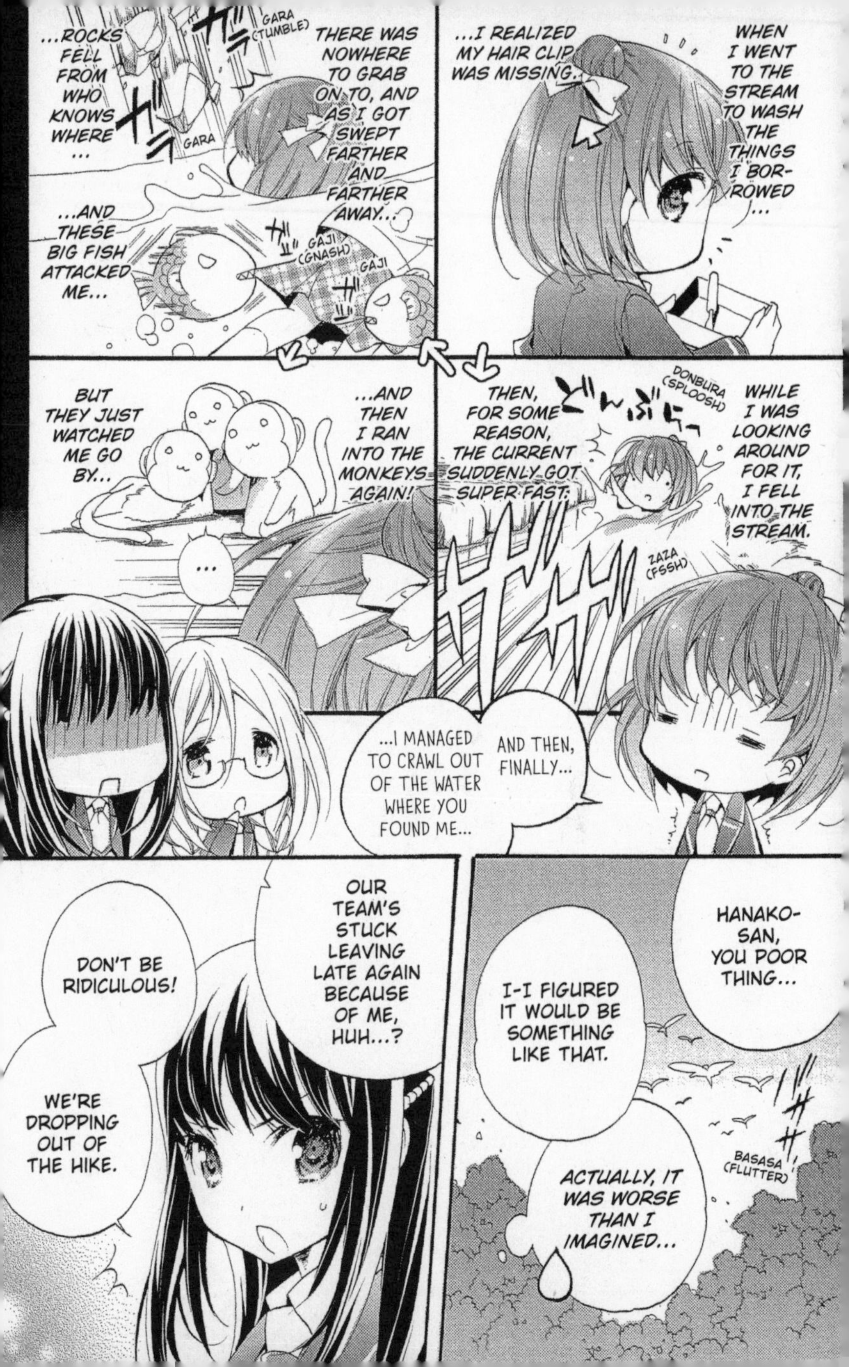
WHEN I WENT TO THE STREAM TO WASH THE THINGS I BORROWED...
...I REALIZED MY HAIR CLIP WAS MISSING...
WHILE I WAS LOOKING AROUND FOR IT, I FELL INTO THE STREAM.
DONBURA (SPLOOSH)
THEN, FOR SOME REASON, THE CURRENT SUDDENLY GOT SUPER FAST.
ZAZA (FSSH)
THERE WAS NOWHERE TO GRAB ON TO, AND AS I GOT SWEPT FARTHER AND FARTHER AWAY...
GARA (TUMBLE)
...ROCKS FELL FROM WHO KNOWS WHERE...
GARA
...AND THESE BIG FISH ATTACKED ME...
GAJI (GNASH)
GAJI
...AND THEN I RAN INTO THE MONKEYS AGAIN!
BUT THEY JUST WATCHED ME GO BY...
...
AND THEN, FINALLY...
...I MANAGED TO CRAWL OUT OF THE WATER WHERE YOU FOUND ME...
HANAKO-SAN, YOU POOR THING...
I-I FIGURED IT WOULD BE SOMETHING LIKE THAT.
BASASA (FLUTTER)
ACTUALLY, IT WAS WORSE THAN I IMAGINED...
OUR TEAM'S STUCK LEAVING LATE AGAIN BECAUSE OF ME, HUH...?
DON'T BE RIDICULOUS!
WE'RE DROPPING OUT OF THE HIKE.

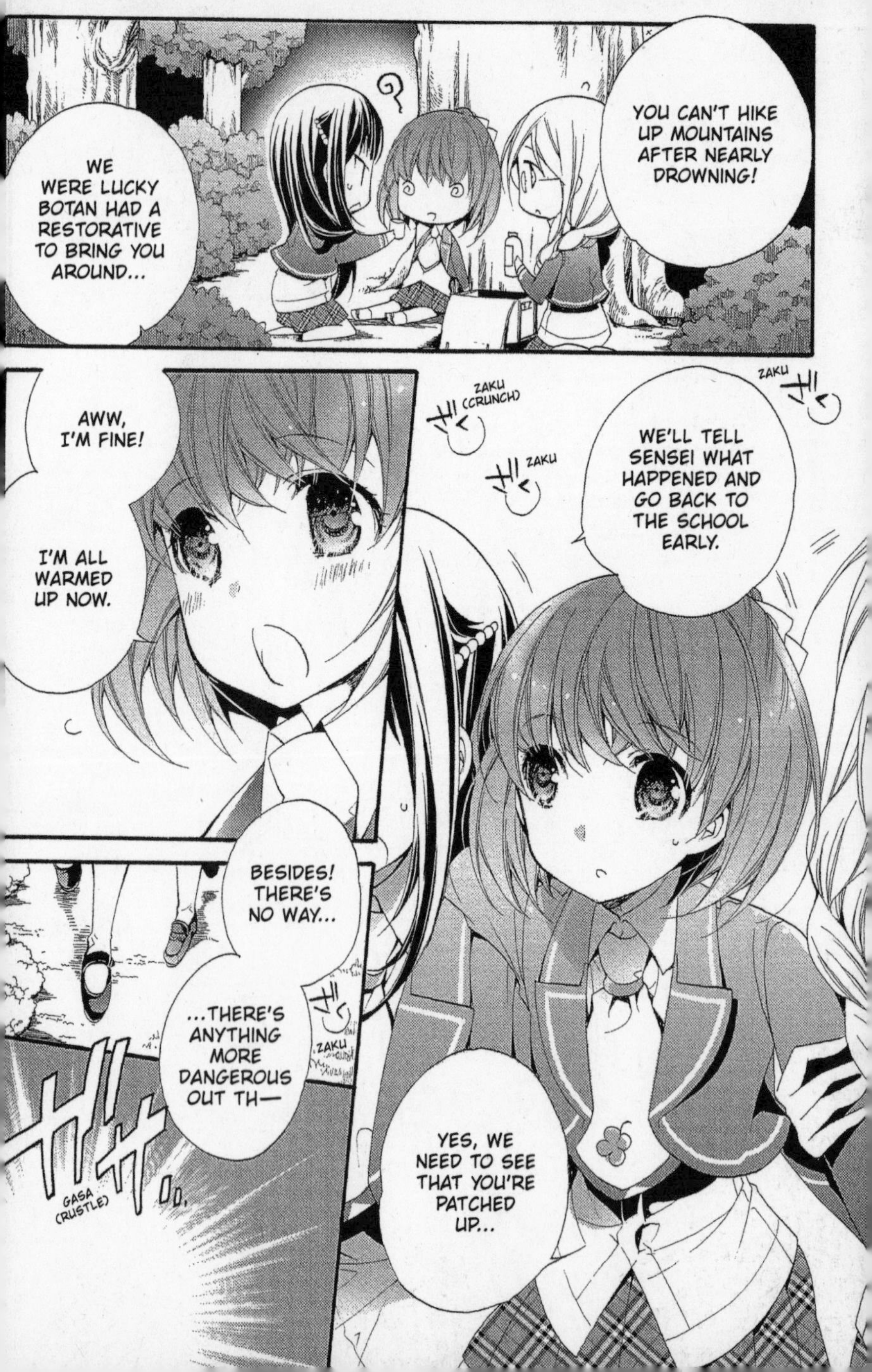
YOU CAN'T HIKE UP MOUNTAINS AFTER NEARLY DROWNING!
WE WERE LUCKY BOTAN HAD A RESTORATIVE TO BRING YOU AROUND...
ZAKU
WE'LL TELL SENSEI WHAT HAPPENED AND GO BACK TO THE SCHOOL EARLY.
ZAKU (CRUNCH)
ZAKU
YES, WE NEED TO SEE THAT YOU'RE PATCHED UP...
AWW, I'M FINE!
I'M ALL WARMED UP NOW.
BESIDES! THERE'S NO WAY...
...THERE'S ANYTHING MORE DANGEROUS OUT TH—
ZAKU
GASA (RUSTLE)

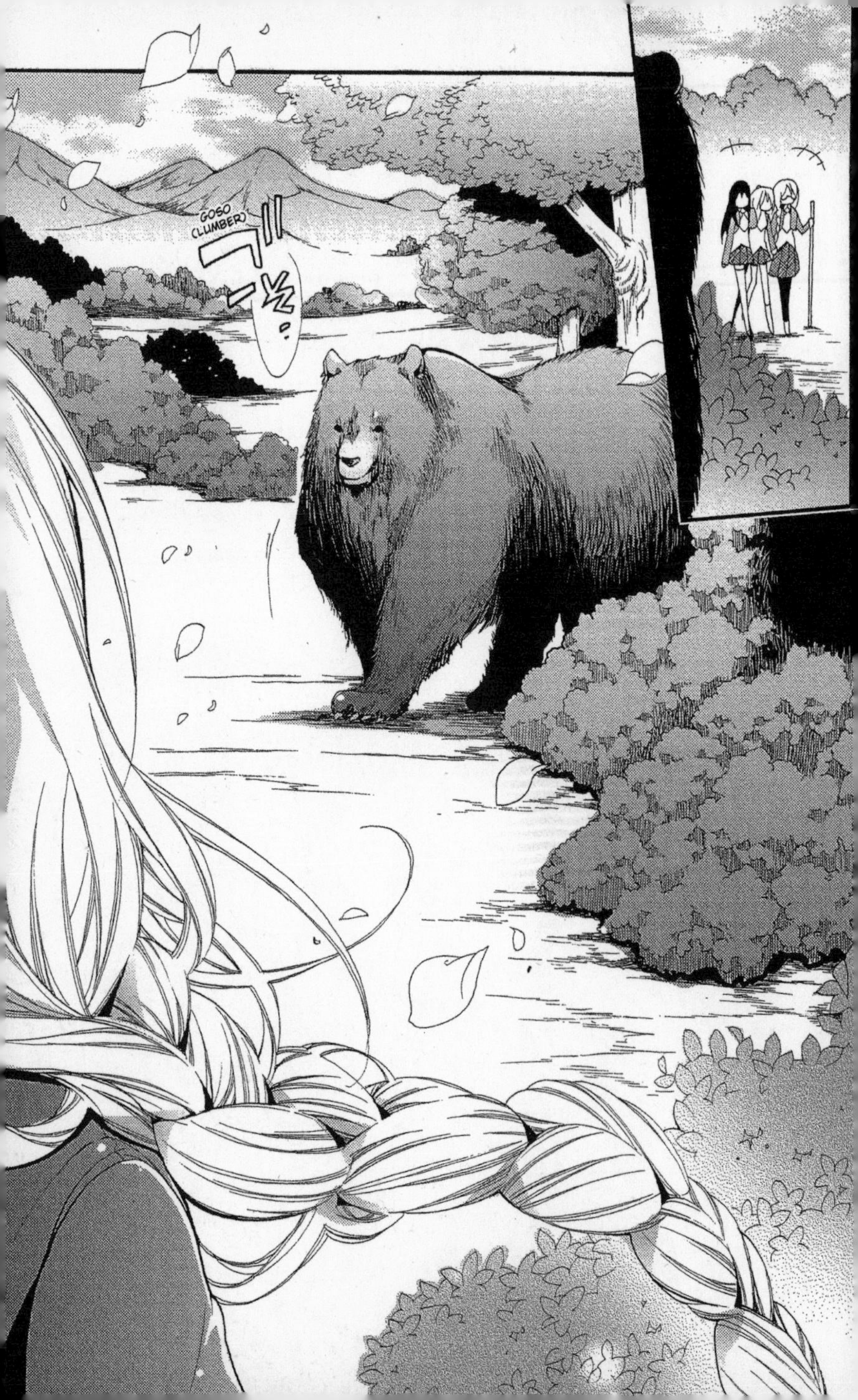
GOSO (LUMBER)

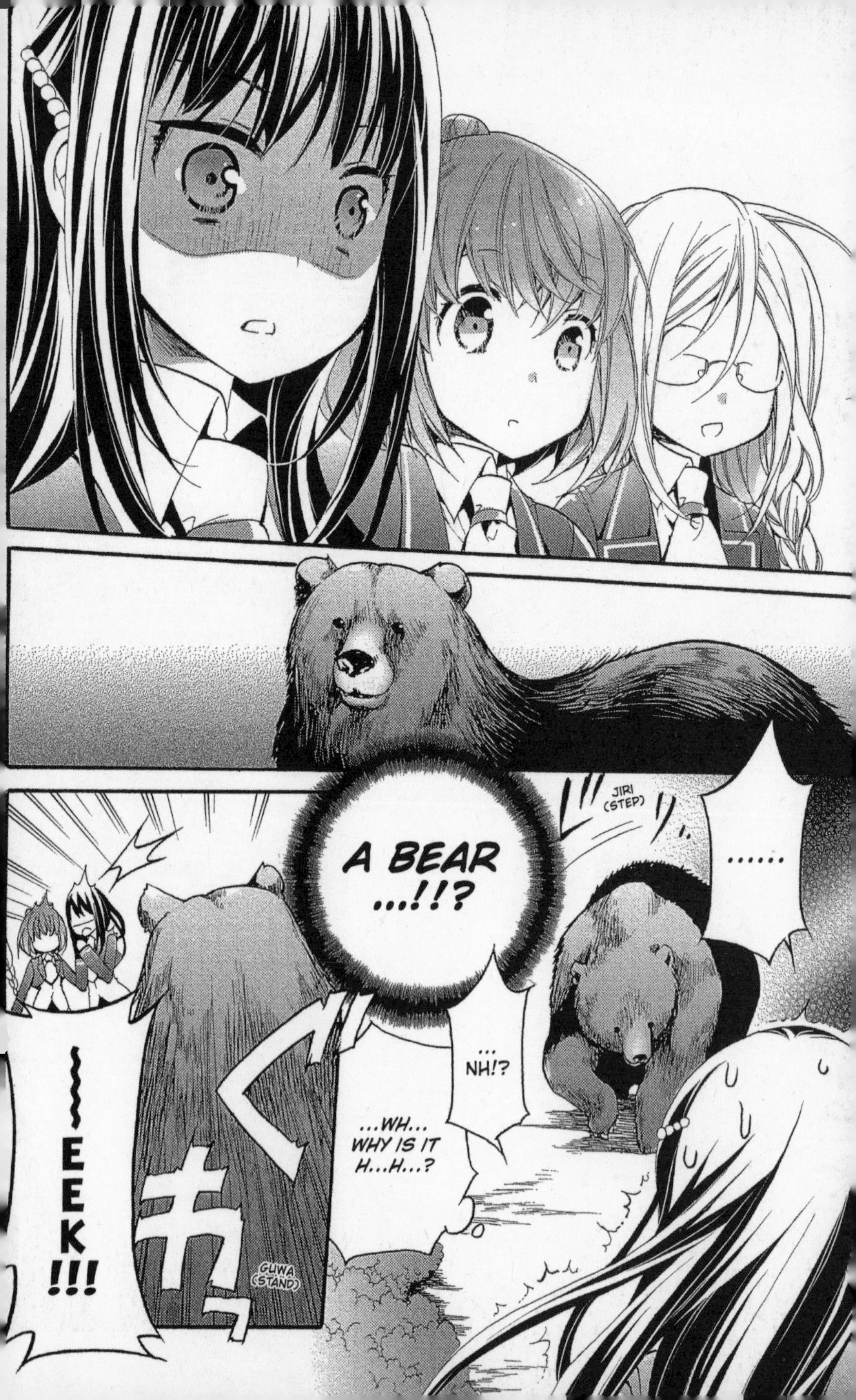
......
JIRI (STEP)
A BEAR ...!!?
... NH!?
...WH... WHY IS IT H...H...?
GUWA (STAND)
キッ
EEK!!!

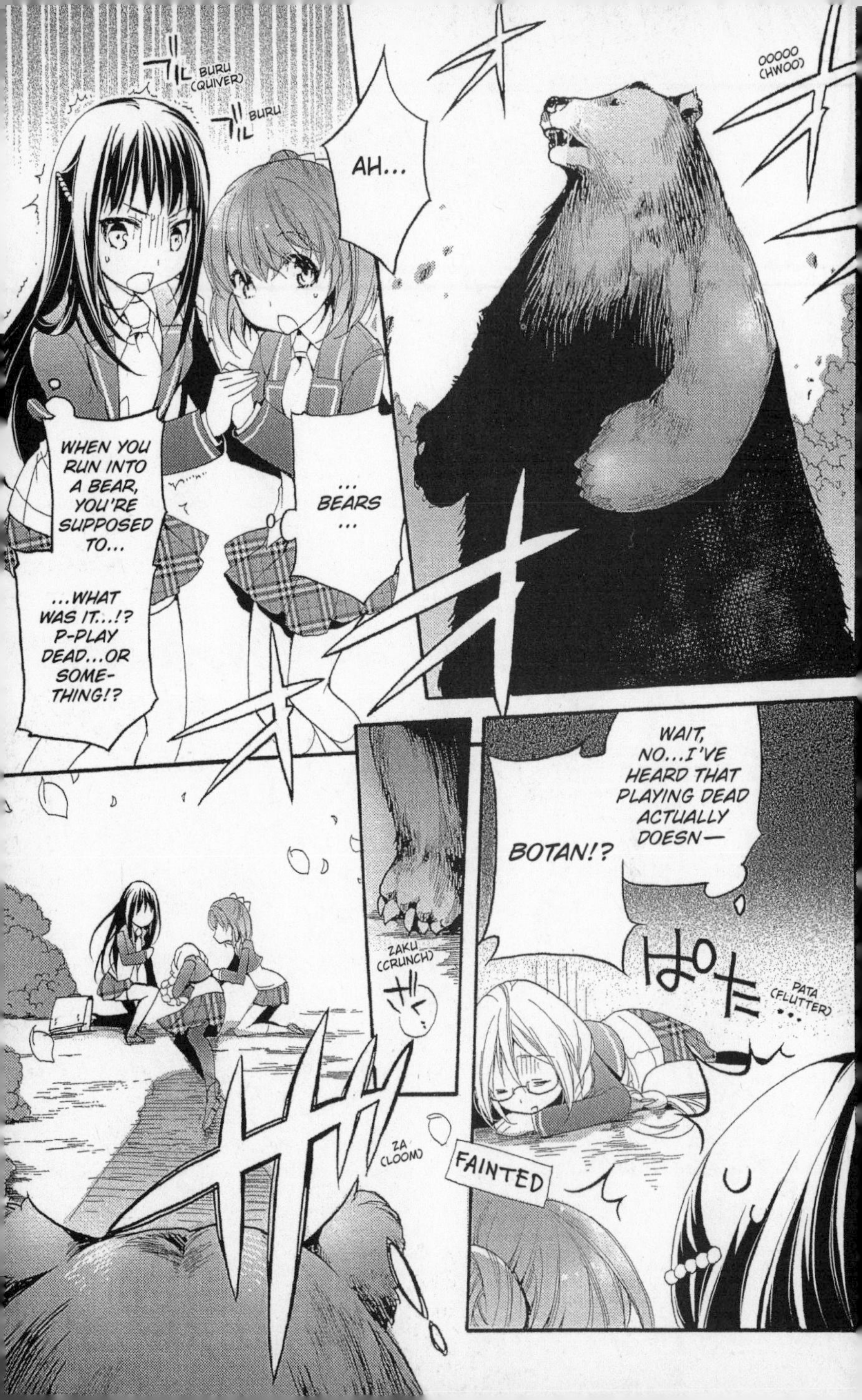
OOOOO (HWOO)
AH...
BURU (QUIVER)
BURU
...BEARS...
WHEN YOU RUN INTO A BEAR, YOU'RE SUPPOSED TO...
...WHAT WAS IT...!? P-PLAY DEAD...OR SOME-THING!?
WAIT, NO...I'VE HEARD THAT PLAYING DEAD ACTUALLY DOESN—
BOTAN!?
PATA (FLUTTER)
FAINTED
ZAKU (CRUNCH)
ZA (LOOM)

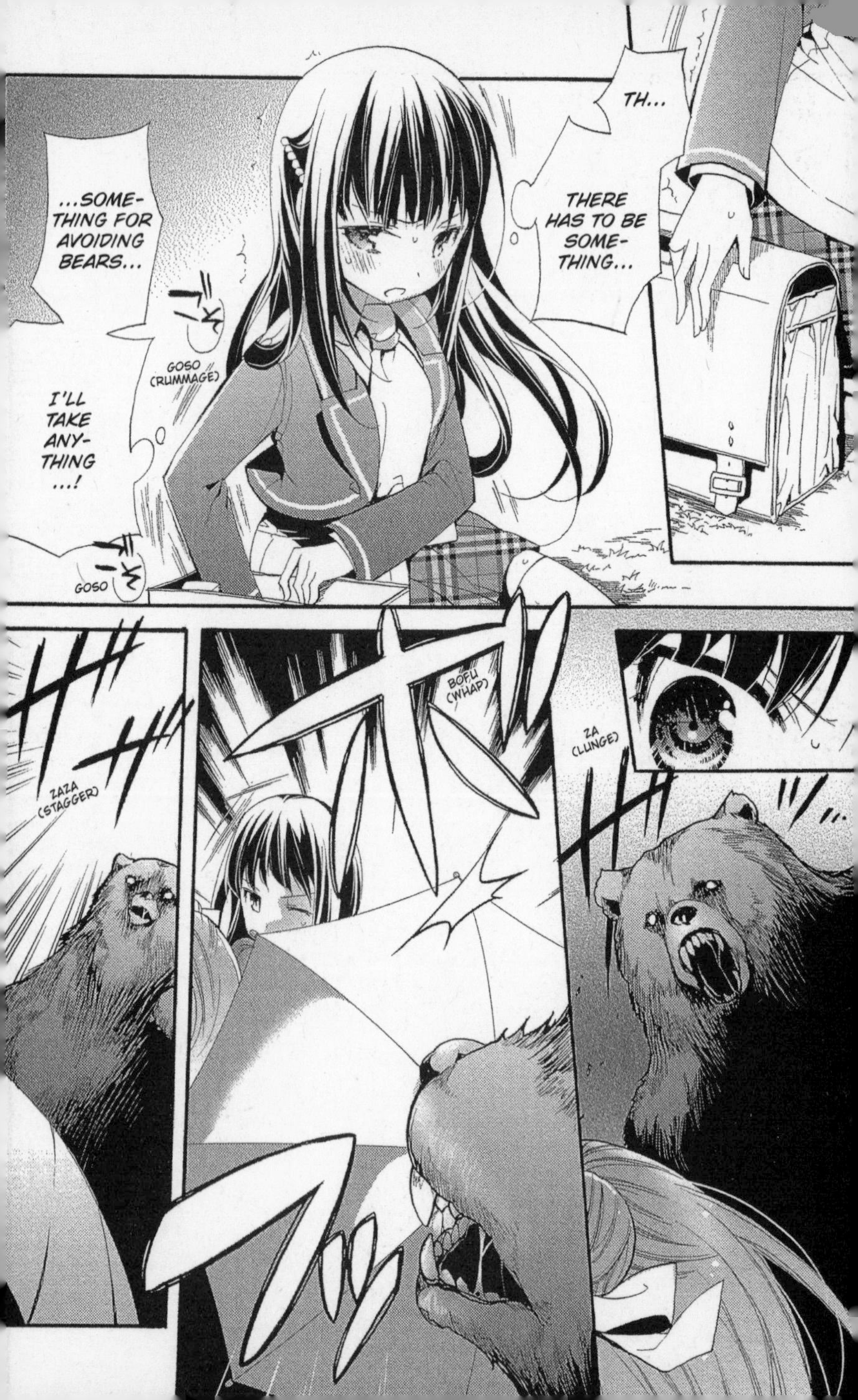
TH...
THERE HAS TO BE SOMETHING...
...SOMETHING FOR AVOIDING BEARS...
GOSO (RUMMAGE)
I'LL TAKE ANYTHING...!
GOSO
ZA (LUNGE)
BOFU (WHAP)
ZAZA (STAGGER)

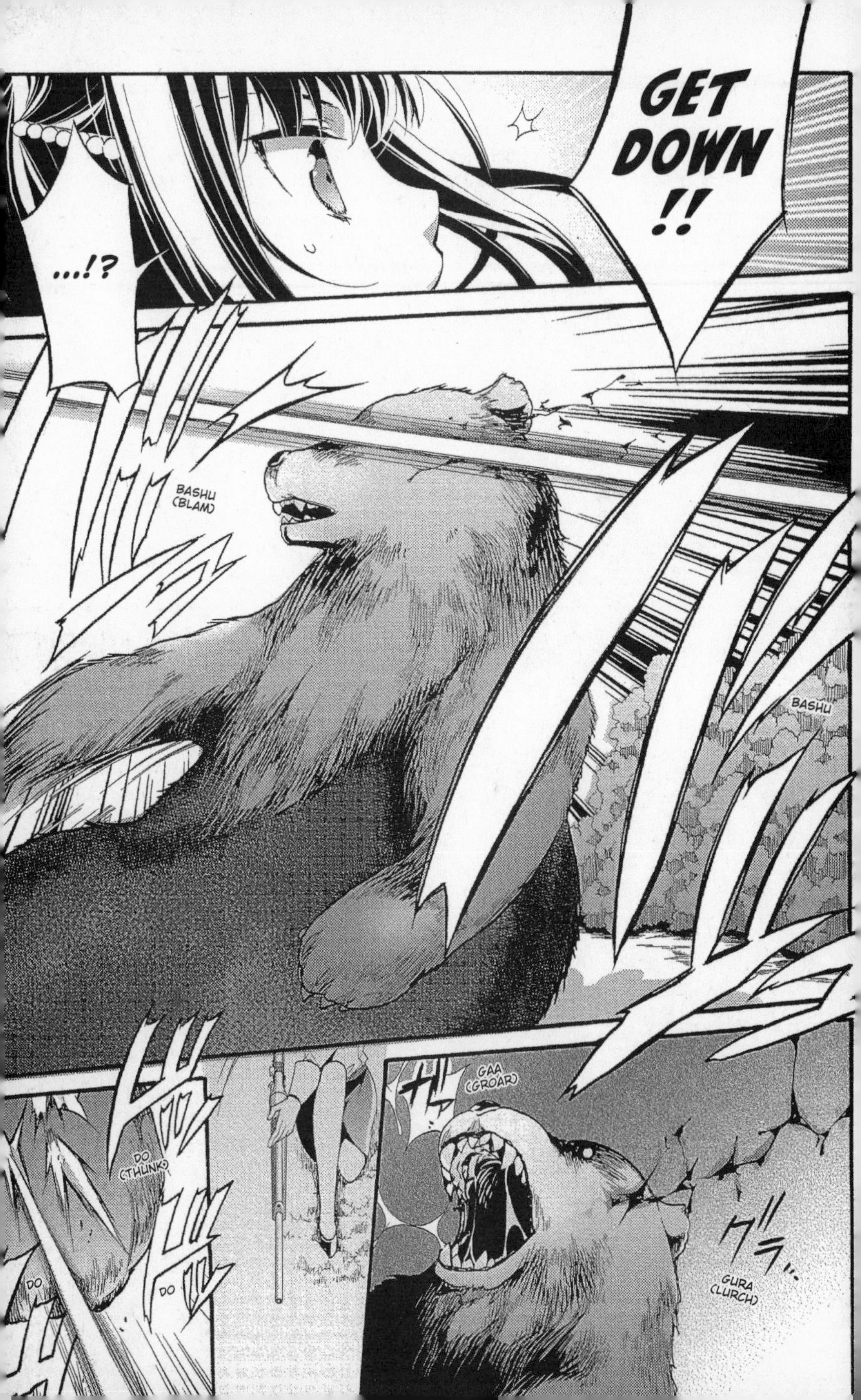
GET DOWN!!
...!?
BASHU (BLAM)
BASHU
GAA (GROAR)
GURA (LURCH)
DO (THUNK)
DO
DO

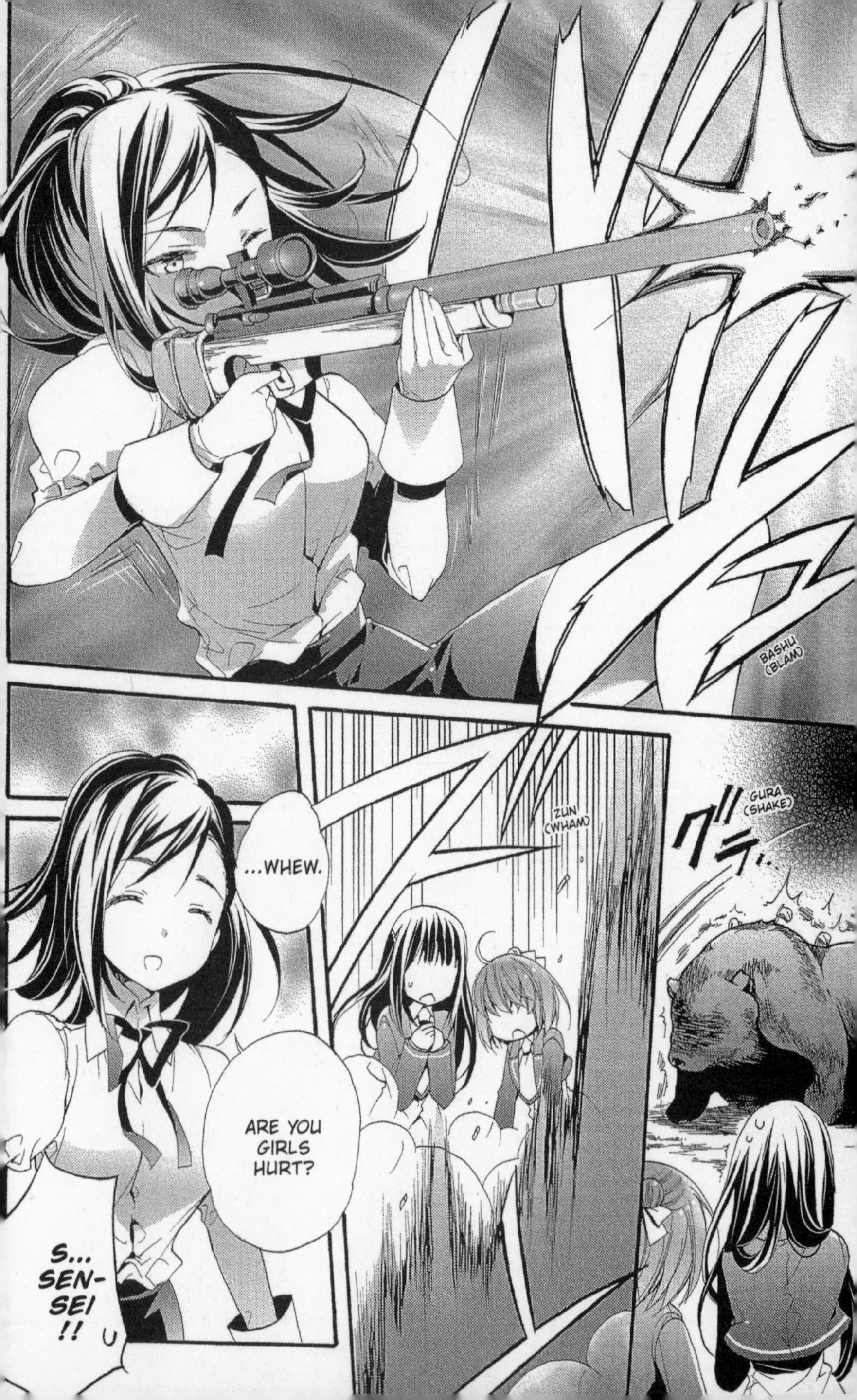
BASHU (BLAM)
GURA (SHAKE)
ZUN (WHAM)
...WHEW.
ARE YOU GIRLS HURT?
S... SEN-SEI!!

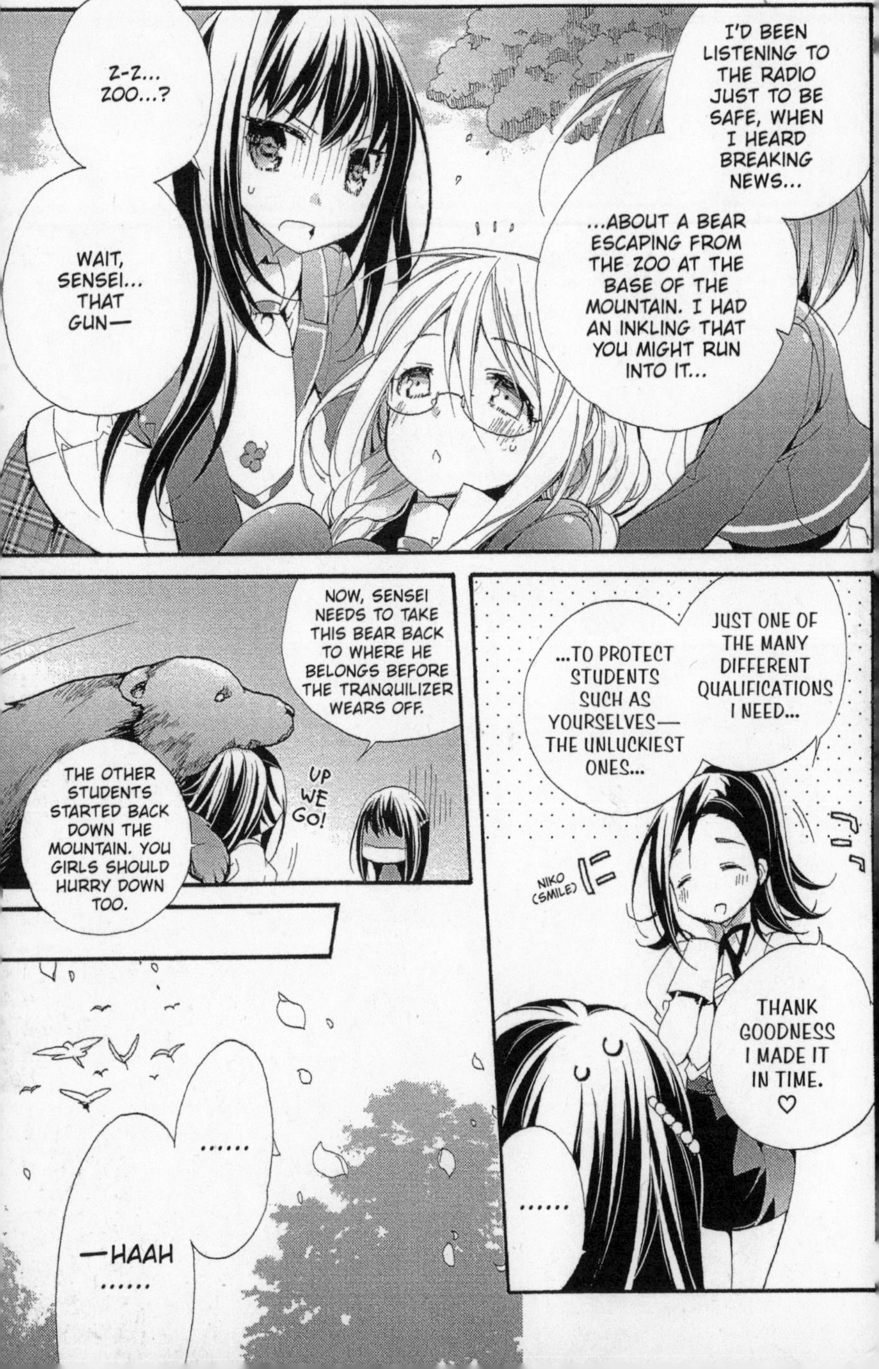
I'D BEEN LISTENING TO THE RADIO JUST TO BE SAFE, WHEN I HEARD BREAKING NEWS...
...ABOUT A BEAR ESCAPING FROM THE ZOO AT THE BASE OF THE MOUNTAIN. I HAD AN INKLING THAT YOU MIGHT RUN INTO IT...
Z-Z... ZOO...?
WAIT, SENSEI... THAT GUN—
JUST ONE OF THE MANY DIFFERENT QUALIFICATIONS I NEED...
...TO PROTECT STUDENTS SUCH AS YOURSELVES—THE UNLUCKIEST ONES...
NIKO (SMILE)
THANK GOODNESS I MADE IT IN TIME. ♡
......
NOW, SENSEI NEEDS TO TAKE THIS BEAR BACK TO WHERE HE BELONGS BEFORE THE TRANQUILIZER WEARS OFF.
UP WE GO!
THE OTHER STUDENTS STARTED BACK DOWN THE MOUNTAIN. YOU GIRLS SHOULD HURRY DOWN TOO.
......
—HAAH ......

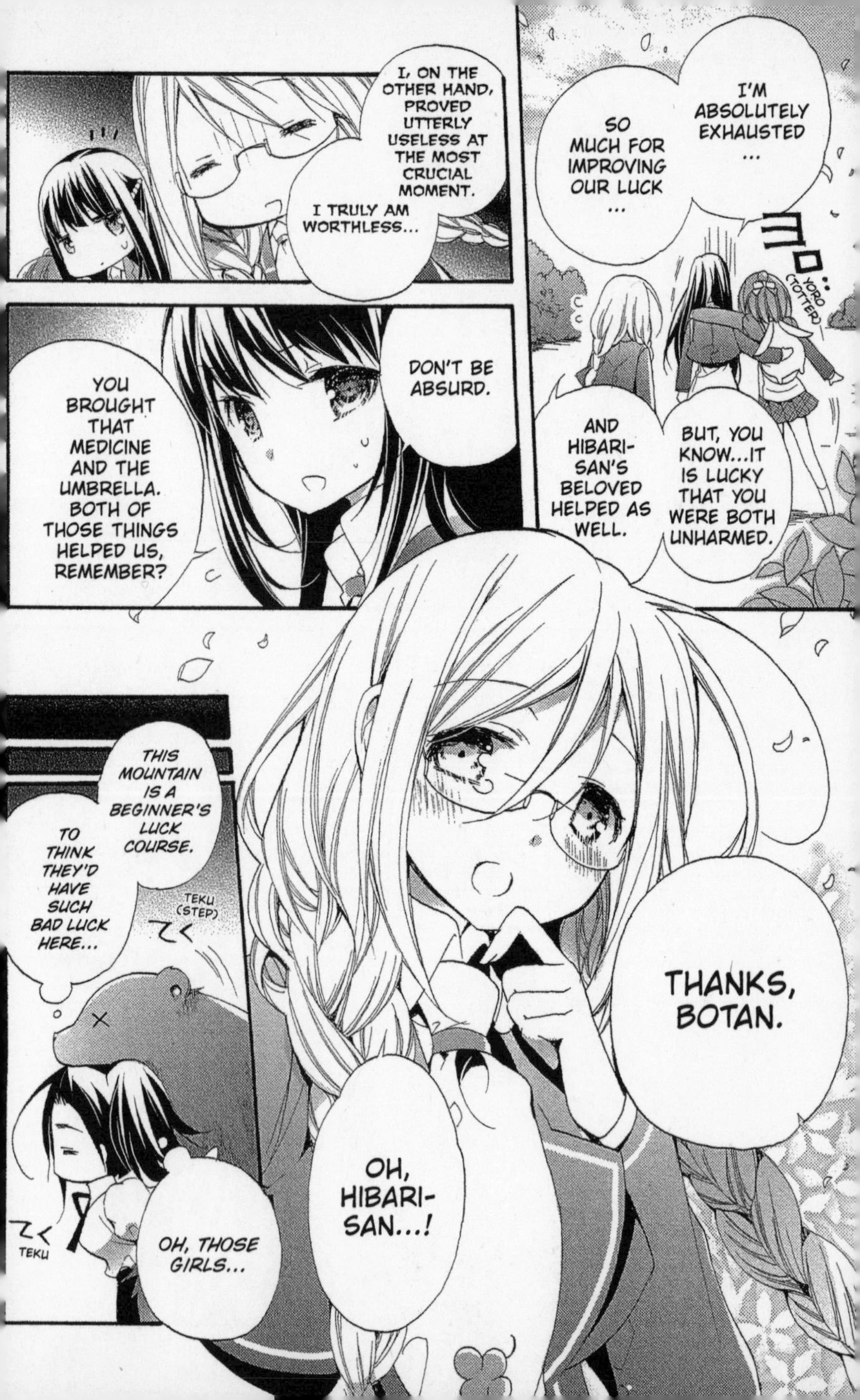
I'M ABSOLUTELY EXHAUSTED...
SO MUCH FOR IMPROVING OUR LUCK...
YORO (TOTTER)
BUT, YOU KNOW...IT IS LUCKY THAT YOU WERE BOTH UNHARMED.
AND HIBARI-SAN'S BELOVED HELPED AS WELL.
I, ON THE OTHER HAND, PROVED UTTERLY USELESS AT THE MOST CRUCIAL MOMENT.
I TRULY AM WORTHLESS...
DON'T BE ABSURD.
YOU BROUGHT THAT MEDICINE AND THE UMBRELLA. BOTH OF THOSE THINGS HELPED US, REMEMBER?
THANKS, BOTAN.
OH, HIBARI-SAN...!
THIS MOUNTAIN IS A BEGINNER'S LUCK COURSE.
TO THINK THEY'D HAVE SUCH BAD LUCK HERE...
TEKU (STEP)
TEKU
OH, THOSE GIRLS...

Anne Happy
unhappy go lucky!

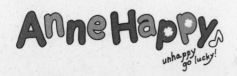

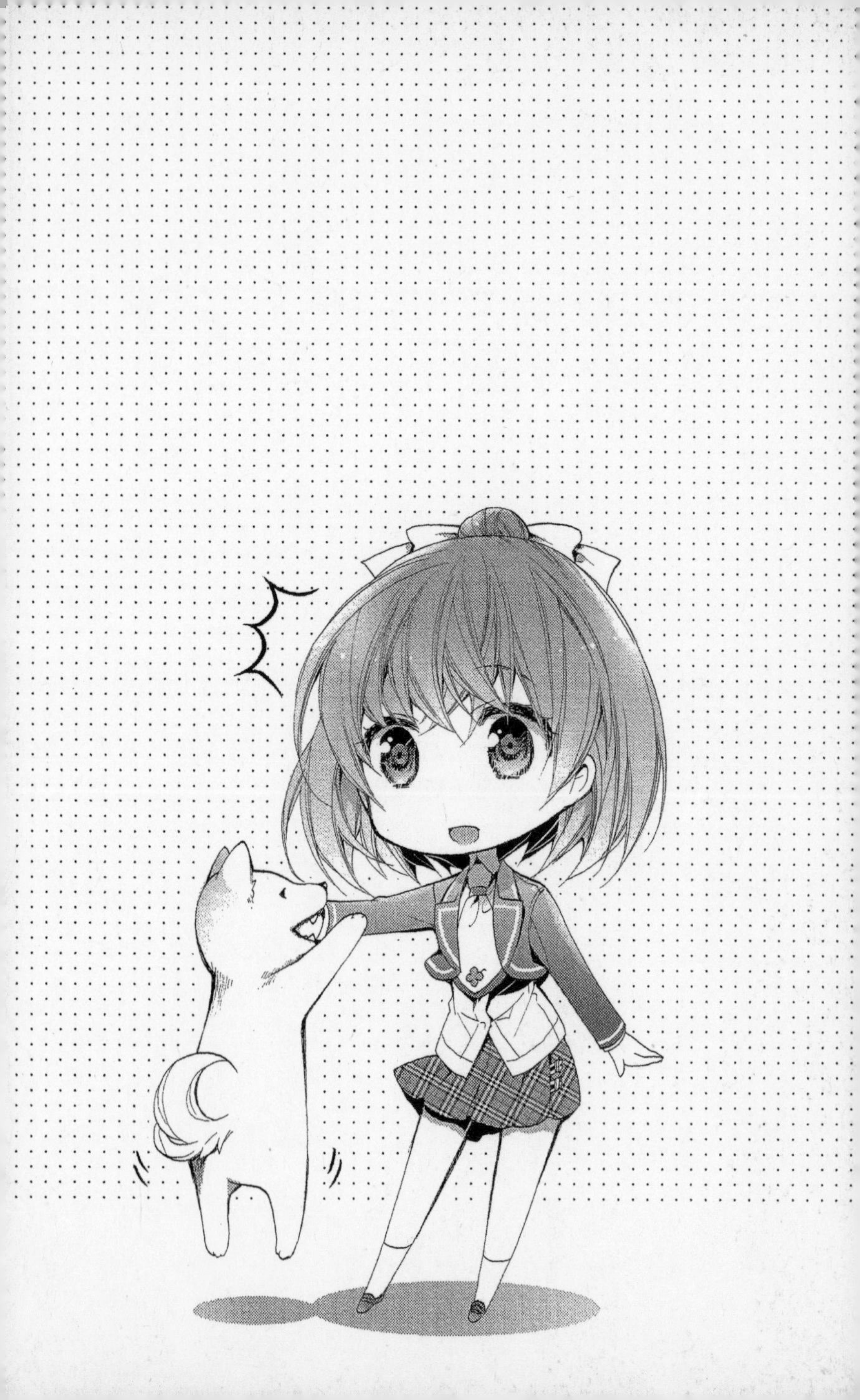

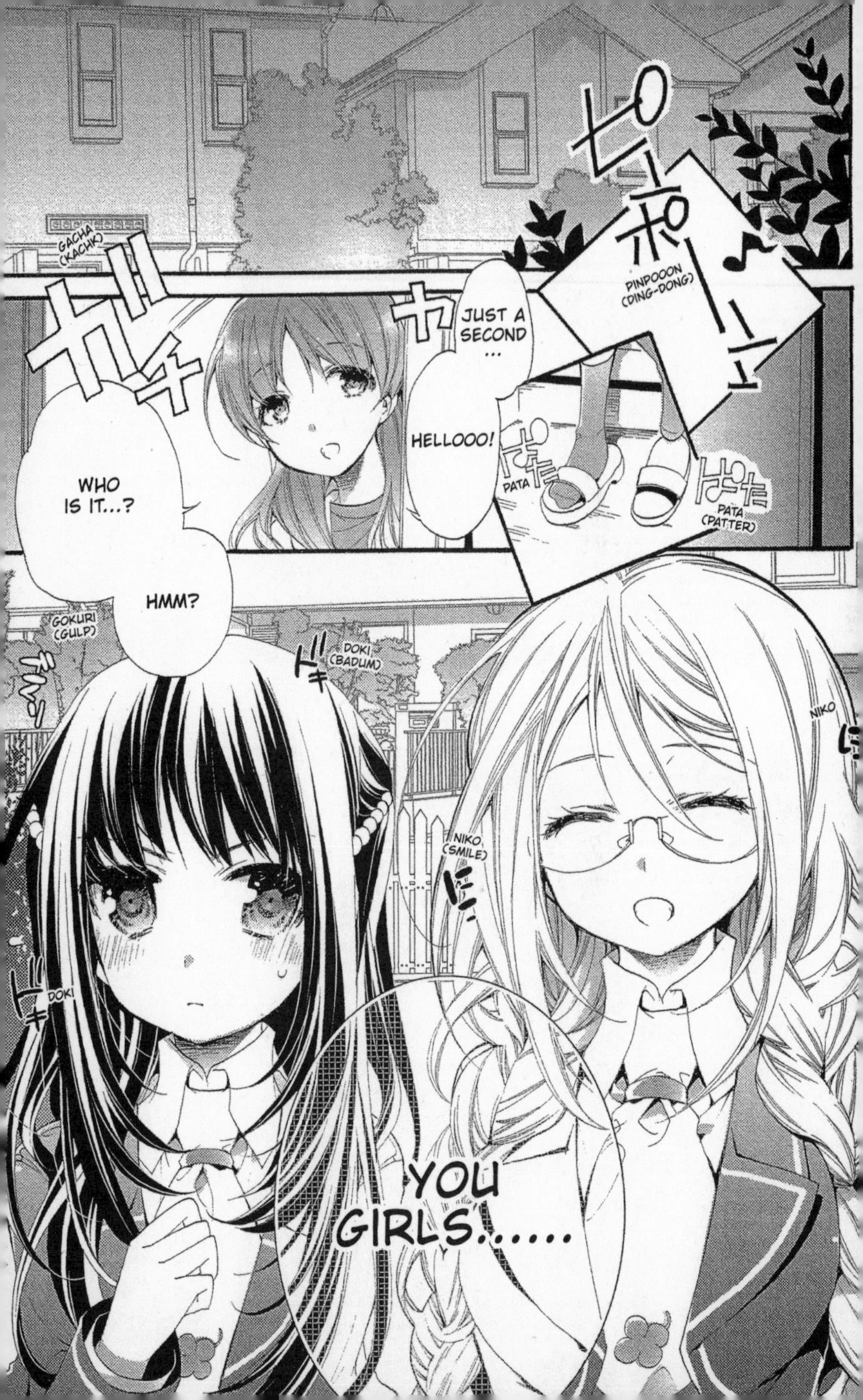
PINPOOOON (DING-DONG)
JUST A SECOND ...
PATA
PATA (PATTER)
GACHA (KACHK)
HELLOOO!
WHO IS IT...?
HMM?
NIKO
NIKO (SMILE)
DOKI (BADUM)
GOKURI (GULP)
DOKI
YOU GIRLS......

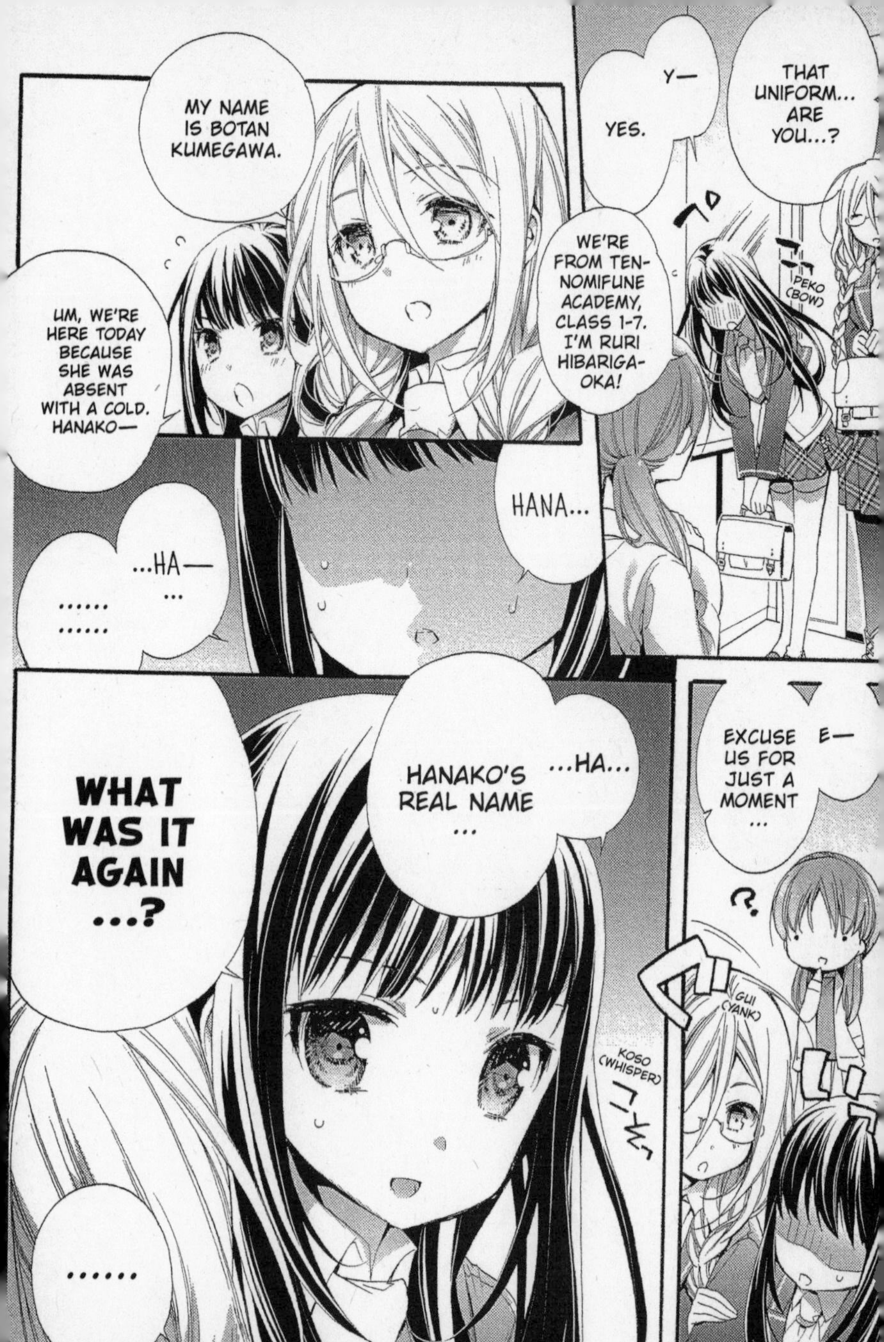
THAT UNIFORM... ARE YOU...?
Y— YES.
WE'RE FROM TEN-NOMIFUNE ACADEMY, CLASS 1-7. I'M RURI HIBARIGA-OKA!
PEKO (BOW)
MY NAME IS BOTAN KUMEGAWA.
UM, WE'RE HERE TODAY BECAUSE SHE WAS ABSENT WITH A COLD. HANAKO—
HANA...
...HA— ... .
E—
EXCUSE US FOR JUST A MOMENT ...
GUI (YANK)
KOSO (WHISPER)
...HA...
HANAKO'S REAL NAME ...
WHAT WAS IT AGAIN ...?
......

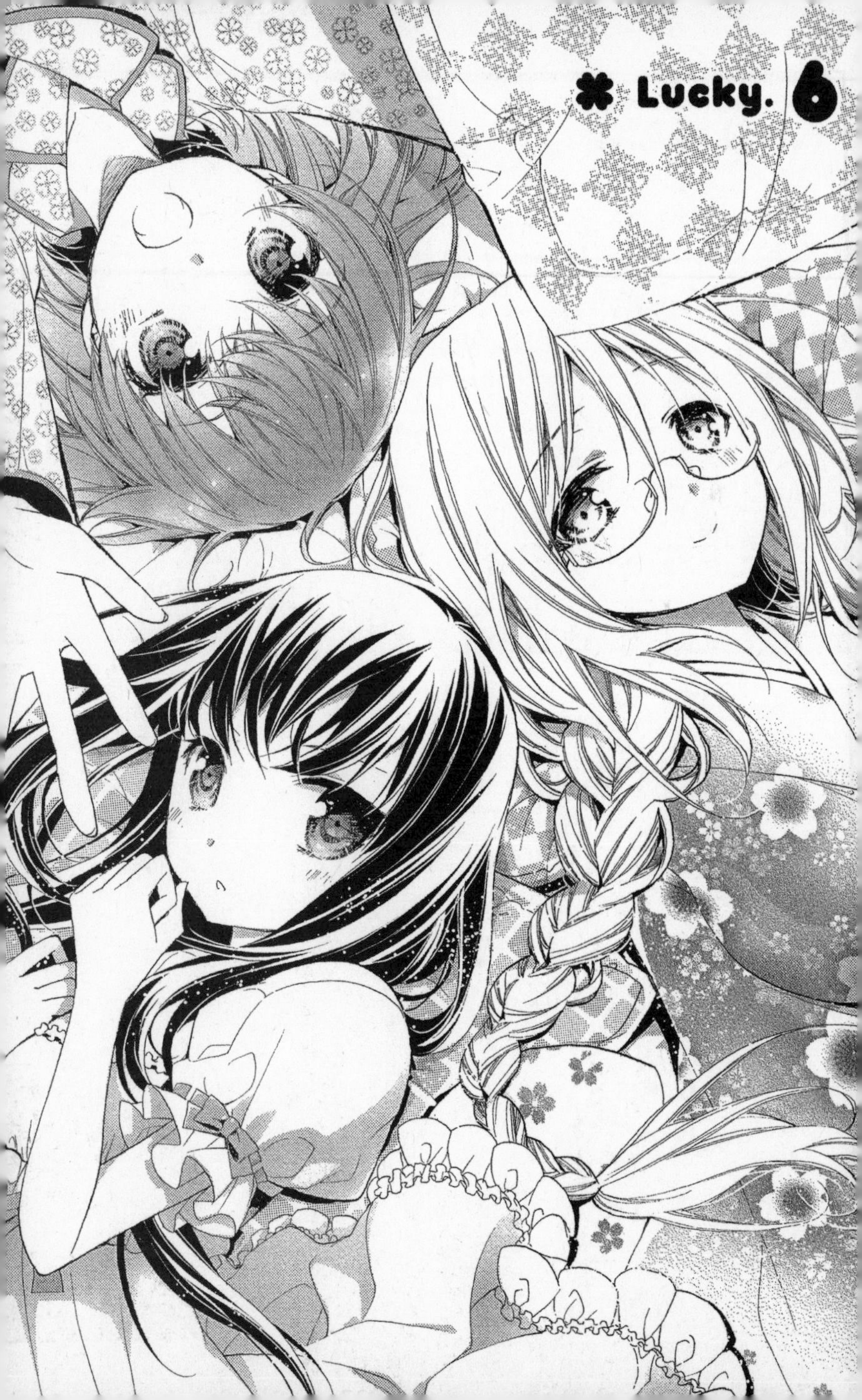
Lucky. 6

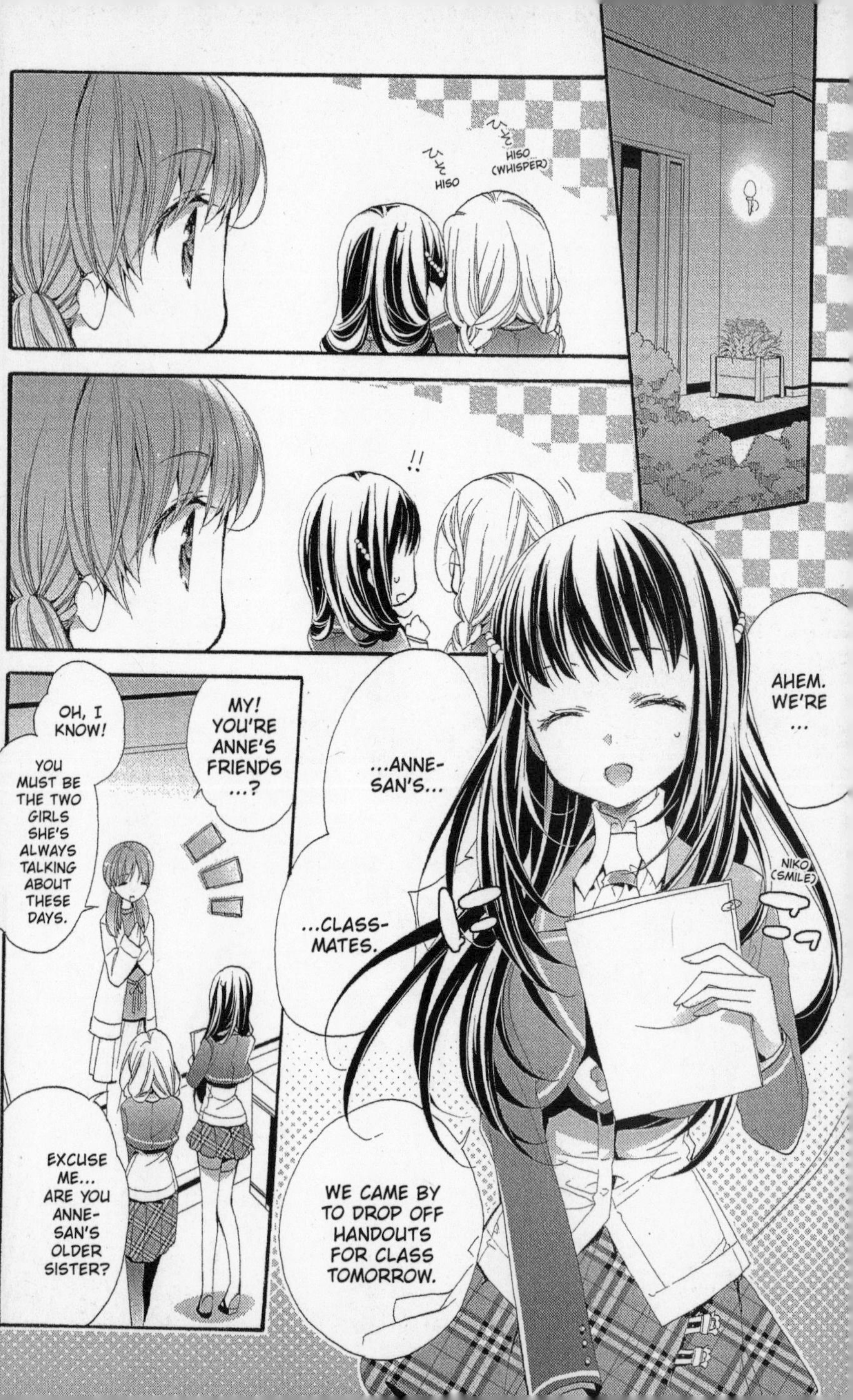
ひそ
HISO... (WHISPER)
ひそ
HISO
!!
AHEM. WE'RE...
NIKO (SMILE)
...ANNE-SAN'S...
...CLASS-MATES.
WE CAME BY TO DROP OFF HANDOUTS FOR CLASS TOMORROW.
MY! YOU'RE ANNE'S FRIENDS...?
OH, I KNOW!
YOU MUST BE THE TWO GIRLS SHE'S ALWAYS TALKING ABOUT THESE DAYS.
EXCUSE ME... ARE YOU ANNE-SAN'S OLDER SISTER?

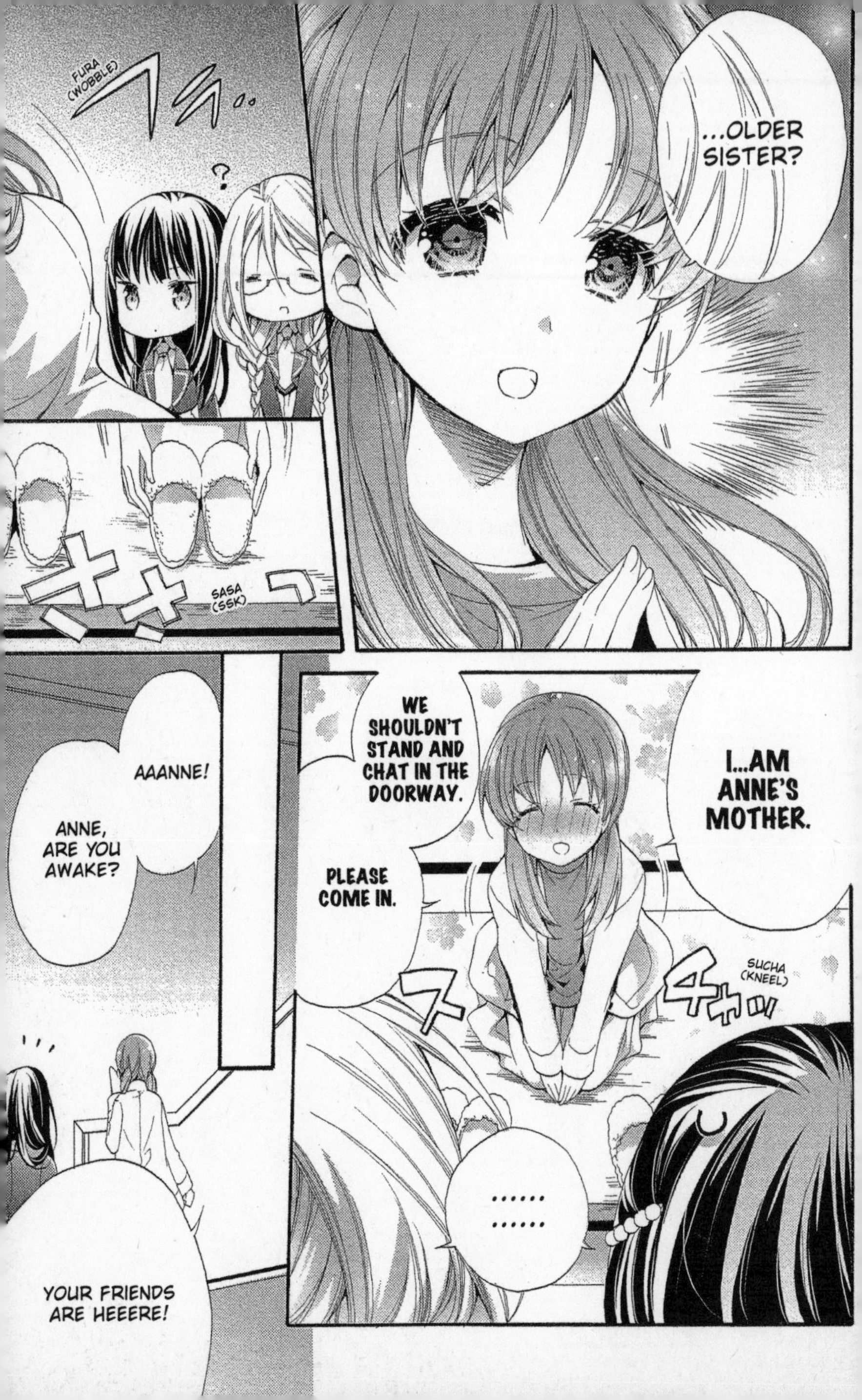
...OLDER SISTER?
FURA (WOBBLE)
SASA (SSK)
I...AM ANNE'S MOTHER.
WE SHOULDN'T STAND AND CHAT IN THE DOORWAY.
PLEASE COME IN.
SUCHA (KNEEL)
......
......
AAANNE!
ANNE, ARE YOU AWAKE?
YOUR FRIENDS ARE HEEERE!

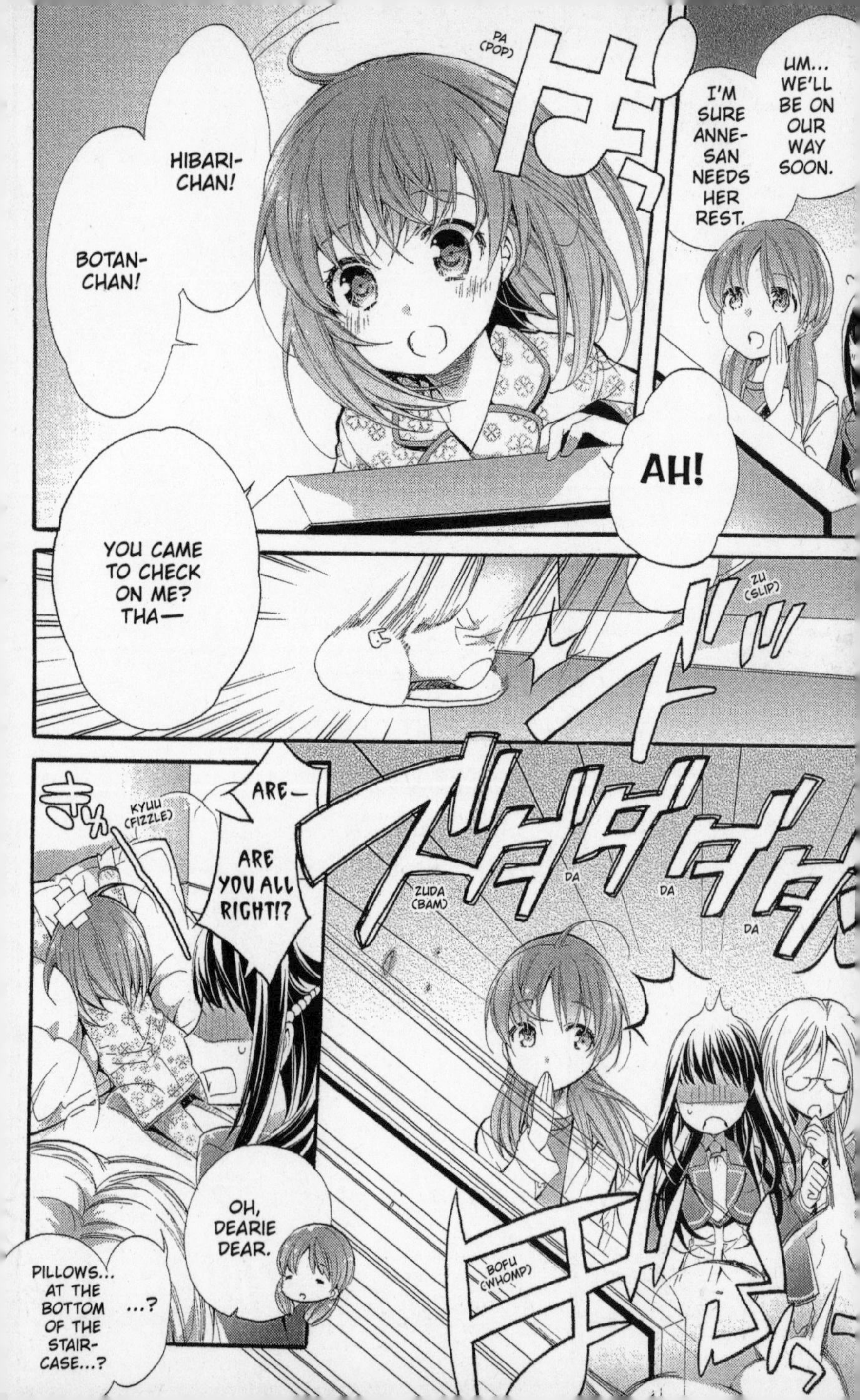
UM... WE'LL BE ON OUR WAY SOON.
I'M SURE ANNE-SAN NEEDS HER REST.
PA (POP)
HIBARI-CHAN!
BOTAN-CHAN!
YOU CAME TO CHECK ON ME? THA—
AH!
ZU (SLIP)
ZUDA (BAM)
DA
DA
DA
BOFU (WHOMP)
ARE—
ARE YOU ALL RIGHT!?
KYUU (FIZZLE)
OH, DEARIE DEAR.
...?
PILLOWS... AT THE BOTTOM OF THE STAIR-CASE...?

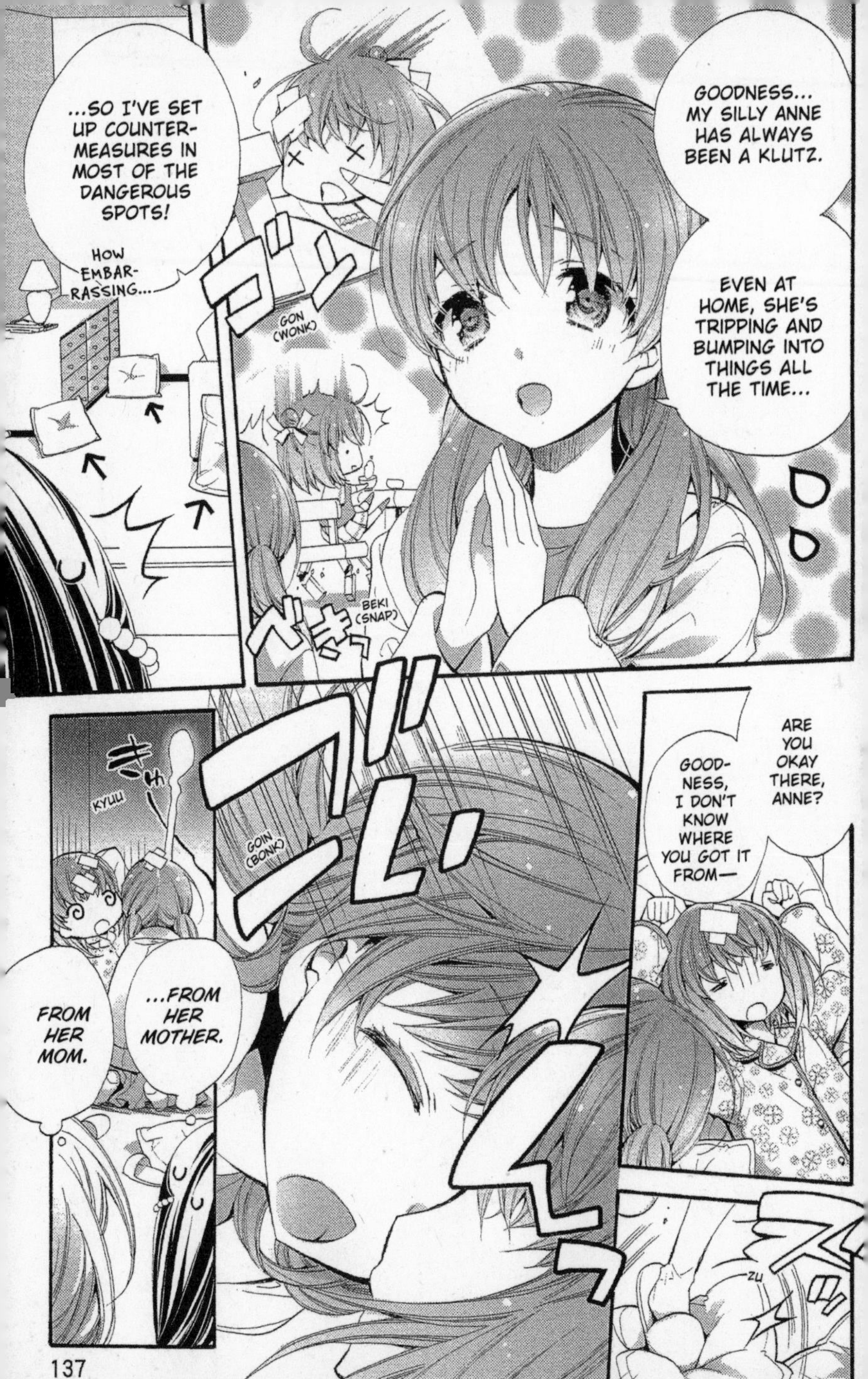
GOODNESS... MY SILLY ANNE HAS ALWAYS BEEN A KLUTZ.
EVEN AT HOME, SHE'S TRIPPING AND BUMPING INTO THINGS ALL THE TIME...
GON (WONK)
BEKI (SNAP)
...SO I'VE SET UP COUNTER-MEASURES IN MOST OF THE DANGEROUS SPOTS!
HOW EMBARRASSING...
ARE YOU OKAY THERE, ANNE?
GOODNESS, I DON'T KNOW WHERE YOU GOT IT FROM—
GOIN (BONK)
ZU
KYUU
...FROM HER MOTHER.
FROM HER MOM.

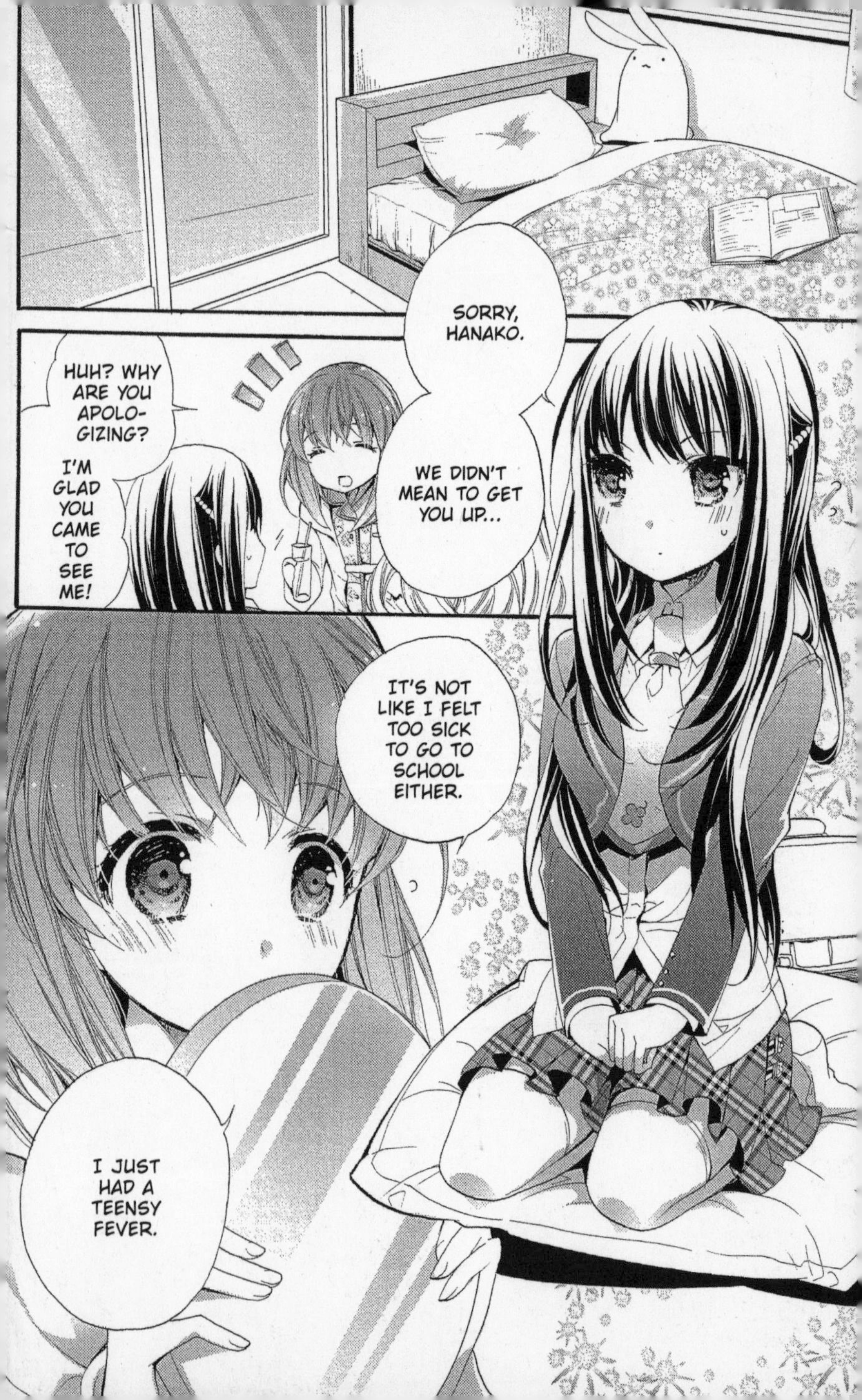
SORRY, HANAKO.
WE DIDN'T MEAN TO GET YOU UP...
HUH? WHY ARE YOU APOLOGIZING?
I'M GLAD YOU CAME TO SEE ME!
IT'S NOT LIKE I FELT TOO SICK TO GO TO SCHOOL EITHER.
I JUST HAD A TEENSY FEVER.

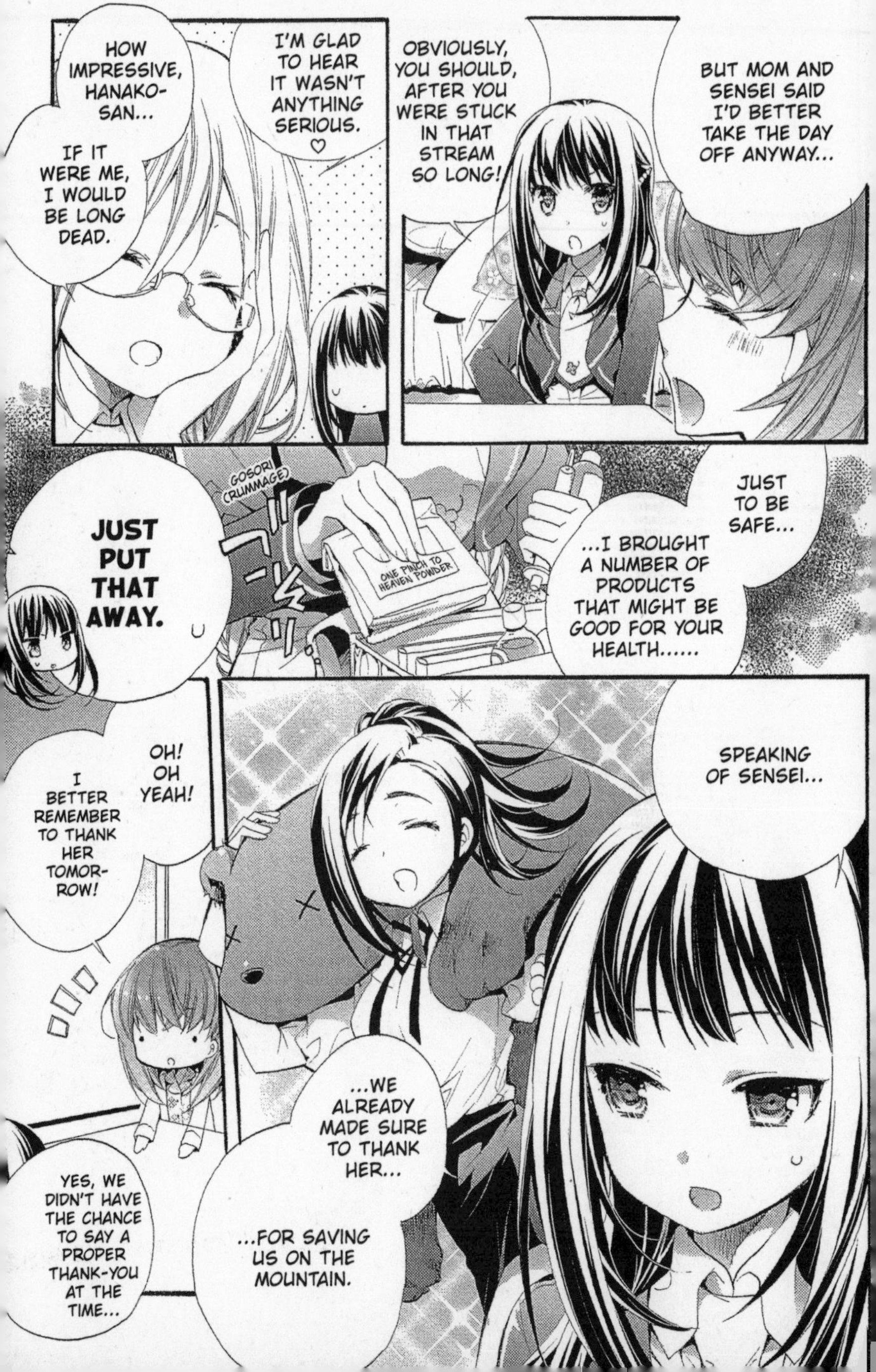
BUT MOM AND SENSEI SAID I'D BETTER TAKE THE DAY OFF ANYWAY...
OBVIOUSLY, YOU SHOULD, AFTER YOU WERE STUCK IN THAT STREAM SO LONG!
I'M GLAD TO HEAR IT WASN'T ANYTHING SERIOUS. ♡
HOW IMPRESSIVE, HANAKO-SAN...
IF IT WERE ME, I WOULD BE LONG DEAD.
JUST TO BE SAFE...
...I BROUGHT A NUMBER OF PRODUCTS THAT MIGHT BE GOOD FOR YOUR HEALTH......
GOSORI (RUMMAGE)
ONE PINCH TO HEAVEN POWDER
JUST PUT THAT AWAY.
SPEAKING OF SENSEI...
...WE ALREADY MADE SURE TO THANK HER...
...FOR SAVING US ON THE MOUNTAIN.
YES, WE DIDN'T HAVE THE CHANCE TO SAY A PROPER THANK-YOU AT THE TIME...
OH! OH YEAH!
I BETTER REMEMBER TO THANK HER TOMORROW!

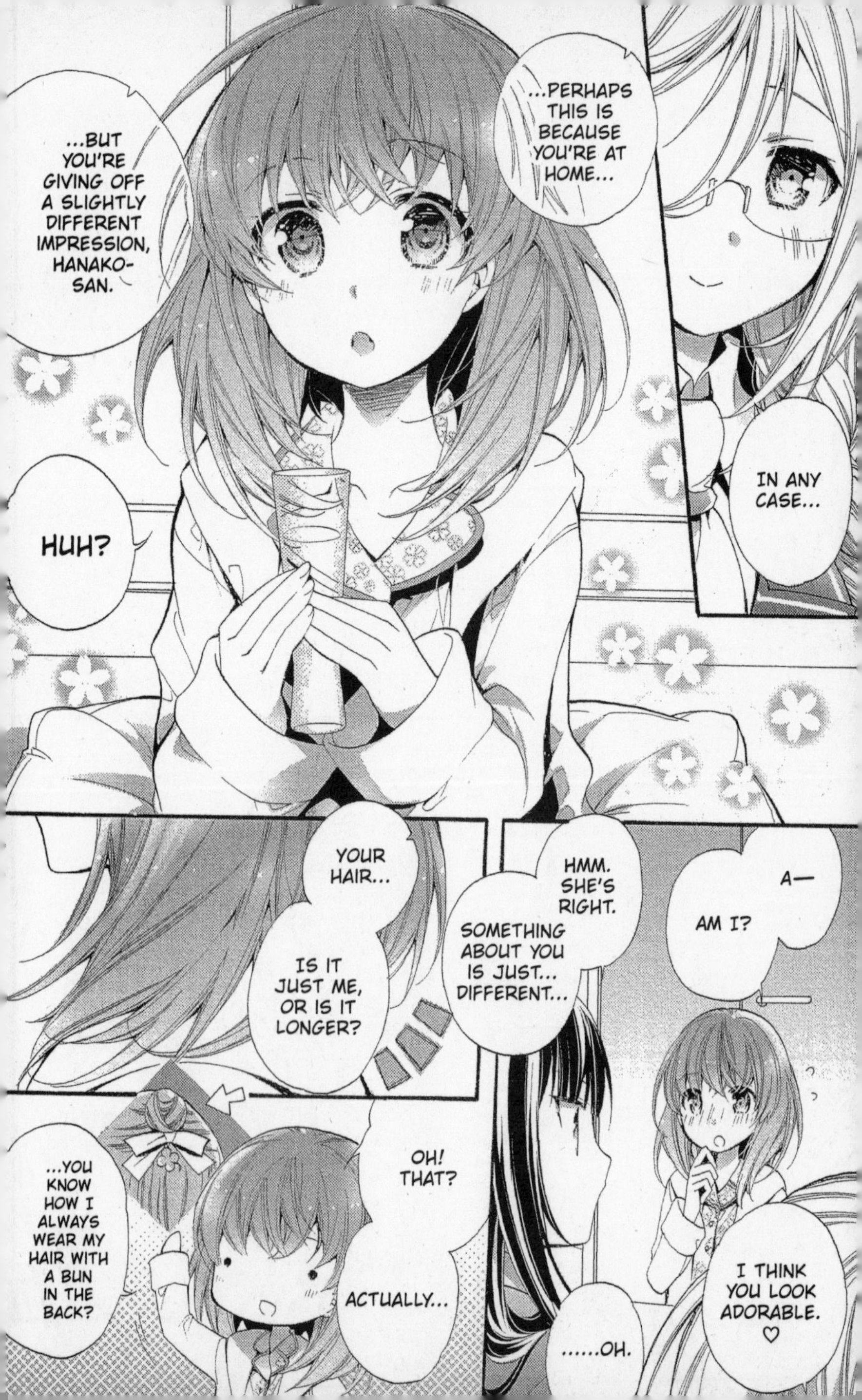
...PERHAPS THIS IS BECAUSE YOU'RE AT HOME...
...BUT YOU'RE GIVING OFF A SLIGHTLY DIFFERENT IMPRESSION, HANAKO-SAN.
IN ANY CASE...
HUH?
A—
AM I?
HMM. SHE'S RIGHT.
SOMETHING ABOUT YOU IS JUST... DIFFERENT...
I THINK YOU LOOK ADORABLE. ♡
......OH.
YOUR HAIR...
IS IT JUST ME, OR IS IT LONGER?
OH! THAT?
...YOU KNOW HOW I ALWAYS WEAR MY HAIR WITH A BUN IN THE BACK?
ACTUALLY...

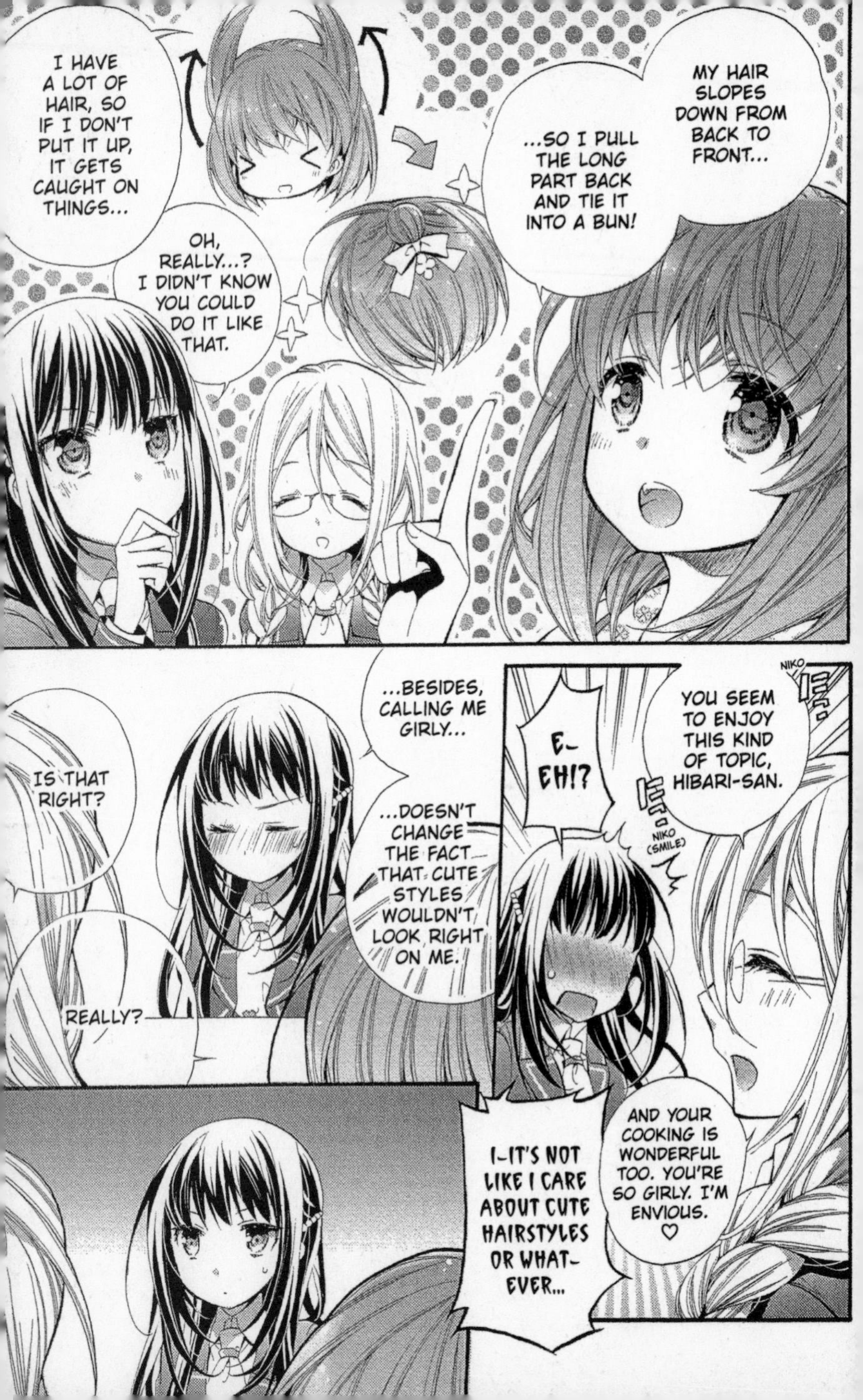
MY HAIR SLOPES DOWN FROM BACK TO FRONT...
...SO I PULL THE LONG PART BACK AND TIE IT INTO A BUN!
I HAVE A LOT OF HAIR, SO IF I DON'T PUT IT UP, IT GETS CAUGHT ON THINGS...
OH, REALLY...? I DIDN'T KNOW YOU COULD DO IT LIKE THAT.
NIKO
YOU SEEM TO ENJOY THIS KIND OF TOPIC, HIBARI-SAN.
NIKO (SMILE)
E- EH!?
AND YOUR COOKING IS WONDERFUL TOO. YOU'RE SO GIRLY. I'M ENVIOUS. ♡
I-IT'S NOT LIKE I CARE ABOUT CUTE HAIRSTYLES OR WHAT-EVER...
...BESIDES, CALLING ME GIRLY...
...DOESN'T CHANGE THE FACT THAT CUTE STYLES WOULDN'T LOOK RIGHT ON ME.
IS THAT RIGHT?
REALLY?

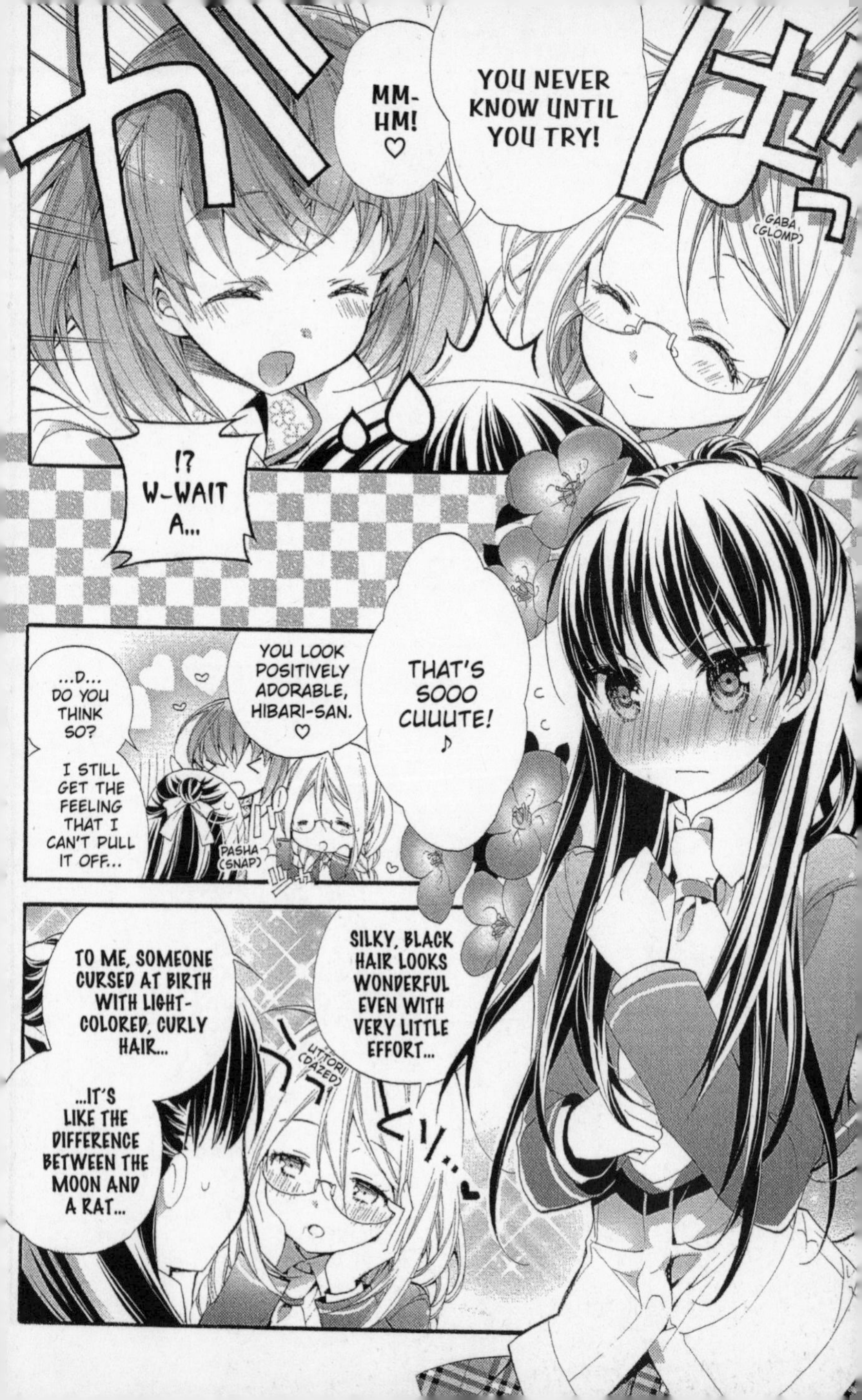
GABA (GLOMP)
YOU NEVER KNOW UNTIL YOU TRY!
MM-HM! ♡
!? W-WAIT A...
THAT'S SOOO CUUUTE! ♪
YOU LOOK POSITIVELY ADORABLE, HIBARI-SAN. ♡
...D... DO YOU THINK SO?
I STILL GET THE FEELING THAT I CAN'T PULL IT OFF...
PASHA (SNAP)
SILKY, BLACK HAIR LOOKS WONDERFUL EVEN WITH VERY LITTLE EFFORT...
UTTORI (DAZED)
TO ME, SOMEONE CURSED AT BIRTH WITH LIGHT-COLORED, CURLY HAIR...
...IT'S LIKE THE DIFFERENCE BETWEEN THE MOON AND A RAT...

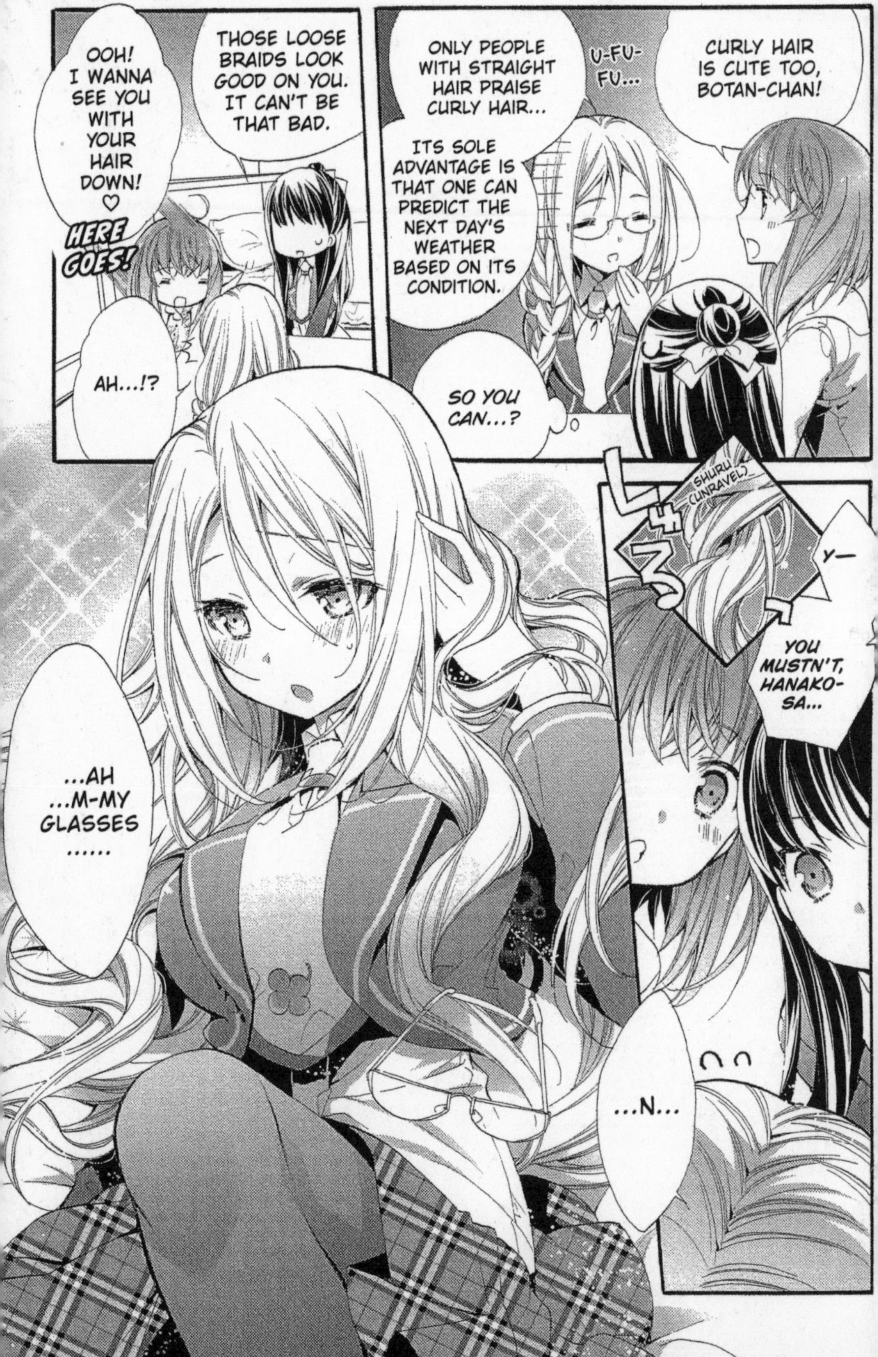
CURLY HAIR IS CUTE TOO, BOTAN-CHAN!
U-FU-FU...
ONLY PEOPLE WITH STRAIGHT HAIR PRAISE CURLY HAIR...
ITS SOLE ADVANTAGE IS THAT ONE CAN PREDICT THE NEXT DAY'S WEATHER BASED ON ITS CONDITION.
SO YOU CAN...?
THOSE LOOSE BRAIDS LOOK GOOD ON YOU. IT CAN'T BE THAT BAD.
OOH! I WANNA SEE YOU WITH YOUR HAIR DOWN! ♡
HERE GOES!
AH...!?
SHURU (UNRAVEL)
Y—
YOU MUSTN'T, HANAKO-SA...
...AH ...M-MY GLASSES ......
...N...

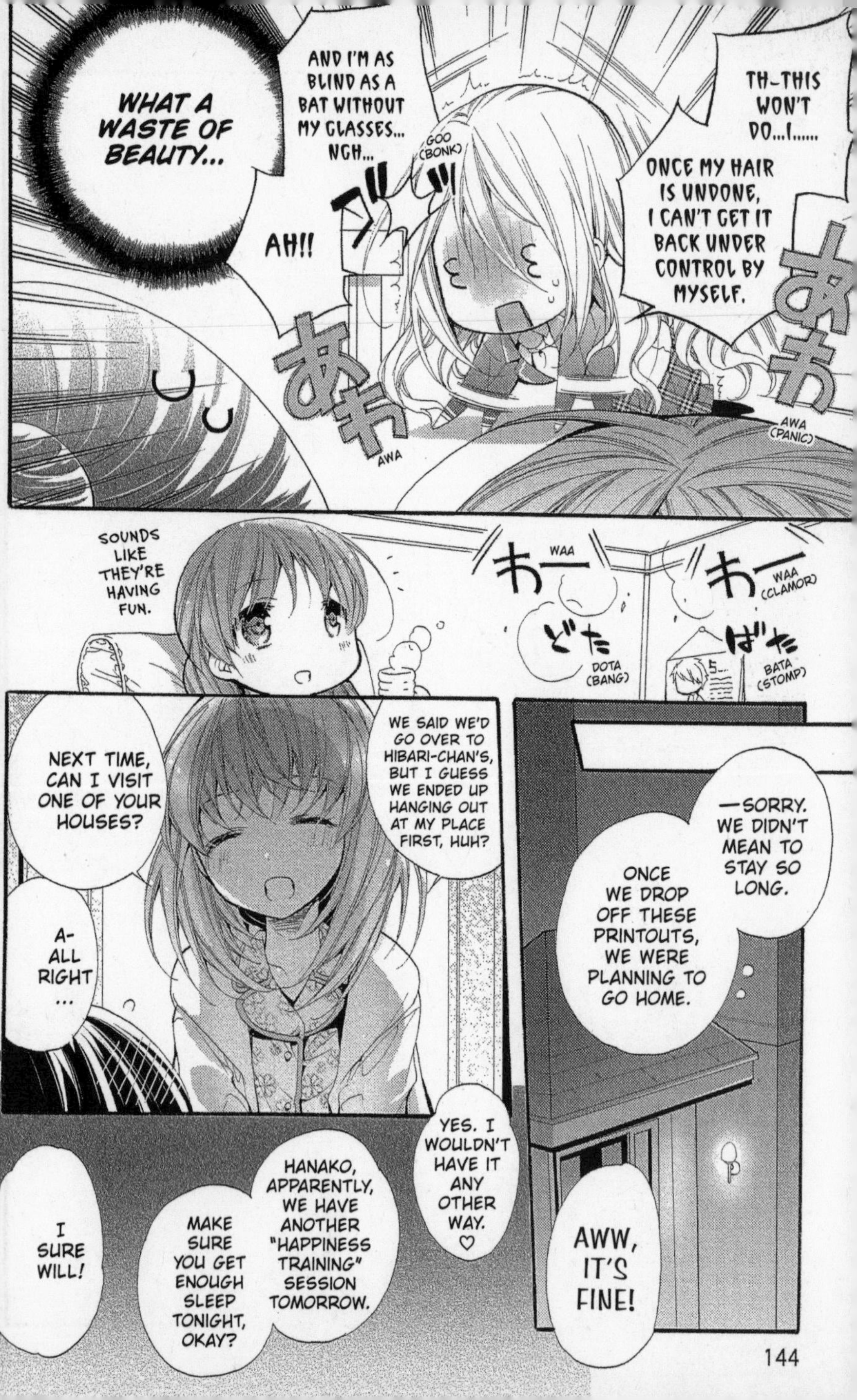

TH-THIS WON'T DO...I......
ONCE MY HAIR IS UNDONE, I CAN'T GET IT BACK UNDER CONTROL BY MYSELF.
AWA (PANIC)
AND I'M AS BLIND AS A BAT WITHOUT MY GLASSES... NGH...
GOO (BONK)
AH!!
WHAT A WASTE OF BEAUTY...
AWA
WAA (CLAMOR)
BATA (STOMP)
WAA
DOTA (BANG)
SOUNDS LIKE THEY'RE HAVING FUN.
—SORRY. WE DIDN'T MEAN TO STAY SO LONG.
ONCE WE DROP OFF THESE PRINTOUTS, WE WERE PLANNING TO GO HOME.
AWW, IT'S FINE!
WE SAID WE'D GO OVER TO HIBARI-CHAN'S, BUT I GUESS WE ENDED UP HANGING OUT AT MY PLACE FIRST, HUH?
NEXT TIME, CAN I VISIT ONE OF YOUR HOUSES?
A-ALL RIGHT...
YES. I WOULDN'T HAVE IT ANY OTHER WAY. ♡
HANAKO, APPARENTLY, WE HAVE ANOTHER "HAPPINESS TRAINING" SESSION TOMORROW.
MAKE SURE YOU GET ENOUGH SLEEP TONIGHT, OKAY?
I SURE WILL!

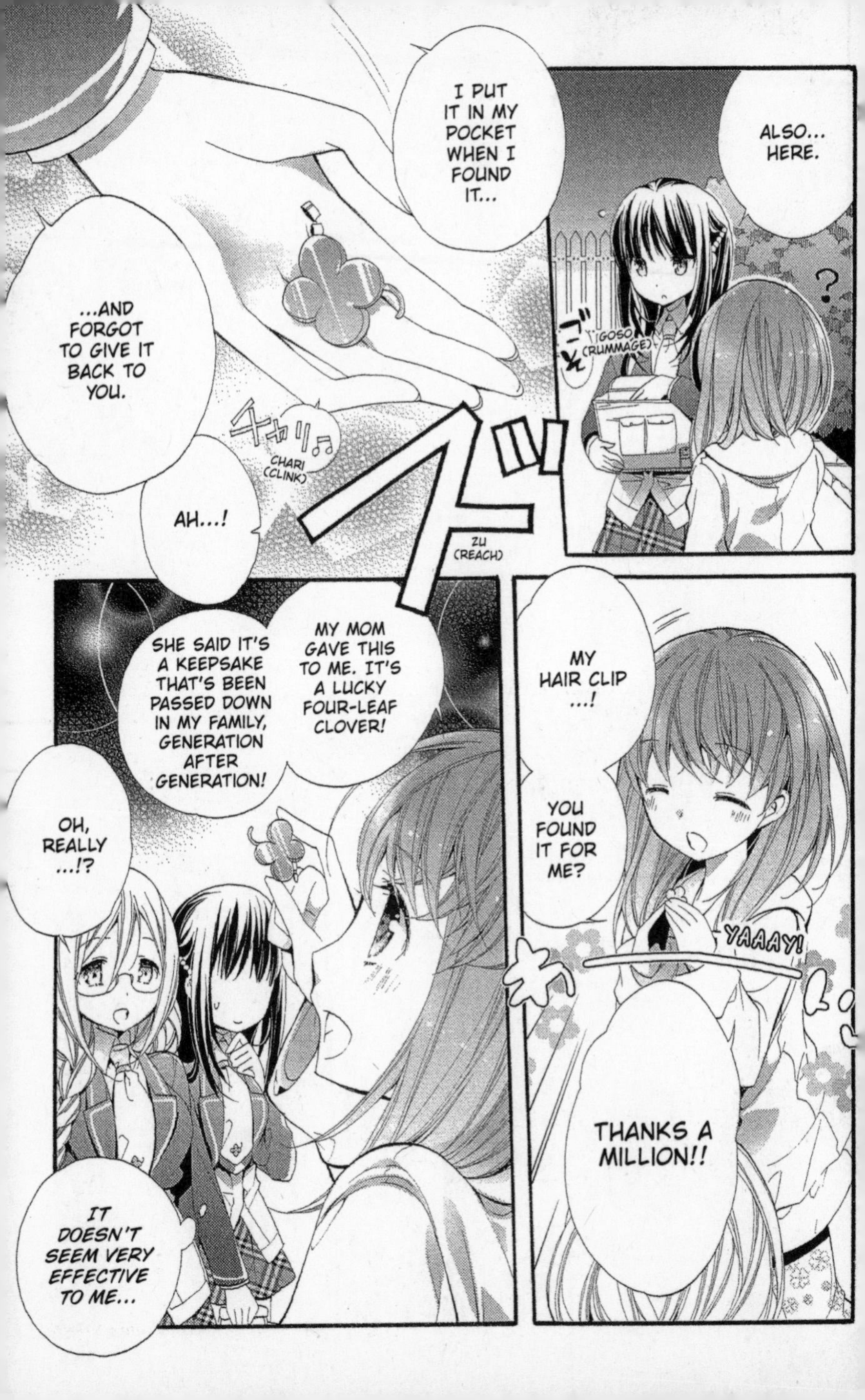
ALSO... HERE.
GOSO (RUMMAGE)
I PUT IT IN MY POCKET WHEN I FOUND IT...
...AND FORGOT TO GIVE IT BACK TO YOU.
CHARI (CLINK)
AH...!
ZU (REACH)
MY HAIR CLIP...!
YOU FOUND IT FOR ME?
YAAAY!
THANKS A MILLION!!
MY MOM GAVE THIS TO ME. IT'S A LUCKY FOUR-LEAF CLOVER!
SHE SAID IT'S A KEEPSAKE THAT'S BEEN PASSED DOWN IN MY FAMILY, GENERATION AFTER GENERATION!
OH, REALLY...!?
IT DOESN'T SEEM VERY EFFECTIVE TO ME...

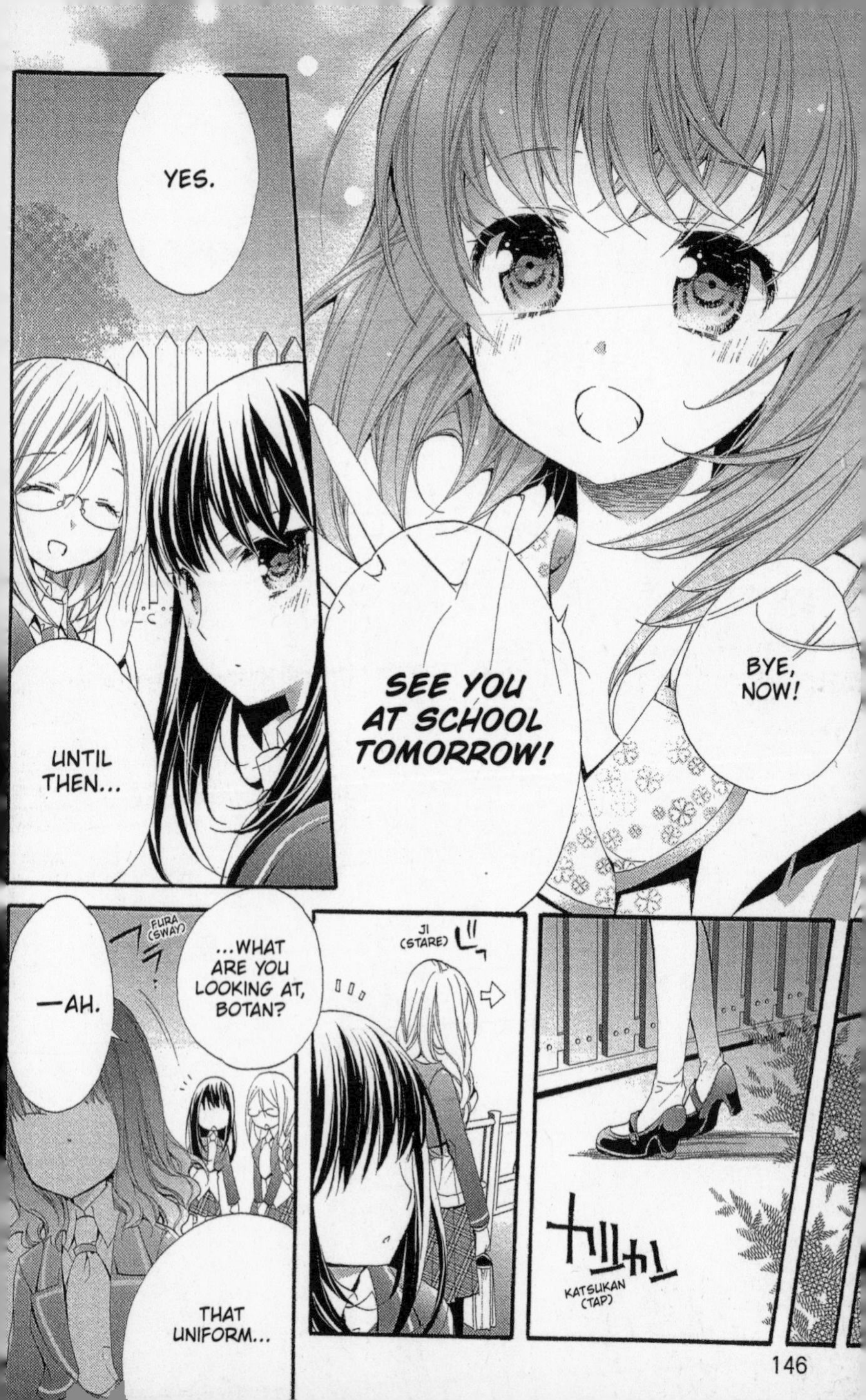
BYE, NOW!
SEE YOU AT SCHOOL TOMORROW!
YES.
UNTIL THEN...
カツカン
KATSUKAN (TAP)
JI (STARE)
FURA (SWAY)
...WHAT ARE YOU LOOKING AT, BOTAN?
—AH.
THAT UNIFORM...

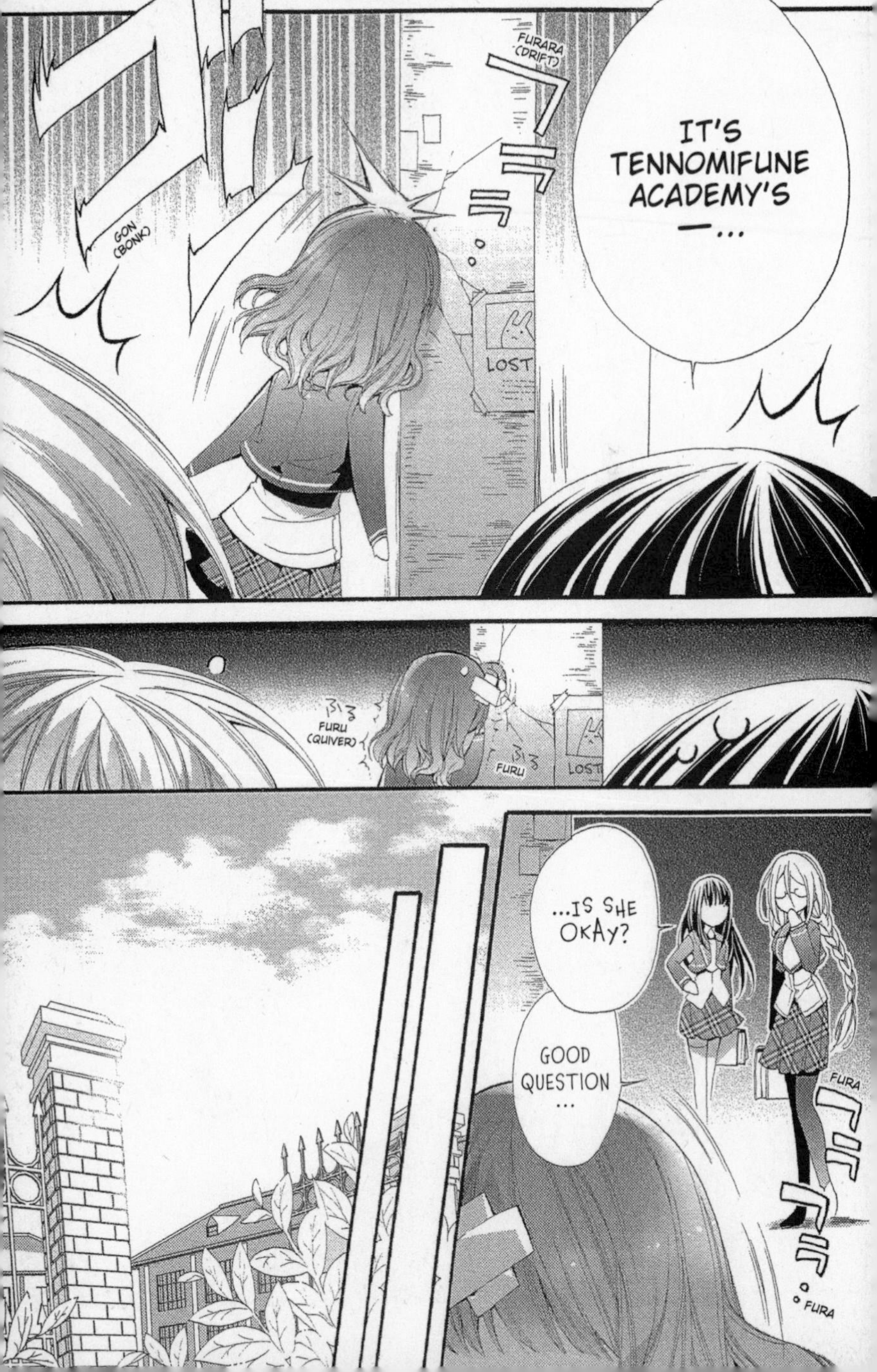
IT'S TENNOMIFUNE ACADEMY'S —...
FURARA (DRIFT)
GON (BONK)
LOST
ふる FURU
ふる FURU (QUIVER)
LOST
...IS SHE OKAY?
GOOD QUESTION ...
FURA
FURA

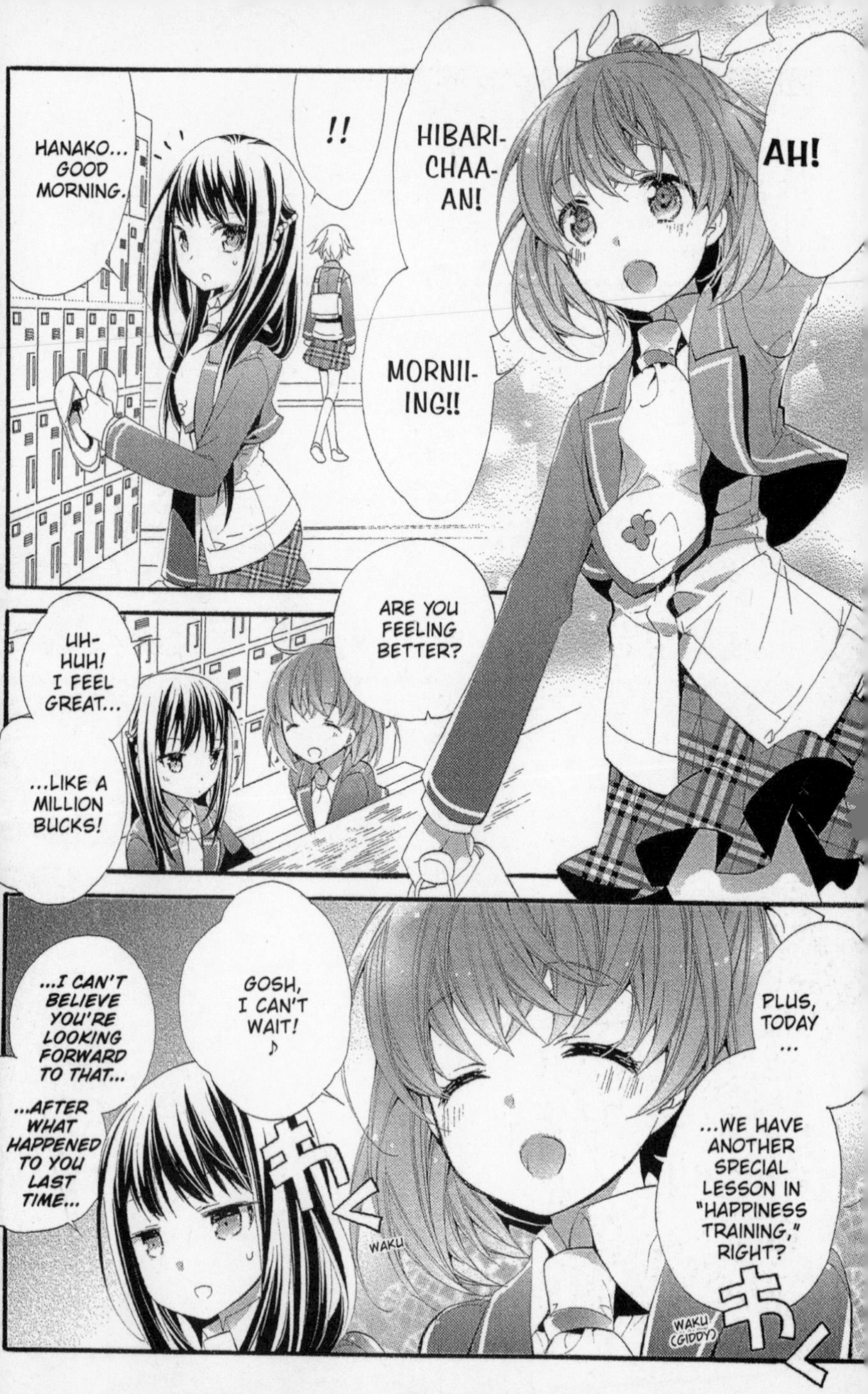
AH!
HIBARI-CHAAA-AN!
MORNII-ING!!
!!
HANAKO... GOOD MORNING.
ARE YOU FEELING BETTER?
UH-HUH! I FEEL GREAT...
...LIKE A MILLION BUCKS!
PLUS, TODAY...
...WE HAVE ANOTHER SPECIAL LESSON IN "HAPPINESS TRAINING," RIGHT?
WAKU (GIDDY)
GOSH, I CAN'T WAIT! ♪
WAKU
...I CAN'T BELIEVE YOU'RE LOOKING FORWARD TO THAT...
...AFTER WHAT HAPPENED TO YOU LAST TIME...

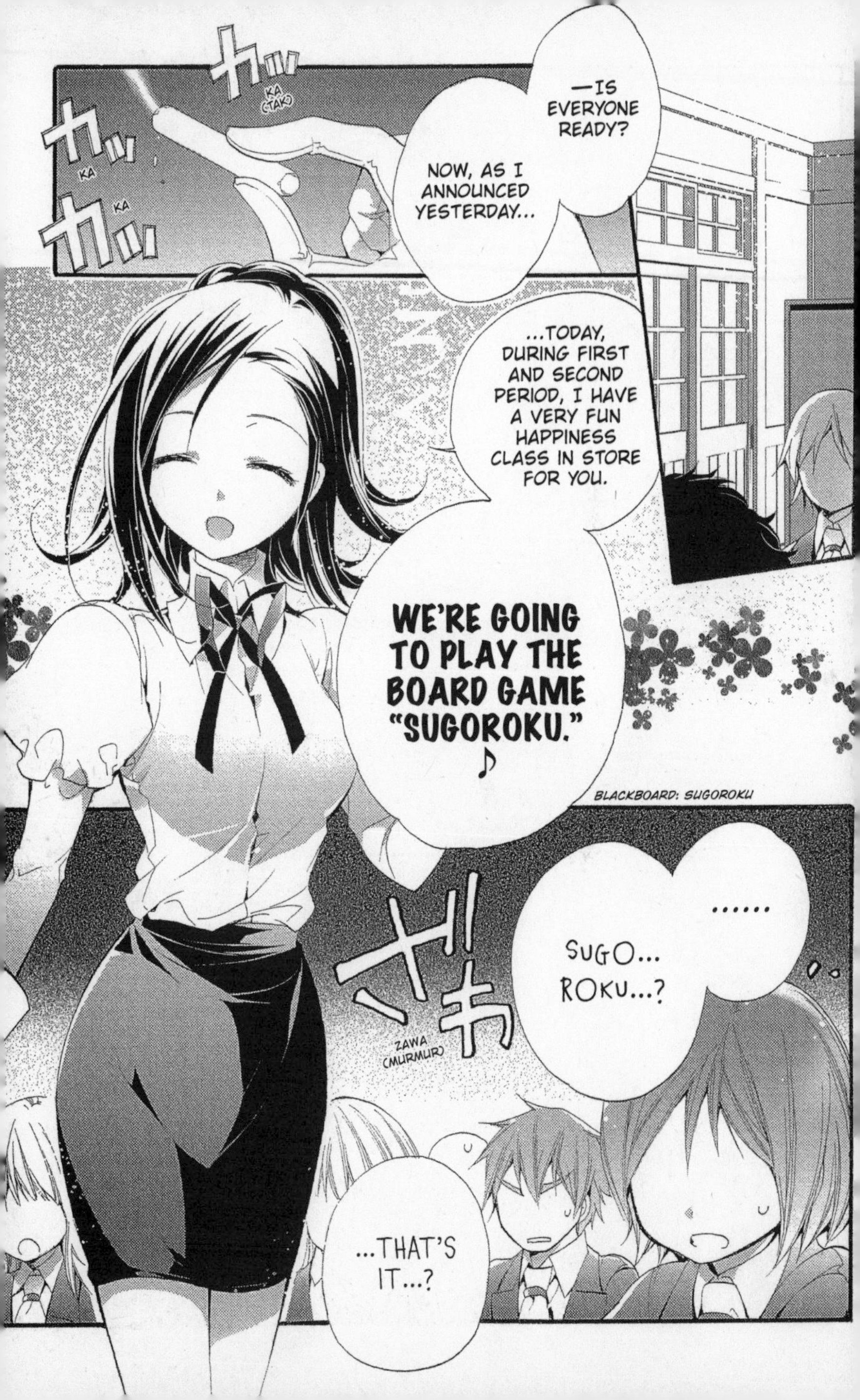

—IS EVERYONE READY?
NOW, AS I ANNOUNCED YESTERDAY...
KA (TAK)
KA
KA
...TODAY, DURING FIRST AND SECOND PERIOD, I HAVE A VERY FUN HAPPINESS CLASS IN STORE FOR YOU.
WE'RE GOING TO PLAY THE BOARD GAME "SUGOROKU." ♪
BLACKBOARD: SUGOROKU
......
SUGO... ROKU...?
ZAWA (MURMUR)
...THAT'S IT...?

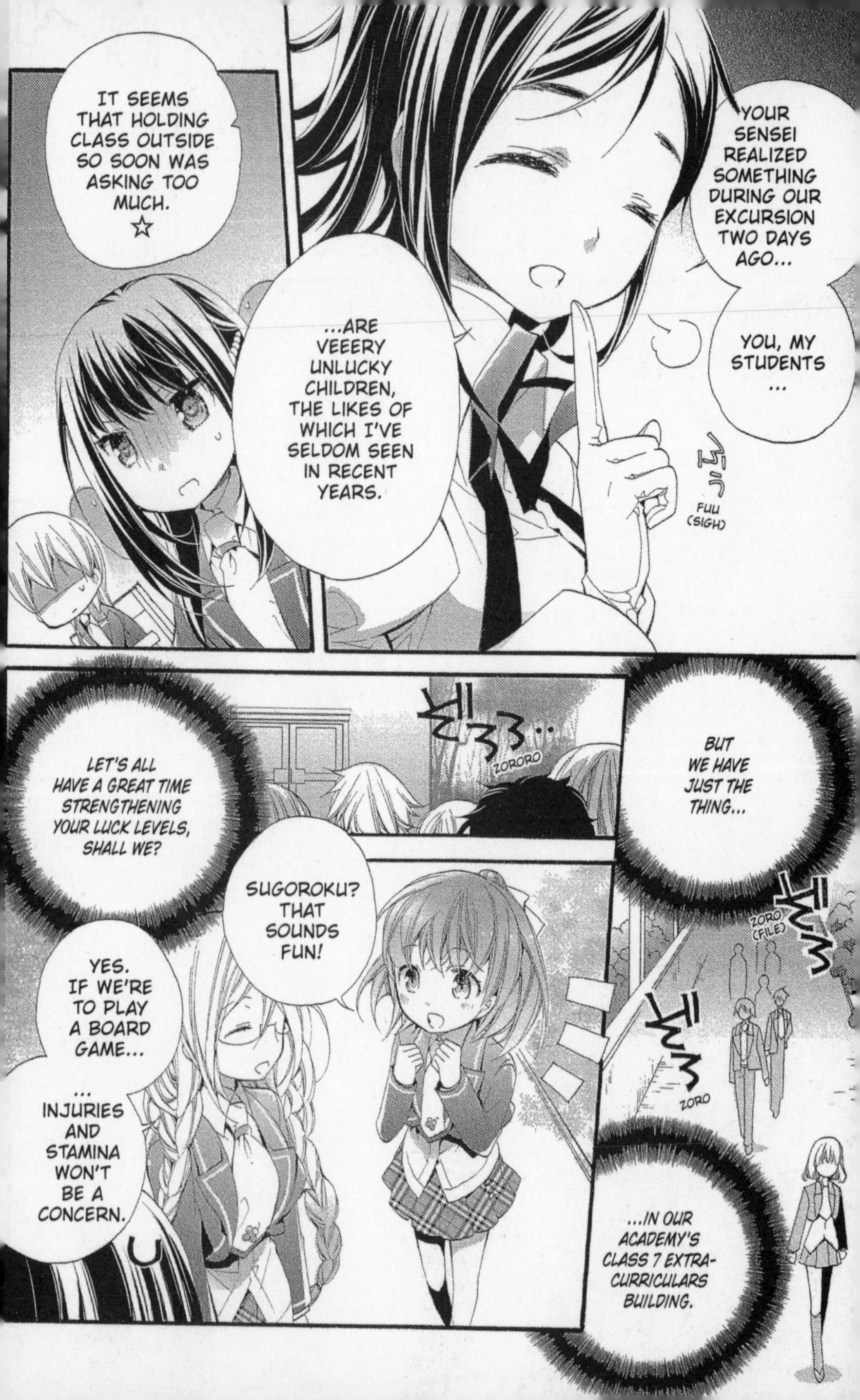
YOUR SENSEI REALIZED SOMETHING DURING OUR EXCURSION TWO DAYS AGO...
YOU, MY STUDENTS ...
...ARE VEEERY UNLUCKY CHILDREN, THE LIKES OF WHICH I'VE SELDOM SEEN IN RECENT YEARS.
FUU (SIGH)
IT SEEMS THAT HOLDING CLASS OUTSIDE SO SOON WAS ASKING TOO MUCH. ☆
BUT WE HAVE JUST THE THING...
...IN OUR ACADEMY'S CLASS 7 EXTRA-CURRICULARS BUILDING.
ZORO (FILE)
ZORO
ZORORO
LET'S ALL HAVE A GREAT TIME STRENGTHENING YOUR LUCK LEVELS, SHALL WE?
SUGOROKU? THAT SOUNDS FUN!
YES. IF WE'RE TO PLAY A BOARD GAME...
... INJURIES AND STAMINA WON'T BE A CONCERN.

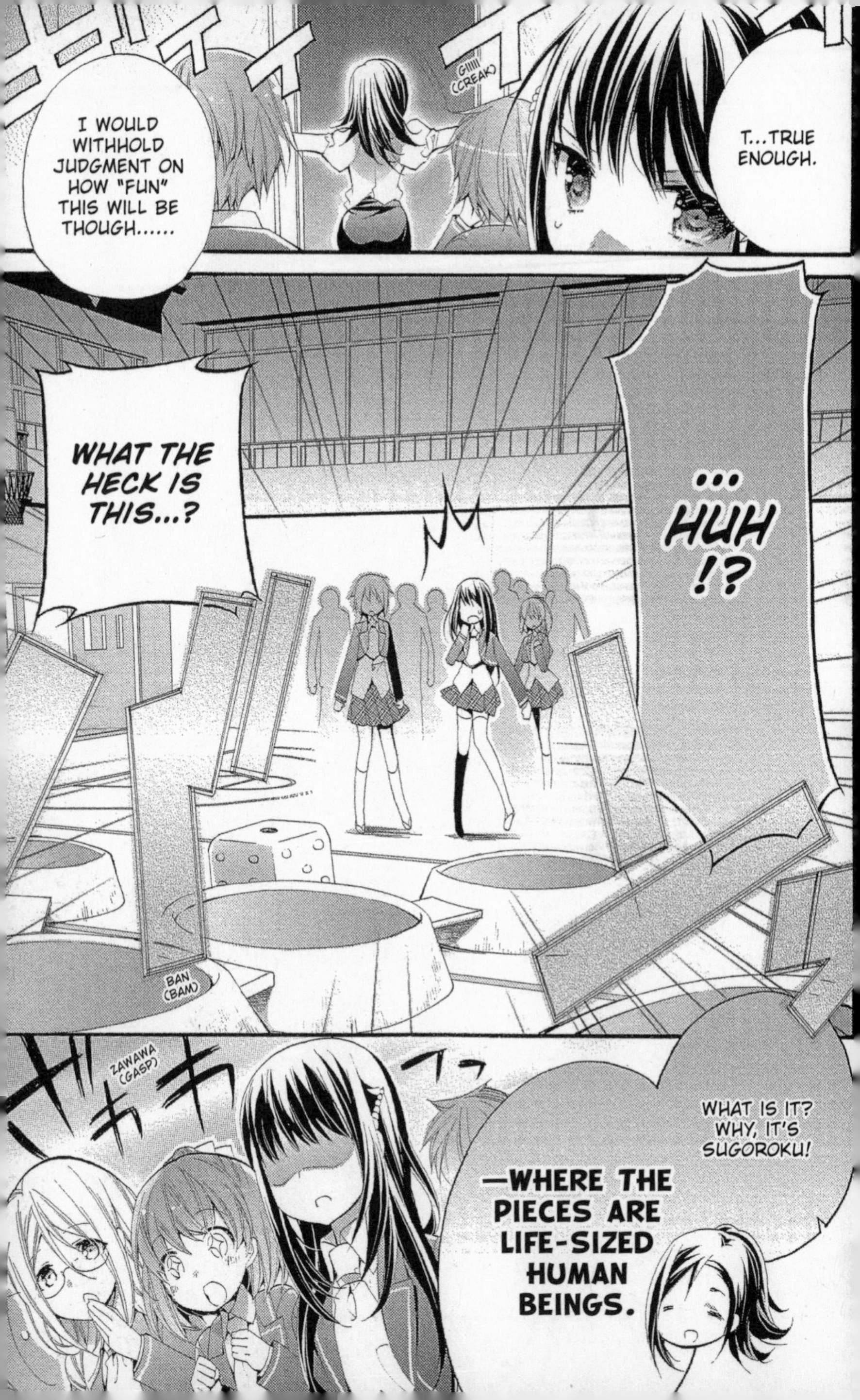
T...TRUE ENOUGH.
GIIIII (CREAK)
I WOULD WITHHOLD JUDGMENT ON HOW "FUN" THIS WILL BE THOUGH......
...HUH!?
WHAT THE HECK IS THIS...?
BAN (BAM)
WHAT IS IT? WHY, IT'S SUGOROKU!
—WHERE THE PIECES ARE LIFE-SIZED HUMAN BEINGS.
ZAWAWA (GASP)

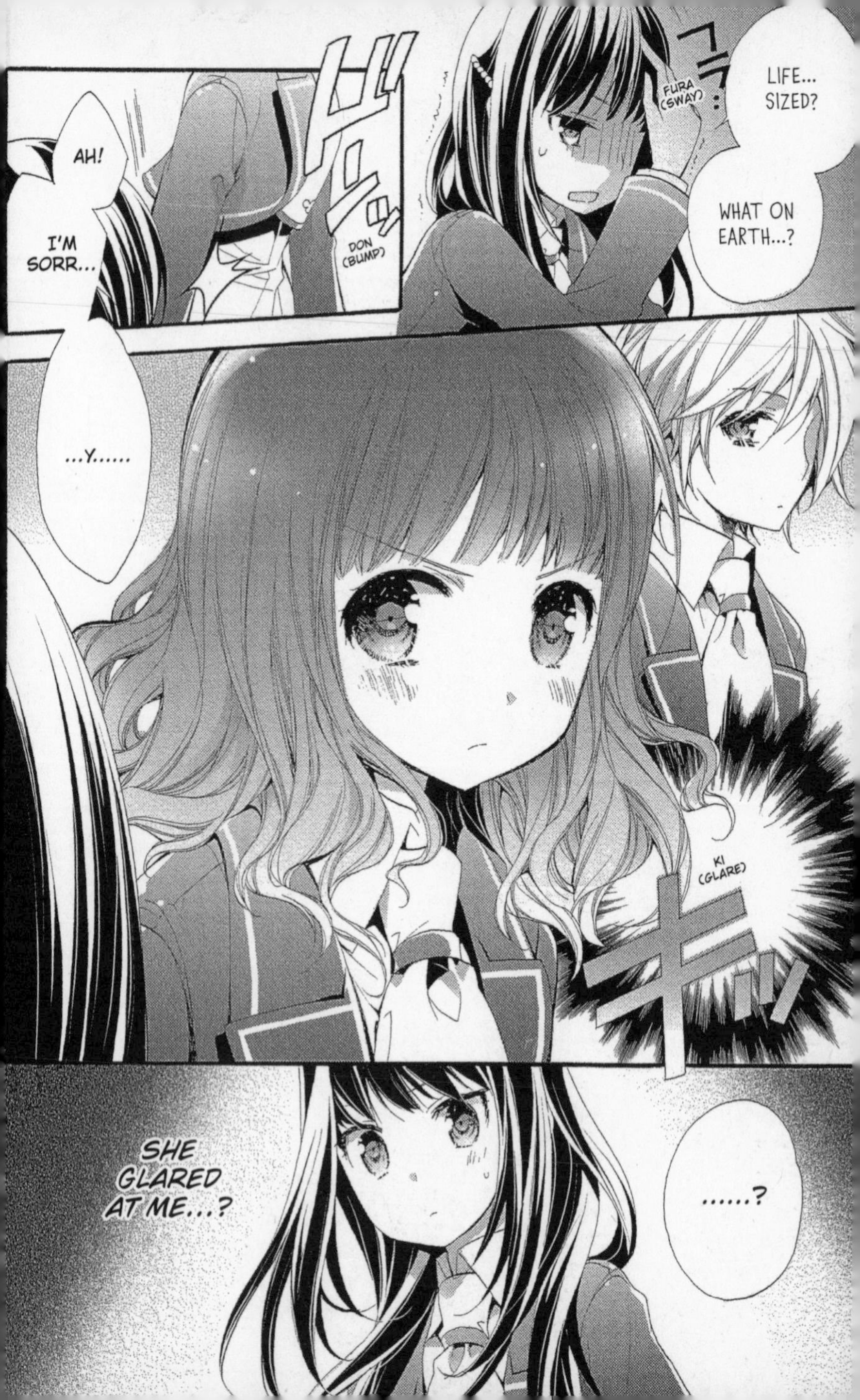
FURA (SWAY)
LIFE... SIZED?
WHAT ON EARTH...?
DON (BUMP)
AH!
I'M SORR...
...Y......
KI (GLARE)
......?
SHE GLARED AT ME...?

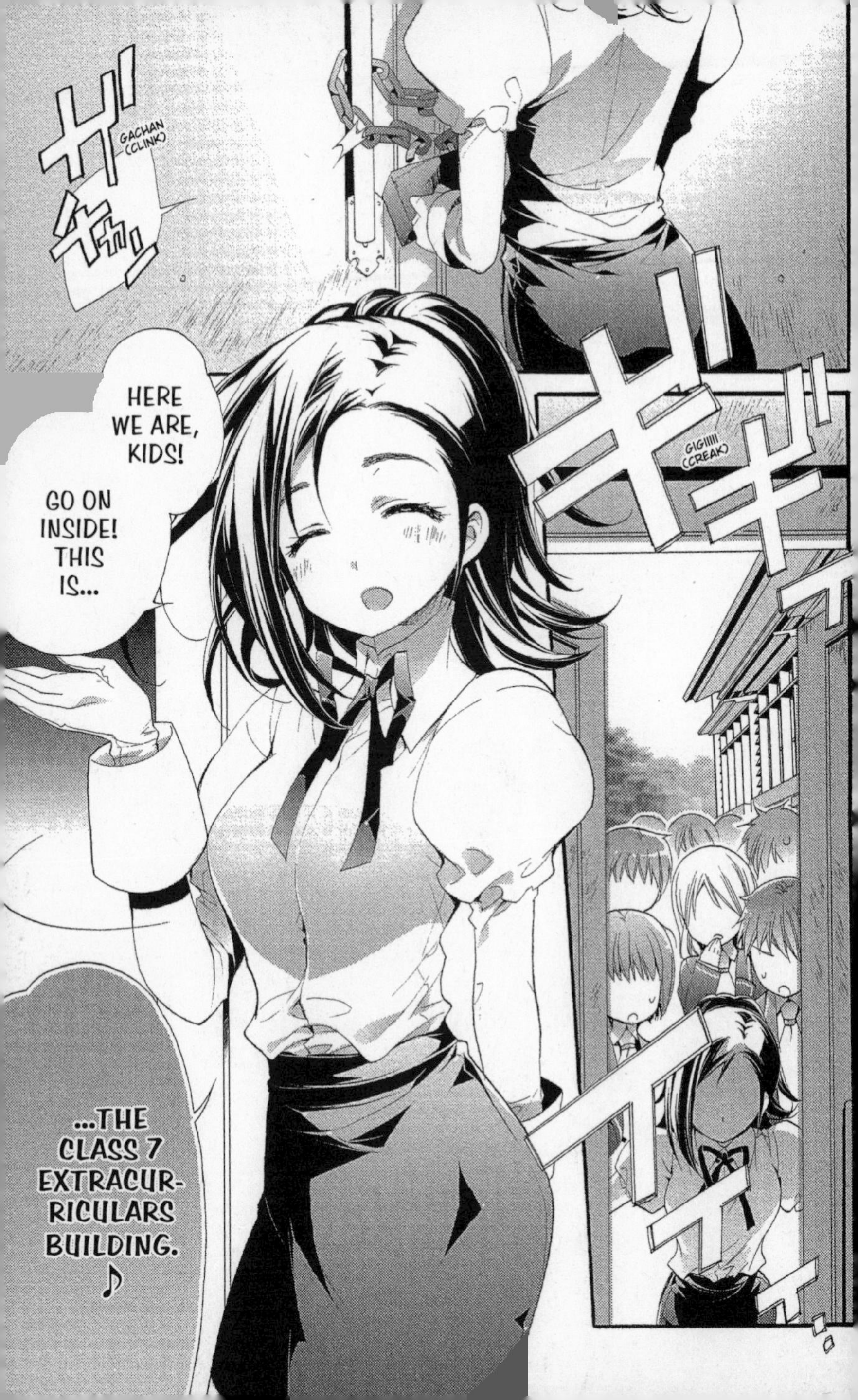
GACHAN (CLINK)
GIGIIII (CREAK)
HERE WE ARE, KIDS!
GO ON INSIDE! THIS IS...
...THE CLASS 7 EXTRACUR-RICULARS BUILDING. ♪

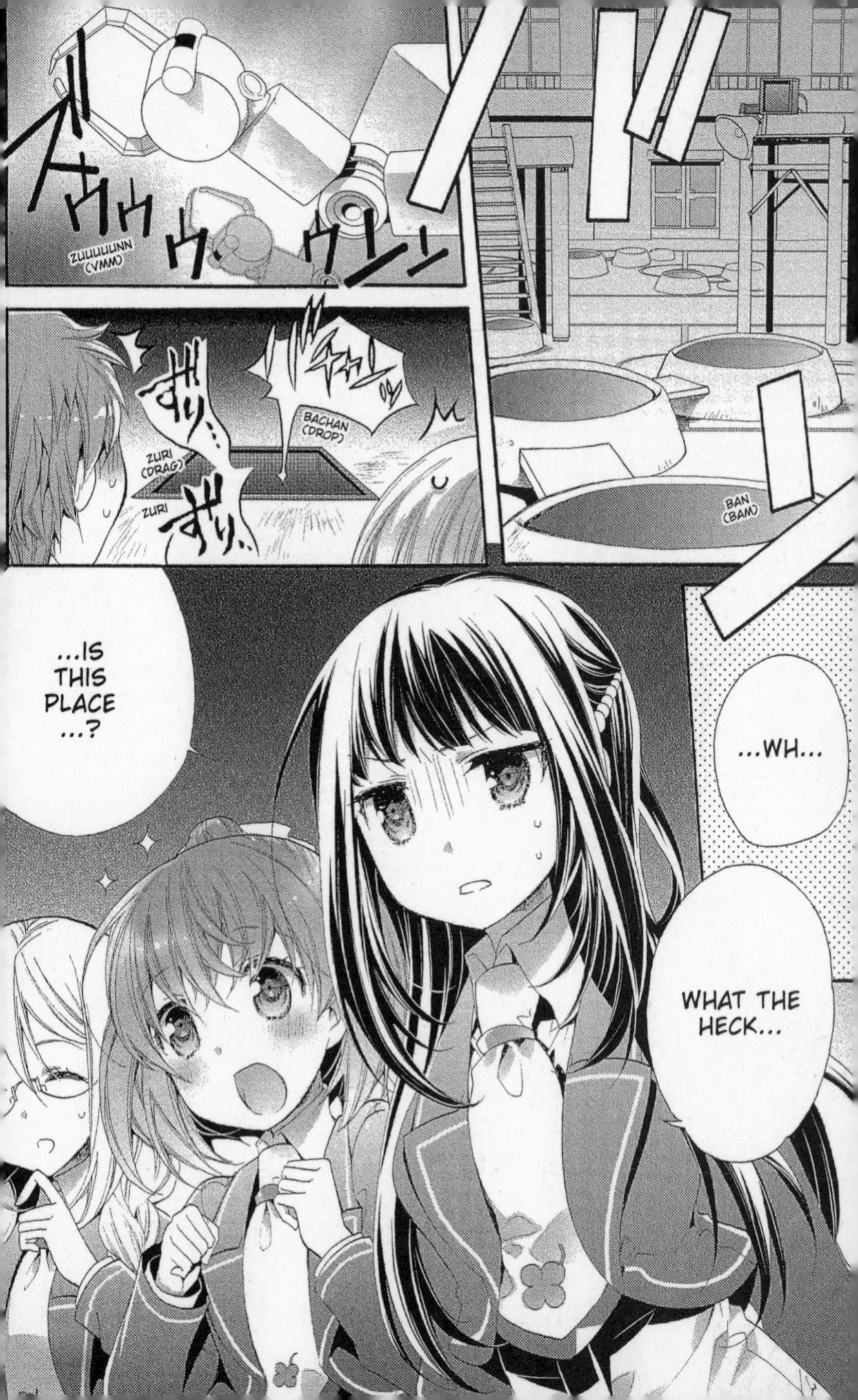
BAN (BAM)
ZUUUUUUNN (VMM)
BACHAN (DROP)
ZURI (DRAG)
ZURI
...WH...
WHAT THE HECK...
...IS THIS PLACE ...?

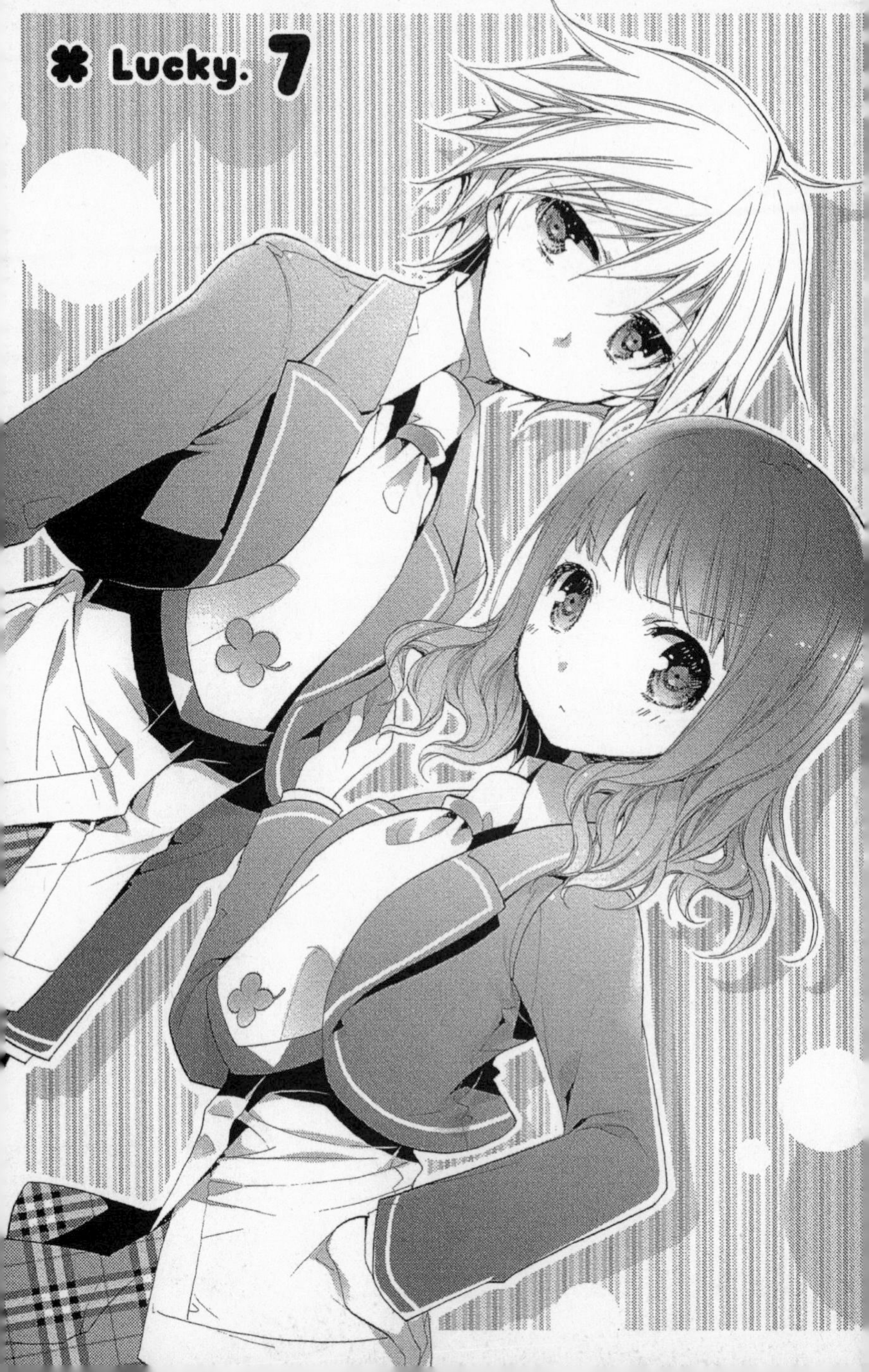
Lucky. 7

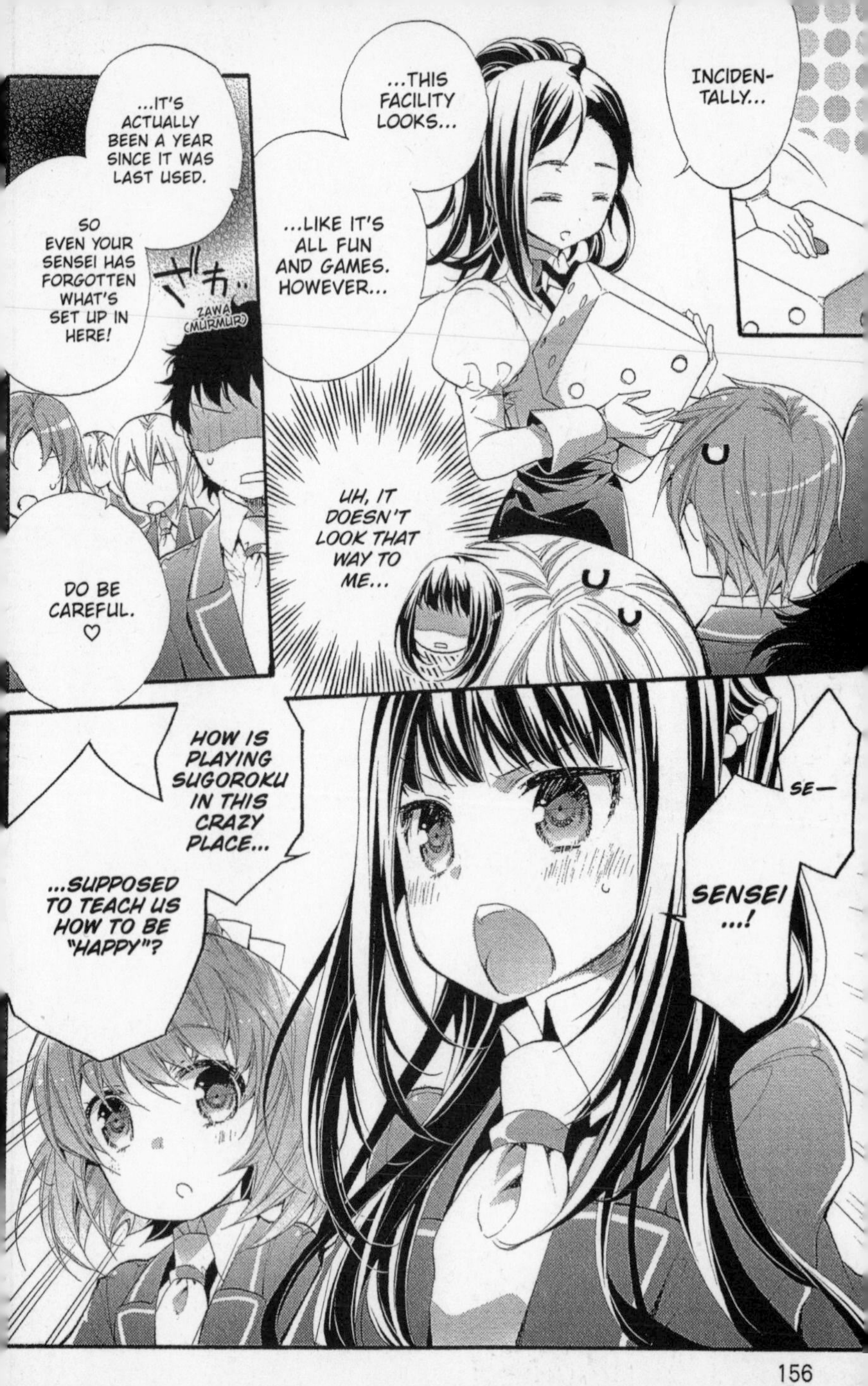
INCIDENTALLY...
...THIS FACILITY LOOKS...
...LIKE IT'S ALL FUN AND GAMES. HOWEVER...
UH, IT DOESN'T LOOK THAT WAY TO ME...
...IT'S ACTUALLY BEEN A YEAR SINCE IT WAS LAST USED.
SO EVEN YOUR SENSEI HAS FORGOTTEN WHAT'S SET UP IN HERE!
ZAWA (MURMUR)
DO BE CAREFUL. ♡
SE—
SENSEI ...!
HOW IS PLAYING SUGOROKU IN THIS CRAZY PLACE...
...SUPPOSED TO TEACH US HOW TO BE "HAPPY"?

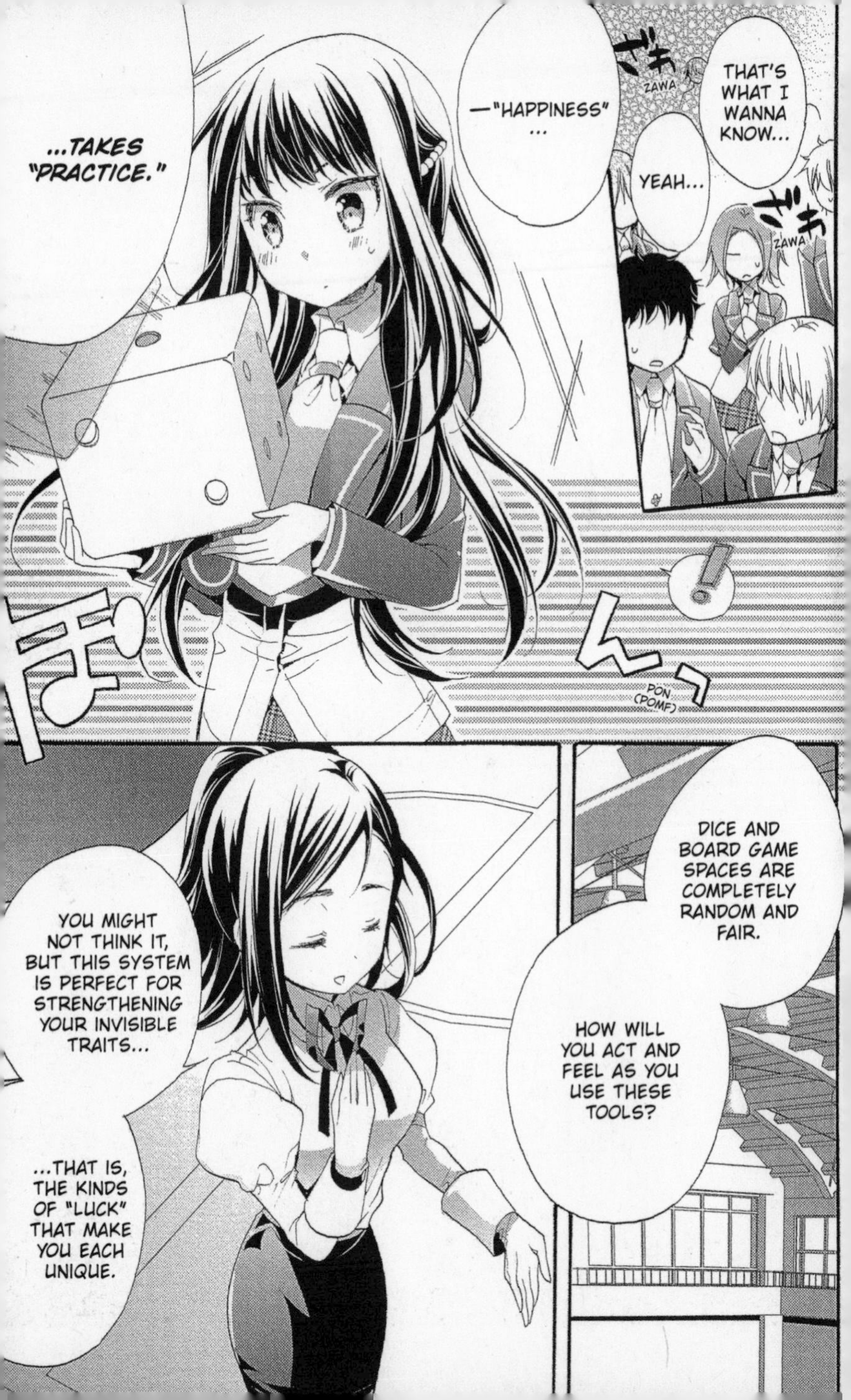

ざわ
ZAWA
THAT'S WHAT I WANNA KNOW...
YEAH...
ざわ
ZAWA
—"HAPPINESS" ...
...TAKES "PRACTICE."
ぽん
PON (POMF)
DICE AND BOARD GAME SPACES ARE COMPLETELY RANDOM AND FAIR.
HOW WILL YOU ACT AND FEEL AS YOU USE THESE TOOLS?
YOU MIGHT NOT THINK IT, BUT THIS SYSTEM IS PERFECT FOR STRENGTHENING YOUR INVISIBLE TRAITS...
...THAT IS, THE KINDS OF "LUCK" THAT MAKE YOU EACH UNIQUE.

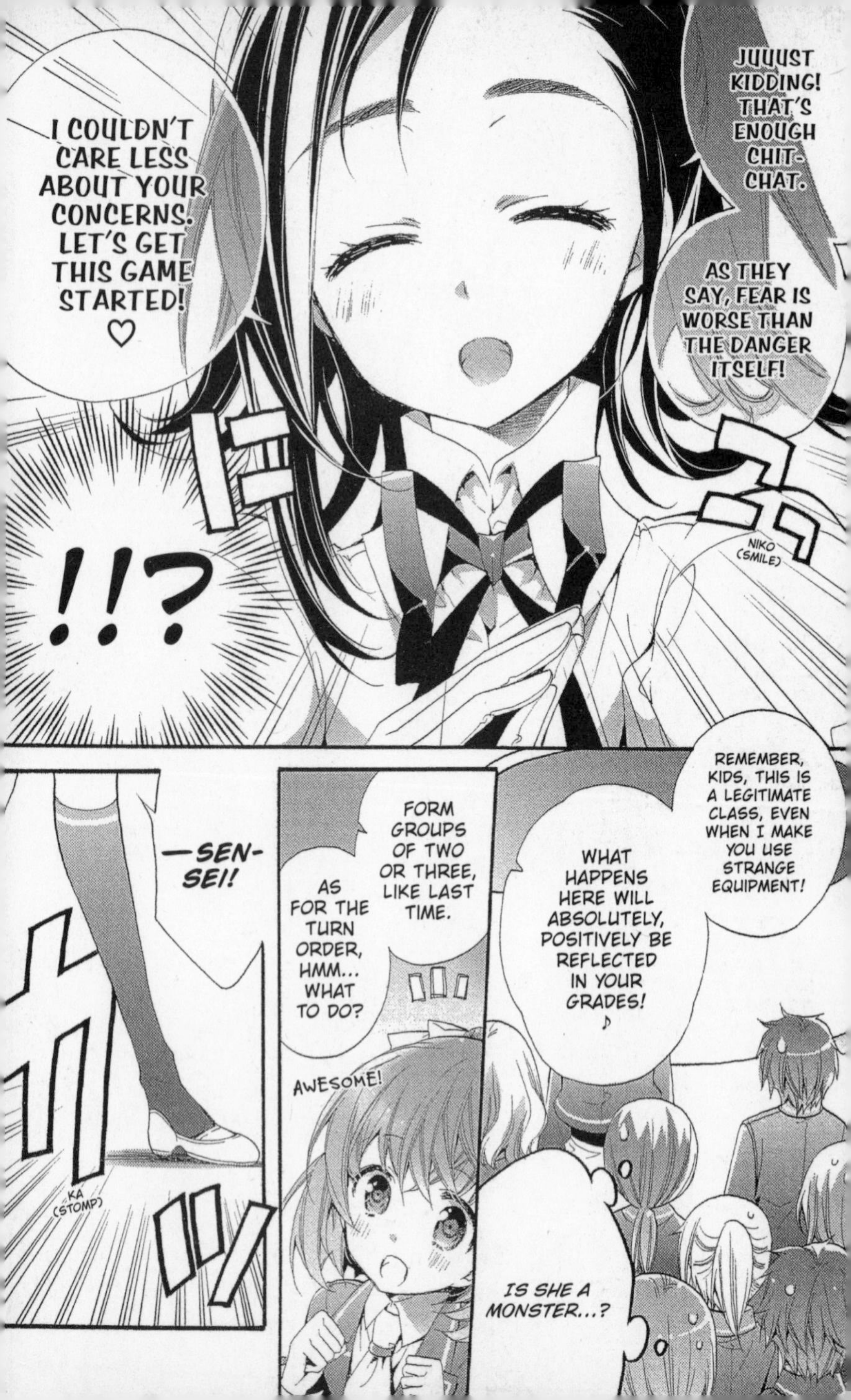
JUUUST KIDDING! THAT'S ENOUGH CHIT-CHAT.
AS THEY SAY, FEAR IS WORSE THAN THE DANGER ITSELF!
NIKO (SMILE)
I COULDN'T CARE LESS ABOUT YOUR CONCERNS. LET'S GET THIS GAME STARTED! ♡
!!?
REMEMBER, KIDS, THIS IS A LEGITIMATE CLASS, EVEN WHEN I MAKE YOU USE STRANGE EQUIPMENT!
WHAT HAPPENS HERE WILL ABSOLUTELY, POSITIVELY BE REFLECTED IN YOUR GRADES! ♪
FORM GROUPS OF TWO OR THREE, LIKE LAST TIME.
AS FOR THE TURN ORDER, HMM... WHAT TO DO?
AWESOME!
IS SHE A MONSTER...?
—SEN-SEI!
KA (STOMP)

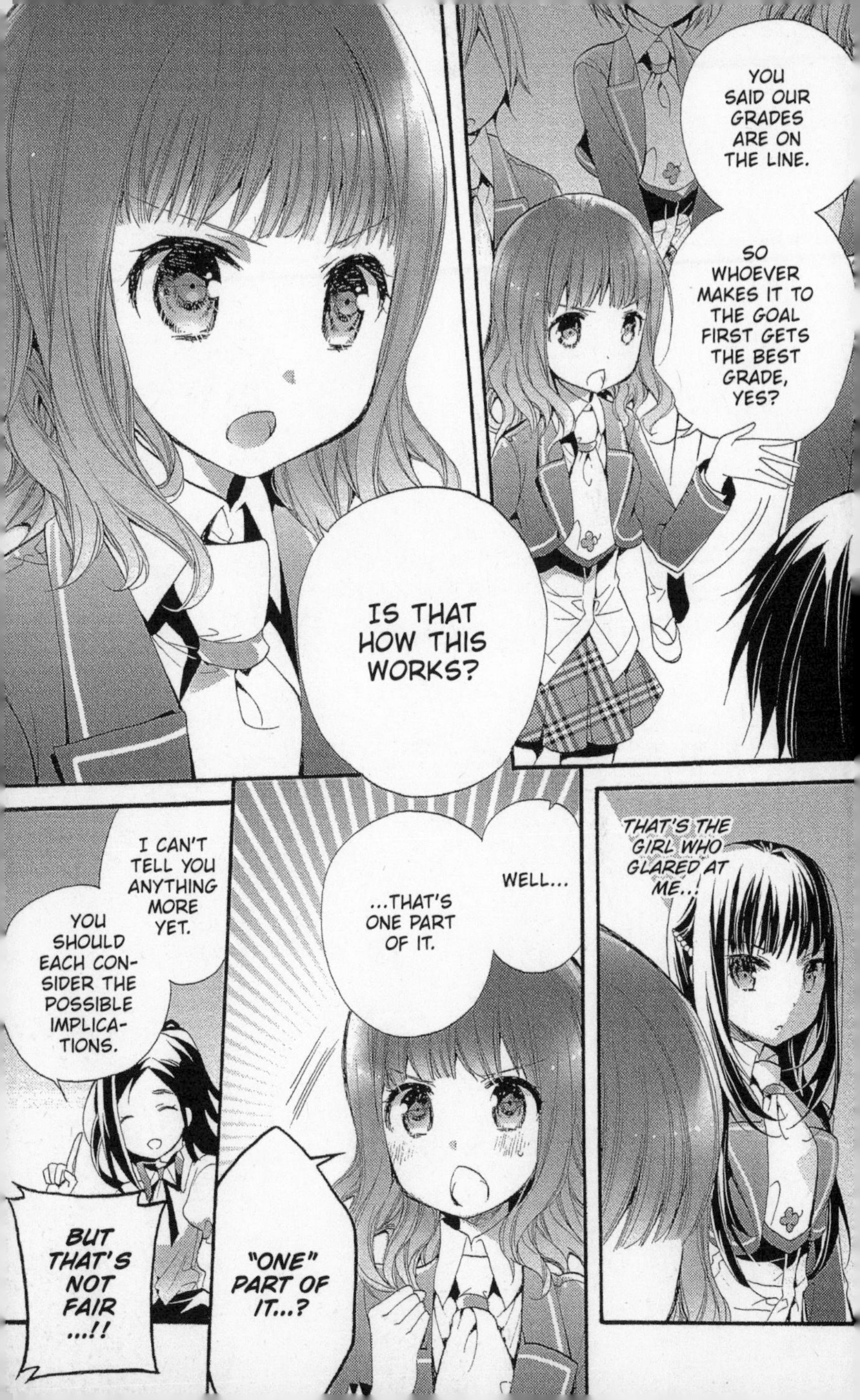
YOU SAID OUR GRADES ARE ON THE LINE.
SO WHOEVER MAKES IT TO THE GOAL FIRST GETS THE BEST GRADE, YES?
IS THAT HOW THIS WORKS?
THAT'S THE GIRL WHO GLARED AT ME...
WELL...
...THAT'S ONE PART OF IT.
"ONE" PART OF IT...?
I CAN'T TELL YOU ANYTHING MORE YET.
YOU SHOULD EACH CONSIDER THE POSSIBLE IMPLICATIONS.
BUT THAT'S NOT FAIR...!!

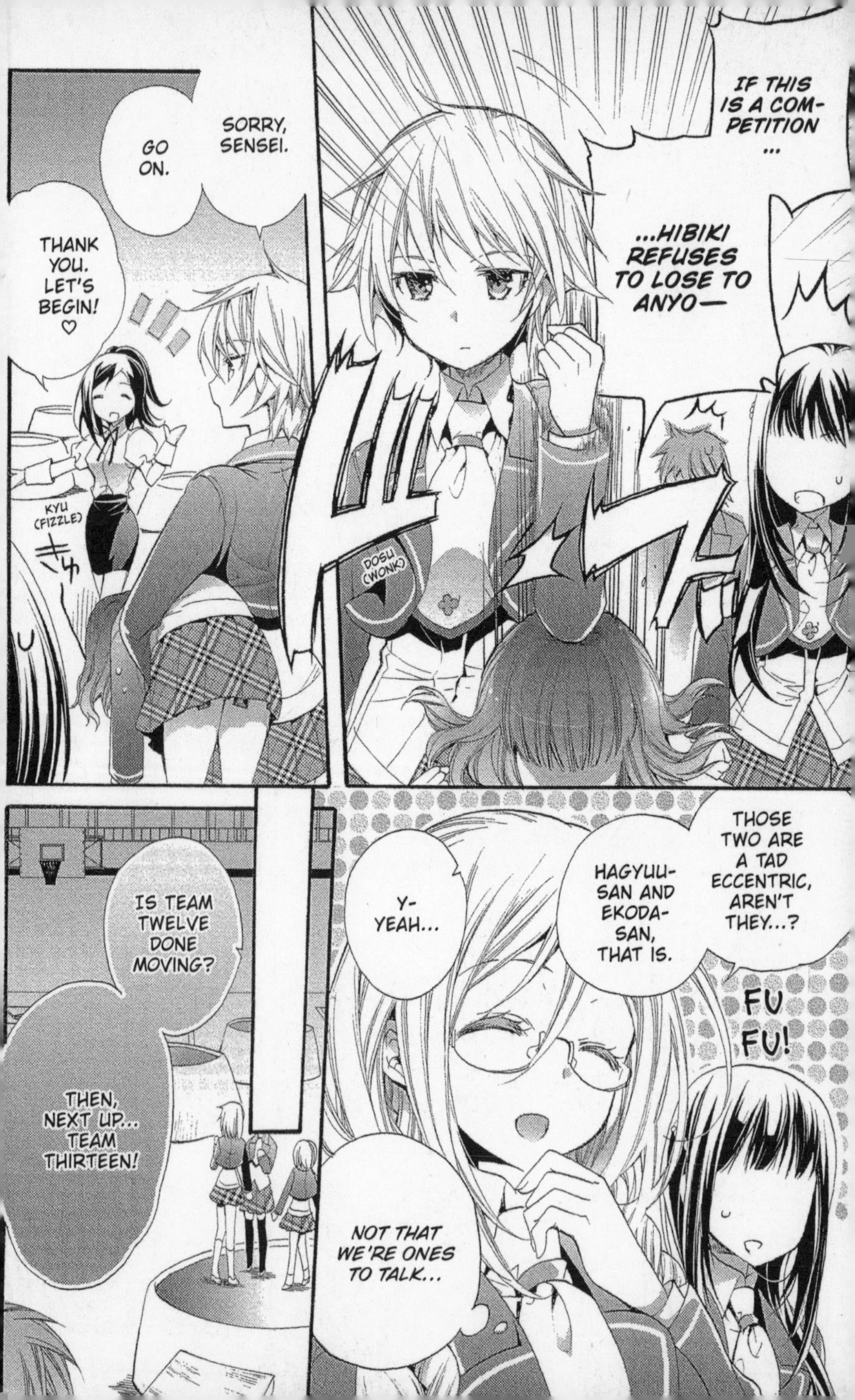
IF THIS IS A COMPETITION ...
...HIBIKI REFUSES TO LOSE TO ANYO—
DOSU (WONK)
SORRY, SENSEI.
GO ON.
THANK YOU. LET'S BEGIN! ♡
KYU (FIZZLE)
THOSE TWO ARE A TAD ECCENTRIC, AREN'T THEY...?
HAGYUU-SAN AND EKODA-SAN, THAT IS.
Y-YEAH...
FU FU!
NOT THAT WE'RE ONES TO TALK...
IS TEAM TWELVE DONE MOVING?
THEN, NEXT UP... TEAM THIRTEEN!

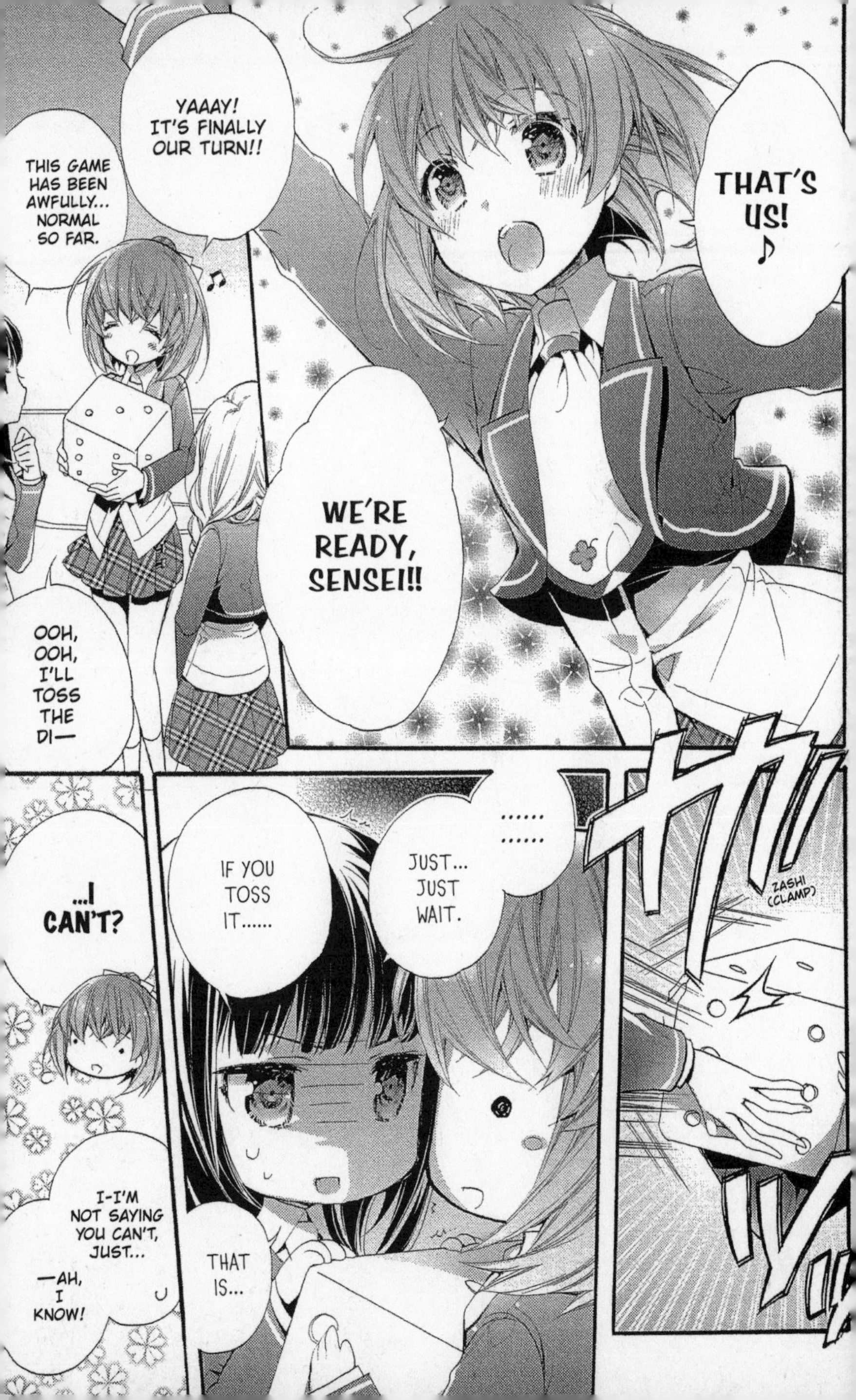
THAT'S US! ♪
WE'RE READY, SENSEI!!
YAAAY! IT'S FINALLY OUR TURN!!
THIS GAME HAS BEEN AWFULLY... NORMAL SO FAR.
OOH, OOH, I'LL TOSS THE DI—
ZASHI (CLAMP)
......
......
JUST... JUST WAIT.
IF YOU TOSS IT......
THAT IS...
...I CAN'T?
I-I'M NOT SAYING YOU CAN'T, JUST... —AH, I KNOW!

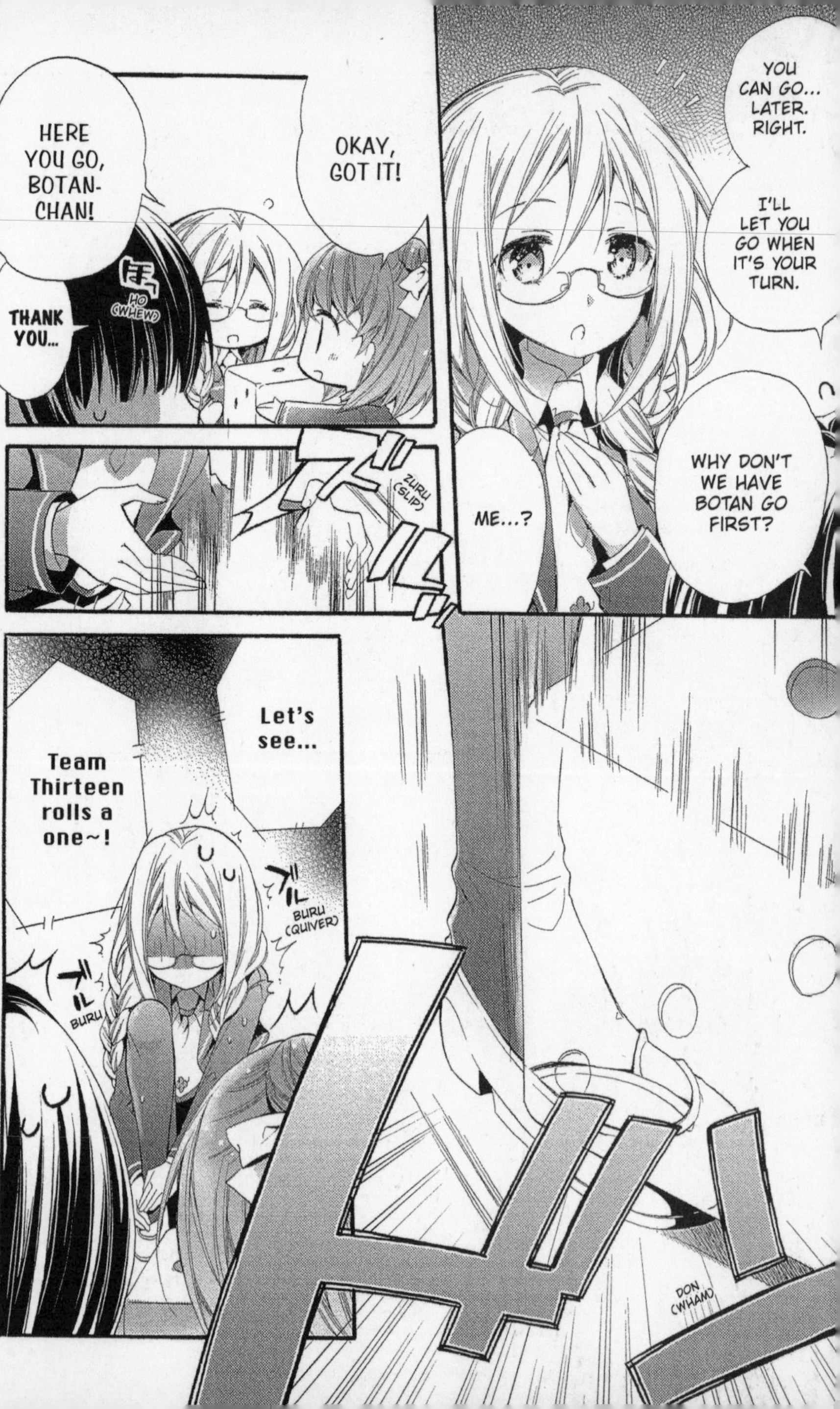
YOU CAN GO... LATER. RIGHT.
I'LL LET YOU GO WHEN IT'S YOUR TURN.
WHY DON'T WE HAVE BOTAN GO FIRST?
ME...?
OKAY, GOT IT!
HERE YOU GO, BOTAN-CHAN!
HO (WHEW)
THANK YOU...
ZURU (SLIP)
DON (WHAM)
Let's see...
Team Thirteen rolls a one~!
BURU (QUIVER)
BURU

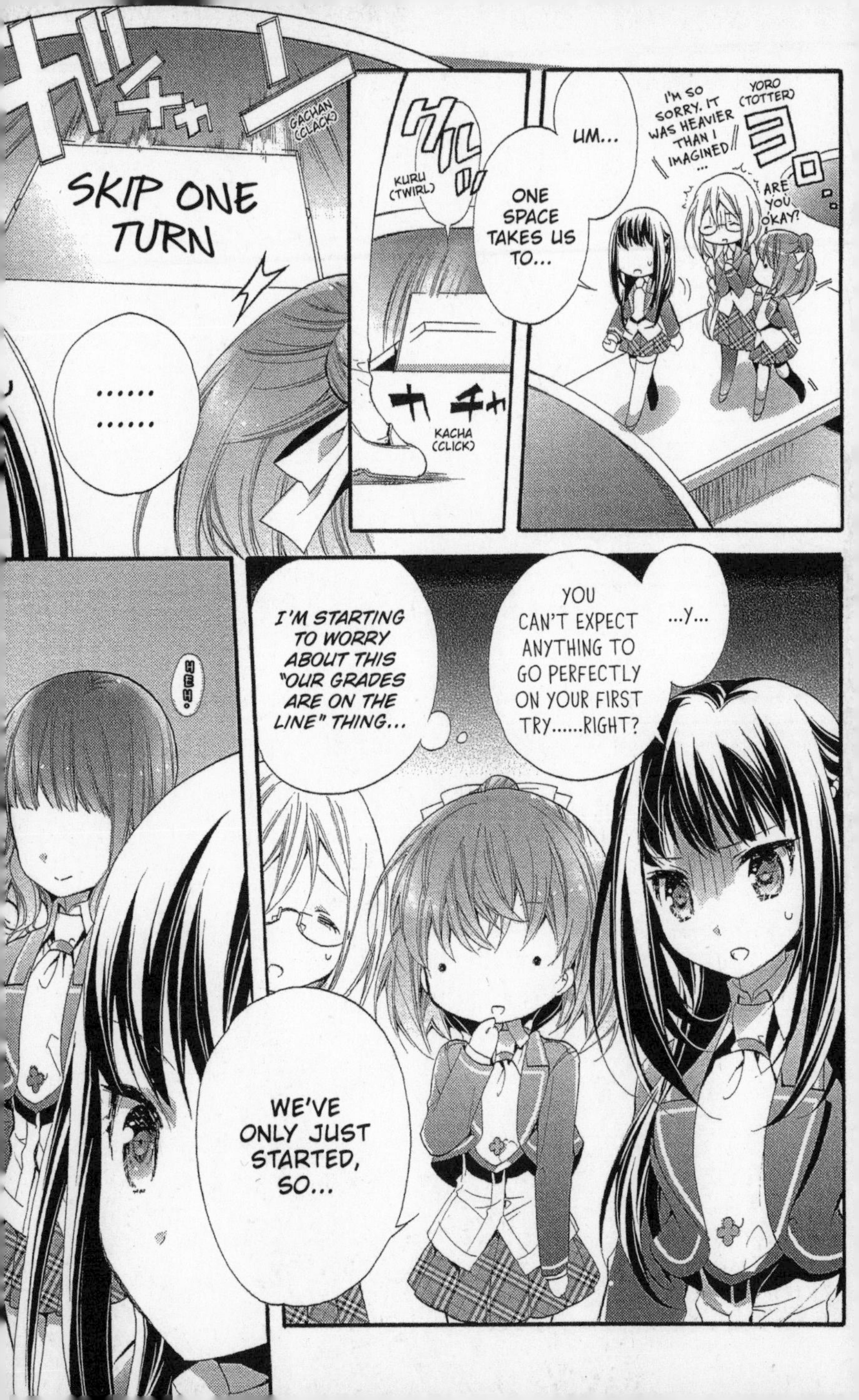
I'M SO SORRY. IT WAS HEAVIER THAN I IMAGINED...
YORO (TOTTER)
ARE YOU OKAY?
UM...
ONE SPACE TAKES US TO...
KURU (TWIRL)
KACHA (CLICK)
GACHAN (CLACK)
SKIP ONE TURN
......
......
...y...
YOU CAN'T EXPECT ANYTHING TO GO PERFECTLY ON YOUR FIRST TRY......RIGHT?
I'M STARTING TO WORRY ABOUT THIS "OUR GRADES ARE ON THE LINE" THING...
WE'VE ONLY JUST STARTED, SO...
HEH.

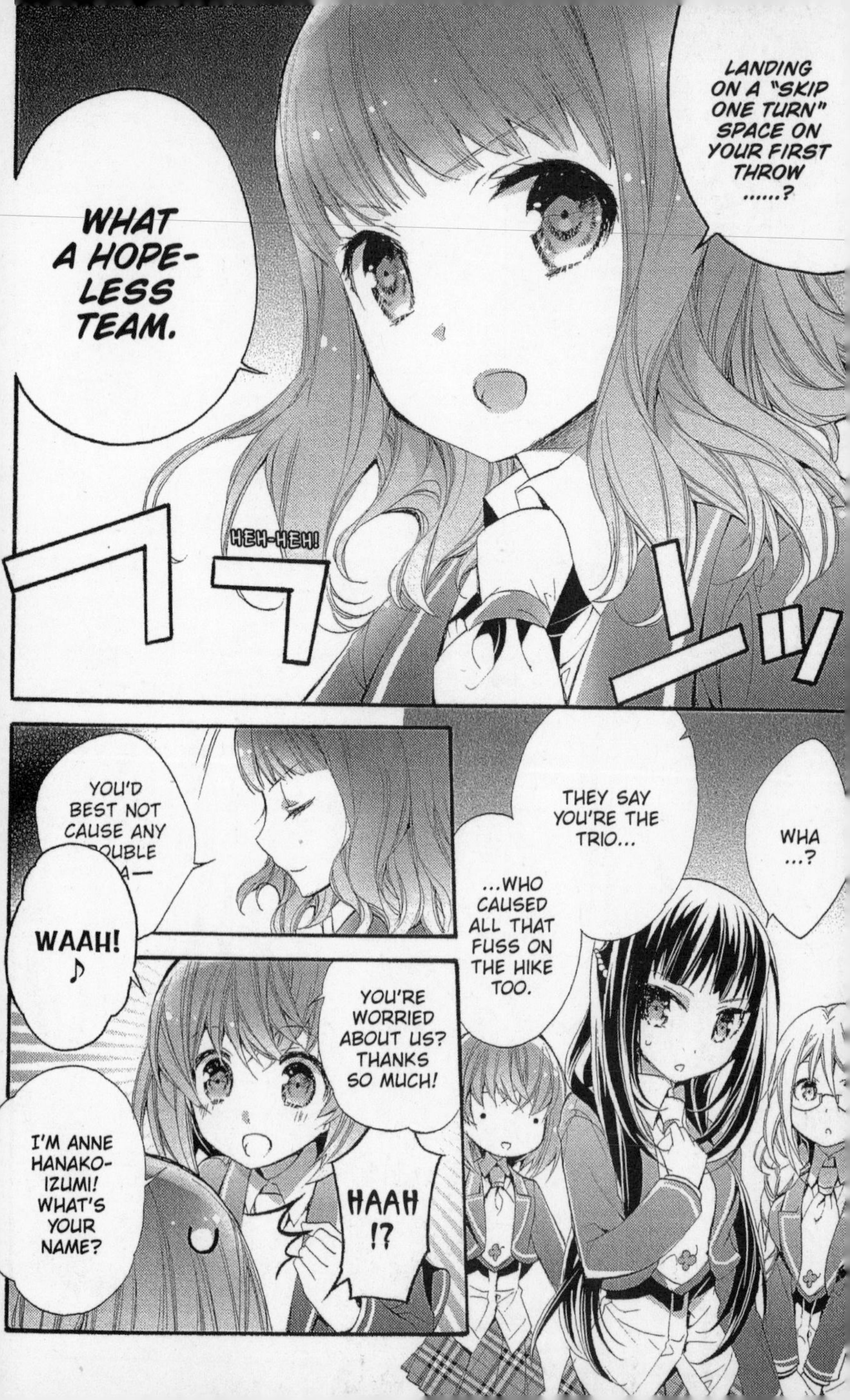

LANDING ON A "SKIP ONE TURN" SPACE ON YOUR FIRST THROW ......?
WHAT A HOPE-LESS TEAM.
HEH-HEH!
WHA ...?
THEY SAY YOU'RE THE TRIO...
...WHO CAUSED ALL THAT FUSS ON THE HIKE TOO.
YOU'D BEST NOT CAUSE ANY OUBLE A—
WAAH! ♪
YOU'RE WORRIED ABOUT US? THANKS SO MUCH!
I'M ANNE HANAKO-IZUMI! WHAT'S YOUR NAME?
HAAH !?

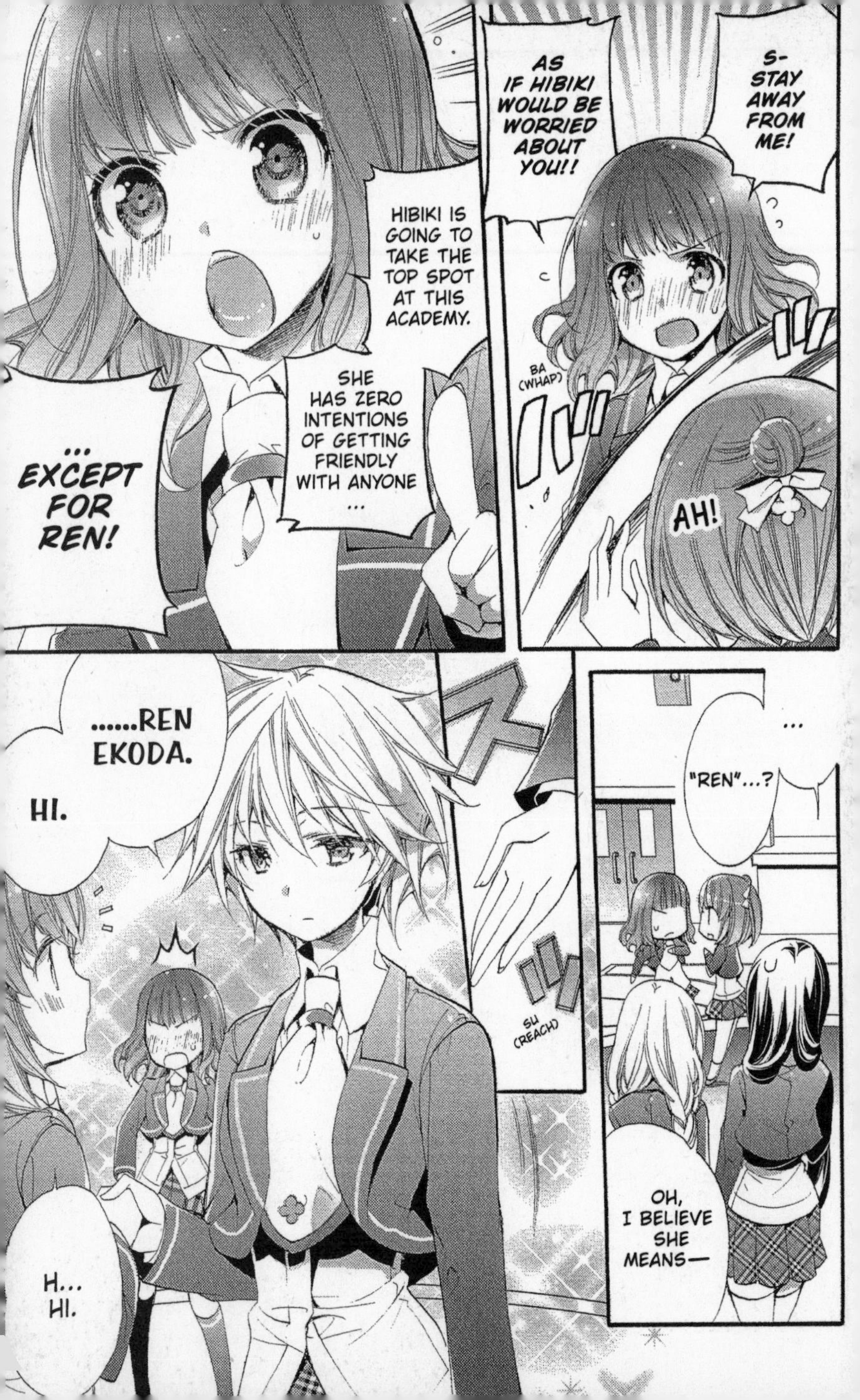
S-STAY AWAY FROM ME!
AS IF HIBIKI WOULD BE WORRIED ABOUT YOU!!
BA (WHAP)
AH!
HIBIKI IS GOING TO TAKE THE TOP SPOT AT THIS ACADEMY.
SHE HAS ZERO INTENTIONS OF GETTING FRIENDLY WITH ANYONE ...
... EXCEPT FOR REN!
...
"REN"...?
OH, I BELIEVE SHE MEANS—
SU (REACH)
......REN EKODA.
HI.
H... HI.

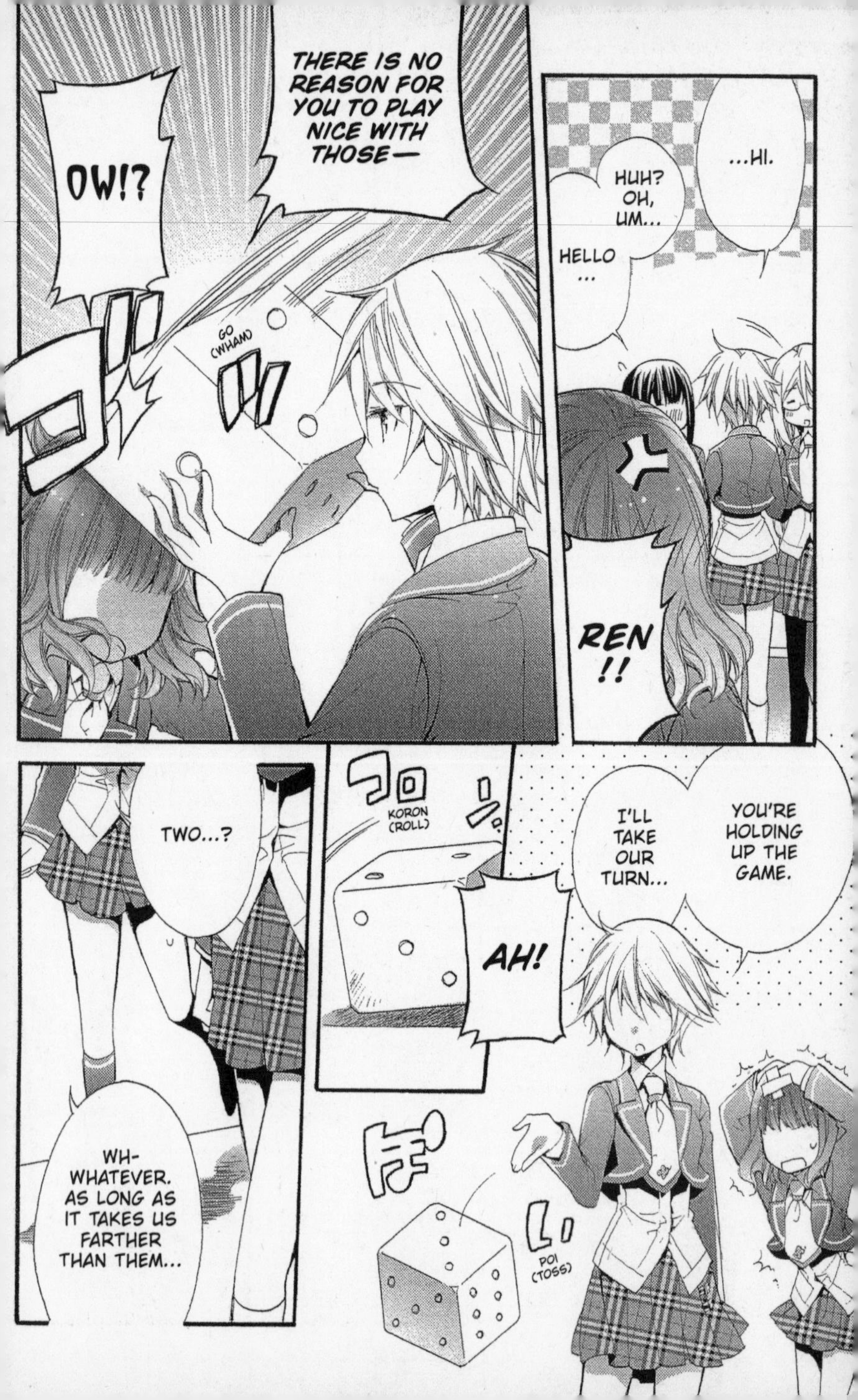
...HI.
HUH? OH, UM...
HELLO ...
REN !!
THERE IS NO REASON FOR YOU TO PLAY NICE WITH THOSE—
OW!?
GO (WHAM)
YOU'RE HOLDING UP THE GAME.
I'LL TAKE OUR TURN...
POI (TOSS)
KORON (ROLL)
AH!
TWO...?
WH- WHATEVER. AS LONG AS IT TAKES US FARTHER THAN THEM...

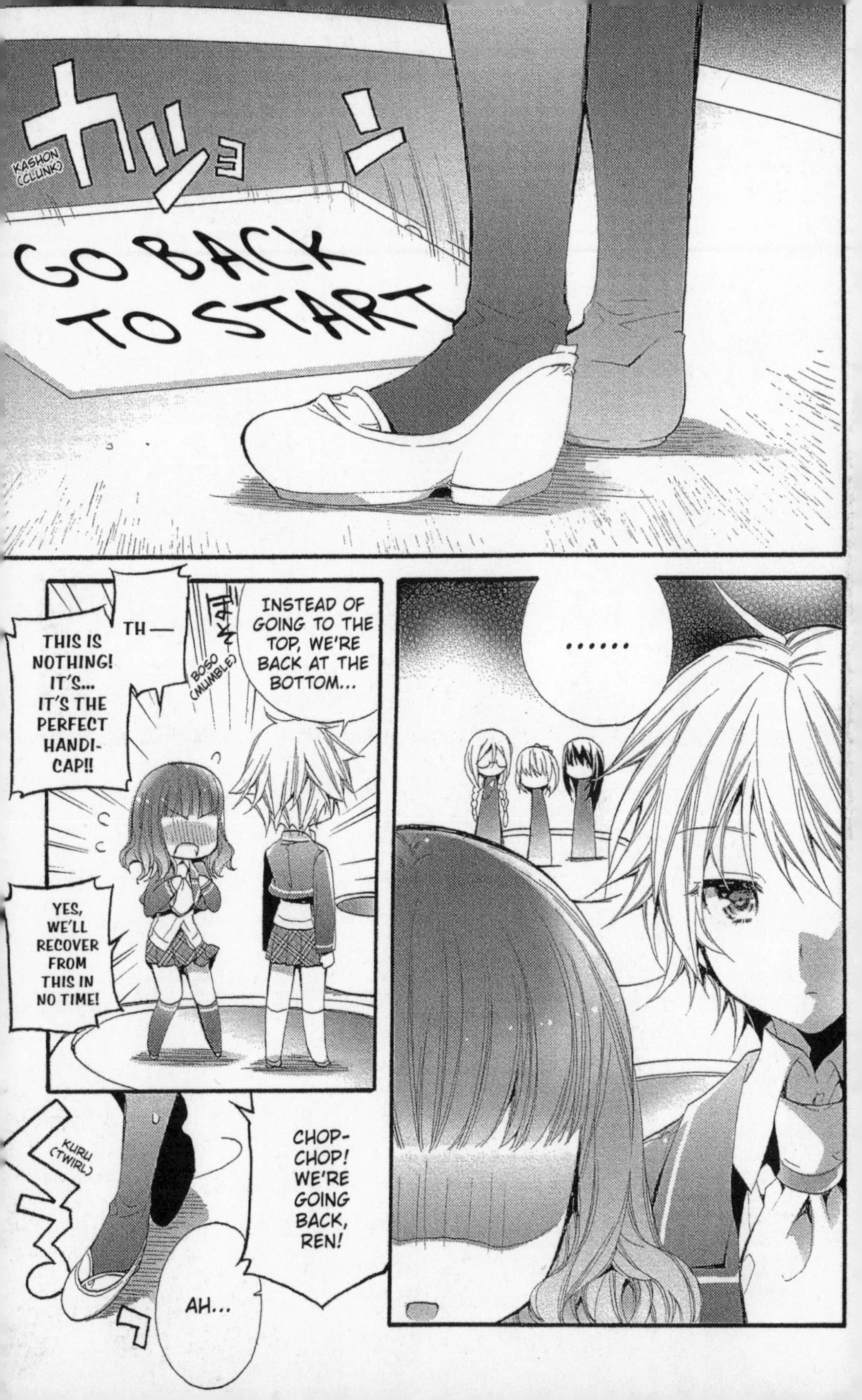
KASHON (CLUNK)
GO BACK TO START
......
INSTEAD OF GOING TO THE TOP, WE'RE BACK AT THE BOTTOM...
BOSO (MUMBLE)
TH—
THIS IS NOTHING! IT'S... IT'S THE PERFECT HANDI-CAP!!
YES, WE'LL RECOVER FROM THIS IN NO TIME!
KURU (TWIRL)
CHOP-CHOP! WE'RE GOING BACK, REN!
AH...

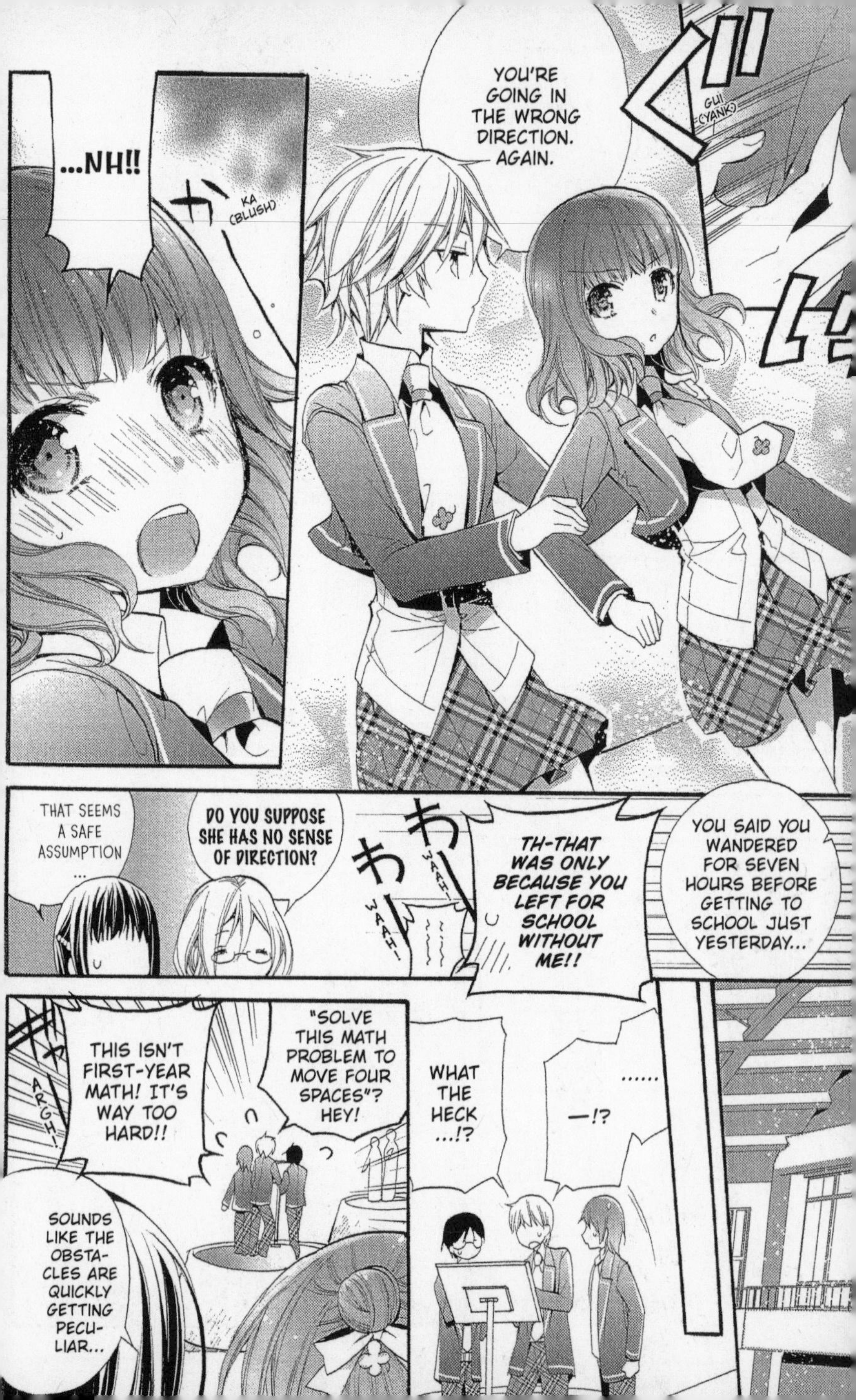

GUI (YANK)
YOU'RE GOING IN THE WRONG DIRECTION. AGAIN.
KA (BLUSH)
...NH!!
YOU SAID YOU WANDERED FOR SEVEN HOURS BEFORE GETTING TO SCHOOL JUST YESTERDAY...
TH-THAT WAS ONLY BECAUSE YOU LEFT FOR SCHOOL WITHOUT ME!!
WAAH! WAAH!
DO YOU SUPPOSE SHE HAS NO SENSE OF DIRECTION?
THAT SEEMS A SAFE ASSUMPTION ...
......
—!?
WHAT THE HECK ...!?
"SOLVE THIS MATH PROBLEM TO MOVE FOUR SPACES"? HEY!
THIS ISN'T FIRST-YEAR MATH! IT'S WAY TOO HARD!!
ARGH!
SOUNDS LIKE THE OBSTACLES ARE QUICKLY GETTING PECULIAR...

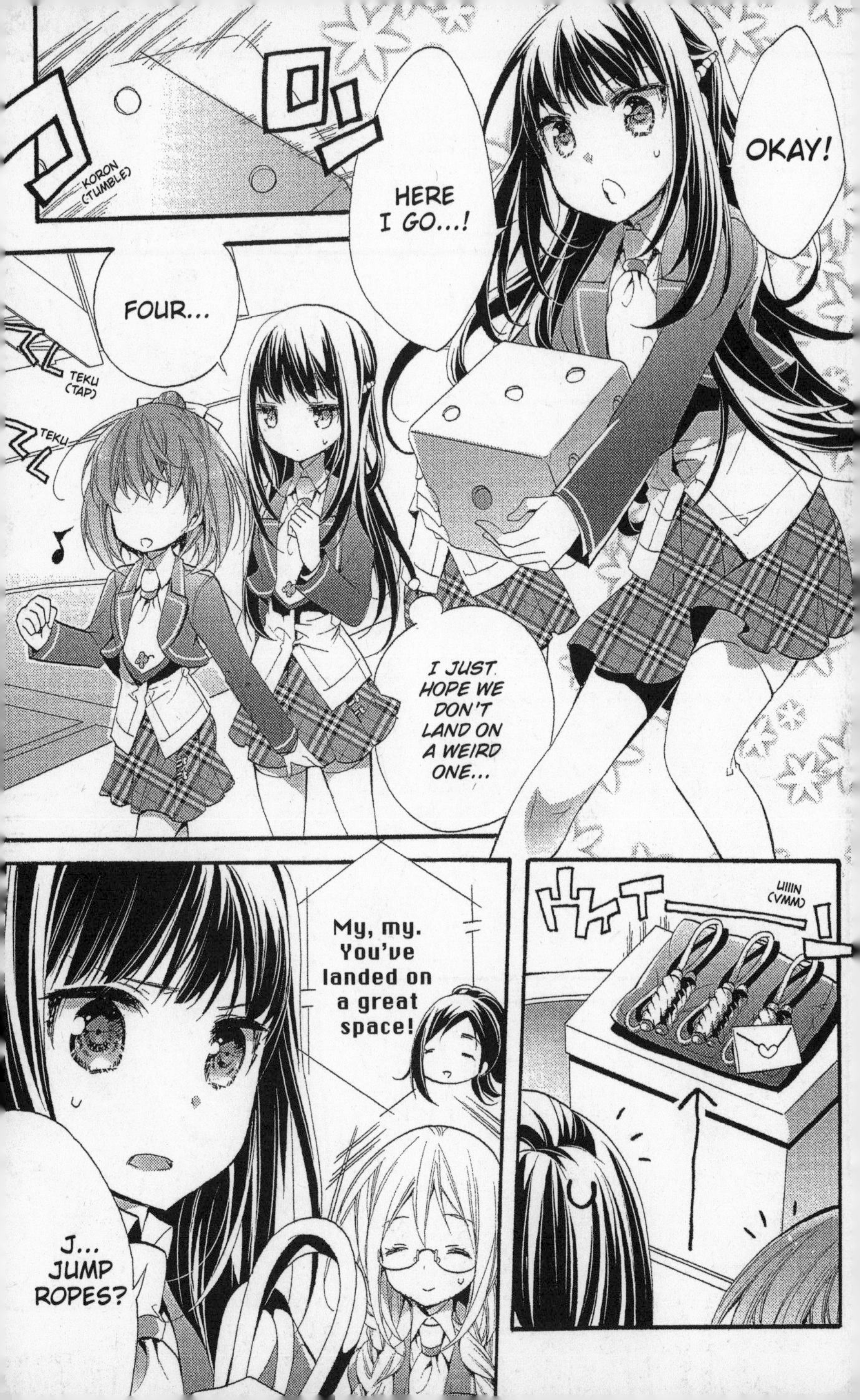

OKAY!
HERE I GO...!
I JUST HOPE WE DON'T LAND ON A WEIRD ONE...
KORON (TUMBLE)
FOUR...
TEKU (TAP)
TEKU
UIIIN (VMM)
My, my. You've landed on a great space!
J... JUMP ROPES?

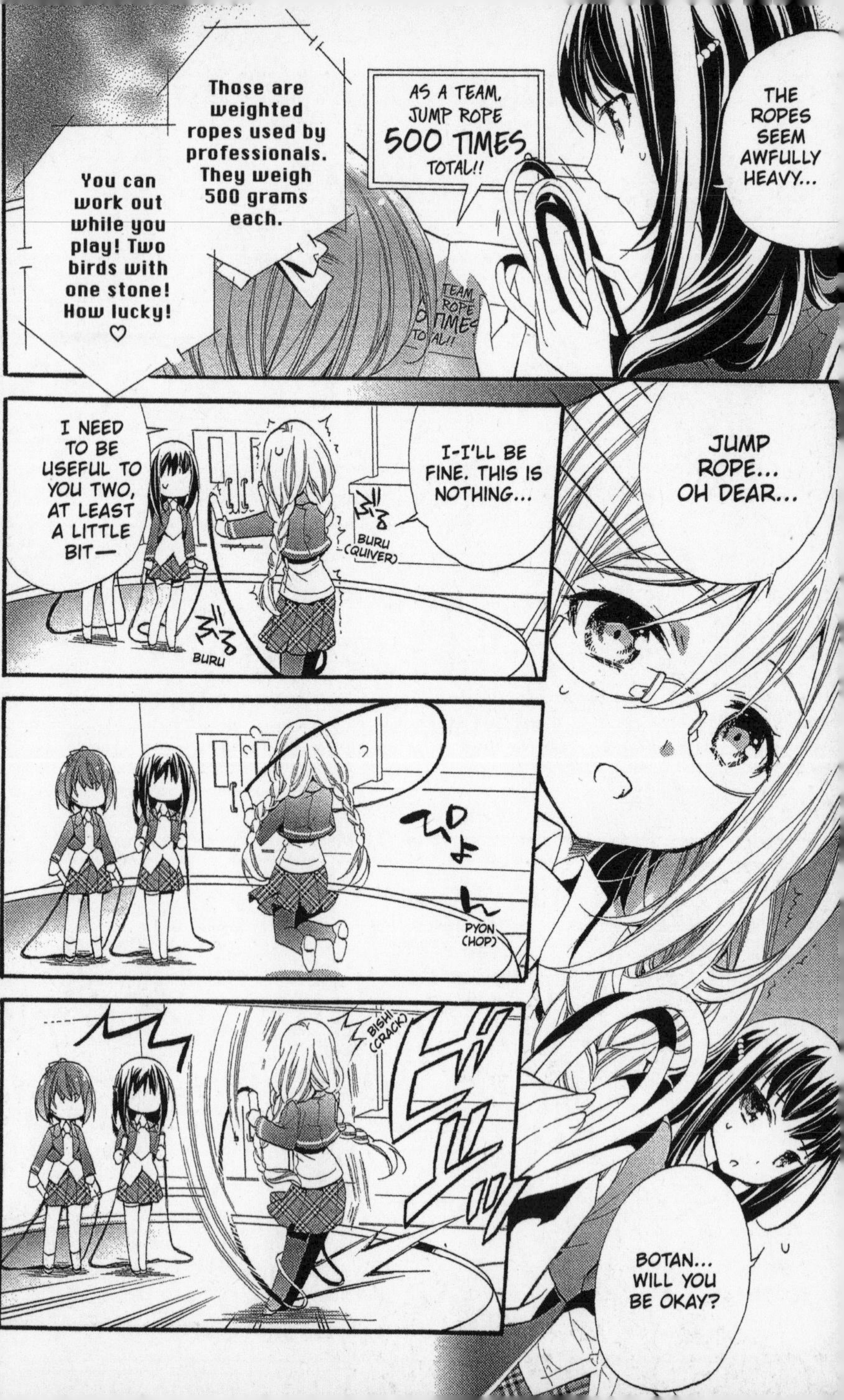
THE ROPES SEEM AWFULLY HEAVY...
AS A TEAM, JUMP ROPE 500 TIMES TOTAL!!
Those are weighted ropes used by professionals. They weigh 500 grams each.
You can work out while you play! Two birds with one stone! How lucky! ♡
JUMP ROPE... OH DEAR...
BOTAN... WILL YOU BE OKAY?
I-I'LL BE FINE. THIS IS NOTHING...
BURU (QUIVER)
I NEED TO BE USEFUL TO YOU TWO, AT LEAST A LITTLE BIT—
BURU
PYON (HOP)
BISHI (CRACK)

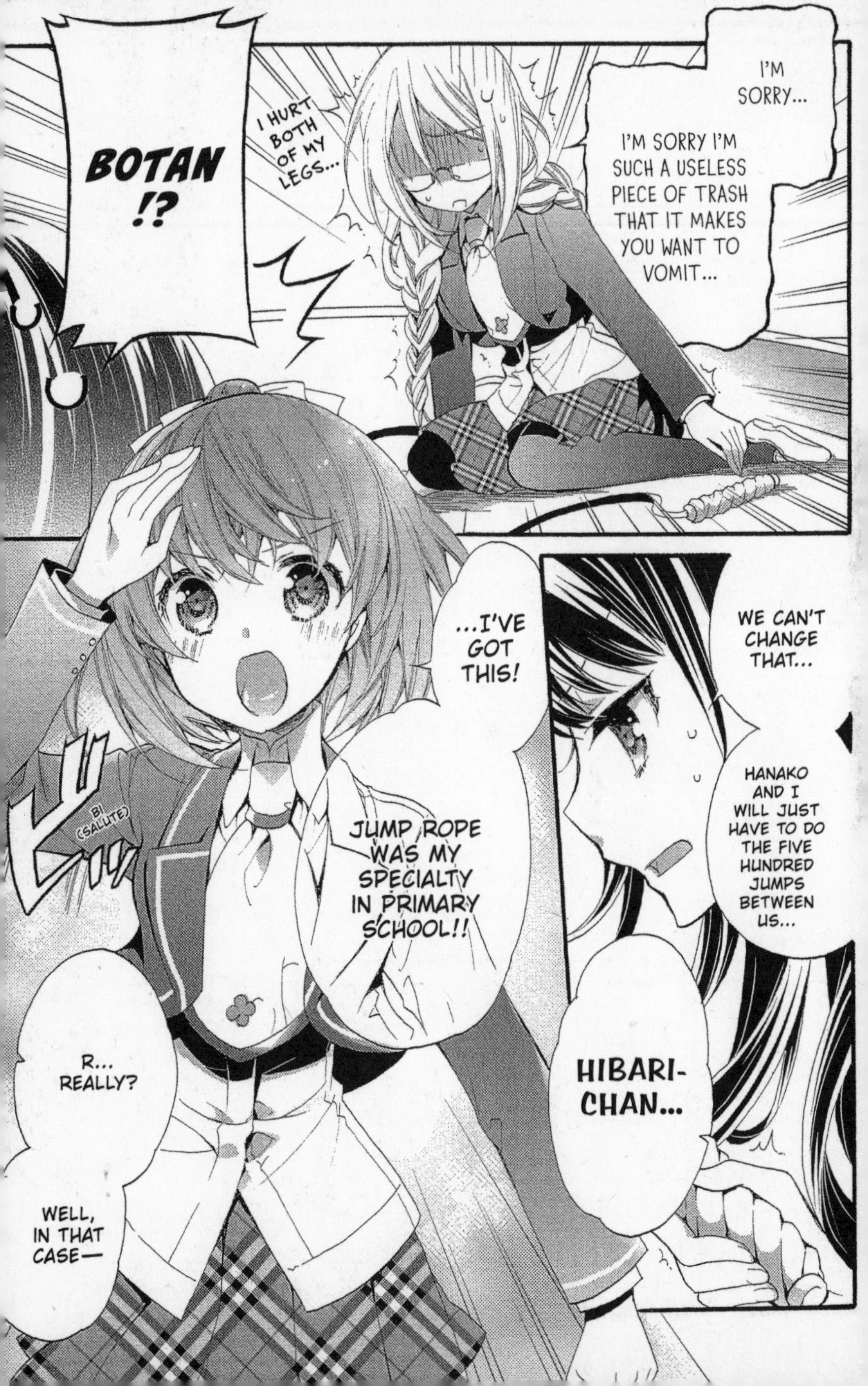
I'M SORRY...
I'M SORRY I'M SUCH A USELESS PIECE OF TRASH THAT IT MAKES YOU WANT TO VOMIT...
I HURT BOTH OF MY LEGS...
BOTAN !?
WE CAN'T CHANGE THAT...
HANAKO AND I WILL JUST HAVE TO DO THE FIVE HUNDRED JUMPS BETWEEN US...
HIBARI-CHAN...
...I'VE GOT THIS!
JUMP ROPE WAS MY SPECIALTY IN PRIMARY SCHOOL!!
BI (SALUTE)
R... REALLY?
WELL, IN THAT CASE—

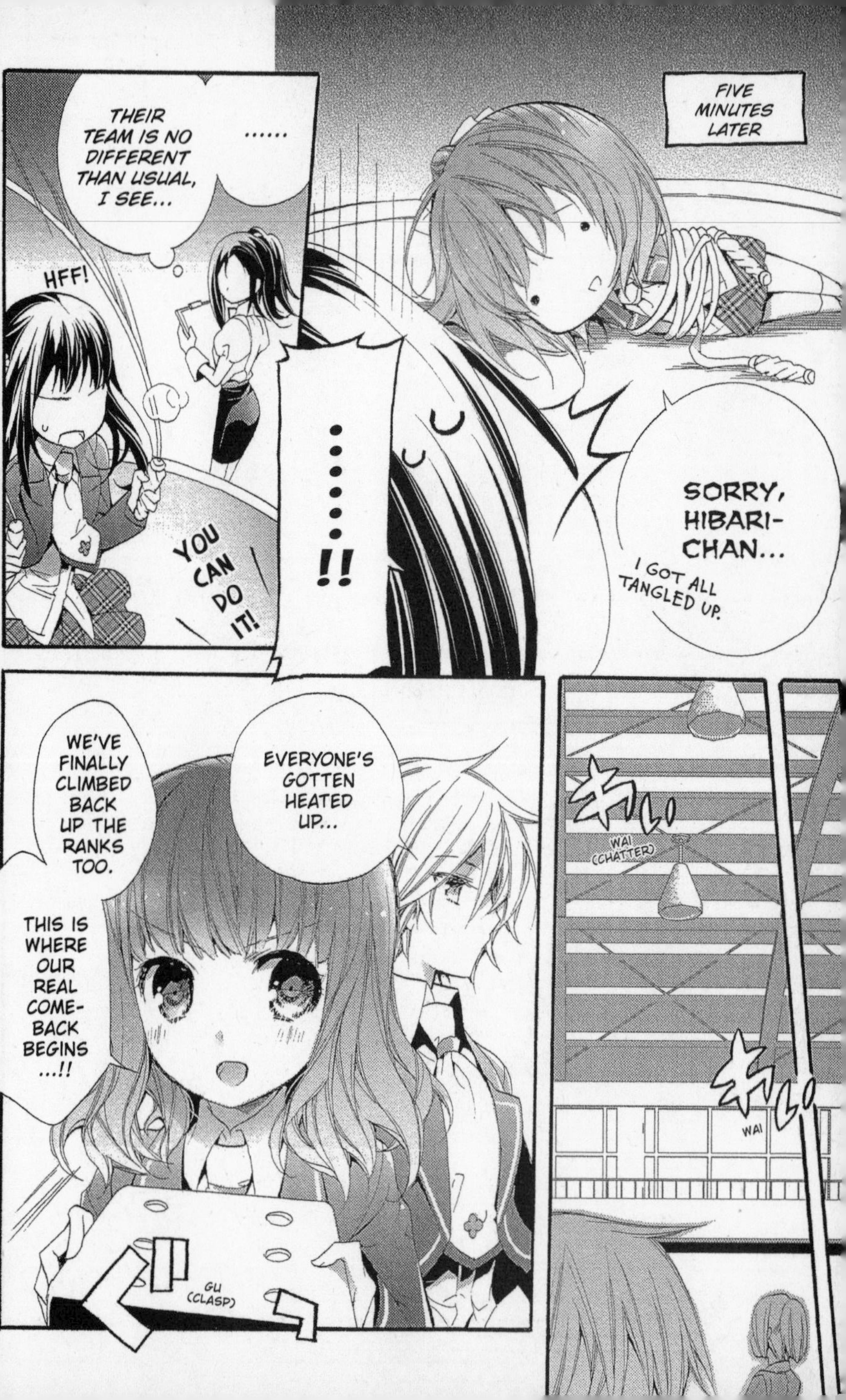
FIVE MINUTES LATER
SORRY, HIBARI-CHAN...
I GOT ALL TANGLED UP.
......!!
THEIR TEAM IS NO DIFFERENT THAN USUAL, I SEE...
......
HFF!
YOU CAN DO IT!
WAI (CHATTER)
WAI
EVERYONE'S GOTTEN HEATED UP...
WE'VE FINALLY CLIMBED BACK UP THE RANKS TOO.
THIS IS WHERE OUR REAL COMEBACK BEGINS...!!
GU (CLASP)

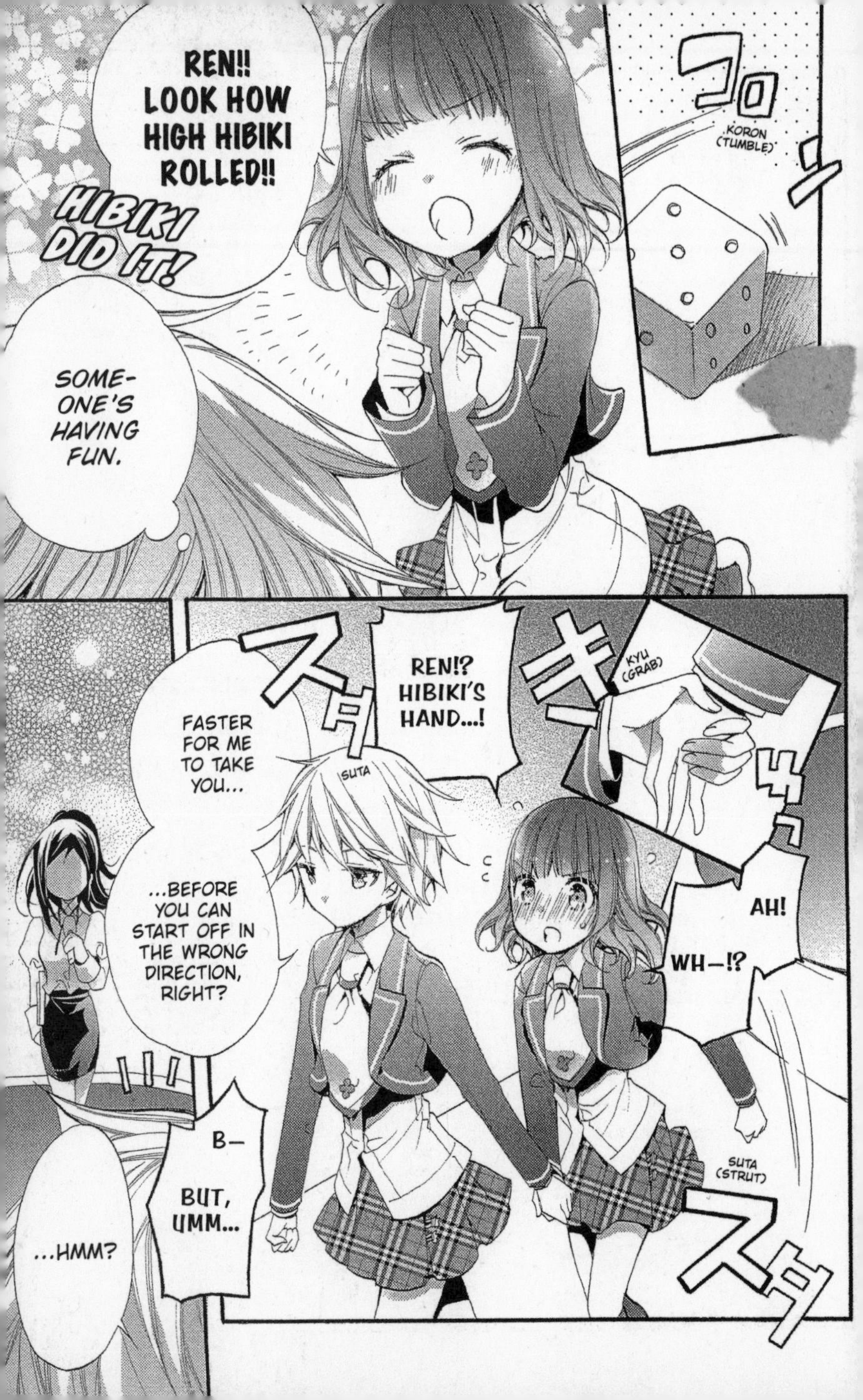
KORON (TUMBLE)
REN!! LOOK HOW HIGH HIBIKI ROLLED!!
HIBIKI DID IT!
SOME-ONE'S HAVING FUN.
KYU (GRAB)
AH!
WH—!?
REN!? HIBIKI'S HAND...!
SUTA
FASTER FOR ME TO TAKE YOU...
...BEFORE YOU CAN START OFF IN THE WRONG DIRECTION, RIGHT?
SUTA (STRUT)
B—
BUT, UMM...
...HMM?

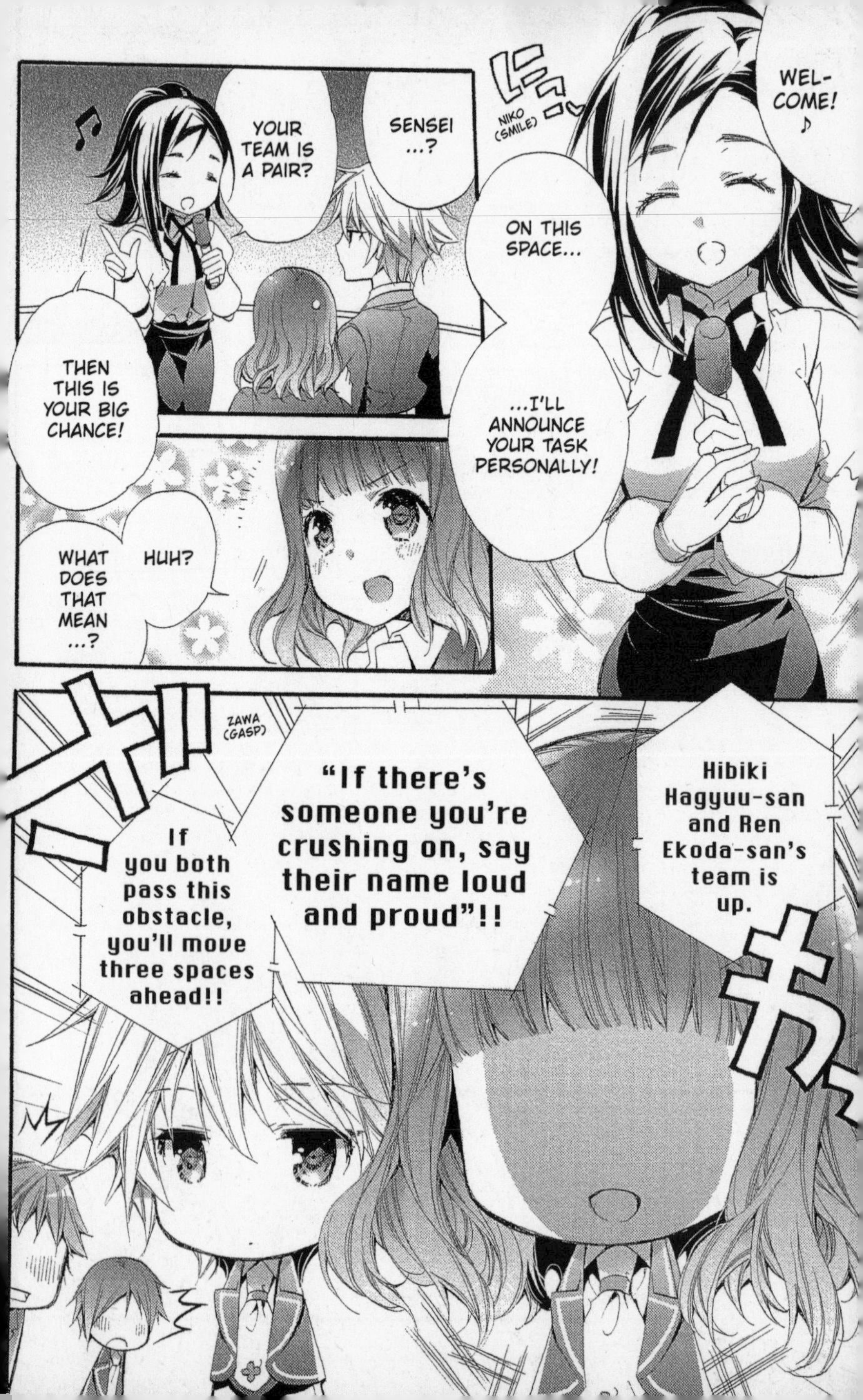
WEL-COME! ♪
NIKO (SMILE)
ON THIS SPACE...
...I'LL ANNOUNCE YOUR TASK PERSONALLY!
SENSEI ...?
YOUR TEAM IS A PAIR?
THEN THIS IS YOUR BIG CHANCE!
HUH?
WHAT DOES THAT MEAN ...?
Hibiki Hagyuu-san and Ren Ekoda-san's team is up.
ZAWA (GASP)
"If there's someone you're crushing on, say their name loud and proud"!!
If you both pass this obstacle, you'll move three spaces ahead!!

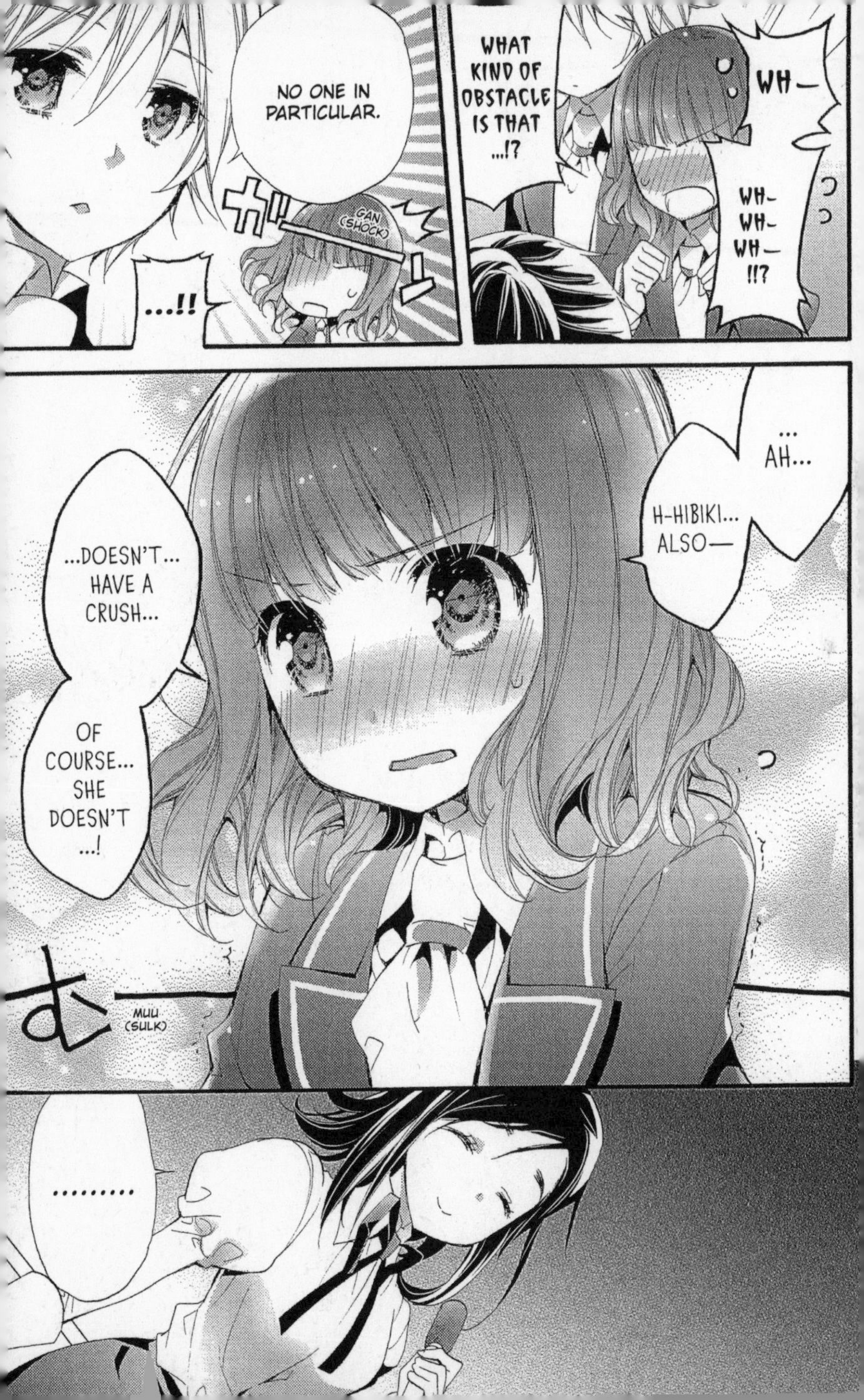
WH—
WH- WH- WH— !!?
WHAT KIND OF OBSTACLE IS THAT ...!?
NO ONE IN PARTICULAR.
GAN (SHOCK)
...!!
... AH...
H-HIBIKI... ALSO—
...DOESN'T... HAVE A CRUSH...
OF COURSE... SHE DOESN'T ...!
MUU (SULK)
....

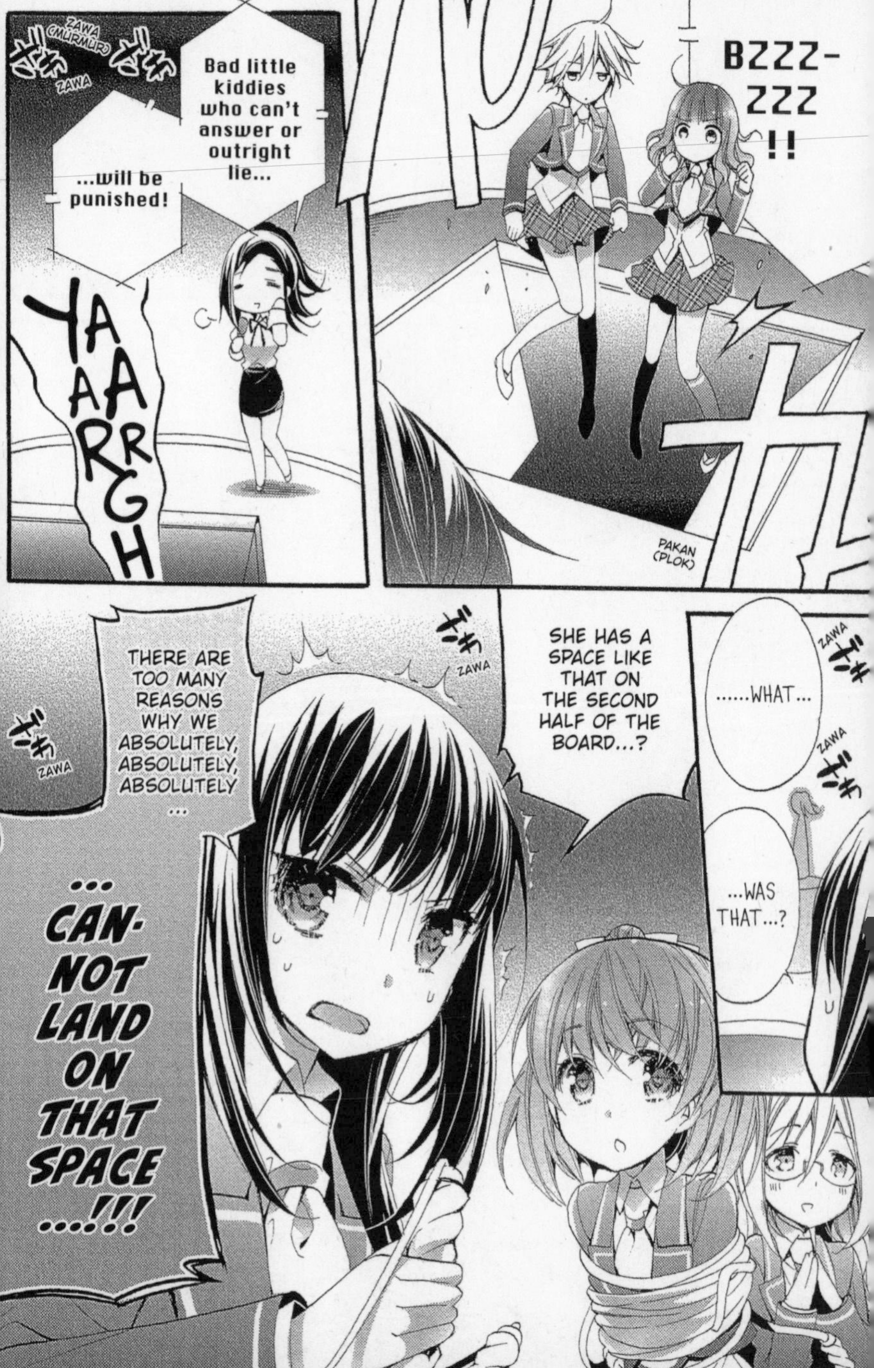
BZZZ-ZZZ!!
PAKAN (PLOK)
ZAWA (MURMUR) ZAWA
Bad little kiddies who can't answer or outright lie...
...will be punished!
YAAARRGH
ZAWA
......WHAT...
ZAWA
...WAS THAT...?
SHE HAS A SPACE LIKE THAT ON THE SECOND HALF OF THE BOARD...?
ZAWA
THERE ARE TOO MANY REASONS WHY WE ABSOLUTELY, ABSOLUTELY, ABSOLUTELY...
ZAWA
...CAN-NOT LAND ON THAT SPACE...!!!